Praise for Sudeep Chakravarti

On *Highway 39*

'Masterly … Replete with stories, a refreshing eye (and ear) for detail.' – *The Telegraph*

'The book should be read for its brazen honesty and by all who care about the idea of a collective, inclusive India.' – *Indian Express*

'*Highway 39* … has yielded spectacular results … Among the very few significant narratives on northeast India.' – *Biblio*

'A gripping read.' – *India Today*

On *Plassey*

'Sudeep Chakravarti's book on the battle of Plassey is popular history writing at its very best … Plassey was a turning point but that battle and the background have not received the attention it merits. Chakravarti's book fills a significant gap and does so in an enviable manner. The book will stand the test of time.' – *Rudrangshu Mukherjee, Chancellor and Professor of History, Ashoka University*

'This work is certainly a *tour de force.'* – *OPEN*

'Sudeep Chakravarti's *Plassey* proves to be as absorbing as the battle it recounts … This is a book that librarians must list and buyers read for what it is worth, if not also for the battle itself that it recounts. Publishers and readers must patiently cradle the deeper talents and prescience of the likes of Chakravarti to build better societies, especially in these times.' – *India Today*

'(*Plassey*) makes for gratifying reading … a strong cast that provides food for delicious storytelling is only part of the equation. In Chakravarti's hands, it also meets healthy analysis and an even-handed study which constantly interrogates the diversity of records and tries to weed out exaggerations in one by holding it up against divergent views in another.' – *Mint*

On *The Bengalis*

'Written with verve, energy and polish, and drawing on considerable resources, both anecdotal and archival, Chakravarti's book takes its place beside other contemporary attempts at "collective" portraiture, such as Jeremy Paxman's *The English* and John Hooper's *The Italians*.' – *The Hindu*

'A compact and brilliant work ... dazzling virtuosity ... The clipped descriptions of Noakhali and Naxalbari are worthy of Hemingway.' – *The Tribune*

'*The Bengalis* is an astonishingly good book, written by an author at the height of his powers.' – *The Pioneer*

'*The Bengalis* is by far the best non-fiction book from India I have read this year.' – *Hindustan Times*

On *Red Sun*

'A book that every MP, MLA and minister should read before entering office. Needless to say, sociologists and bureaucrats should read it as compulsory study material.' – *The Hindu*

'Chakravarti adopts a questioning attitude towards Maoist opponents and Maoist sympathizers alike. The result is a remarkably objective book ...' – *Far Eastern Economic Review*

'Chakravarti does a valuable job in fleshing out the human stories that lie behind the headlines ... This [is] essential reading.' – *Business India*

'The sombre story of India at war with itself.' – *Deccan Herald*

Other Books by Sudeep Chakravarti

HISTORY, CULTURE, GOVERNANCE, CONFLICT

Plassey: The Battle that Changed the Course of Indian History (2020)
The Bengalis: A Portrait of a Community (2017)
Clear.Hold.Build: Hard Lessons of Business and Human Rights in India (2014)
Highway 39: Journeys through a Fractured Land (2012)
Red Sun: Travels in Naxalite Country (2008)

NOVELS

The Baptism of Tony Calangute (2018)
The Avenue of Kings (2010)
Tin Fish (2005)

THE EASTERN GATE

War and Peace in Nagaland, Manipur and India's Far East

Sudeep Chakravarti

SIMON &
SCHUSTER

London · New York · Sydney · Toronto · New Delhi

First published in India by Simon & Schuster India, 2022

Copyright © Sudeep Chakravarti, 2022

This book is copyright under the Berne Convention.

No reproduction without permission.

® and © 1997 Simon & Schuster, Inc. All rights reserved.

The right of Sudeep Chakravarti to be identified as author of this work has been asserted by him in accordance with Section 57 of the Copyright Act 1957.

1 3 5 7 9 10 8 6 4 2

Simon & Schuster India
818, Indraprakash Building,
21, Barakhamba Road,
New Delhi 110001.

www.simonandschuster.co.in

Hardback ISBN: 978-93-92099-21-2
eBook ISBN: 978-93-92099-26-7

The views and opinions expressed in this book are the author's own and the facts are as reported by him which have been verified to the extent possible, and the publishers are not in any way liable for the same.

The author has made all reasonable efforts to contact copyright-holders for permissions. In case there are omissions or errors in the form of credits given, corrections may be made in future editions.

Typeset in India by SÜRYA, New Delhi

Printed and bound in India by Replika Press Pvt. Ltd.

FSC
www.fsc.org
MIX
Paper from
responsible sources
FSC® C016779

Simon & Schuster India is committed to sourcing paper that is made from wood grown in sustainable forests and support the Forest Stewardship Council, the leading international forest certification organisation. Our books displaying the FSC logo are printed on FSC certified paper.

For
Lanusangla, Penmi and Nandini, my sisters
Audrey Tiasen, Chloé Kilensüngla, Noyingroni, Lumchilo,
and Hannah, my nieces

CONTENTS

A Note on Reading *The Eastern Gate*

A work of non-fiction is sometimes defined by a template driven by its genre: history, politics, conflict and conflict resolution, anthropology, foreign policy, geopolitics, internal security, human rights, travelogue, reportage, narrative non-fiction, commentary, and so very much more.

The Eastern Gate is a collective, if you will, of several of these genres. As a chronicler, historian, writer, storyteller, analyst, columnist, journalist—these are placed with no particular emphasis—my work has always attempted to engage multiple experiences and approaches.

For this work, I've added a 'dispatches' element: in the narrative employing news breaks as they happened, information and messages received and exchanged, notes and thoughts as preparatory to writing, notes and records of meetings, recapping a work-day, snippets from travel diaries, snatches from the notebook, slices of life …

These lend immediacy to events, an unvarnished rawness that reveals layers of truth and perception. That is why I opted to weave several of these elements into the narrative in the original form instead of sanitising them or, to use an equally unlovely phrase, processing them. I hope it enhances your travel to *The Eastern Gate* and beyond to so very many Wheres, Whens, Whos, Whats and Whys that envelop this dynamic and charged region of the Indian subcontinent.

SC
Socorro, Goa
October, 2021

Key

AFSPA. The Armed Forces (Special) Powers Act, 1958 permits the army and its adjuncts wide powers of investigation, interdiction and killing even on suspicion. Offers constitutionally mandated legal prophylactic for such actions. Applied in various parts of Northeast India. Across all Nagaland, most of Manipur, parts of Assam, Meghalaya, Arunachal Pradesh. Similar law applied in what was earlier the state of Jammu & Kashmir. Such laws persist despite several government committees recommending their dilution and repeal. Several states of India apply similar special laws that accord local police AFSPA-like powers.

Alternative Arrangement. A demand by several Naga tribes under the umbrella of the United Naga Council, the apex organisation of Naga people of Manipur, for Naga homelands to be delinked from the administrative ambit of the government of Manipur to deal directly and autonomously with the central government in New Delhi. A major sticking political point in Manipur, often used by UNC and its affiliates to trigger strikes and shutdowns in Naga homelands to squeeze Imphal Valley.

Article 371. Provisions of various sub-sections of this article India's Constitution that accords special provisions and guarantees related variously to customary law, land ownership, degrees of administrative and judicial autonomy, among other things, in Nagaland (371A), Assam (371B), Manipur (371C), Sikkim (371F), Mizoram (371G) and Arunachal Pradesh (371H). Article 371A in particular has guarantees that are very similar in nature to Article 35A, abolished in 2019, which accorded special residential and other guarantees to citizens of the former state and now-bifurcated territory of Jammu & Kashmir. The Bharatiya

Janata Party and the BJP-led central government maintained that Article 35A hampered development, but Article 371A and other 'sister' subsections continue to guarantee similar provisions in far-eastern India.

Asian Highway. Two so-called Asian Highway routes that pass east to northwest through India. Asian Highway 1 (AH1) on paper runs from Tokyo to Istanbul. The Indian aspect begins in Moreh in southeast Manipur, at the border with Myanmar, then cuts through Bangladesh to Kolkata and mimics the old Grand Trunk Route across to Pakistan. AH2 runs from Denpasar in Bali, Indonesia to Khosravi in western Iran. The Indian aspect begins at Moreh and after traversing Manipur it takes a different route through northeast India and Bangladesh to re-emerge in India and tracks a more northerly route than AH 1 across northern India to pass into Pakistan. There are several smaller aspects of various other AH designations that criss-cross India.

CAA. The controversial Citizenship Amendment Act, 2019 that was revived as a controversial Bill by the BJP-led national government when the coalition won a second parliamentary term in May 2019—and passed by parliament in December that year. It sought to offer citizenship to non-Muslim citizens of Indian origin from present-day Pakistan, Afghanistan and Bangladesh; and reduced the waiting time for citizenship by nearly half. CAA is seen by many in far-eastern India, particularly the communally-charged hotspot of Assam, as legitimising migrants—even Hindu migrants. Cause of unrest across the region and violence in Assam. At the time of publication of this book, the central government, specifically the Ministry of Home Affairs, which repeatedly sought extensions to frame rules that will govern CAA, was yet to do so.

Chakhesang. A Naga tribal collective, evolved from the Chokri, Kheza and Sangtam tribes. Now recognised as a separate tribe in Nagaland. They have homelands primarily in the Phek region in south-eastern Nagaland and in contiguous areas in north-eastern Manipur.

CorCom. The Coordination Committee was formed by seven Manipuri rebel groups in July 2012. It quickly came to be known as CorCom. The United National Liberation Front (UNLF), Revolutionary People's

Front (RPF has as its armed wing the PLA or People's Liberation Army), Kanglei Yawol Kanna Lup (KYKL)—along with UNLF and PLA, the current trinity among these groups—Kangleipak Communist Party (KCP), People's Revolutionary Party of Kangleipak (PREPAK), a faction PREPAK-PRO or PREPAK progressive, and United People's Party of Kangleipak (UPPK). UPPK was expelled from CorCom in early 2013. CorCom and its members, as a collective and as individual entities, has allied with NSCN (K) and the Independent faction of ULFA or United Liberation Front of Asom (Independent), to conduct operations against the Indian Army, paramilitaries and police. NSCN (K) openly offered refuge to these other rebel groups like factions of Bodo rebels from Assam and Kamtapuri rebels from northern Bengal, an arrangement which weakened after implosions within K since 2017 and subsequent operations by Myanmar's military.

Framework Agreement. An agreement signed in New Delhi between NSCN (I-M), the largest Naga rebel group, and the Government of India on 3 August 2015, in the presence of Prime Minister Narendra Modi, Rajnath Singh, home minister at the time, and Ajit Doval, national security advisor. The signatories were R.N. Ravi, at the time government-appointed interlocutor for Naga peace talks, and Thuingaleng Muivah, general secretary of NSCN (I-M), the expanded form of which is National Socialist Council of Nagalim (Isak-Muivah). It was an agreement to come to an agreement to formally end conflict with Naga rebels and take to a logical end an uneasy ceasefire with I-M signed in 1997.

ILP. The Bengal Eastern Frontier Regulation Act, 1873 created a system of the Inner Line Permit, or ILP, to regulate the entry, period of stay and movement of non-locals in several parts of far-eastern India. After 1950, non-locals came to mean citizens of India and it was applied to Arunachal Pradesh, Nagaland and Mizoram. In the wake of the fracas over CAA, it was extended to Manipur. Meghalaya has since consistently pushed for extension of ILP to that state.

Kaladan Multi-Modal Project. A work-in-progress project to link Aizawl in Mizoram by road due south to the Kaladan river jetty in

Myanmar, and, via the port of Bay of Bengal port of Sittwe, link the port at Kolkata. A road and railway project to link Agartala in Tripura to the border town of Sabroom and then on to Chittagong port in Bangladesh for further links to various points on the Indian seaboard is a smaller but significant project which, like the Kaladan project, was born of the Look-East Policy announced by Prime Minister P.V. Narasimha Rao in 1994.

NRC. The National Register of Citizens, like CAA pushed a pet project of the BJP-led central government. Thus far aggressively applied in Assam, it is seen by many as a target to identify and eject—although nobody is certain where to—those outed as illegal migrants from Bangladesh. Nearly two million, mostly Hindu, were corralled under NRC with a time-consuming appeal process and several cramped camps have come up in Assam since 2019 to house those deemed to be illegal by Assam's government. The NRC net snagged numerous citizens of India as well as some who had served in the Indian armed forces and paramilitary organisations. NRC is generally welcomed in Assam and has been held out as an election-stump threat by the ruling party in other states, particularly West Bengal.

NSCN. The National Socialist Council of Nagaland, formed in 1980 in the wake of disappointment and anger among some Naga rebel leaders, including Muivah, at what they saw as the capitulation of other rebel leaders of the rebel-led Federal Government of Nagaland, who signed the so-called Shillong Accord in 1975. This cemented Nagaland's relationship with the Republic of India even more solidly than the peace deal of 1960 which led to the creation of Nagaland as a state of India in 1963. The Shillong Accord accepted the supremacy of India's Constitution, among other clauses that bound Nagaland to India. Muivah, Isak Chishi Swu and S.S. Khaplang led the NSCN, which continued armed action against India forces, police and administration. It became a parallel government in Nagaland and all Naga homelands, both in India and Myanmar. In 1988, Khaplang violently broke away after differences with Muivah and Khaplang and formed what is known as NSCN (K) with its base in Taga, in northwest Myanmar. Both groups later singed ceasefire agreements with India, I-M in 1997 and K in 2001, but K broke away from ceasefire in early 2015. Meanwhile, both I-M and K suffered several fissures and breaks. These breakaway groups, all of them sporting various NSCN appellations—for instance U, K-K, K-Khango, K-Sumi—have since in 2017 entered into peace talks with the government of India, a situation I-M has viewed as unacceptable—because it dilutes its claim to speak for all Naga peoples and interests.

Phizo. Angami Zapu Phizo is a Naga rebel icon. Along with colleagues he led the evolution of the Naga National Council, which first pressed for autonomy and then independence in 1951, with a landmark plebiscite which the government of India dismissed. Phizo emerged as the hard-line face of the pushback against India, and, in short order, leader of the rebel government, Federal Government of Nagaland. He escaped in 1960 with help of a British missionary, the Reverend Michael Scott, first to east Pakistan and eventually to the United Kingdom. He settled into a life of a gentleman-rebel in Kent. After his death in 1990, his remains were brought to Nagaland amidst an outpouring of emotion and his funerary ceremonies attended by massive crowds. He was interred near the Nagaland secretariat and Assembly complex in Kohima. Phizo was born in 1913 in Khonoma, the Angami village famous for its resistance to the British and, then, India.

Tatmadaw. The collective by which Myanmar's armed forces (army, navy and air force) and its auxiliaries and militias, is known. Tatmadaw has for long controlled everything from the government to the economy, except for a few short years after independence from Great Britain in 1948. A military coup in 1962 ended democracy until 2011. An uneasy practical alliance with the party of former opposition icon Aung San Suu Kyi ended in early 2021, when Tatmadaw arrested Suu Kyi and her senior colleagues and took control of the government. Even with their occasional operations against anti-India rebels, Tatmadaw officials have regularly negotiated quid pro quo with various groups of Naga, Meitei, Kuki, Assamese and Bodo rebels, among others. Payments have been made in cash—to simply remain in Myanmar or to free a Manipuri rebel leader, for example—and kind—such as occasionally providing perimeter security for Tatmadaw and even pitching in for operations against Myanmarese rebels.

Zeliangrong. A Naga tribal collective, formed from the very distinct Zeme, Liangmei and Rongmei tribes. They have homelands in west and northwest Manipur, primarily the districts of Tamenglong and Noney (hived off from Tamenglong in late-2016) and the contiguous area of Peren district in south-western Nagaland.

Introduction

There is a story behind the naming of *The Eastern Gate*.

I was in Imphal in early November 2009 on one of several visits to the capital of Manipur and elsewhere in the state to research a book set in this far-eastern region of India. In a way that book, *Highway 39*, published in 2012, was a prelude to this one: it sought to explain the history and root causes of some key conflicts in far-eastern India, and the despair and distress of several decades. It was an attempt to unravel the remarkable and brutal recent history of Nagaland and Manipur, their conjoined and restive present, and their uncertain yet desperately hopeful future. It portrayed a picture of a people brought repeatedly to breakdown through years of political conceit and deceit, poor and presumptuous governance, immense ethnic tensions, rebellions on account of a great disrespect of local identities and aspirations, outright conflict, human-rights horrors, a cumulative and wrenching insecurity—and, yet, coming through it all with inspirational resilience.

The story of this region, what India's political etymology calls its 'Northeast', is a story of our times.

While there is much to be healed and much to be done, there is now active talk, and its occasional walking, of reconciliation with various factions of Naga, Meitei, Kuki, Assamese and Zomi rebels in the region, among several other ethnically charged fronts; their rehabilitation; and non-violent participation in their futures. Alongside—and that is a loaded word in politics, geopolitics and their practice—this strategic gateway region to India's myriad eastern ambitions and security ambit has ever more become the mirror to India's 'Look East' policy announced by the Indian government in 1994. At the time, P.V. Naramsimha Rao was prime minister. A subsequent 'Act East' policy was announced in November 2014 at an India-ASEAN meeting in Myanmar, the first significant eastern flourish of the government of Prime Minister Narendra Modi. In the process it bridged this common outlook of two vastly different administrations with different agendas: one led by the relatively centrist Congress, and the other by the overtly right-wing Bharatiya Janata Party.

But whatever the political constructs and policies for integral nation with the overhang of fevered nationalism, for several years I have understood that there cannot be a Look- or Act East Policy by overlooking Northeast India—what I prefer to call Far-Eastern India. India's relations with this region will mark the country's engagement with its northern and eastern neighbours—China, Bangladesh, Nepal, Myanmar and Bhutan. Equally, there can be no doubt whatsoever that India's relations with these neighbours will have a direct bearing on how this region thrives, or falls by the wayside, in the future. The success or failure of India's policies—and it will ultimately fail if 'Northeast' India is not an intimate part of it—depends on this understanding.

Indeed, the power of such collective dynamics—alongside manmade impulses such as climate change and migration—might decide whether there will remain a 'Northeast India' as we know it today.

And yet, for all its importance and relatively recent policy initiatives, far-eastern India has suffered from several decades of mandated ignorance and apathy. A deliberate apathy that is rooted right from hundreds of millions of childhoods, as in Mainland India textbooks for long-ignored key histories, major historical figures, tribes, cultures, and even geographies beyond the most cursory mention of the Brahmaputra river that helps to feed and hold together much of eastern India and Bangladesh. One of India's two central school boards introduced the history of Northeast India into the curriculum as late as 2014–2015, as an afterthought, and with scant, ideologically whitewashed tools with which to teach it, in the history syllabus. It was a beginning of sorts.

This is the region to which the Japanese drove up in 1944 from their fresh conquest, Burma. It was a die-hard bid to push back the British and attack India's east in a plan to move steadily into the subcontinent. The Allied pushback, aided massively by British-Indian troops and the often-forgotten contribution of peoples who call this region home, ensured a different history. This is where India's more benign outreach begins, at least as stated in its policy curriculum vitae, a pivot to secure its interests in the neighbourhood through strengthened diplomatic ties, securing strategic bridgeheads and routes, and communication, commerce and investment.

The Eastern Gate seeks to background the ambit of that ambition in this geo-strategic, geo-economic sweet spot with a combination of research and reportage in a narrative that draws in policymakers from politicians and bureaucrats to academicians and analysts, players of every hue from rebels to intelligence operatives, and people in whose name policies and plays are made. Equally, in a narrative that begins in mid-2014—around the time the first BJP-led government of Prime Minister Modi was just weeks away from winning the general elections to Parliament—*The Eastern Gate* also seeks to highlight the mechanics and the pressures and counter-pressures of peace-making that has the potential to transform and elevate this region: the Naga peace process that saw an uptick in mid-2015; and the crucial, often misunderstood ethno-political umbilical that ties it firmly to Manipur and, to a lesser extent, to Arunachal Pradesh and Assam. Slips-ups, obtuseness, arrogance, and that great contributor to failure, being too-clever-by-half in the process of conflict resolution, could unleash dynamics that could destroy the notion that so often celebrates the absence of war as peace. Alas, the process has already witnessed an unfair share of all-of-the-above.

Even with the overwhelming superiority of India's security apparatus, the simple truth is that, if conflict were to resume on account of a collapse of ceasefires triggered by dead-end peace negotiations, disagreement by a major faction, or perception of massive loss of face to a rebel group in particular—and, by extension, to the people it seeks to represent in general—then there would be an immediate, visible rise in public sympathy for the rebel cause. 'Tables could turn very quickly,'

as a Naga acquaintance close to the peace talks between Naga rebels
and the government of India explained to me by way of an example.
And, rebel-cause could be a fresh cause to reflect the times: millennial
rebels carrying millennial resentment and dissent, not just in Nagaland
but across this region.

This aspect is important. Rebels held out for decades in various ways
with the direct and indirect help of support at home, as it were, as much
as support by the agencies of neighbouring governments which at one
time or another found it useful to train, supply and offer safe passage
and haven to numerous rebel groups rooted in Nagaland, Mizoram,
Manipur, Assam, Tripura, Arunachal Pradesh and Meghalaya. Despite
being under severe pressure from Indian security forces and geopolitical
realities that have triggered a steady squeezing of their havens in
Bangladesh and Myanmar, and despite being seemingly out-of-step with
their semi-Maoist ideologies or, occasionally, Che-romanticism, such
rebel groups—especially those representing Manipur's majority Meitei
community and identity—continue to hold emotional cachet among
the public. It's an umbilical link rooted in history and culture—and
the wrongs, real and perceived, by India.

The Naga peace process and Manipur—the two that find far greater
primacy and detail in this book on account of their interconnected and
regional impact—is fraught with righteous perceptions of the same
suggestion, or outcome, that can seem equally just for one community
and unjust for another.

This G-spot, as it were, rivals the Afghanistan-Pakistan (or Af-Pak, in
seminar-speak) G-spot to India's west, and stretches from eastern Nepal,
to Bhutan and the uneasy Tibetan Administrative Region of China, to
Myanmar and Bangladesh—countries with which this region of India
shares borders just shy of 5,200 km.

Indeed, the very meaning of neighbourhood is different here.

The region, which accounts for nearly a seventh of India's landmass
and is home to nearly 50 million people, can most easily reach the ports

of Bay of Bengal through Bangladesh and Myanmar. The easiest trade and land communication routes linking far-eastern India and eastern India—in simpler terms, say, Agartala in Tripura to Kolkata in West Bengal—are right across Bangladesh, as was the case before the Partition in 1947 cartographically and callously divided the subcontinent.

As aircraft fly, the distance from Guwahati—northeast India's largest city and the commercial hub of Assam, the region's largest and most populous state—to Kunming, the commercial and strategic hub of south-western China, is just over 1,100 kilometres, about an hour and half in a passenger jet, perhaps thirty minutes in a modern fighter. The Tibetan Plateau is even closer. Lhasa is 389 kilometres away as the eagle flies. Sylhet, an important hub in north-eastern Bangladesh, lies less than 150 kilometres south of Guwahati, and is much closer to Shillong and Silchar. Dhaka, with which Guwahati had rich riverine commerce before Partition—as did much of eastern India—is at a little over 300 kilometres; and, border controls permitting, a day's drive south. In comparison, New Delhi is about 1,500 kilometres away by plane (and Beijing, 2,700 kilometres).

A combination of wishful strategic thinking and hopeful strategic planning visualises that, in the near-future, within a day you may be able to drive down straight to the south of Guwahati, and be deep inside Myanmar's mineral- and energy-rich regions, or access a port on the Bay of Bengal to reach Kolkata and beyond. With current border controls and awful infrastructure on the Indian side, the overland aspect would take three days or more. (Of course, the combination of occasional pandemic and a perennially heavy-handed military in Myanmar must first permit such movement.)

From here beckon points further east: overland to Thailand, Vietnam, Lao, Cambodia, Malaysia and Singapore, and other nations of south-east Asia, adding a significant layer to existing sea and air routes, boosting hinterlands, investment, markets and interdependent and interlocking alliances. It would also be a part of India's delayed and sometimes knee-jerk overture with its 'golden necklace', if you will, to China's brash, set-in-stone strategy of the 'string of pearls' which marks that emergent superpower's presence across Asia, and the Indian Ocean that is Indian only in name.

You get the picture.

So, this book also reiterates the need for a necessary pivot: India has also to see things from the perspective of this region, not merely push the perspective of mandarins in New Delhi. Because here in far-eastern India it's also about a future in relation to this region's two largest and ever-more ambitious neighbours: If there is Mainland China, there is also 'Mainland India'. This is a geographical, geopolitical and psychological truth.

For it all to work out, of course, there needs to be absence of restiveness or absence of conflict in this far-eastern region of India that is home to more than two hundred ethnic communities and more than two hundred languages and dialects. Calm along its borders with Myanmar, China, Bangladesh, and Bhutan. And, naturally, calm in all these countries.

India's eastern elixir is a seductive, stunningly complex cocktail.

The implication of it all was brought home to me like nothing else one evening in Imphal, as I attended a felicitation ceremony for a protest icon, Irom Sharmila. She was at the time jailed, and intubated for force-feeding—she was on a years-long hunger strike. It was Sharmila's protest against a massacre of civilians by troopers of Assam Rifles, an operational extension of the Indian Army, in 2000. Her refusal to eat was interpreted as attempted suicide by local courts. Indian penal law prescribed jail time just shy of a year for such offence. By this time, she had been in jail for nearly nine years (and would remain there until 2016), a ludicrous circus of release-and-arrest to conform to the letter of that law.

Sharmila was to be fêted at this ceremony by two other protest icons. One was Mahasweta Devi, the ageing, unwell and still formidable activist-litterateur who arrived from Kolkata. The other was Yumnam Mangol Devi, a long-time leader of the Meira Paibi. This tiny octogenarian was a legend among this group—literally, women torchbearers—on account of torches that bands of ladies would carry during their dramatic night marches and vigils, protesting a range of things from alcoholism to the abuse of human rights.

As with the welcome accorded to Mahasweta, Ima Mangol—Mother Mangol—was received as a warrior, not just the elder, the grandmother, she also was. Applause followed her from the driveway to the auditorium where the ceremony would be held. Women and men, young and old, greeted her with folded hands. Some rushed to touch the ground before her feet.

Such respect wasn't unusual here. Women like Ima Mangol— generations of Meira Paibi—have for more than a hundred years taken protest and outrage to the rulers of Manipur. These manifestations of nupi lan or women's war have been both relatively small and big. In 1904, several thousand women surrounded Lt Col. H. St P. Maxwell, Manipur's British Resident, over an order by him to renew the hated practice of forced labour. Earlier imposed by Manipur's maharajas, the system of lalup forced males between the ages of seventeen and sixty to offer set days of free labour to be used at the pleasure of the administration. In a book, *Nupi Lan*, there is a telling of how Maxwell referred to these protesting women: 'It is very difficult to know how to treat a mob of wild cats like this, but I shall take care to disperse them next time before they become numerous.' As it happened, Maxwell was compelled to call off lalup. In Manipur, this episode is referred to as the First Nupi Lan.

There have been others. Women protesters were beaten and bayoneted by troopers of Assam Rifles in 1939–1940 during what is called the Second Nupi Lan, over the issue of rice being exported from Imphal valley by a compact of British colonial overlords and Manipur's king, and the transaction completed by Marwari traders of the time. It created massive shortages of this staple, coming as it did after floods in 1939 that devastated crops.

They have witnessed other indignities wrought by quirks of history and rulers.

Like the seemingly innocuous incident in early 1972 set some Meitei nationalists on edge. On 21st January that year, Manipur was formally declared a fully-fledged state of India. The attitude and optics of that announcement remain controversial in nationalist circles five decades later and is likely to remain controversial as history is increasingly written by those from Manipur instead of sanitised and redacted histories processed by central-government mandated educational institutions in New Delhi.

Aesthetic publicity posters for the inauguration showed classic, if somewhat stereotypical, Meitei symbols. A Manipuri dancer of the Raas Leela form was the centrepiece. Typical of this dance embodying the 'divine love' of Radha and Krishna—and the numerous bewitching gopis without whom this romance is incomplete—she was shown wearing the ethereally beautiful costume, potloi, with its distinct, stiff cylindrical skirt, the kumin. This late-18th century form is credited to the court of a Meitei king, Bhagya Chandra, who reigned a few decades after Hinduism was mandated as the state religion by King Pamheiba. The dancer in the poster was accompanied by far older symbols. The mythical Kangla-sha, a creature with a lion's body and a dragon head, sacred to Meitei heritage, and the ancient practice of Sanamahi—that Pamheiba sought to demolish—was to her right. To the dancer's left was coiled Pakhangba, the dragon-snake central to the Meitei origin myth for both religion and royalty.

The legend read: 'Manipur. A New State Inaugurated by Prime Minister Smt. Indira Gandhi.'

While it was pitch-perfect for a prime minister fresh off a stunning military victory with the surrender of a huge contingent of Pakistan's armed forces in East Pakistan-now-Bangladesh, the poster was tone deaf in two significant ways.

First, it portrayed the centrality of Meitei culture and people to the exclusion of all other peoples of the state—an attitude that is ironically pointed out by the Naga, Kuki and Zomi citizens of Manipur.

And second, the 'new state' the government of India and its outreach announced was actually an old state. The name Manipur dates from the time of the formal ingress of Hinduism, which predates both the

British Indian empire and the spread of the East India Company in the subcontinent. Manipur existed as a kingdom and confederacy that traces its origin to the early centuries of the Common Era, and was over time known by several names—Kangleipak evidently being the most prominent.

The kingdom of Manipur segued to complete British control after the Anglo-Manipur war of 1891. On 15 October 1949, Manipur formally merged with India—an act by the last king of Manipur, Bodhchandra, who signed a treaty of accession with India on 21 September that year. Both dates and events remain riotously controversial. They are interpreted by Meitei nationalists as Bodhchandra having been pressured by a newly-independent India, with an or-else signing ceremony in Shillong, where Manipur's royals maintained a residence. Bodhchandra signed what is known as the Manipur Merger Agreement with V.P. Menon, who was at the time secretary in the ministry of states, among other things tasked with integrating—sometimes with unabashed pressure—the several hundred kingdoms and 'princely states' into the Indian dominion. Manipur remained a relatively minor state within the union for several years. In 1956 Manipur was redesignated an Union Territory, governed directly by the central government under the direct administrative control of the home ministry before being made a state in 1972 with full federal privileges and powers—on paper, at any rate.

'It is our wish,' Indira Gandhi announced somewhat imperiously at the formal inauguration, 'that Manipur may shine like a gem and impart beauty to the whole of India.'

Indira had been pushed to make even that concession.

A recap of the times from a digital archive of Manipur Police records it in a bland—but telling—manner:

During 1969–70, the demand for statehood of Manipur became violent. A black flag demonstration was also staged before the Prime Minister of India, Smt. Indira Gandhi on 23rd September 1969 when she visited Imphal. The police had to open fire to control the mob. During this period, the subversive revolutionary groups also came out with different names. The Police had a tough time in controlling the activities of Meitei State Committee and R.G.M. (Revolutionary Govt. of Manipur), in addition to handling the agitation for statehood by different political parties and students.

On the law and order front, the Meitei State Committee, which was badly mauled in 1970–71, ceased to exist during 1971–72 with the surrender of its top leaders in May 1971. Some members of another organization namely RGM (Revolutionary Government of Manipur) reached Jiribam [a town in southwestern Manipur, near Silchar in Assam and a major hub of interstate movement of both people and goods], possibly for want of other suitable harbour after the liberation of Bangladesh, with a large quantity of arms and ammunition. The self-styled leader and some of his lieutenants were arrested there as a result of an excellent follow-up by the police. Another top-ranking leader was also arrested by the police at Imphal. This finished RGM almost completely. Thus, the police achieved a great success in almost eliminating these two underground organizations.

The troubles continued through the subsequent years of Indira's iron hand, including imposition of an Emergency in 1975–1977, through her electoral defeat in 1977 and her spectacular victory in India's premiership league in 1980. Indeed, those years formed the bedrock of Manipur's many rebellions today. As the police archives tell us:

During 1978–79, 13 Police Outposts were opened in Central District to control the activities of the Meitei extremists under the leadership of N. Bisheswar Singh, who wanted to revive the subversive activities of the group called R.G.M. A group of 16 Meitei youths led by him went to Lhasa secretly for training sometime in 1976 and after returning to Manipur committed a series of crimes. Their organisation came to be known as PLA (People's Liberation Army)—the name of the Chinese Army. Following their violent activities, the whole of the Central District was declared disturbed area on 21/7/78. A few other insurgents [sic] groups like PREPAK, etc. also emerged, and they continued to indulge in violent activities such as looting, murder, snatching of arms and extortion, etc. The police mounted a relentless attack on these organizations and achieved a great deal of success.

In 1980–81, the activities of the subversive Meitei extremist groups namely PLA, PREPAK and KCP assumed serious proportions. They carried out 21 ambushes and killed 67 persons, in addition to injuring 57 persons. Those killed and injured included men of Civil Police, Manipur Rifles, CRPF, RAC, Army, and civilians. They also took away some weapons while committing these crimes. The police, however, reacted with determination and achieved a great success. They killed 25 insurgents and captured 440 insurgents. A *large number of arms and ammunition were also captured. As a result of this pressure, 83 insurgents surrendered to the authorities, as well.*

There was indication of other rebellions. There was the Naga rebellion that steadily spread to the Naga homelands to Manipur's north—another future flashpoint of conflict and conflict resolution in the millennial Naga peace process. And there was the continuing burn of the Mizo rebellion, an ethnicity and territory with which Manipur shares an easily crossed border to the south:

Simultaneously, the Underground Nagas also resumed their violent activities especially in the Manipur East District. There was a very fierce ambush on an Army convoy on Imphal-Ukhrul road in which Army lost 20 personnel and large number of weapons,

In the Manipur South District, the Mizo National Front was active and indulged in collection of money/ration, etc. from the villagers bordering Mizoram.

Such matters remain emotive. In fact, Manipur's merger with India remains an emotive issue more than seven decades after the fact, with Meitei rebel groups calling for a state-wide shutdown each year on 15th October. Their statements always highlight the primary accusation: that the signing over of Manipur to India was done 'under duress'; some even describe the signatory king as having been 'incompetent'. The shutdown is usually more effective in Imphal Valley, not the hill regions.

(The kingdom of Tripura's merger with India also took effect on the same day. Kanchan Prava Devi, the regent of Tripura, was the signatory; she had signed a treaty of accession—the 'instrument' of accession—over two years earlier, on 13 August 1947. As we shall discuss later in greater detail, the merger remains an emotional issue among the Tripuri—not immigrant Bengalis but those who answer to the Tiprasa ethnic groups; but the merger-emotion, as it were, is relatively less explosive than in Manipur. The problem in Tripura is more on account of ethnic tension and misgovernance than the merger.)

Since the 1980s, when conflict began to rage here between agencies of the government of India and rebels and non-combatants alike—citizens that India ironically claimed as its own—it sometimes appears to be a blur of nupi lan with scant breaks.

Outraged nupi took to the streets in 2000 to protest the massacre that also began Sharmila's fast.

In 2004, ten middle-aged women marched to Imphal's Kangla Fort, disrobed, and screamed at the resident Assam Rifles and 'Indian Army' contingents to rape them as they did their 'daughter'. They accused troopers of raping and killing Thangjam Manorama, a suspected rebel proxy, in a burst of extra-judicial terror. The incident created global headlines, deeply embarrassed the governments of India and Manipur, blew the lid off rampant extra-judicial killings as nothing before had, and quickly led to Kangla Fort, the spiritual hub for Manipur's majority Meitei community, to be formally returned to the 'people' in a partial gesture of reconciliation.

Ima Mangol sat still on the dais for more than an hour before her turn. She spoke in Meiteilon. In measured, unwavering tones she underscored the need for 'integrity in protest and resistance'. If things didn't change in the basic construct and relationship of Manipur and India, she said a set of doors might open, and another set would close. She had invoked a saying in Meitei lore to send India a message.

Nonpok thong haangba spoke to 'opening the eastern gate'.

Nongchup thong thingba meant 'closing the western gate'.

Some years later, my friend Debabrata 'Bobby' Roy Laifungbam said much the same thing to me during a conversation at his home in Imphal about politics and identity. A human rights and development activist who eschewed the profession of doctor, and son of a fiercely independent-minded Manipuri princess and writer, Binodini Devi, Tamo Bobby, or 'elder brother' Bobby, was as animated in responding to India and Manipur's many missteps as Ima Mangol.

Either way, they both articulated an enduring thought—even though interpretations of the 'gate' has changed over time. For many in this far-eastern region of India, geographically as well as intellectually 'Mainland India' lies to the west, beyond the western gates that can so easily be shut. Unless India's entire far-east enables it—and India in turn enables and empowers its far-east for that privilege—India's expectations of journeying thought the eastern gate will remain a chaos of bad faith, bad policy and fractured dreams. Mainland China will not have done it, not entirely at any rate. Its main competitor in the region, Mainland India, will have.

To the gates.

Book One

SMOKE

1. Guns and Runners:
À la Carte at the Eastern Gate

Dining room at Imphal Classic full of diplomats. Reps from missions, dy high comm and consulates of UK, US, Japan from Delhi and Cal/Kol. For ceremony to commemorate Battle of Imphal in WWII. Field Marshal William Joseph Slim's grandson here too. Slim was Lt. Gen. in Dec 1944 when he was knighted near Imphal along with 3 of his corp commanders by the viceroy Field Marshall Archibald Wavell. Reward for finally pushing back Japanese Army that July. Hope Slim the younger has had time to visit the sometime bungalow of his granddad in Kangla Fort just to the south of Classic. Breakfast a great mix even without the diplomats. Japanese filmmaker tracking WWII history. Evangelist family (Yanks). Elderly Tamil couple: bureaucrat parents, family? En route Moreh to visit family? Pit-stop before returning home? A Marwari bizman greets his local guests and, evidently, key contact, with loud cry of 'UNKEL! How are you?'

Trip to Moreh cancelled on a/c of bandh/blockade called by Thadou Students' Association to protest perceived falsification of complaint & inaction by sec forces re mid-June incident of violence against some of the community. And this is India's bridgehead to Myanmar and SE Asia! Part of Asian Highway 1! Good paper plan but thus far, geo-economic + geopolitical joke! Prefer to call this ongoing hoax 'Indo-Myanmar road'. Boipu texts to say blockade should lift on NH 102 (Imphal-Moreh stretch of old NH 39) but United Naga Council ban on 'construction of government project works like railways, Asian highway etc in hill districts'.

Blockade politics is as bizarre. Whoever does it blames one or more ethnic or political group or govt. In any case usually they all blame India.

Looking forward to Ratha Jatra feast at Nobo's place. Unique yet wonderful to see Jagannath's chariots being pulled along in so many neighbourhoods in Imphal. No escaping the juggernaut of 18th C. Hindu-Sylheti-Bengali-

Brahmin-caste ingress and conversion by royal decree. Unsurprising so many traditionalist/nationalist Meitei dislike king Pamheiba!

Fabulous feast. 20 course, mix of Meitei + Bengali. Nobo's dignified wife politely introduces me to four dignified ladies invited to lunch as 'victims of domestic violence, they now make bags and other things'.

Can't forget chat with US consul general from Cal/Kol. We'd travelled to Imphal on the same flight. Discussed pathetic dev in Manipur, massive corruption, fractured pol situation, iffy conflict resolution. Spoke of her meeting with Ibobi. She queried the CM about development and he diverted the conversation to how China was a threat. Am not a diplomat, so laughed aloud. CG smiled politely. Diplomatic equivalent of belly-slapping laughter.

History, politics, ethnicity, econ, gender issues, cuisine, culture and govt attitude. All between breakfast & lunch. Let's see what Moreh has in store!

T is an excellent host.

'Beretta? Glock? Llama?' he offers a few top-of-the line 9 mm handguns. T smiles; he can see I'm impressed. 'Browning? Smith and Wesson?'

He then begins to show off the aperitifs. The Beretta .380, a design first developed by American handgun legend John Browning as the Automatic Colt Pistol in the early years of the 20th century, and has steadily morphed into a deliverer of ever-punchier, ever-quicker bullets. There is also the more delicate .32 Beretta, quite deadly, that carry slimmer 7.65 mm rounds. 'Maybe for your girlfriend, nah?'

T's face twitches with mirth and methamphetamine. His hands shake as he tries to hold a small mug of milky tea to his lips and after a futile attempt at sipping gently, gives up. The mug rattles as he sets it down on the tabletop between us. His fingers twitch before he firmly sets them on his track pants. His other accessories are a plain T-shirt, single-strap slippers popular across this region, and a slim gold chain. Out of politeness I too set down my mug, floral-patterned, Made-in-China ware that adds more colour in a room of scattershot décor: a few photographs of Christ, homilies, an awkwardly posing family, a kaleidoscopic and quite worn sofa, a large new television set and a set-top device that beams a football match in Europe, muted for our meeting. T's glassy eyes reflect the green and red of a football pitch that carries rampaging players of Manchester United. My behaviour calms him, aided by the soothing words of our go-between without whom this rendezvous in one of Moreh's crowded wards would not have come about. I'm safe, my interlocutor assures T, he can speak freely.

Reassured, T offers a collectors' favourite, an antique 9mm masterpiece of a handgun from Germany's über-alles years. 'Luger?'

The made-in-Spain Llama retails for ₹1,50,000 at T's weapons deli. The very American Smith and Wesson is marked up at ₹1,80,000. The Italian Beretta, now also manufactured in the United States, and the slick Austrian Glock at ₹2,00,000 a piece. Second hand. New weapons that come in 'packing' carry significant premium. Either way, it's cash only. Indian Rupees also work across the border in north-western Myanmar. Naturally ammunition is extra, and keeps the well-greased after-sales market running robustly.

T is one of several weapons procurers in town who feed some Kuki rebel groups, occasionally a Naga rebel faction, and an assortment of other rebels in far-eastern India. Specifically, T is more like a distributor to the area's connoisseurs—politicians, crime lords, the occasional politician-crime lord. They also top-up small rebel groups. Well-established and relatively large Naga and Meitei rebel groups and factions, for example, don't need those like T—even though they have reached him, and those like him, from time to time, for supplies to be collected in Churachandpur and Imphal, even Dimapur. They usually deal directly with the aggregator-suppliers in Myanmar who have their long reach into China, Thailand and of course Myanmar black-and-grey markets, watched over by their armies. The National Socialist Council of Nagalim (Isak-Muivah), for instance, has for long run its own supply chain from Myanmar to reach adjacent Ukhrul district of Manipur—a significant I-M haven on account of ethnic ties—and also into two eastern districts of Arunachal Pradesh bordering Myanmar, also Naga homelands.

T agrees to let me record our conversation and take notes, but requests anonymity. In a place with a population of about 20,000—roughly double if one counts Moreh's hinterland—and tightly-knit communities of Kuki, Meitei, the Meitei Pangal, and Tamil, Sikh and Nepali folk displaced by Myanmar's decades-old ethnic cleansing, all stuffed in nine small wards, the tiniest clue can be a giveaway. T claims he would then be open to 'harassment' by—and which might include more payoffs to—rogue elements in Manipur's police, Indian government paramilitaries, and various factions of rebels in Manipur who play protector. Worse, he might end up dead.

It's time for the main course. I ask T: How about some assault rifles?

He offers several Kalashnikov copies and variants. These are new and used AK 47s brought in courtesy of Thai suppliers, and from the autonomous Shan state in Myanmar's east, bordering China, Thailand and Lao; AK 56 and Type 81s 'from China', a steady trickle of that country's jettisoned and leached supplies that find a ready local, regional, even global, market. There are ageing American M-15s and M-16s sourced from Thailand, which remains a conduit of Vietnam-era supplies alongside more recent models. The lively and the leaky among Myanmar's army are also occasional suppliers.

I've seen several such weapons during several visits to camps of various Naga rebel groups from 2009 onwards. During one such visit, to the main camp of the Unification faction of the National Socialist Council of Nagaland (NSCN) in Kehoi, east of Dimapur, I spent time talking to some cadres after interviewing a top official. These cadres were lounging about in the courtyard outside the hut where I had conducted the interview. They were cleaning handguns. There were two 9mm weapons, and a .32 calibre one. This last was an Astra, of Spanish manufacture. One of the 9mm weapons was a Smith & Wesson, the other a Spanish Star with Myanmar army markings in Burmese script. It wasn't the only time I've seen such marking on rebel weapons. And, during a visit to Camp Hebron, the administrative and military headquarters of NSCN (I-M), I saw both female and male cadres carry all manner of assault rifles and hand guns: a well-equipped mini army which it was—is.

As with the handguns, a la carte assault weapons cost around

₹3,00,000 each for used, double and more for 'packing'. Accessories are quite easily available, T assures me. Ammunition, sniper scopes, laser guidance, silencers for both assault rifles and handguns. After payment it takes approximately four days for the order to travel from the supply and finance hub of Mandalay to Tamu; cross-border, cross-cultural delivery that cuts through the Amazon of logistics, unofficial red-tape and rebel-tape.

What else? Landmines, grenades, RPGs—all 'made in China,' T says reassuringly, although the demand for landmines in this side of the border is low even if it remains a bit of a rage with Myanmar's army.

Were I hungry, I joke with T, such a menu would lead to the onset of a food coma.

But you haven't had dessert, he shoots back with a smile that momentarily dispels the glaze in his eyes, the twitching on his face, the air-piano playing fingers. How about a GSG, a German .22 calibre sports rifle, telescopic sight thrown in at a discount?

Moreh is billed as India's key transit point to Myanmar on the ribbon of two planned Asian Highway routes—Route 1 and Route 2—linking Southeast Asia with West Asia through India and Bangladesh. It's mostly a route on paper and emblazoned on hopeful distance markers and signboards. A Land Customs Station is being upgraded; it is to be integrated with immigration facilities. A truck park is planned. There's been talk of a mineral park for limestone, copper ore and such from Myanmar. (The route would dovetail with a proposed BCIM, Bangladesh-China-India-Myanmar economic corridor that since the 1990s has attempted to move along a corridor to connect Kunming in China's south-western Yunnan province and designated hub for all policy and practical outreach in this part of the region, to Myanmar and then, via Bangladesh, to Kolkata. India, wary of the C in BCIM, has remained selective about its options. India has also eyed with suspicion a project by China National Petroleum Corporation (CNPC) to transport crude oil and gas from the Bay of Bengal through an 800-km pipeline to

Kunming in Yunnan province—not dissimilar to India's own plans to link Mizoram, or to ship hydrocarbons and other products to Kolkata and beyond via Myanmar.)

Plans have for several years—at least since the early 1990s—called for products and people from both countries and points beyond to move seamlessly—officially—through this eastern gate at Moreh, giving the town a dimension greater than its daily-market-town persona. It has always been preferred as a more upgraded enterprise than the daily-market exchange at Behiang, the border town southwest of Moreh in Manipur's Churachandpur district. This is along the old Tiddim Road, which heads due south from Imphal through Behiang and right to Tiddim, or Tedim, about 130 km south from this border in Myanmar's Chin state. This is the road the imperial Japanese army travelled up to fight the battle of Imphal during the Second World War.

That's the hazy future. For now, the underbelly is the belly. Weapons that come in to India. Narcotics of various shades and grades that travel both ways. Animals for the food and pharmacy markets of Southeast Asia and China.

Red sandalwood from the forests of India's Karnataka and Tamil Nadu states. This is highly prized and smuggled to Myanmar and onwards to the contraband and finance transhipment hub of Mandalay to the Shan State and through to southwest China, fetching four to five times what it costs in far-eastern India. Another route moves red sandalwood to Thailand through points like Chiang Rai and Mae Sot in Thailand—Mae Sot a point on a proposed 'Trilateral Highway' that would run through about half the length of Myanmar to link it to Moreh. A select few among Moreh's small but influential Tamil community have the reputation of a long reach from the eastern end of the subcontinent to its very south, a reach that survives a route traversing several thousand kilometres and several Indian states. One such Tamil gentleman at the apex of this trade and whose name is spoken both admiringly and carefully, carries a reputation that opens doors in every state capital that lies on the route, from Imphal to Chennai, and is reputed to hold some strings in New Delhi and Nay Pyi Taw as well.

Sometimes, when the scrutiny on Moreh and the Manipur route is high, trucks carrying red sandalwood—as investigation from their occasional interdiction in Assam show—head to Mizoram, for secretion across that state's 510-km border with Myanmar. Besides several jungle tracks into Myanmar that's typical of the entire border stretch from Arunachal Pradesh to Nagaland, Manipur and Mizoram (adding up to 1,643 km), there's a border-trade crossing at Zokhawthar in eastern Mizoram, along the Tiau river, which demarcates the international border here for over nearly 200 kilometres. Across the border a secondary road links up with the old Tiddim Road. Like water, trade usually finds a way.

There are more innocent products: Indian-made pharmaceuticals, fabric for the ubiquitous Myanmarese longyi—also made in Kolkata and Chennai, as manufacturers' tags proclaim in stores in several regions of Myanmar—juices and fruit-flavoured beverage, chocolate, infant food, tyres for Bajaj autorickshaws. I've ridden these Made-in-India vehicles several times on a 15-minute ride from Nanpharlong just across the border from Moreh to Tamu, the nearest town in Myanmar that falls within the radius in which Indians are permitted to travel without a visa, from morning until 5 pm. In a reverse flow arrive LED lamps, blankets, toys, consumer goods, Godzilla brand mosquito repellent, even the delicious, long green beans—yongchak—practically worshipped in Manipur and elsewhere in far-eastern India.

Official trade data for Moreh with the Ministry of Development of North Eastern Region placed two-way trade at a little over ₹4 crore or ₹40 million for 2010–2011 (which increased to a over ₹16 crore or ₹160 million in 2017–2018; border trade statistics are notoriously slow to be updated in central government records). Largely, betel nut was imported, cumin seed exported. Mostly agricultural products and medicine are permitted to be traded without application of duty.

Unofficial trade figures? Officially incalculable. Although an intelligence operative in Imphal told me that his best estimate is ₹100 crore a day—a billion rupees—'incalculable' seems a safer option. Incalculable too is the quantum of cut paid to government officials, security overseers, and rebel groups—even rebel groups in ceasefire with the government of India, and, occasionally, the government of Myanmar.

The same uneasy economy applies to narcotics, Moreh's plasma. As with weapons, this web connects several communities, both ethnic and economic.

One morning in July 2014, after a breakfast of excellent fresh idlis and chutney in Moreh's Tamil neighbourhood, adjacent to the border with Myanmar, I headed to one of its Kuki neighbourhoods, set a little further back from the border than the Tamil neighbourhood. Here, a little further back can mean just a couple of hundred metres; it's a serpentine border, much like local and cross-border equations.

The hillside of the veng—a ward in the Kuki-Chin-Mizo languages—had dumps of hundreds, thousands, some even containing tens of thousands of emptied pseudoephedrine strips; blister packs as well as all-foil packs of medicine usually used to treat nasal congestion and the common cold. There had clearly been some attempt to burn the evidence, but it appeared half-hearted, even brazen, like brushing things under a carpet. There were small clumps of melted plastic fused with foil. Amos Holdou Khongsai's grave held a memorial plaque, but no decoration except dried leaves and a forest of empty strips that began right at the tomb. The strips showed a mix. I counted four different brands from as many Indian manufacturers.

The medicine is extracted and then transported to Myanmar for use in manufacturing methamphetamines. 'Speed' comes from it, but that's an old-fashioned name. A derivative is the caffeine-spiked Yaba, which means 'crazy medicine' or 'mad drug' in Thai, the production engine for which is located largely in the north-eastern Shan State in Myanmar—mainly in the autonomous region controlled by the Wa. (A briefing on narco-terrorism by an Indian source just before that trip was instructive: 'According to our information there are twenty-four small to large factories making WY in Myanmar—three in Rakhine state, two in Kachin state, the rest in Shan State, bordering Kachin and Thailand.')

In far-eastern India, the pills usually come in the brighter colours of the spectrum that sell with the imprint WY. This cousin of the purer crystal methamphetamine, or crystal-meth—or Ice—has spawned a new moniker: World-is-Yours. Plentiful, cheap and, even as I visited, blanketing this region of India and neighbouring Bangladesh.

It wouldn't do to linger. This wasn't the main street of Moreh where Mandalay beer from Myanmar, Tiger beer from Singapore and the Chinese Dali are so openly, reasonably available alongside Indian brands of rum and whiskey—this last a steady trickle courtesy of bent security forces in this geography, as my hosts told me, reiterating a claim I've heard here for several years. The supply of liquor is always plentiful in this border town, far more than at Pallel, the entry point to these south-eastern hills on the road to Moreh. Numbers can vary depending on upticks of security alerts, but there are usually six checkpoints between Pallel and Moreh. Most travellers and traders to and from Moreh are checked, usually by troopers of Assam Rifles. It sometimes turns brutal at these checkpoints, as I have witnessed several times over the years and written of it: the act of stripping vehicles to find contraband, drugs and weapons can often extend of stripping citizens of their dignity—including queries in colloquial Hindi as to their ancestry and proclivity for incest, the extent of their knowledge of Hindi, and their patriotism towards India. Yet such streams never run dry.

This part of the veng was no place for an outsider and people were beginning to notice. I left after hurriedly taking photographs and a grabbing a fistful of empty strips.

In comparison, there was a feeling of relative comfort at Ima B's heroin hutch. It was a small house in one of Moreh's back alleys, in a multi-ethnic neighbourhood. The portly, jolly matron leaned back on a small bed that functions as a settee. That was the sanctum. I sat across from her on a chair. She was busy, and indicated in her gravelly voice after several minutes that we could begin our conversation—naturally with the caveat that she would take time out whenever business calls.

Ima, as everyone called her, was calmly efficient. She measured heroin—No. 4 in parlance—from a hollowed-out bamboo bowl into a kokta, a tiny metal container usually used to measure ground tobacco and spices. It's ₹100 a kokta. Most buyers prefered to stay in a covered space adjacent to the sanctum, shoot up with a puriya-worth of substance, a 'shot'. Like the young man who came to Ima B's centre of operations—her bedroom. This main room of the house was tiny, the bed by a tiny window with grills. He handed over a syringe with a plunger removed. Ima poured ₹50 worth of No. 4 into it. He returned to a low wooden table with a couple of ashtrays and candles and carefully poured a measure of water from a plastic jug—water from the well in the backyard—placed the plunger in the tube of the syringe and gave it a good shake for a minute or so. He sat, then heated the thin needle over the flame of a candle, gave it a while to cool down, flexed his bare arm with its ready streams of vein, and with the delicacy of a caring nurse inserted the needle into a vein and, very gently, shot up. He leaned back on the chair and closed his eyes.

There were a dozen or so men and three women seated there on plastic chairs around a scattering of plastic tables with a scattering of match boxes and cheap plastic lighters, and lit candles. Some of the men were in vests, a few bare-chested. They spoke in low tones if they spoke at all. An attractive lady who looked to be in her mid-30s but could have been years younger got up to go to the well, drew a bucket of water, and poured it over her head, over her T-shirts and jeans and after shaking off excess water and chit-chatting with a couple of men near the well, resumed her place in the hutch. A few smoked No. 4. Some snorted it. All were unmindful of the quality of the heroin, uncaring of whatever other substance it was 'cut' with, or whether it was an opiate or mostly opioid. Not everyone stayed. Some heavy users revisited up to five times a day. Some took a two- or three-day supply and went off to their villages.

We hit a busy patch. I counted seven buyers in a 10-minute stretch as my translator, a young lady who worked with a local NGO, explained my presence. Ima responded with a series of 'Hmm's without missing a beat of the trade or barked instructions. I borrowed the kokta, and in a burst of *Scarface* fantasy I dipped a little finger into it and then licked the powder, as I've seen policemen and anti-narcotic agents do in Hollywood movies. It was acrid, intensely chemical. I made a face.

Ima, the translator and a customer burst out laughing. Comic relief during a long day. Ima's shop opened at 3:30 each morning and closed at 7:30 in the evening.

Among an estimated 150 such sellers in Moreh, of which she claimed a fifth were 'Manipuri'—shorthand for Meitei, her ethnicity—Ima B claimed to sell about eight grams of No. 4 a day to residents and visitors. Kukis formed the majority of the remainder, but there were Tamils and other communities in the game too. Ima B profited by ₹1,000 daily from a sale of ₹8,000 worth of substance a day. She said she received her supplies from an 'agent' in Moreh who also fronted the money, and who in turn received it from 'Burma'. This agent, her sponsor, pocketed the rest. And, like her sponsor, she also needed to pay the police, which she conflated with 'police commandos'—an elite force in Manipur's police with an unlovely, proven history of thuggishness and staging encounters, a power unto themselves—and the local bureaucracy. She named specific forces, specific designations among the police and bureaucracy, who received monthly payment. It was all organised. When police came to collect, they carried a list of sellers and methodically checked it off. That's how Ima B, who had been in the business for thirteen years as I met her, knew of the number of No. 4 sellers.

She was a widow. Her husband had tuberculosis and was unable to work or pay for medical bills. No. 4 offered a relatively easy way out to pay the bills, run the house, bring up the children. Trials leading to a trap wasn't an uncommon story in these parts.

From what I gathered from several conversations, people like Ima B didn't deal with 'UG' or political parties. That devolved to the handful of 'agents' who work their deals with rebel groups and politicians in the district and in Imphal. For heroin, WY, the lot. This was a part of nearly every conversation I've had on the subject since the mid-2000s in this region, or about this region and, indeed, in Moreh from the first time I visited this border town in 2008, and during subsequent visits here.

In February 2014, just months before my visit to Moreh's ephedrine dump, Ajay Chaudhary, a colonel of the Indian Army and five others, including a soldier with the Territorial Army and locals, were arrested on charges of ferrying from Imphal to Moreh pseudoephedrine tablets of various well-known brands valued at between ₹150 million and ₹200 million. The colonel's car sported defence ministry plates and a beacon. Two other cars in the convoy had 'Army' pasted on the windshields. Police chased them down when the officer breezed past a check post flashing his credentials. Another of those arrested was an Imphal-based security official with an airline. Shipping such medicine as bulk couriered consignments wasn't uncommon. Neither were articles in media about consignments seized at Imphal's airport, or unclaimed packages that, after investigation were found to contain pseudoephedrine tablets.

'You have heard about the arrest of a colonel,' an official with a central intelligence agency later told me in Imphal. 'If he can do it at his level then what about brigadier, senior officers, ministers of Manipur? The colonel has done many runs. He got caught.'

Was it an accident or was Col. Chaudhary tracked? I asked, over coffee in my hotel room, away from the CCTV cameras and public attention in the hotel's lobby and restaurant.

'We got information that he's been indulging in such activities for the past one and a half years. He was even being watched by Manipur commandos.' He meant police commandos. 'MI [Military Intelligence] has started looking into other officers. For example, with 26 Sector AR in Pallel. Brigadier.' He mentioned a name. 'He cleverly left.'

Even so, the interdiction of a colonel was a rarity in this regional trade that security personnel I spoke to placed at several billion rupees a year. They pointed to the involvement of at least a dozen rebel groups of all ethnic persuasions such as Naga, Meitei, Kuki, and Zomi, active in Manipur; and that of the political, bureaucratic and security establishments. All feed off the narco-economy. All want to control it. All find some accommodations, find a level.

This level hasn't been without conflict—indeed, for some decades. In an entry for November 1992, just before NSCN(I-M) ratcheted up a genocidal campaign on Kukis for control of land, a project commissioned by United Nations High Commission for Refugees recorded a comment on the region's narcotics trade. The entry by the Minorities at Risk project noted that Kuki and Naga armed groups 'have frequently clashed in the past for control of the lucrative heroin trade route through Moreh, an Indian outpost close to the Burmese border'. It added: 'Both groups have a powerful vested interest in prolonging communal conflicts in order to divert attention from their profitable smuggling of timber, gold and heroin. Both the Kukis and the Nagas see this trade (especially heroin), as the best way to finance their guerrilla wars against the Indian government.' And—the observation didn't add—against each other.

To the north and south of the Imphal-Moreh artery lie narcotic havens cradled in hilly terrain. In Ukhrul district to the north, a stronghold of Naga rebels, poppy and cannabis are grown—with the south and east of the district favouring poppy and the west, cannabis. Poppy is a favoured crop to the south in Chandel and Churachandpur to the south-west, which like Ukhrul border Myanmar; here Kuki, Zomi and Meitei rebels have sanctuary. Cannabis is largely absorbed into north-eastern India, eastern India and Bangladesh. Poppy, often with poppy seeds supplied by patrons in Myanmar, as I'm told in the course of several interviews in Imphal and Moreh, has more of to-and-fro from raw material to finished product. Poppy sap is cooked into a base to manufacture heroin. It is then transported by couriers using steep mountain trails into Myanmar, with their financiers billing 'transportation charges' of between ₹15,000-20,000 a kilo. It returns as heroin, distributed using various channels, including Asian Highway 1.

T Mongbuh (Tongneh Mongbuh) not T Mongbung as I first wrote it, BK corrects me. Good to have BK around, he speaks Thadou-Kuki. Around 300 pop., 20–30 houses. Western edge of Valley, west of Loktak lake. Gorgeous: impossibly green plains to rolling green hills, cloud-crown, rain swept afternoon. Quiet.

LK, 23, is a duo-crop farmer like most in this hamlet. Paddy in the family's five-acre farm just over the crest of the first hill. After harvest in Oct-Nov, poppy. No option, he says. Nine children just in the house he lives in—'they consume a lot'. Rice for subsistence and some surplus sale, poppy for everything else. Payoffs the responsibility of buyer though he does shell out to the adamant cop. Reluctant to speak of UG links—although most Kuki UG are now AG! They have weapons, connections, LK and his family have mouths to feed. I ask where the poppy sap—also called jelly, kaami goes. 'Burma.' Uses old name for Mynamar that many people still do. Then he checks himself, worried. 'I don't know.' (See int with narc/spook: he talked of trails from Ukhrul to Myanmar, CC'Pur to Myanmar. Carriers paid INR 30K to transport sap consignments weighing 30 kg or so.)

Also ref int with AMADA official. Big name. All Manipur Anti-Drug Asscn. Big mission. Change farmers over from narc to regular crops: pea, yam, potato, maize. Trying to work thru govt agri dept to do soil testing & identify appropriate seed type in Ukhrul, east of Senapati, Tamenglong, Valley fringe areas. Uphill task. 'Actual financiers not from the farming areas,' AMADA guy Phoney says. UGs, bureaucrats, pols. Villagers want to make 'easy money'. That's how financiers convince villagers to plant poppy. Becomes a tussle between what's 'right' and what's 'economic'. Investors track output. Sometimes change plantation location after 2/3 yrs as soil nutrients diminish. When farmers see good R.O.I. they sometimes begin planting poppy even without investors. Guy clams up when I probe deeper about connections, pushback from financiers via govt and open threats from UG to not cut poppy & marijuana, incl. providing weapons to farmers to guard crop. Seeing my disappointment suggests I try bora—pakora—made with poppy leaves. LOVE bora!

CHK claim of NGO guy + cop, both Meitei, that AMADA and CADA—Coalition Against Drugs & Alcohol—have 'supporting groups'. Says AMADA is KYKL & that's why AMADA's POA is more extreme, mirroring KYKL ideology; CADA links = UNLF. But what about Valley groups benefitting from narc? Clams up. Won't be pushed.

Pride of place in LK's largish hut, crowded, musty main room is an old Philips TV. The other prominent display is a framed poster of the Last Supper. A Bible-belt makeover of the original earthy da Vinci I had coincidentally seen just months earlier at Sta. Maria delle Grazie. But as powerful as that experience was, the kitschy copy is no less powerful in this small homestead, in its context of faith and survival, and with its additional message: 'I am the Bread of Life. Whoever comes to me will never be Hungry.' A booster message on a table by the door, is from John 6: 35. 'Whoever Believes in me will never Thirst.'

Paddy, poppy and prayer. So it goes.

Here, security forces live cheek by jowl with militant groups that are either actively belligerent or have suspended hostilities as part of negotiations with the government. Either way, there's coexistence in a food chain from financier to farmer to seller to buyer—and protectors. The occasional interdiction of narcotic consignments, occasional destruction of marijuana and poppy fields, is just for 'namesake', a lady with an Imphal-based legal-aid group for HIV-AIDS echoed the comment of an Imphal-based intelligence officer with the central government who once showed me, and later texted me, photos of a well-known rebel commander from Northeast India in the middle of poppy fields in the borderlands of India and Myanmar.

When I visit the office of the sub-divisional police officer in Moreh, the ranking civilian law-enforcer in town, the gentleman offers a suitably surreal interview. The officer of Manipur Police is nervous, evasive. He denies there is any smuggling in Moreh, let alone any sale, trade or trafficking in narcotics and weapons. He claims there are no representatives or proxies of rebel groups in Moreh. He cannot of course speak for what happens in other parts of Manipur, or just across the border in Nanpharlong, or Tamu—that's Myanmar's problem. It's also Manipur's problem, I don't have the heart to tell him what he already knows. Some of his senior colleagues in Imphal and some sources in local rebel movements spoke to me of how politicians, bureaucrats, contractors and even some large NGOs take a skim from projects—over and above their own skim—and often 'arrange' to have these funds delivered in Tamu, where 'VBIGs', or Valley-based insurgent groups as they are called in security parlance, maintain residences and camp-offices.

Indeed, the police officer claims there is hardly any crime in Moreh.

His colleague, a superintendent of the local operations of the emphatically named Customs Preventive Force, is equally evasive. He claims he hasn't heard of trafficking in contraband. He has heard nothing of raw materials for the drug trade being shipped from Moreh and points to the north and south across to Myanmar. He knows nothing of refashioned drugs, from WY to No. 4, making their way back. He knows nothing of weapons supplies, or the purported methods to smuggle them. He knows nothing of the other lucrative and long-term revenue stream in Moreh: the highly prized, and priced, red sandalwood. Like all local government officials when speaking on record on matters of policing, security and contraband, he knows nothing of the shadowy cabal of Tamil gentlemen who control the trade from their base in Moreh, easily maintaining footprints in Manipur and Delhi and southern India; who, with the impressive facility of the cosmopolitan fluently speak Tamil, Burmese, Meiteilon, English, Hindi, and a dialect or two of the Kuki.

Moreh is the first hub of denial. There are many hubs of denial—Tengnoupal, Pallel, Lilong—all the way back to Imphal and to points far beyond.

Waiting for word from the Anjuman Islahi Uashrah @ Lilong for 4 pm mtng. No point hanging around Imphal, so head on past Lilong past Thoubal (didn't see aloo-puri lady outside Thoubal mkt area, too late in day, next time) & Wangjing to Khongjom. Such a dramatic place. Khongjom War Memorial hugely significant marker: memorial to Anglo-Manipur War of 1891. Formal end of Manipur as independent kingdom. As significant a year as 1949, seen by most when M pressured to formally accede to Indian Union. Bitter-sweet history since, on balance more bitter than sweet.

Stunning 360° view from tree-shielded hill. Memorial monolith from 1972 encased in polished granite on hilltop. Quotes Paona Brajabasi, major in Manipur army, executed here by Brits: 'The enemy's shell can land in our camp … Whereas ours cannot in theirs my fellow countrymen! It is a disgrace to die fleeing, death is now sure for us but we will never retreat.' Paddies all around, rectangles of silvery water, western cordon of hills in CC'Pur far, nearer hills to the east just a few ranges & gorges away from Myanmar. Absolute stillness. Even young couples are quiet.

Head back to Lilong for meeting with Anjuman. Meitei-Pangal/Muslim hub. Using differentiator advisedly as not all Muslims here are Manipuri. Most I see aren't. Many eastern Indian faces, faces seen in borderlands of Myanmar/Bangladesh. It's like a different world within Manipur, this patch east & west of Imphal-Moreh highway, half-hour south of Imphal. Skullcaps, headscarves everywhere, many ladies in burqa. Shop names common in other parts of India: Zam Zam Tailors, Shah Travels. Go west, cross slim river and travel in several kms. No churches, Hindu temples, traditional Meitei Sanamahi shanglen, just mosques & madrasas. With add-on topography & flora, could be B'desh. Could be eastern fringe of Bengal.

Anjuman's four-storey office is down a sharp slope. Lower floors house offices, upper floors are where narc addicts/users are kept. The upper-floor windows facing front are crowded as I walk in. Meet Maulana Habibullah Nadwi and Mohammad Mohiyuddin, a community elder. We speak in Hindi. The two aren't Meitei-Pangal. The maulana is aware of the havoc narc has caused in this area, and the unsavoury rep Lilong carries even in a region of unsavoury reps re narc & conflict. Cops, NGO-wallahs speak of Lilong as narco transhipment hub. Frequent news of busts, as elsewhere in the Valley and some parts of hills, but tiny fraction of flow. Maulana speaks of narc-related problems burning through Lilong. Theft. Molestation & rape. 'Inko khatam karna hai,' he says. Noble pursuit!

50–52 inmates in the Anjuman, getting a mix of punishment + prayer. 'Yeh aspatal bhi hai, ek tarah ka jail bhi hai,' Mohiyuddin says bluntly (MORE DETAIL IN RECORDING + PIX). Mix of hospital and jail. Says no law ('ain nahin hai') here, constable to judge. Sometimes sec forces, cops, anti-narcs, AR/army catch folks with heroin, say 'maida, atta'. 'Then they release the culprits. Everyone goes free. Then they threaten us. We don't have weapons. Our weapons are the Quran & Hadis.' He says it's faith vs INR 30 lakh/kg for kaami, base for brown. No. 4 is INR 2,400/gm.

They pull out a register to show names of inmates and seized narcotics ++ in two years. Neatly handwritten in English with each head numbered:

(1) Syrup: 9717 bottles—7549 = 2168 bottles [assuming minus botts of cough syrup used for med purposes!] (2) S.P. tabs = 2,96,452 tabs [Spasmo-Proxyvon painkiller] (3) M. Doxine = 1,360 strips (4) Solucuf = 16,650 strips [contains pseudoephedrine] (5) Lupin D = 16,660 strips (6) No. 4 = 84 gm (7) Kaami = 2 kg 900 gm (8) Wine = 829 litres [booze nt wine] (9) N-10 = 6,467 tabs [sleeping pills, basically] (10) Vehicles = 25 (11) Machine for Kaami manufacturing = 2 nos.

ADD ON: Drugs sold openly in Imphal. More exp than Moreh but still cheap comp with Mainland. Been seeing pushers, users in North AOC area for years, short walk from my regular hotels & near where buses to Kohima-Dimapur & Ukhrul leave every morning. SP aka Spasmo-Proxyvon = painkiller.

Ganja. No. 4. WY. Entry-level No. 4 ₹50/shot. Double ++ for hooked user. Bizarre to see it all near barracks + offices of Manipur cops, CRPF, BSF, AR. Have jogged often in the morning from North AOC past the veng & thru Minuthong Hatta north & east along Kangla Fort perimeter to the CM's res & Secretariat! At night, tricky place. Users, sex workers, pushers ... Tell me of alarm system when irregular folks like unpaid cops and similar show up. Hit electric poles. Noise telegraphed down the street. Everyone disappears for a bit. Not tonight. They have time to talk. Users and SWs sit around listlessly. Couple of men & a woman are in a stupor. They're going nowhere, slowly, painfully. Done deal.

Drug-rehab workers say numbing out also come from alt stuff. Diazepam brands eg Valium, PKs eg Lobain, even adhesives eg Dendrite & nail polish. Brilliant briefing from Ms Kimboi & Ms Phamila at the HIV/AIDS legal aid place near Chingmeirong crossing (CHK notes earlier pages). Men, women both affected with drugs + HIV/AIDS but women have it worse. As ever. Steady slide.

Various reasons over the years, multiple conflicts & tensions. Kuki-Naga, Kuki-Meitei, Meitei-Meitei Pangal, Kuki-Zomi/Hmar/Paite ...

In fact the last not that well known. But a chk of Manipur Police records show, e.g., tension way bk in 1960 when Manipur's security apparatus had bn busy wt Naga rebellion that had travelled south by then!

'There were many encounters with the Naga hostiles in Tamenglong Sub-Division where the Manipur Rifles and Civil Police exhibited extra-ordinary courage and devotion to duty,' according to an archival note. 'During the encounter, quite a few police lives were lost, but there were quite a few losses on the side of insurgents also.'

But significant mention of other tensions:

'In 1960 Police had to face a lot of stress and strain in controlling clashes between Kukis and Hmars in Churachandpur, Jiribam and Tamenglong Sub-Divisions. But with the help of the Bihar Military Police, this situation was controlled. Again the Socialist Party and the Communist Party launched demonstrations demanding the Assembly. These situations were also tackled. Further, there were some encounters as well, with the undergrounds.'

++ displacement from dev projects like dams, like Khuga Dam in mid-2000s. Collateral damage—that awful, chilling phrase to mask death and destruction for operational purposes or development for the so-called greater good.

Using could begin with selling veggies to feed habit to selling bodies—'as a last stop,' Phamila says. Women worst affected, & the children. Jobless, orphans. No help from govt when complaints are made about harassment and/ or torture by cops, other security bec they're flotsam & jetsam. Society's debris.

Poster in the tiny office shows a starburst of prostitution hubs in and around Paona Bazar, a part of Imphal's largest and busiest market zone. Another quotes a news headline ref Supreme Court Justices Markandey Katju & Gyan Sudha Misra from their 14/02/2011 judgement on a case of killing of a sex worker:

'Poverty, not pleasure, forces women into prostitution'; and 'Sex workers are also entitled to the protection of life of dignity (Article 21 of the Constitution of India).'

O tempora! O Morehs!

It is now evening. There's the promise smoked fish, Myanmar and Mandalay brand beer or the smoother Dali from China—available openly in Moreh, part of a state where prohibition is law. There's even the Indian middle-class staple of Blenders Pride whisky that vendors say is sourced from the 'army'—a mark of authenticity in a den of counterfeit alcohol—to pass on to eager customers at ₹750 a bottle.

Trading freely isn't quite the same thing as free trade, but in Moreh, like much else in far-eastern India, it doesn't really matter. It's a part of the grand palace of smoke and misleading mirrors where nobody knows anything and everybody knows everything. Ordinary citizens occupy the crumbling outhouses and stables, and the rebel leaders, politicians and bureaucrats—both local and their visiting patrons from New Delhi, Guwahati and Shillong—the many-splendoured suites.

2. 'There Won't Be a Manipur'

The middle-aged Naga rebel looks out of the window. Hard rain masks the jade-green hills in this unspoiled northern suburb of Kohima. It's a tranquil afternoon in early-August. We're at the home of a mutual acquaintance, sharing tea and conversation.

The former deputy chief of NSCN(I-M)'s army glances at the Walther PPK handgun on a table by his side. For some minutes he had inspected the Walther, a wedding gift to our acquaintance from the faction's army chief at the time, Phungthing Shimrang. Our host had brought it out from a safe to briefly show it off and kept the weapon by the tea service before leaving the room.

Ramkathing Varah opens and inspects the emptied magazine, slides it back in, thumbs off the safety, primes the slide, aims down the barrel at the teakwood bookshelf at the end of the room, and pulls the trigger. Click. It is all fluid motion that lasts seconds. He gently replaces the Walther on the table, and responds to my query about what could happen if a political understanding isn't reached about securing the Naga homelands in Manipur.

'Manipur nathaki jabo,' he says simply.

There won't be a Manipur. More precisely, there won't be a Manipur as we know it. According to Varah, it's a possible outcome of one of the deadliest games of political chess being played in India.

He maintains that if the government in Manipur, Nagaland's southern neighbour with homelands of several Naga tribes across more than a third of its territory, doesn't agree to the demand of its resident Nagas for administrative autonomy—dealing directly with New Delhi—Manipur will break. It's what the apex agency of the Nagas in Manipur, the United Naga Council (UNC), terms 'Alternative Arrangement'.

Varah's observation is not an idle one. The man carries combat reputation and has spawned lore. In his younger days Major General Ramkathing Varah is said to have ridden a bicycle to the Imphal home of Yangmaso Shaiza, a former chief minister of Manipur, and shot him dead in front of his family. Varah escaped in the ensuing fuss. That was in 1984, in the glory days of united NSCN—four years before a split into its first set of factional alphabets, I-M and K—the hit in evident retribution for Shaiza's insistent attempts to bring electoral politics and administrative autonomy to Manipur's hill districts—and into direct confrontation in its pocket borough. Several years later, after NSCN's first bloody split in 1988, I-M's iconic army chief, V.S. Atem, depended on Varah to build up that faction's armed strength, training and operations. I've heard Atem and Varah being collectively described as the 'backbone of the Naga army'.

More recent lore has Varah planning I-M's attack on the camp of the Unification faction in Vihokhu, southeast of Dimapur along the Naga hills. In late-2007, a hundred I-M officers and cadres had broken away, bloodily, and set up this camp not far from I-M's own HQ in camp Hebron. Besides bad blood, both camps were separated by badlands, forests, the highway to Kohima, and competing egos and ethnicities, but united in their competition for prestige, territory and taxation—primarily extortion in the name of a cause that feeds the parallel economy of rebels alongside diversification in narcotics and weapons. The kidnapping and execution of an I-M cadre in early 2008 by elements of the Unification breakaway had primed for greater explosion in an already explosive battlefield where Naga rebels were at war with other Naga rebels even as they all remained in a ceasefire with the government of India. It was essentially a power-roulette of I-M versus K and now, by early May 2008, U expediently allying with K. A statement had to be made.

On 16 May 2008, around 5.30 a.m., I-M cadres ambushed and chased down a group of their former colleagues. After a battle lasting nearly seven hours, a short distance from Nagaland's commercial capital and headquarters of the Indian Army's 3 Corps—tasked to watch over these far-eastern borderlands and China—fifteen Unification cadres lay dead. A fortnight later, I-M attacked the U camp at Vihokhu. More than a dozen Unification cadres died. In another attack three weeks later, the camp was entirely overrun. An estimated ten Unification cadre died, the rest scattered in the wind—and in the evident care of India's security apparatus which would later arrange another campsite for U to regroup. (I would in October 2009 visit this new under-construction camp, at Kehoi, also near Dimapur, to interview Kughalu Mulatonu, a senior U official, an interaction detailed in *Highway 39*).

Rebel lore also records that Varah expected to be made longvibu, or army chief, after his mentor Atem. But Thuingaleng Muivah, the emphatic and wily 'M' in I-M to Isak Chishi Swu's relatively benign 'I', had picked a loyalist—loyalist to Muivah's power centre that is—to be chief of its army because, in this constantly shifting game of power-chess it wouldn't do to add more heft to Atem. Muivah's play happened in 2009, a year after Varah thought his spot as chief of I-M's army was secure.

And here's Varah now, five years on, an executive member of that army's steering committee, a compact man with economy of movement staring down the barrel at Manipur. As we speak, he and his group's army is estimated at between 7,000 and 8,000—in numbers, second at this stage in South Asia only to the strength of the Communist Party of India (Maoist).

Do you think there can be an understanding? I ask him. After all there's a new government in Delhi. There's talk of a new government interlocutor for Naga peace negotiations.

'Ajit Lal ase, na?' Varah continues in Nagamese, and mentions the just-retired chair of India's Joint Intelligence Committee, which primarily pools information and expertise from the Intelligence Bureau, R&AW, and the intelligence services of the army, navy and air force. Lal had retired on 31 July 2014. He had just days earlier been formally endorsed for the job by Rajnath Singh, India's home minister, and the recommendation sent along to the prime minister's office for clearance. Varah and I meet on 5 August. 'Ekta-duita meeting hobo pare,' he says. The direction the new government wants to signal will become clearer after a couple of such meetings with the new interlocutor. But the government will need to make an offer—'Offer koribo lage.'

For its part, I-M is being proactive, he says. Muivah, who also maintains a 'ceasefire' residence in New Delhi's Lodi Estate—more precisely, it's maintained for him by the home ministry, a bungalow of the sort parliamentarians and armed forces brass are sanctioned, located between the nearby fashionable hubs of Khan Market and the India International Centre—has reached out to the new government. 'Uncle Muivah', Varah says, using a prefix Nagas employ for an elder, expects to meet Prime Minister Modi before the month is out.

That might indeed come about owing to a new government eager for optics, I concur, but what of real solutions? For Naga groups to sign on the same piece of paper for a common peace and common future could be the relatively easy part—as tortuous as even that process would be, I didn't say aloud. But any conciliatory future, surely—this part said aloud—depends on the realities of Manipur. Indeed, I vent a little to the old rebel, I've been writing for several years in columns, essays and a book about just how intertwined the Naga peace process is with Manipur, about a compact with all the people of Manipur. But beyond Manipur, the understanding of this integral aspect of any peace deal, any reconciliation and rehabilitation, is still limited. And, surely, this compact mustn't just be with the Kuki and Zomi people, but also the Meitei, without whose primary participation and buy-in nothing can move ahead.

'Meitei manukhaner mogoz ase,' Varah responds to that nudge. 'Tribal manukhaner mogoz nai.' The Meitei have brains. Tribal folk do not.

He sees my raised eyebrows and smiles as he delivers another wry observation in Nagamese. 'Meitei tabla marishe, Naga-Kuki nachishe.' The Naga and Kuki dance to the Meitei rhythm.

Then it's a torrent of the usual non-Meitei POV for several minutes, much of it on point, and as clear as to the causes of resentment as these are confounding to resolve. And, of course, how I-M is poised to deal with it all.

Notes: Mtng wt Ramkathing:

The Naga pol & one of the go-betweens of I-M and govt and Nagaland and Manipur establishments says I-M can 'deal with' Manipur police and Manipur Police Commandos 'without any problems'. For all their training Manipur Police aren't trained to deal with seasoned/trained troops/rebel troops, but more into raids & interdiction of relatively weak/isolated targets, or in support of Indian paramilitaries and Indian Army. Only Indian Army, Assam Rifles, CRPF and BSF can handle I-M and other overground/underground rebels. Thus far haven't heard any substantive disagreement with this theory by any cop/spook/security specialist I've spoken to.

Varah's verbal torrent is mainly about Manipur's geography and volatile ethnic mix. Of the 23,000-odd square kilometres that comprise Manipur, Imphal Valley is around 1,810 square kilometres. The remaining 92 or so per cent comprises hilly terrain.

The majority Meitei community comprises about 60 per cent of the population, and lives mainly in Imphal Valley—with its eponymous capital. The valley is surrounded by hills where live tribes, mainly Naga, the Kuki—the two largest non-Meitei groups in Manipur—and the Chin, who have sub-groups sometimes collectively known as the Zomi, or the Zo people. ('Zomi' is an etymologically flipped version of 'Mizo', as those who live in Mizoram are known—Mizoram is literally the land of the Zo people). On account of this demographic heft, the plains have 40 seats in Manipur's Assembly, compared to 20 for the hills.

Varah's tribe, the Tangkhul, the second largest Naga tribe after the Konyak and among a dozen Naga tribes which have homelands in Manipur, have for long contended that the non-Meitei and by extension, the Valley, have since 1972 taken the cream of both development and infrastructure funds, and opportunities for jobs in government. As we have seen, that was the year Manipur was administratively upgraded from a Union Territory governed directly by the central government to a state.

Besides Manipur-based Naga tribes, which claim majority in the three hill districts of mineral-rich Ukhrul, Senapati and hydrocarbon-rich Tamenglong, other tribes too claim institutionalised discrimination in Manipur. As Varah and I speak, these three districts, and the hill districts of Chandel—claimed by both Naga and Kuki nationalists and rebels—and Churachandpur, mainly inhabited by Kuki and Zomi peoples, ring the four Valley districts of Imphal East and Imphal West, Thoubal, and Bishnupur. We were still a while away from the creation of more districts.

Just days earlier, leaders of the UNC—ironically, a world apart from the Naga Hoho, the apex organization of Naga tribes in Nagaland—had in a conversation with me reiterated the need for what they term 'Alternative Arrangement'. This dismissed autonomous hill district councils which UNC claims dance to Imphal's tune, and demanded direct administrative interaction with New Delhi. UNC considered Nagas elected to such councils as puppets: another irony—as we have read, the assassinated chief minister Shaiza had his democratic streak held against him by Muivah and his colleagues who have not looked kindly to any political process that would dilute their influence. This insistence, bolstered by economic blockades that UNC has for several years regularly employed to choke the Imphal Valley in an attempt to make political points and gain concessions, has prompted six tripartite meetings since 2010, attended by representatives of the governments of India and Manipur, and UNC. There had been no movement beyond bland assurances by the government.

Now, UNC wants to cut loose. More ominously, what many senior officials in Manipur and New Delhi consider the backers of UNC—NSCN(I-M)—wants to cut loose. The killing of the vice-chairman of the Ukhrul Autonomous District Council and member of council, Ngalangzar Malue, on 12 July is being seen as an indication.

Malue was a man marked by I-M and persona non grata in the hills. He had driven up from Imphal to visit his mother at their village home in the district. As the hired van he was being driven in approached Finch Corner, an important tri-junction 21 km short of Ukhrul that links both Ukhrul town and the strategic border village of Kamjong in the south-eastern part of the district to Imphal Valley, assailants opened fire.

Coincidentally, I had passed Finch Corner not long before the hit, driving a borrowed SUV, an overworked but reliable Scorpio that belonged to an Imphal-based NGO, and was on my way back from Kamjong to Imphal. Some Naga and non-Naga insiders I queried later that day attributed the hit to the orders of Phungthing Shimrang, the chief of I-M's army—the person whose appointment allegedly tripped up the ambition of our contemplative I-M general with the Walther and tea, Varah. But Phungthing remained untouchable—thus far.

Just days before the killing at Finch Corner, Seth Shatsang and I had driven up from Imphal to Senapati for a meeting with UNC officials. Gentle, insistent rain accompanied us from the time we left Imphal to travel north to Senapati, the headquarters town of the eponymous district. Seth's clunky Bolero was our chariot of the day, and he had let me drive, saying he hadn't slept for close to two days—too much was happening for the president of the All Naga Students' Association Manipur to take his foot off the pedal, but my offer to drive allowed him to do so.

It was a beautiful drive despite the deplorable, cratered road that degenerated every so often into rubble, a ride like an intense rally and more so in the monsoons. I had earlier written of this national highway, No. 39, that connected Assam, Nagaland and Manipur in an umbilical from the Assam refinery town of Numaligarh, near the Kaziranga Sanctuary, south to Dimapur, southeast to Kohima, due south to Imphal, and then southeast to Moreh, as the highway to hell. Nobody objected. They wouldn't object now either, even though the highway had been redesignated No. 2 and No. 102, as if two could handle the pressure better than one. It remained among the worst-maintained and most crucial arterial stretches in India and was also a part of the paper project called Asian Highway System, and designated AH 1.

Cool, mist-laden breeze had calmed us as we passed the old WWII airfield at Koirengei, just north of Imphal. To our west, lush green hills with a crown of clouds, the marker of near-yet-far Tamenglong made distant with terrain and decades of administrative apathy, greeted us right after we passed the small Valley village of Sekmai. It is famous, or infamous from the perspective of the Meiteis' moral majority, for its eponymous and indigenous firewater made from rice. A cloudy, gentler version is atingba, taken with cucumber and a little chilli, or a savoury salad with piquancy like a mule's kick, singju. A mix perfect for the rains, but it would have to keep. It was early morning, we had work to do, and time only for some chai at the Nepali village of Charhajare—with its provenance traced to Gorkha soldiers, another contribution of WWII—at the northern tip of the Valley, or the Kuki-dominated town of Kangpokpi farther along before reaching the mostly Naga lands of Senapati.

We settled for Charhajare. 'The Valley needs the Hills, the Hills need the Valley,' Seth told me over chai that a young Nepali girl, her people now as rooted in Manipur as Seth's, brought to us. He was now refreshed after a nap even through the everyday chiropractic trauma of the road. 'But most of all we need our identity, our land, our future. That comes first. The interdependence, the relationship between the Hills and the Valley will continue anyway.'

But he knew it was a complicated interdependence, a complicated relationship, and complicated sense of identity—not to mention a complicated history. Indeed, nothing symbolised it more than the multi-ethnic mix on the stretch of road we were on. Potential volatility is precisely why such habitations are marked on army maps, such as the one I saw at the headquarters of the 59th Mountain Brigade of the Indian Army during an earlier visit to Senapati. Tasked to watch these borderlands in the entire northern and southwestern aspect of Manipur, the brigade also maintained an eagle's eye on the 60-km stretch of highway that was our home for the day.

Here, the largely Meitei communities gave way to mixed ones as the highway left the plains north of Imphal to approach the hills. Kuki-dominated villages were marked with tiny pink flags, those with Nepali majority were marked with yellow, and Naga villages with green flags. Tracking the highway south-to-north: Kanglatunbi was Nepali, Thingsat was Naga, Motbung was of the Kuki, with four more Kuki clusters of Phaijang, Songlung, Kholep and Saitu. Closer to Kangpokpi was Haijang, a Kuki village that had to its north the Naga village of Daili, and to the north of that, the Nepali village of Turibari.

To the left of Senapati was a big cluster with three colours nearly at arms-length: Shongyangjang and Maokot were marked in Kuki pink; Dhoragari and Simili are marked yellow for Nepali, and the lone Naga holdout was Akutpa.

To the north and east of Senapati, to the borders with Nagaland and Myanmar, the markers were all Naga green. Deeply forested Tamenglong district, which abuts Assam to its west and Nagaland to the north, was almost entirely green with Naga concentrations.

Marking was the easy part. Ensuring the security of identity and livelihood in the present as well as a post-conflict future required superhuman patience, diplomacy and planning from both citizens and those who governed in their name. In Manipur demarcations were a matter of life and, as recent history has frequently shown, death.

Reach meeting site of UNC some kms before Senapati town. Turned left off highway. Uphill for a bit to a large clearing. UNC's new HQ planned here. All senior UNC officials present, meeting in open field under shamiana. Called tent here but it's okay, Seth jokes that I'm allowed to use Mainland lingo as a Mainlander! We're told committee meeting will spill over to my time of meeting L. Adani (same-same but different, this one Mao, that one money!) so meeting shifted to 1630 hrs to current UNC office, downhill from 59 Mountain Brigade HQ & camp.

Grace Shatsang comes by to say hello when she spots Seth. First head of Tangkhul Shanao Long. Sure she will be prez of TNS again or other top roles. Smiling eyes, sharp eyes. Formidable. Says she read my writing on NE. Says heading to Chiang Mai for reconciliation talks on Sunday (06/07) with other FNR members + several Naga factions: I-M + K-K + NNC/FGN. No K—Khaplang. Something brewing?

Cracked joke about Naga fondness for Thai cuisine. And about football match in Chiang Mai as with previous FNR peace meets which all made for a major photo-op outcome. Will K come, or substitutes needed for team? Can Photoshop if no photo-op. GS laughs freely. Seth shakes head, but smiling, respectful before GS. He knows my gallows humour, but GS is a boss.

Great, simple lunch at Paul Leo's home in his village, about 3 km north of Senapati. Leo at UNC meeting. GOI has asked UNC to send two reps for committee for Alt Arrangement. Leo part of comm, also chair of UNC's own comm for AA. His wife welcomes Seth and me. Seth well known to her. Me unknown. Typical Naga hospitality. Typical NE hospitality. Unquestioning if visiting with known person and/or open heart & mind + politeness + transparent purpose. Then doors always open. ALWAYS.

On way to meeting, see some new graffiti in large white capitals across the large clearing. 'We demand our homeland.' 'Nothing can stop Nagas.' I see the Peace Monument is still there upslope from the market square. Basalt slab topped with white dove carrying blue olive sprig. 'Erected on Aug 1, 2004 in commemoration of cease-fire declaration in Nagalim on Aug. 1, 1997.' Symbolic defiance in I-M zone, seeing as how things blew up in 2001 in Manipur + completely ignores K ceasefire of 2001.

NTS: Careful with political jokes.

There was a sticker at UNC headquarters some might find a bit odd, considering that it suggested a political line that had for several decades been the aspirational mantra of Naga rebel groups, in particular I-M. 'Free Nagalim.'

There was a less incendiary lead from the Old Testament, Proverbs 31:8 & 9. 'Speak up for those who cannot speak for themselves, for the rights of all who are destitute,' urged No. 8 in everyday English. No. 9 urged as compassionately: 'Speak up and judge fairly; defend the rights of the poor and needy.'

It seemed like a mood-setter for a discussion on the future of a people: the Nagas and, in particular, Nagas in Manipur—UNC's raison d'être.

What will be the approach with the Alternative Arrangement? I had asked Adani. Particularly as in this region your approach cannot be in isolation; it's all interconnected. The government of Manipur is trying to move in a particular way. Nationalist elements of Meitei society are moving in their own way. Different groups of whom you call 'national workers'—here I meant Naga rebels—each have their own dynamic. The government of Nagaland and the people of Nagaland have their aspirations. The government of India has its priorities. Developments in Myanmar and the attitude of the government in terms of its relationship with Naga rebels operating out of, or seeking refuge in, Myanmar, and that government's bilateral state of play with India, let alone the shadow of China, would affect future outcomes.

So, there were many things linked to UNC's aspiration. What would be the solution acceptable to UNC? Will it be anything less, as UNC has demanded, than the hill districts of Manipur be directly administered by the central government?

'For simple people like the Nagas ...' Adani began.

'Simple, sir?' I couldn't help interrupting. 'I don't believe that for a minute.' There was laughter and smiles all around. 'I've been hearing "the Nagas are a simple people" for a long time. Forgive me for interrupting—you're not that simple, otherwise you would not have continued to do what you have for so many years.' I meant the decades-long rebellion, uneasy ceasefire, holding out for politically demarcated homelands, and such.

'We take things to a great extent as they are seen, and understood,' Adani continued, unruffled. 'So the sophistication in reasoning and anticipating, that would be limited.' Even so, there was complete clarity on certain matters: '... We want our own real land. We want to rule over ourselves; we want to develop ourselves—in the ways and manners we feel are good. That stands out from the bigger struggle.'

He claimed a persistent concern was the steady erosion of protections, which were 'twisted' and not worth the paper they were written on. For instance, the Manipur Land Revenue and Land Reforms Act, 1960, passed by the Parliament at a time when Manipur was a Union Territory, administered by a New Delhi-appointed satrap, a halfway house while transitioning from a 'princely state' in 1949 to a state of India with its own legislative assembly and elected chief minister in 1972. 'There is a protective provision: it will not be applicable in the hill areas.'

The actual wording in Part I of the Act is: 'It extends to the whole of the Union territory of Manipur except the hill areas thereof.'

'Actually, it's supposed to mean "tribal areas",' Adani said. 'Now what they have been doing relentlessly is to get around this Act. The foothills have all been brought under the Act. So, when land is brought under that Act it becomes part of a revenue district, land is surveyed, and it becomes a purchasable commodity.'

Stripped down to the basics, Adani claimed that many areas of the foothills, particularly in Senapati and Churachandpur districts had been denied the exclusion provided by the 1960 legislation by the simple expedient of passing administrative orders marking several villages as 'plains' villages rather than 'hill' villages. This immediately took such repurposed land away from the purview of customary law applied by hill tribes, where land—including minerals—belonged to a particular tribe, indeed, a particular village, and the community was the primary arbiter of such ownership. Correct?

'Ya, ya.'

It wasn't a new story. The whittling away of hills-to-plains began back in 1962, within a couple of years of the Land Act being legislated. A further complication was that, unlike other areas in northeast India where tribes were protected under the Sixth Schedule of the Constitution—in Nagaland, Arunachal Pradesh, Mizoram, parts of Tripura and Assam—the hill areas of Manipur were not accorded that protective umbrella. This had for long been perceived by the tribes of Manipur as largely a Meitei conspiracy.

Adani and his colleagues were irked by what he termed 'transferring districts', specifically, police jurisdiction. For instance, he said, 'Now they'—the government of Manipur—'are transferring villages which are in Ukhrul district, which is a Naga district, to police stations in Imphal district, under the police of Imphal East …'

So the government was going about it at a tangent, shifting police jurisdiction as a first step to shifting administrative jurisdiction?

Not just that, Adani maintained. The government had also put out a discussion paper on their proposed New Land Use Policy for Manipur—I had heard rights activists in Imphal, mostly Meitei, being

incensed about it too, but more for reasons of their opposition to
the possibility of environmental destruction and land grab by various
businesses than affecting ethnic boundaries.

'So they are going about the hills trying to convince people this is
good, categorising land for effective use and all,' Adani offered, 'but it is
a ploy to get around the Land Act, actually … They keep on relentlessly
pursuing this.'

Added to this, to hear Adani tell it, was the undemocratic indignity
of the steady erosion in the structure and functioning of the Autonomous
District Councils for the four hill districts of Ukhrul, Tamenglong,
Chandel and Churachandpur—affecting Naga, Kuki and the Zo people
alike. This diminished the aspect of self-government as specifically
mentioned in an act of Parliament from 1971.

'And government of Manipur … said we cannot give Sixth Schedule
to the tribals because that will lead to disintegration of Manipur … In
the talks also—we have had talks—all the while government of Manipur
has been using Acts—gazettes, notifications, rules, whatever—so that the
benefits do not reach us. Now when we assert ourselves for our rights
they say "No, if we give it, it will lead to disintegration of Manipur".'

Adani had begun to warm to the theme. '… We are down at the
base, beneath the level of consideration and consultations. Because of
this absolute majority dominance, na? Our voice is not heard. Forty
MLAs from the plains, 20 from the hills—tribals. Out of these 20, 10 are
from the Chin-Kuki group, 10 are Nagas. Within the Nagas also'—he
waves an arm—'he's a Congressman, he's NPF, he's this, he's that …
The equation is such …'

It was difficult to move, and to move together?

'Ya. It's designed, actually,' Adani laughed.

A part of that argument was of course a stretch: after all, the
successive governments of Manipur didn't design the territory of
Manipur and its ethnic mix. They inherited it. The population density
of a particular area contributed to it becoming a constituency—in much
the same way as anywhere else in India. The 40:20 plains-to-hills spread
in Manipur's assembly was born of this reality.

But the political and, by extension, administrative command-and-control structure that skewed things was a reality too. According to the UNC, there appeared to be minimal benefit to actually having these 20 representatives from the hills in Manipur's legislature. All 20 of these MLAs were members of the Hill Area Committee of the Manipur Legislative Assembly, which was empowered by a 1972 law with oversight to 'safeguard the interest of the people of the Hill Areas' through governance and development—even budgets needed to be referred to them as a procedure, not for consent but as a FYI.

'Now the formation is such,' Adani smiled as he delivered a rhetorical coup de grâce, 'the Hill Area chairman and also the members, in order to save their positions, they have to abide by what the chief minister or cabinet says. Even the [various government] departments have their pressure on the Hill Area Committee. So it's a white elephant … No real powers. One chairman'—of Ukhrul's district council—'complained he didn't have the power to buy paper to write notes.'

That was a way of saying: politically and administratively emasculated.

'So provisions are there, everything seems to be quite okay, it's only the stupid Nagas and tribals who are complaining, and when we raise our voice …'

As simple Nagas.

'Ya,' he smiled, 'the simple Nagas.'

Talks to reach a solution about the Alternative Arrangement first began in September 2010, after several months of near-breaking-point stress for Manipur which exposed the deep-set paranoia the Valley had about Naga aspirations and the overhang, in particular, of NSCN (I-M). The talks were tortuous.

And, as with nearly everything in these parts, the reason was a tortuous recent history that painted everything in Manipur and would continue to paint everything in Manipur—and that, in turn, was like a raging bull in a China shop that was the Naga peace process.

It began with a ceasefire.

3. Talk-Talk, Fight-Fight

Notes: Ref articles: The lawyer & human rights activist Nandita Haksar has this great anecdote about how the Naga peace process got an uptick. It's a story typical of the grey areas that exist—even thrive—in far-eastern India's overground-underground.

She writes that it began during a 'dinner party at the home of a senior police officer, Peter Chiphang.' Among the invitees were Deepak Dewan, who edited a weekly, North East Sun, and Grinder, one of Muivah's nephews. Dewan wanted to scoop an interview with Muivah, which if it came through, would be a first with an 'Indian' publication. 'Grinder helped him get that interview and after reading the interview, Muivah gave Grinder permission to contact minister Rajesh Pilot.'

Tracked the chronology. At the time of the dinner, Peter Ngahanyui Chiphang, an officer of the Indian Police Service, held the rank of inspector general of police and was posted in Imphal. The interview, which unsurprisingly made a great splash, was published in 1993, and catapulted Dewan to a sort of celebrity status in certain circles as the person who had the ear of the chief of the third largest rebel group in India after the two leading Maoist conglomerates. Pilot was at the time a junior minister tasked with internal security at the home ministry.

One thing led to another, word from Grinder to Pilot and from Pilot to his boss, Prime Minister P.V. Narasimha Rao. 'As a result of these meetings in July 1995 P.V. Narasimha Rao,' writes Haksar, 'met the two NSCN leaders'—Muivah and his colleague, Swu—'in Paris.'

That segued after Prime Minister Rao's tenure to the United Front coalition government, and the successive administrations of H.D. Deve Gowda, with his meeting I-M leaders in Zurich; and during I.K. Gujral's tenure as PM, the ceasefire agreement taking effect on 1 August 1997—all with due process with the Parliament being informed.

In late-January 1997, I-M leaders met the Indian prime minister at the time, H.D. Deve Gowda, at a hotel in a Zurich suburb. Deve Gowda, elevated to premier by the United Front coalition government, was on his way back from the annual meeting of the World Economic Forum in Davos. Some of us who had accompanied him as a part of an Indian media delegation recall that stop, which led to about an hour's delay in the departure of Air India 001, the prime minister's designated flight. All that an acquaintance in the prime minister's office would concede is that something big was brewing with Naga rebels. In July 1997, when Inder K. Gujral had followed Deve Gowda as the head of that coalition government, I-M signed a ceasefire agreement with the government of India, which came into effect from 1 August—and was subsequently renewed each year. The ground rules for the ceasefire were finalised on 12 December, and a ceasefire monitoring group formed on 20 December. (The ceasefire protocol in 2001 with the Khaplang faction was similar.)

It was a big deal. I-M was the largest faction of Naga rebels, ahead in strength and influence only to the NSCN faction headed by arch-rival Shangwang Shangyung Khaplang, or NSCN-K. I-M was often billed as the mother of rebellions in northeast India for its propensity to offer expertise and sanctuary-for-a-fee to numerous regional rebel groups in a swathe from West Bengal and Assam to Tripura, a reputation that K too had for its Myanmar-based strongholds. And now I-M had agreed to dial down. (NSCN-K would follow with its own separate ceasefire with the government of India in April 2001, during the premiership of Atal Behari Vajpayee in the BJP-led National Democratic Alliance government. It was a formalisation of K's informal arrangement that first began with a two-month ceasefire with the government of India in November 1998, and signalled a hopeful future.)

It also brought into focus a bizarre ceasefire.

Both I-M and K factions were permitted to maintain what came to be called 'designated camps' in Indian territory. I-M established its headquarters near Dimapur. The K faction, by virtue of its leader, Khaplang, being a Hemi Naga from Myanmar and being headquartered in Taga, about 40 km due east of the Indo-Myanmar border in Nagaland, didn't relocate to Indian territory but maintained several such designated camps in Indian territory. Both factions were permitted to retain weapons, recruit cadres and actively train them. I-M continued to maintain its Alee Command, or overseas command—groups of cadres stationed outside Indian territory, in Bangladesh and Myanmar but with a preference for Myanmar after a relatively India-friendly government led by Sheikh Hasina took office in 1996—and which, with a gap after 2001, has continued uninterrupted in office since 2009.

Both I-M and K carried on their parallel administration even after they signed ceasefire agreements, in Nagaland, and the contiguous Naga-dominated areas in neighbouring Manipur, Arunachal Pradesh and Assam. They, particularly I-M, even maintained bureaus in several district headquarter towns in Nagaland. They continued to intrude into everything from neighbourhood disputes to assembly elections and parliamentary elections and influence the outcome. They continued to run a donation-and-extortion-led revenue stream in the name of 'national work' that tapped into every economic and development activity and even government payroll, in these areas. They monitored the flow of funds that Naga citizens—even government officials—and businesses operating in Nagaland—even the driver of an autorickshaw—contributed every month, quarter or year.

The most emphatic presence on Indian territory was undoubtedly that of I-M. Its headquarters at Camp Hebron—landmarks of this group that mixes Christianity, socialist ardour and brute force have biblical references—hosts much of its army and administration, the Government of the People's Republic of Nagalim. It's a short drive southwest of Dimapur, Nagaland's commercial hub.

Flags here proclaim Nagalim: A light-blue background striped with red, yellow and green curving from about mid-section to the left and arcing to the right, and topped by a white six-pointed star of Bethlehem. On a visit to Camp Hebron I saw clocks proclaim 'Nagalim Time'—thus far, Indian Standard Time—symbolic of its territorial claim in India and a slice of northwestern Myanmar. From here NSCN (I-M) runs its administration, and its parallel administration from across all Naga areas in India. It makes a mockery of the governments of India and Nagaland, and has co-existed because an uneasy peace with occasional skirmishing was seen as being better than outright war.

This ceasefire was driven entirely by realpolitik in another respect as well: it technically extended only to Nagaland, not Naga homelands in other Indian states.

A ceasefire was not peace, Anil Chauhan, who commanded the 59th Mountain Brigade at the time of one of my earlier visits to Senapati in 2009, told me. He said clinically it was nothing more than an understanding 'between two belligerents'. That understanding became even more crucial for both security forces and rebel armies in Manipur, Arunachal Pradesh and Assam. For instance, Naga rebel camps in Manipur were governed by the quirks of ceasefire. As these cannot officially be 'designated camps', these were regarded by the Indian security forces as 'TNO', or 'taken note of' camps, in ceasefire parlance.

'Isn't it tricky for people like you who operate in an environment of ceasefire but not in a zone of ceasefire?' I had asked Brigadier Chauhan. 'It's a really thin line, isn't it?'

The responsibility for counterinsurgency operations, or 'CI', lay with the army along with Assam Rifles, he explained. 'What technique you will apply, what force—that is your business. And how you interpret a situation is your business.' Maintaining law and order, Brigadier Chauhan said, was the job of the police and civilian administration. 'But as you said, it's a thin line.'

'By "thin line" I meant parameters of the ceasefire. When I-M or the K faction is present in Manipur state, technically the ceasefire doesn't apply. Correct?'

'Correct.'

Again, however, this was left to interpretation, the brigadier explained. 'As far as I-M is concerned, they are very particular that they should not violate the ceasefire. They go to great lengths actually to see that at least here'—in Manipur—'the situation is not disturbed.'

'That's a good thing.'

'That's a good thing. But they are doing it in a way that follows the letter of the agreement but not the spirit.' I-M pushed the envelope in every way they could. But his job, as the brigadier repeatedly reminded me, was to remind the rebels that India's army was around in force, should that force be required.

I once asked Phungthing Shimrang, general of I-M's army, about the intricacies of managing this ceasefire yet not quite a ceasefire, during an interview in his residence in a Dimapur suburb some of my Naga friends and I jokingly refer to as Beverly Hills, for its sprawling bungalows and estates of several of Nagaland's fat cats—ministers, bureaucrats, rebel officials.

'It's a headache,' Gen. Phungthing had laughed in rare agreement with his long-time enemies.

In 2001, that headache exploded spectacularly. On 14 June that year, at the conclusion of talks in Bangkok between I-M leadership and the Indian delegation, India's interlocutor for Naga peace talks at the time, K. Padmanabhaiah, announced that the extension of ceasefire for another year would be 'without territorial limits'. In effect, in Nagaland and beyond.

Logically, it made sense. The Naga rebellion has from its earliest days in the early 1950s had traction, militarily and psychologically, in all Naga homelands. Latter day rebels, wherever they were headquartered—in secure permanent bases or in ever-shifting Oking, as HQs are formally referred to in all rebel orders and 'tasking'—held sway across Naga homelands. But for the non-Naga people of Manipur, particularly the Meitei, by implication it amounted to formally recognising that Naga homelands in Manipur were a part of conflict resolution; and, by extension, the first step to virtually ceding the Naga regions of the state—in the hilly districts of Senapati, Ukhrul, Tamenglong, Chandel and some parts of Churachandpur district inhabited by the Zeliangrong Nagas—to the idea of contiguous, formally recognised Naga homelands in the future. A map of a people, not a map of a province, a state.

There was another aspect that troubled many non-Nagas in Manipur and elsewhere too, an aspect that few would speak of openly. (And when I did so in my writing, for instance, in columns in the media and during some public interactions, I received disturbing phone calls and messages as to how I should be careful while travelling in Nagaland and certain parts of Manipur!). In a rigidly cast Naga society, where tribal affiliation and a tribe's homeland still comes before all else—and relatively cosmopolitan hubs like Dimapur and, to a lesser extent, Kohima, are a rarity—in a post-conflict Nagaland, there's no real future for key Naga rebel leaders from I-M and much of its cadre who were—are—Tangkhul Naga from Manipur's Ukhrul district.

Local elections in Nagaland are contested along tribal lines, irrespective of affiliation to a political party. It is as yet inconceivable that a local politician from Wokha in Nagaland—the eponymous town and district, a homeland of the Lotha people—will contest elections from adjacent Mokokchung, homeland of the Ao people. The Tangkhul simply wouldn't have traction in Nagaland—unless Nagaland itself expanded one day to include contiguous Naga homelands. Similarly, Ukhrul district, homeland of the Tangkhul people, is reasonably considered the pocket borough of much of I-M's leadership, considering that Muivah is Tangkhul, so are his succession of army chiefs—Atem and Phungthing, for example—chief spokespersons, key officials in the civilian structure, and numerous cadres.

Isak Chishi Swu, the I in I-M, was respected and was from the Sema or Sümi tribe, which has its homeland in the Zunheboto region in central Nagaland. Swu had for long been projected as the unifying factor among the outreach to tribes, and to some extent it buttressed the idea that I-M had not, at least since its split with Khaplang in 1988, become a Tangkhul project. But Swu, the Yaruiwo, or chairman to Muivah's Ato-kilonser, or prime minister, increasingly focused on prayer while Muivah focused on building and maintaining the organisation, and appointing loyalists to key posts.

Muivah's future, which at this point appeared to be somewhat tied to a territorial or organisational insurance policy, as it were, had for long fuelled Meitei fears that a Naga peace deal would involve ceding of Manipur's territory. So, a ceasefire without 'territorial limits' was seen as that done deal. Eventual legislative paperwork for it would merely be acceptance of a fait accompli.

Imphal Valley erupted, all the more remarkable as the state was at the time under President's Rule—directly administered by Delhi and with heavier-than-usual application of security forces. Several tens of thousands of mostly Meiteis took to the streets of Imphal and other large towns of the Valley on 18 June 2001, four days after the announcement by Padmanabhaiah. In Imphal, mobs stormed the State Legislature and set fire to it. Government vehicles and buildings became targets.

Eighteen people died in retaliatory firing by security forces. Imphal-based media severely criticised the central government's move. Meieti youngsters, several with heads tonsured in sympathy for those who had died in the firing, swore to die to save the territorial integrity of present-day Manipur. On 24 June, the prime minister at the time, Atal Behari Vajpayee retracted the Bangkok announcement, in effect limiting the ceasefire with NSCN (I-M) to the state of Nagaland. Status quo was restored.

It had been touch and go. As related in an article in *newspapertoday.com*, an online paper I edited at the time for India Today Group, Atem, then the commander of I-M's army, threatened to go back underground and resume war if the ceasefire was not extended across all Naga-inhabited areas. But his organisation and he had backed off. Realpolitik prevailed.

Ever since, nationalistic Meitei organisations have marked 18 June as Integrity Day—not formally acknowledged by the government of Manipur but by many citizens in the Valley. There's a memorial to the dead by the northeastern perimeter of the Kangla Fort complex. It's now as potent a reminder of Meitei pride as the fort itself: besides being a commemorative enclosure that celebrates Manipur's kings, the fort complex contains separate places of worship for the seven ancient Meitei clans which lore describes as having first settled in the Valley.

And, ever since, Naga organisations, including UNC have periodically reminded the Valley who controlled access to the Valley, by cutting off that access, blockading the north-south highway into the Valley as well as the west-east highway that extends from the tea, timber and trading hub of Silchar in southern Assam, via Jiribam and Tamenglong district, into the Valley.

It's a potent, persistent meld of fear, concern, paranoia, politics and animosity. The Naga rebels know it well.

Nine years after the deadly fallout over the extension of ceasefire, I met Muivah in his government-provided New Delhi residence for a wide-ranging interview.

As we said our farewells, Muivah and I talked about his home in Ukhrul district of Manipur, in the Tangkhul Naga village of Somdal. 'I haven't been to my village for forty-seven years,' he said wistfully, quite another plane from the firm, angry tones he had frequently employed during our conversation while discussing the Naga rebellion and the Indian government's quite transparent strategy of attrition and divide-and-divide-again to deal with rebel groups in general and I-M in particular. 'I'm thinking to go there.'

He attempted to do so within days of our meeting in April 2010. Muivah first headed to Dimapur and then to Kohima, an hour's drive away from Nagaland's key border crossing point for Manipur at Mao Gate. His core team set up a camp office at the village of Visvema in Nagaland, close to the border. The date for his visit to the Naga areas of Manipur was fixed for a week, 3-10 May. The plan, of which India's home ministry and its senior minister at the time, P. Chidambaram was aware, had Muivah crossing over into Manipur at Mao Gate—no relation of China's strongman Mao Zedong, but emblematic of the Mao, a Naga tribe with homelands in Senapati district—and travel to Imphal with celebratory stops along the way. It was all very proper. I-M had formally sent the request on to the home ministry through India's newly appointed interlocutor for Naga peace talks, R.S. Pandey. The ministry had in turn requested Manipur's Director General of Police, Y. Joykumar Singh, to provide Muivah security during his travels in the state.

After visiting Imphal, Muivah would travel to parts of Tamenglong and Chandel districts before visiting Ukhrul, his 'home' district. Muivah would visit Somdal on 8 May. He would visit his family home, where his elder brother Shangreihan now lived. He would visit the graves of his parents. Attend prayer meetings. Mark an intensely sentimental and intensely political homecoming.

The government of Manipur barred his entry. The state's Congress chief minister, Okram Ibobi Singh's decision to prevent Muivah's entry defied the request of India's home minister, also from the Congress, the party which led the United Progressive Alliance government in New Delhi.

At a mid-afternoon meeting on 30 April, Manipur's cabinet voted to prevent Muivah's entry into the state. As I received news of it only minutes later, I couldn't help thinking of a message I received from a contact some weeks earlier, about how a very senior I-M official, a former general, lost his cool at a meeting at Hebron to discuss the extent of Naga territory during Muivah's visit to Hebron in March 2010. 'If this time the Meiteis create roadblocks we will just invade Imphal Valley,' the person had reportedly remarked before he was calmed by his equally incensed colleagues. 'What can they do? Nothing!'

Later in the day, on 30 April, a spokesperson of the Congress-led Secular Progressive Front government in Manipur told media persons that his government's decision was taken to limit 'possibilities of disturbances threatening peaceful coexistence of the communities if the NSCN-IM leader comes to Manipur'. Besides, he added, as the ceasefire between I-M and the Government of India didn't extend beyond the geographical boundary of Nagaland state, in Manipur Muivah was technically still a hostile, his organisation technically still at war. The spokesperson said the government's decision had been faxed to India's Home Minister Chidambaram.

The situation was already on edge. ANSAM, the apex Naga Students' organisation in Manipur, had already begun an economic blockade to protest the Manipur (Hill Areas) District Council Act, 1971 (3rd Amendment, 2008), a legislation to propose long-delayed elections to autonomous district councils in the hills. While it certainly acquiesced to the Naga demand for holding such elections, the legislation was now seen by Naga organisations as a ploy to advance the state's agenda using puppet candidates, which they feared would further reduce the power of village councils. The legislation was also interpreted as an attempt by Ibobi to begin his long game of trying to create more districts with the ploy of breaking a largely 'Naga' district like Senapati into Naga majority areas and non-Naga majority areas.

The blockade attempted to choke the Valley. Those who tried to run the blockade, mostly trucks carrying supplies and fuel, were attacked. Several trucks heading south to Imphal were torched by Naga activists. Most major media outlets in Manipur were vocal with suggestions that the violence was conducted at the instigation of I-M; they also sharply criticised Home Minister Chidambaram for precipitating the crisis. In turn, Muivah criticised the governments of India and Manipur.

On 6 May, the situation worsened. Naga organisations from Nagaland, among these the Naga Students' Federation and several women's organisations arrived at Mao Gate to protest Manipur's bar on Muivah, and attempted to force their way through massed security personnel—Manipur Police commandos and regular police. The protesters were charged and fired upon. Three died and close to a hundred were injured even as Ibobi rushed to Delhi for meetings with Chidambaram, India's Finance Minister Pranab Mukherjee and Defence Minister A.K. Antony.

Naga organisations in Nagaland and the hill districts of Manipur totally shut down the two highways—south to Imphal from Kohima, and another smaller artery via Ukhrul to Imphal, in protest. Within days, Imphal Valley, the redoubt of Meitei life and opinion, was squeezed for lack of essential supplies. The only other way into the Valley, the node of three main highways criss-crossing Manipur, was from Silchar and Jiribam in the west. Massively deteriorating road conditions on account of the monsoons that had by then arrived and a protest-lockdown of Tamenglong district through which it passed had in any case made that inoperable.

Muivah continued to force the issue—it was for him both a pressure point and a matter of prestige. In early June he moved from the Nagaland border village of Viswema east to Pfütsero in the region of Chakesang tribes, ostensibly to try and reach Ukhrul using the smaller artery. His team spun the move as a 'peace mission', but by then it was clear to everyone it was a political play to reinforce the idea of Greater Nagaland and I-M's stake in that stand, and recoup whatever mileage he could from the aborted trip.

Manipur's government moved quickly to pre-empt that and rushed several hundred police to the Naga villages of Liyai Khunou and Jessami near Manipur's border with Nagaland. Significantly, the Border Security Force, a paramilitary which answers to the central government, deployed personnel—evidently ordered by a now exasperated home ministry that had hoped Muivah would back off. The incident had begun to draw significant political attention in New Delhi as well: even as the central government contemplated the airlifting of essential supplies, including medicine, into Imphal, senior BJP officials visited Chidambaram to insist that the territorial integrity of Manipur be protected—adding to the already volatile circus of opinion and emotion. It was also a significant BJP byplay to stake its political claim in Manipur—a state with a significant Meitei population that largely worshipped according to Vaishnav tenets and was therefore seen as a significant toehold for that party.

More crucial byplays took place alongside Muivah's will-he-won't-he visit to Manipur—and also helped to set the tone for the Naga peace process over the next several years. Several Kuki organisations openly criticised Muivah and his attempts to enter Manipur. And some Naga rebel factions also took the opportunity to tear into Muivah. Adinno, rebel icon Angami Zapu Phizo's daughter and the leader of a faction of Naga National Council and the so-called Federal Government of Nagaland, in an email interview to Manipur's *Hueiyen News Service* lashed out at Muivah and I-M. Among several insults, she contemptuously termed Muivah a 'nonentity' in Nagaland affairs, and claimed that 'as the keeper of the soul of Naga nation, NNC has the final say on war and peace'. Kughalu Mulatonu, a senior functionary of NSCN-Unification, whom I met several months earlier at the group's Kehoi Camp near Dimapur, announced in an interview with *India*

Abroad News Service: 'Muivah is a terrorist and his terror designs were reflected when he used hundreds of innocent Naga civilians as a human shield to try to enter Manipur and visit his birthplace.'

Muivah had 'no business to curb the human rights of the people of Manipur', declared the ever-agile Mulatonu, who with several colleagues had violently broken with I-M—and which, among other things, invited that violent counterattack from Varah, my companion over tea and Walther PPK in Kohima. 'We warn Naga civil society groups not to hold Manipur to ransom by blocking trucks from entering Manipur via Nagaland … you cannot do that as it violates all basic norms of human rights … We want that the Meiteis of Manipur and the Nagas cohabit without any animosity.' This position went against I-M's stand, and also played into Manipur and India's hands at the same time—whether by design or default was difficult to gauge.

By the time ANSAM lifted the blockade on 18 June 2010—the first of several such 'lifts' and re-impositions over the following two months—the plains areas of Manipur were panicked and in despair, battered by scarcity and induced inflation. And very angry. A newspaper headline in Imphal read: 'Torture of 2.5 million Manipuris by ANSAM.'

Several Nagas who lived in the plains, mainly in Imphal, headed to the hills for safety. Among these were friends, acquaintances, contacts—people I had interviewed over several years. I received outraged emails from Meitei human rights activists who spoke of the Nagas' need to secede being at the root of all ills. Some acquaintances and friends, Naga and Meitei, who routinely, and together, took on the governments of Nagaland, Manipur and India on issues related to human rights, displacement of project-affected people and environmental degradation, now turned on each other as issues of identity rather than change and reconciliation took centre-stage.

The decision to lift the blockade came after a meeting attended by representatives of Naga Students Federation, Naga Hoho—the apex organisation of tribes in Nagaland—UNC, and Naga People's Movement for Human Rights. An article in *The Telegraph* of Kolkata summed it up:

'In a joint statement, the Naga organisations said they took the decision to "temporarily suspend" the blockade in deference to the request of Prime Minister Manmohan Singh, Home Minister P. Chidambaram and leader of Opposition Sushma Swaraj.

'However, the meeting endorsed the United Naga Council's decision to declare the ADC polls in the Naga areas of Manipur as "null and void" and sever all ties with the state government. It demanded that the Centre make alternative arrangements for the Nagas in Manipur. It also urged the Centre to remove Section 144 CrPC'—a statute of the Code of Criminal Procedure that prohibited the gathering of four or more persons—'and withdraw state forces from the Naga areas. Condemning the declaration of UNC and ANSAM leaders as offenders, they decided that the agitation would continue till the aspirations of the Naga people were fulfilled.'

This intervention by top Naga organisations from Nagaland and Manipur revealed more than perhaps was intended: it presented the issue as being far beyond the scope of a students' organisation protesting a set of elections. It exhibited a clear agitational agenda and, for a time, a stated unity among several key Naga organisations from both states.

Muivah left for New Delhi on 15 July. He had lost face. But I-M's agenda remained intact—even strengthened to some extent. Ironically, divisions were reinforced as a part of conflict resolution.

Meanwhile, in Muivah's long-ago home of Somdal, residents had put up a banner. 'Welcome home Avakharar,' it proclaimed at the entrance gate to the village, in anticipation of the visit of the person they called Elder Father.

They would have to wait. It seemed likely that Muivah, like his one-time mentor Angami Zapu Phizo, the iconic Naga leader Muivah once dismissed for not strongly opposing what he and several of his colleagues felt was a dishonourable accord—the Shillong Accord of 1975 between a group of Naga rebels and the government of India—would return home in a coffin, taken not by rage and rebellion, but by age.

With such ethno-political layering, strategies, egos and bruising histories, it was unsurprising that UNC's talks with the government of India hadn't really gone anywhere. In any case, to begin with these talks were, tellingly, between UNC and the government of India—not the government of Manipur. There were several meetings in New Delhi and Senapati, UNC president Adani said. 'They would patiently listen to our side of the story, and all the time say "But Manipur is a Meitei ethnic thing, we have to take into consideration the interest of other people,"' Adani paused to sip some tea, '"the state government has to be involved ..."'

Fair enough.

'... that was a passing on the buck approach. Then we confronted them: It is government of India's duty and responsibility to intervene. You have a mechanism to look after the people, that mechanism is not working, that system is not working. We cornered them. The result is, in the last talks ...'

The one in February 2014?

'Ya, ya. The government appointed a committee to go into the demand and translate it into reality. That was the first time Manipur government was represented politically. Their opinions were sought. They said, "Manipur is a multi-ethnic community, the voices of all the people have to be heard, government of India would best come out with a solution"—nah?—"that considers the views of everyone."'

They passed the buck back to the government of India.

'Ya.'

And so, UNC were formally introduced to the concept of death-by-committee—but I let that wisecrack pass unsaid.

A series of very Indian bureaucratic and political dynamics then began to intervene. Adani began to explain it all in a disjointed manner. 'So we said "See the government of Manipur is also here ... we have to take it forward." So the joint secretary at that time ... Assam and Arunachal had a border problem ... Right from the time he stepped into the hall he started pleading for, you know, early leave. "Please let me leave, the helicopter came late, I have a situation." You cannot leave unceremoniously like that.'

That official was Joint Secretary in-charge of the Northeast in the home ministry, Shambhu Singh, the ranking bureaucrat who was, coincidentally, an Indian Administrative Service officer of Manipur cadre—the state pool assigned to him when he joined the service.

'Ya, ya ... Finally he said "Okay, committee will be formed. When you reach (New Delhi) you talk with the minister."'

Once Sushil Kumar Shinde, who had succeeded Chidambaram as home minister okayed the plan for the Committee it would need to run the gauntlet of the PMO—prime minister's office. As it happened, general elections to parliament were announced, and on 5th March the Model Code of Conduct designed to prevent any last-minute policy initiatives by an incumbent government kicked in. A senior bureaucrat in the home ministry would have been abundantly aware of the imminent announcement of elections.

'That day itself we were at the JS-Northeast's cabin,' Adani continued. 'He was looking at the TV and said: "Oh, code of conduct".' The UNC president claimed the joint secretary gave his team a 'written assurance' that the process wouldn't stop, but of course it was dependant on the election process.

The entire gauntlet of review would again need to be run, as the central government would change. A BJP-led National Democratic Alliance government, with Narendra Modi as prime minister and a new operative crew at the PMO had taken over on 26 May 2014. According to UNC, they wrote to the home ministry on 3rd June and received a response from the joint secretary 'within two hours' time through his Blackberry'. The official replied, says Adani, assuring UNC that the matter had been flagged to the new home minister, Rajnath Singh, on his first day at the job. Shambhu Singh conveyed the minister's message, asking UNC to 'wait for some time' as he would need to discuss the matter with the prime minister. Meanwhile, the parliament's Budget Session intruded, and the waiting continued.

'We have left it at that, very confident that we have things in black and white, it is already registered.' The bottom line: the four hill districts of Chandel, Tameglong, Senapati and Ukhrul 'should not be under the government of Manipur'. They should have the same independence of politics and purpose the Naga homelands in Nagaland, answerable to 'customary laws' protected by the Constitution of India and governed by autonomous district councils with the direct responsibility of New Delhi, not Imphal, to prevent any discrimination in development, infrastructure and employment opportunities.

But for all the rhetoric, I sensed a vagueness. When I asked about specific details beyond broad statements, such as how exactly the administration would work, were there detailed plans for each district, the response essentially was that they were working on it. That, unsurprisingly, played to suspicions in Imphal and New Delhi that UNC's demands, whatever the language of autonomy it was couched in, was a part of tactical and strategic leverage by I-M.

How do you see the government of Manipur taking to this? I pressed on. Meitei intellectuals, politicians, administrators, had frequently made statements to media, and written in media that the Alternative Arrangement was a terrible idea. They mentioned centuries-old ties between the Naga people in the hills and the Meitei, how the 'elder brother' stayed in the hills and 'younger brother' came down to the plains ...

'Their mind is set on it,' Adani said. 'Whatever they may say—"two thousand years of history cannot be ignored"—that's their assertion. We will not deny two thousand years of history—it might have been more than that also—but it was never a shared history of governance, administration ...'

Surely there was social and cultural interaction?

'Ya, ya. But [selectively] picking and snatching from history will not make it coherent. Even as of now tribals in general—not just the Nagas—are not happy with the Meiteis. And Meiteis, they have no willingness to respect the tribes. Everything is Imphal-centric.'

How?

'Development is Imphal-centric. We speak Manipuri, but I can't speak Manipuri with the idiom, phrases, the decorum that a Meitei has. And because of that they get angry. Meaning, they look down on me. Because I can't speak with the etiquette that a Meitei has. That chauvinism is very, very strong.' He spread his hand. 'Who wants to protest, ask for things, just for the sake of it?'

But what of the concern or the paranoia among the Valley Manipuri that the Alternative Arrangement is the first step for 'Nagalim' or a ploy for an integrated homeland for the Naga people?

'It's a made-up kind of paranoia ... What they are scared about is, should there be autonomy for the tribal people what is Imphal-centric in terms of arrangements, all benefits that flow down to the Valley, that will be in danger. They use that excuse to refute and reject—nah?—the genuine aspiration of the tribes ...'

Even with his rhetoric, he acknowledged that the ongoing 'higher negotiations', such as with I-M, would impact how UNC demands were viewed. Besides, the political and ethnic dynamics of Nagaland and Manipur, and India's continued wooing of Myanmar in a bid to gain geo-economic and geopolitical advantage as well as the purpose of denying rebels of Northeast India sanctuary in that country, would ensure that a seemingly simple demand for autonomy would have many implications, would be seen though several different lenses.

As I left, I asked Adani about the story behind another poster, this one pasted on a metal cabinet. It showed Muivah and Prime Minister Manmohan Singh. Muivah was on the left, in a smart dark suit, eternally dark hair in the fashion of many ageing men from the east, large steel frame glasses. He was placed above the flag common to Naga rebel groups since the flag was first raised by officials of the Naga National Council in Kohima on 14 August 1947—tellingly, symbolically, the day before India formally gained independence. Prime Minister Singh was shown in a white kurta favoured for decades as a costume by Mainland politicians and now adopted in the northeast as well, and his trademark light-blue turban. His face sat atop the Indian tricolour flag and its Ashokan dhamma-chakra, a synthesis of the way of the Buddha. 'Long Live', proclaimed a slogan. As with such flags, both depicted identity, purpose, empathy, justice.

'This is from (the time) when Muivah was about to visit his native place,' he said.

Somdal.

'Ya, right. Somdal. That was the time ... it was a sort of a campaign kind of thing. Pasted all over.'

And then we know what happened.

Adani nodded.

4. 'It Is a Known Secret—Everybody Knows It'

Off to Kamjong early morning. Collect our 'insurance policy', an official of Tangkhul Naga Long, at Finch Corner. Ukhrul 21 km north from here, Kamjong 59 km to southeast. Love driving here. Mix of impenetrable forest and jhum areas of pineapple, banana & other growth. Fog, mist, narrow winding road, glimpses of gorge and stunning rhododendron. Crawling along, low viz, never more than 20 metres. Occasionally making way for AR trucks. Tricky business passing on these rain-slicked roads; the Scorpio isn't exactly a compact vehicle.

Big AR camp in Kamjong, 44 Bn. Very close to Myanmar border. Counter-insurgency factor. Before reaching Kamjong passed 'CI Post' of 49th Bn BSF near turnoff to Thoubal, AR 16th Btn post at Shangshak Khullen.

Timber smuggling hub. Massive logs everywhere in the interior. Kenbo mopeds brought in from Myanmar about in Kamjong village, no number plates. This is a two-way transit area for narcotics and one-way for weapons from Myanmar, and buffaloes too esp during Christmas season.

About 260 households, says a local official; TNL person said 1,000. More than CI and smuggling a factor here. Naga-Kuki too. An indication on way to Kamjong was Khangkhui Khullen village. Earlier Kuki, called Gamnom. Kuki moved out during Naga-Kuki clashes. Kamjong is an uneasy mix, uneasy truce. Tangkhul two-thirds, Kuki one-third. Kuki area is Kamjong-Chassad. After police lines, where road to border forks downhill at Huimin Thana, is the Tangkhul part. A shop just across into the 'Naga' part has a sign: 'Farewell to Manipur. Welcome to Nagaland.'

More slippage in these parts. This time among Nagas. This is South Ukhrul dist. Diff politics from North Ukhrul dist. 'Southern' Tangkhul feel a little looked down upon by the heavies, admin and I-M, from the north and west. Entity called Manipur Naga Revolutionary Front. Backed by UNLF—say intel sources. UNLF can go about in some parts of south Ukhrul dist. (Who

says Naga and Meitei can't get along? They do here. They do in Myanmar
with NSCN-K. My enemy's enemy is my friend, et cetera ...)

Resplendent among the rundown roads—and demands for 'at least
Jeepable roads'—and frontier feel of the borderlands of country, district and
ethnicity, is the large, sparkling 'village' home of local MLA Victor Keishing.
His father Rishang Keishing was once Manipur's Congress chief minister. VK
is also Congress. Same-same but different.

There isn't any love lost.

The UNC wouldn't be pleased at the manner in which they are
viewed—have for long been viewed—at the Secretariat in Imphal, but
the severity of it might have surprised them. At any rate it surprised
me as I met the chief secretary of Manipur, about a month after my
conversation with Adani.

It's a busy area, Babupara—in modern-day, irreverent translation
quite literally the neighbourhood of bureaucrats. It lies south of a
T-junction, just past the chief minister's residence, a mini fort at the
southeast corner of Kangla Fort. I was last here to meet the previous
chief secretary D.S. Poonia, a soft-spoken, careful, often glib bureaucrat
with a habit of steepling his fingers, and Ibobi Singh's administrative
right hand until 2013. That was the year when the brusque and direct
Pachau C. Lawmkunga became chief secretary.

Their ethnicity hardly mattered. Poonia was a Jat from northern
India. Lawmkunga is Mizo. Their appointment was a marker of India's
administrative cosmopolitanism, as well as the chief minister's fancy as
acquiesced by the nabobs in New Delhi—those nearer the top of the
food chain of power and privilege.

The large desk with its rows of chairs in front was still there in the
functional room. The wonderfully detailed map of Manipur on the
wall facing the compact Lawmkunga was there too, and I couldn't help
turning to it as the chief secretary took a couple of phone calls after
my explanations as to the purpose of my visit. Such maps were the
privilege of government—the administration and security personnel—

and it applied to every state of northeast India. This stood out as in the 'Mainland' maps of each state, sometimes, even districts, were easily available to the civilian. Even with the increasing spread of Google Maps and Google Earth, such digital applications were sometimes meaningless across vast rural swathes of Northeast India where connectivity remained poor. But India's map companies didn't bother with smaller states of far-eastern India. Manipur, Nagaland, Arunachal Pradesh, Mizoram, Tripura, Meghalaya and Sikkim were usually clubbed into an overall 'Northeast Map' along with Assam, a collective afterthought.

Manipur's top bureaucrat was done with his calls, and he shuffled some papers. I had led in with the hit at Finch Corner from the previous month, and UNC's massive uptick in rhetoric.

'It's very simple,' he spoke bluntly, roughly, none of the tangential by-lanes of his predecessor for this man. 'Our stand is very clear on this matter. The Ukhrul incident is the culmination of—what you call—the illegal activities carried on by this NSCN (I-M) …'

'Right.'

'… NSCN (I-M) over the last so many years. Despite the fact that ceasefire agreement has not covered Manipur … this was 1997, July 25 … UNC and I-M insisted that all Naga-inhabited areas in Manipur and Assam and even Myanmar should be included in the ceasefire. We are not agreeable to this, we're totally against this.'

'The so-called Greater Nagaland?'

'Yes, Greater Nagaland, Nagalim, whatever they want to call it, they have to keep it confined (to) Nagaland. But now they want Manipur, Assam … I am talking on behalf of Manipur only.'

'Now, do you think the UNC is being rigid …?'

'The UNC is very unreasonable. UNC is nothing but a front organisation of I-M.'

I burst out laughing, partly in surprise, partly in journalistic glee: few in any position of power in this region spoke as bluntly. He reminded me of Mhathung Kithan, Nagaland's blunt-talking home commissioner who held back nothing of his contempt for both rebels and the government—but that was several years earlier.

'This is an open book that can be read by everybody,' Lawmkunga was back to his rapid-fire deadpan delivery after a brief smile. 'They totally boycotted Government of Manipur. They are asking for AA. We met twice or thrice in Delhi and here. I asked them, "What do you mean by AA"—Alternative Arrangement? They could not answer specifically what do they want.' Here Lawmkunga echoed my unease about UNC's lack of detail, opting for a battering ram when precise proposals would better serve a genuine purpose. 'What they wanted is that they should pilot the agenda of this I-M overground. Though they *are* overground'—the bureaucrat acknowledged the reality of ceasefire—'they are having total nexus with this I-M. It is a known secret, everybody knows it.'

I let him run with it.

'Now, why did this Ukhrul incident happen? Because these I-M people, despite the ceasefire not being extended to Manipur, they have been carrying on many illegal activities: kidnapping, killing, ambush—everything—for the last so many years. Since 1997. And government had also reported to home ministry many a times, but home ministry did not act, taken proper action as much we wanted (them) to do. But they have the opportunity when they killed the ADC member (from Ukhrul)'—Ngalangzar Malue.

'We want to show there is a government here, so we raided their hideout in Ukhrul and arrested eight of them ... with all the incriminating documents, and now they are in jail. They [I-M] are creating problems all over, even for the Ukhrul people.'

It had been a remarkable show of force from Manipur government for Ibobi to send in state police to arrest eight I-M cadres. Indeed, employing police when the government was usually content to let Assam Rifles or BSF and CRPF handle such forays into Naga homelands and specifically one which was the pocket borough of I-M. It seemed Ibobi was getting ready to pull an ace or two from his sleeve in Manipur's shape-shifting powerplay.

Ref recorded conv with local IB head spook ref I-M & Finch Corner hit. Tricky situation with Ibobi's decision, he says, because 'there's another group waiting to target the Manipur Police group when it comes back from Ukhrul ... they are there, south side of Ukhrul town.'

I-M ambush?

'Yeah, yeah ... Anyway you know what happens to those who are seen to go against their wishes.'

So Finch Corner hit is a I-M hit—according to you?

'Yeah. The directions came from the man on the top. He was sure he wanted some of these ADC members knocked off.'

He? Phungthing? Muivah?

'Muivah. He of course never talks directly on the telephone so it's always passed on through a cut-out ... we're very sure I-M's done it and we also know the nicknames of the persons who have done it ...'

Naturally P&M connection will never be proven, but spooks/govt will logically conjecture for negotiating pressure + add more dossier fodder. Foot soldiers anyway take the fall. Not quite end of story.

While the arrest of I-M cadres for the Finch Corner hit appeared to be escalatory, I was receiving a lot of radio chatter, if you will, about another underlying reason. Ibobi was well into his third five-year term and, besides incumbency, the chief minister carried the baggage of leading an administration that had commissioned and condoned massive human rights violations and massive corruption—all of it recorded. These were remarkable even by standards of Northeast India in general and Manipur in particular.

The first aspect, which ranged from kidnapping and torture to extra-judicial killing across the Valley and beyond, was copiously documented by human rights organisations in Manipur, such as Imphal-based Human Rights Alert and international watchdogs like Human Rights Watch, and media. (Since 2009 it has formed an appreciable part of my own reportage and commentary in media, and several incidents and aspects were documented in *Highway 39*).

The matter of staggering misappropriation of public funds and corruption was documented in several reports of the Comptroller and Auditor General of India—official, and all available in the public domain and, despite occasional mention in media, largely buried in public discourse and nearly absent from discussion in Parliament. That stasis was evidently on account of Ibobi's deep connections with the Congress leadership in New Delhi, and on account of Manipur being at the leading edge of conflict and conflict resolution—precisely the reasons that have also prevented investigations into wastage and corruption in most other northeast Indian states, particularly Nagaland. As ever, the economy of conflict proved to be more seductive than the economy of peace.

Ever since Ibobi was first elected to chief ministership in 2002, the year after the disastrous events of 18th June over the extension of I-M's ceasefire to areas beyond Nagaland, he also employed another hook of appeal. He projected himself as the protector of the integrity of Manipur. He became more vulnerable with the transitioning of the Congress-led central government in May 2014 into one in the control of BJP—a party with a firm eye on psychologically and politically capturing the as-yet-unconquered bastion of northeast India for that party with the help of the massive, well-funded, well-oiled support machinery of institutions collectively known as the 'Sangh'. In Manipur, the mark was on the Meitei population in the hope that a flourishing practice of Vaishnavism and a drumming up of a Hindu narrative despite the fact that the relatively gentle Vaishnavism of Manipur was far removed from the transparently hard line, brazenly aggressive and, often, regressive, Hinduism of the Sangh, would sway this pivotal community. It wasn't exactly a surprise, then, that the politically vulnerable Ibobi would raise stakes in the game of political one-upmanship.

Great to meet MB in Imphal. Been a while. One of the nicer 'seniors' from college, now he's one of the nicer babus, I tease him. Drinks & dinner at his home in the senior bureaucrats' enclave, catch up about friends, and talk about

work, politics, peace. He shares my views about BJP govt in Delhi not pushing the Naga issue in Manipur. Too much at stake. 'Not beyond a point, because it would destroy their chances in Imphal Valley which basically is the only place they have a chance.' Yup. Assembly elections due by early-March 2017 as assembly term expires mid-March.

Ibobi would be strengthened in the Valley and non-N areas, MB says, if BJP/NDA govt gave in to Alt Arrangement. Nagas is Nagaland 'don't really' want the Tangkhul in Nagaland, but AA is not happening because there's too much at stake in the big picture.

What about talks with various rebel groups?

MB loses it—in his scale, that is! Voice goes up a couple of notches. 'They have no interlocutors. They are just drifting from SoO to MoU, with no game plan beyond divide-and-rule and drift. There's no vision beyond survival.'

Always good to have validation from the belly of the beast.

Told him hoping to meet his boss, the CS, in a few days. He won't tell you what I have, MB says. Yes, but he will say other things, and I'll have it on record. 'Don't mention my name,' he says, 'We haven't met, we haven't spoken.' Of course, I agree. Who're you?

Agree to meet after he returns from Del. IMF-DEL-IMF. Along with DMU-DEL-DMU & GAU-DEL-GAU, surely the busiest and longest-standing conflict perpetuation routes in South Asia excluding DEL-SXR-DEL & ISB-KBL-ISB!

Raising the stakes appeared to be Ibobi's way out. Several people I spoke to in Imphal from all political and ethnic spectrums all pointed to Ibobi's 'internal problems' within the restless local Congress party structure. The police foray into Ukhrul, they explained, was perfect to shift the focus.

'Everyone feels the CM is fighting this war, so to say, with the UNC,' explained a senior police officer. 'They have to support the CM or they will be labelled as anti-Meitei or whatever. So, everyone has kind of fallen in line—and that suits the CM.' He insisted that it wasn't 'such a big issue—that's not to say the murder of a person is a small issue—but things like this have happened in the past but never have things been taken to this level'.

He meant the Manipur government's response: station between 500–600 police, including a large presence of police commandos, in Ukhrul town for an extended period, 'continuously' impose laws to prevent large and 'unlawful' gatherings. 'So, everyone recognises CM is doing this on account of his own internal problems.'

Indeed, the internal buzz was that Ibobi was ready to escalate matters further by stationing large numbers of police commandos in Senapati and Tamenglong districts as well—the other districts where I-M had a 'certain amount of hold', as the senior police officer mentioned. But he felt Tamenglong, where 'K is still giving I-M a run for its money' would for Ibobi be less of a security investment for political returns, quite like Chandel district, where the Naga influence—I-M's influence at any rate—was relatively low as compared to Ukhrul and Senapati districts, places of intense 'future issues'.

But I-M, like other rebel groups, wasn't without its own one-upmanship quotient. So—I asked Chief Secretary Lawmkunga even though the answer was becoming increasingly clear—do you think I-M is doing all this as a pressure tactic so that it could be leveraged in its negotiations with the Government of India, and set the stage for possible peace talks? Formal peace talks, not just a review of ceasefire rules and complaints that have continued, almost pro forma, since 1997?

'That much I cannot say, but we have lodged our protest with the Government of India, ministry of home affairs.'

Officially, from the government of Manipur?

'A very strongly written letter to Government of India saying that these illegal activities have been going on for the last so many years, and it is the home ministry's responsibility to put them under control, because the state government does not have anything to do with the ceasefire. We are not a party to that. It is the responsibility of the home ministry to put in rein all these people.'

Lawmkunga has forgotten his tea, a ritual sacred to his predecessor.

'Now the state government has taken action because of compulsion,' he said. 'Compulsion in the sense that we cannot allow anyone to kill, kidnap, extort money.'

I was about to interject with a wisecrack, to politely query if such intent applied only to Naga groups, or did they apply to Meitei rebel groups as well, but Lawmkunga's scowl prevented me.

'We are trying our best to prevent all this. Despite best efforts we have not been able to do as much as we wanted but we are doing our best to prevent the occurrence of all these things. And those who are involved and are perpetrators of this crime will not be spared.'

The government of Manipur and its adjuncts and, of course, several non-Naga communities, weren't the only ones wary of UNC or the heft of I-M. The reality was that, the same as I-M didn't speak for all Nagas—as one of the rebel groups, albeit the largest one, it only presumed to speak for all Nagas—the UNC was not the only organisation. For one thing, it's ambit was limited to Manipur. For another, as with Naga tribes everywhere, each Naga tribe in Manipur had its own organisational structure. And some weren't enamoured of the Tangkhul-heavy nature of I-M's leadership, and the inescapable fact of the tribe's heft in numbers.

It certainly included the two gentlemen of the Zeliangrong tribes—an etyomological collective of the Zeme, Liangmei and Rongmei people who call Manipur's Tamenglong district home, besides adjacent Peren district in Nagaland, and a small nearby slice of Assam. One was a top functionary with the All Zeliangrong Students Union of Nagaland, Manipur and Assam. Another was a senior official of the Zeliangrong Baudi, or Union, that represented the Zelingrong peoples across their homelands in these three states.

Both were nervous about meeting me and insisted I don't disclose their identities as that would cause problems within UNC and, possibly, invite from I-M retribution that so readily formed a part of the rebels' playbook. They also insisted we meet in my hotel room in Imphal, so as to avoid prying eyes and ears. They had arrived separately to further allay the suspicion of any observer. Both rebel and security apparatuses liked to keep tabs.

'We have to play a delicate balancing act,' the student leaders said as his older colleague nodded in agreement.

The younger man wore a T-shirt printed with a map of the Zeliangrong homelands, highlighted by a flame within a circle. 'MAKLAM MEI RUI GUANG TU PUNI,' a slogan below the flaming circle declared. One day the Zeliangrong people will have their own land.

It was more defence than offence. While they were as one with Naga aspiration, they believed in the need for preservation of their own identities across Manipur, Nagaland and Assam—besides their economic interests, a crucial aspect in the Zeliangrong homelands that were rich in hydrocarbons. But their movement and aspiration is not voiced too strongly, the Zeliangrong leaders tell me, in order to not derail the greater Naga movement.

'So we have to be a bit gentle, a bit careful, the Baudi official said. 'We are for the Naga question or Naga problem to be settled, but we would like our Zeliangrong question or problem to be settled along with the Naga question or problem.'

While this sentiment extended to other tribes too, few would risk the wrath of the controlling superstructure. But the Zeliangrong have for long carried an independent streak even within the Naga construct. Two iconic figures dominate Zeliangrong history. One is Haipou Jadonang, a Rongmei Naga leader who, until his death in 1931, had in his 26 years managed to unite the tribes that later came to be called Zeliangrong against the ingress of Christianity and British dominion. The kingdom of Manipur was at the time a British protectorate as a direct result of the loss of the Anglo-Manipuri wars of the late-19th century. Pou Jadonang, as he is known, also propagated the tradition of Heraka, a mix of a social and religious movement that essentially preached nature worship stripped off many rituals, and stood against the ingress of Christianity—a British-driven project that would in a few short years spread across most of far-eastern India, except the bulk of present-day Assam, Imphal Valley, and the bulk of Tripura. The British hanged Jadonang at Imphal jail on the charge of Jadonang's complicity in the death of four Manipuri traders.

For the British, he was a nuisance put down. Jadonang had been arrested earlier, in 1929. It was the year a group of Naga elders, largely of the Angami and Ao tribes, are said to have petitioned representatives of the Simon Commission to be left to their own devices. Jadonang, who had earned extra icon-stripes with his arrest, upon his release set up a small army. Jadonang had to go.

Only, he left behind an acolyte, as fiercely independent-minded about the Zeliangrong people as Jadonang himself had been, and perhaps even more controversial in the Naga nationalist and Manipuri nationalist schema: Gaidinliu. Like her cousin Jadonang she was arrested by the British, in 1932, after skirmishing with troopers of Assam Rifles. An interaction in Shillong jail with Jawaharlal Nehru, which evidently impressed him, led to her being called Rani by India's future first-premier. The prefix stuck.

After India's independence 'Rani' Gaidinliu went head-to-head with both Christianity and the idea of Naga nationhood. She battled the first by professing Heraka. She battled the second by pressing for an autonomous homeland for the Zeliangrong people, pretty much what the present-day Zeliangrong map showed. This led to her being dismissed by Naga rebel leadership of the time as an agent of the government and she ended up a target for the Naga National Council—compelling her to go underground until 1966. Going against the largely Baptist Naga religious convention to favour an indigenous form of worship didn't endear her to Naga conservatives either. The colourful Zeliangrong leader with a penchant for Rongmei indigenous clothing and sunglasses—even a commemorative postage stamp issued by India showed her wearing a pair—remained an icon until her death in 1993. And, perhaps, even more so since.

The Zeliangrong United Front, then, did not come as a surprise. Indeed, especially with UNC's strident push for Alternative Arrangement in Manipur from 2011. The intelligence grapevine, both government and not, spoke of ZUF having received the support of NSCN's Khaplang faction—sworn enemies of I-M—for staking its claim to protect Zeliangrong homelands. Its claim was that of a separate homeland within the Indian construct, an alternative arrangement within the Alternative Arrangement, as it were. There was also talk of tacit support from non-Naga, and non-Zeliangrong Naga communities in Manipur—anyone who had anything to gain by being away from the I-M, UNC and the Meitei superstructure.

Skirmishing between ZUF and I-M broke out almost immediately. Then, on 30 May 2012, a gun battle broke out between I-M and ZUF cadres between Oktan and Ijeirong villages, in an area within the jurisdiction of Tamenglong's town police. Two ZUF cadres were killed. I-M claimed a cadre of the K faction was killed too, besides claiming that the encounter had tacit support of other Naga factions like NNC and the Indian security establishment. More encounters would follow.

At any rate ZUF was now an emphatic acronym in the region's alphabet soup of armies and ambitions. Or, to use a more dramatic analogy, another piece on the chessboard of war and peace.

5. Zale'n-gam: Stories of Lands and Freedoms

To Langol for interview with Kuki Inpi prez. Langol is NW of Imphal, by the hills, not too far from Singda dam. The roadside singju & atingba at Singda dam is terrific, no time for it on this trip! Pass the Games Village—from the time National Games were held in Imphal in 1999. City's massive garbage dump is on the way. Inpi prez's house is a modest, neat one, part of Games Village template. Says his family is away—'I'm a bachelor!' His colleague, a VP of the Inpi is an elderly man—'I'm a bachelor also!' He makes tea for us. Very touched.

I apologise for not expanding on Kuki history & aspiration in 'Highway 39'. Tell him I hope to shortly correct that anomaly in another book. Apology accepted. Prez gifts me a 'special' Kuki shawl. Shall treasure it along with other gifts of various Naga, Meitei, Karbi, Axomiya shawls and scarves & the 'Tangkhul' jacket Muivah gifted me. My wardrobe of amity.

Zale'n-gam, which translates as 'Land of freedom' in the Thadou-Kuki dialect—is the Kuki nationalists' ideological and ancestral claim. Zale'n-gam is ubiquitous in Kuki history and memory, besides books, journals, blogs and social media. I've seen it carved in capital letters on the backrest of large made-to-order wooden settees at a furniture workshop in Moreh, on gaudy calendars in impecunious homes, and as neat needlework in more prosperous ones. The remembered and aspirational Zale'n-gam that various Kuki clans inhabited includes contiguous parts of Northeast India, with slices of Manipur, Nagaland, Assam and present-day Mizoram; to present-day Sagaing Division in northwest Mynamar (parts of Chindwin and Kale-Kabaw valleys); and the Chittagong Hill Tracts of Bangladesh.

Caught in the churn of subcontinental geopolitics and politics in which the Kuki are essentially bereft of numerological majority in any province across three countries, Kuki nationalists and chroniclers usually point to recorded history. As with the Nagas and several other peoples in this region who carry a longer tradition of oral history than the written, these relatively older histories were sometimes recorded by those not from the community. In several instances, such histories are disputed. Equally, such records or impressions are sometimes used to cement a community's residency as much as its history.

For instance, Kuki chroniclers, researchers and politicians point to a reference of Kuki chiefs in puya—ancient Meitei sacred texts that deal with genealogy and rituals, among other matters—who are mentioned as being allies of the near-legendary Pakhangba, considered by many to be the first Meitei king, in the early years of the Common Era. While the origin of Pakhganba is shrouded in Naga-Tai-Kuki-Chin origin myths and royal liaisons of that king, in any case, goes the argument, if Kukis were associated with Pakhangba, surely Kukis existed for a considerable time prior to that association.

Some origin theories are as colourful, like the often-quoted suggestion by Col. Adam Scott Reid in an 1893 work that the term Kuki is derived from a Bengali word meaning 'hill people' or 'highlander', although Reid's rationale for that translation is lost to the Bengali people and their robust and inclusionary language. The works of British civil servants in India like William Shaw, and officers like Col. John Shakespear, a British officer who fought campaigns in the Chin-Lushai Hills in the 1880s and 1890s and wrote about the peoples (including *The Lushei-Kuki Clans*), attempted to list various clans and tribes to denote the Kuki. A classification and reclassification in post-Independence India has led to some complications about exactly which tribes are 'Kuki', but undeniably there were—and are—Kuki in the geographies in which their residency was recorded. The aspiration of Zale'n-gam might be of mythical proportion, but this particular reality is not.

Kuki chroniclers and community elders also point to what they call the Anglo-Kuki 'wars' of the mid-19th century, which some Naga and Meitei commentators unsurprisingly downgrade to a series of 'skirmishes'. To be fair, these were indeed skirmishes, albeit fierce, between 1845 and 1871, to stall British Indian ingress into parts of what is present-day south-eastern Assam and Chittagong Hill Tracts, areas in which the Kuki collected taxes.

During the Kuki uprising over 1917–1919, in the waning years of WWI and the immediate post-war years, there was an attempt to buttress anti-British sentiment when a few key chiefs, including the chief of Chassad reached out to 'militant nationalists from Bengal', as I read in *Zale'n-gam: The Kuki Nation*, a compendium of the community's history, claims, and a lengthy list of atrocities committed against it. There is a claim that these Bengalis helped to broker an understanding with Germans, the main Axis opposition which also—and this is a matter of historical record—attempted some anti-British ploys in Bengal and Odisha. Later, there was an attempt to unite against the Allies during WWII by offering active support to the Imperial Japanese Army and the pro-Japan Indian National Army led by Subhas Chandra Bose. Kuki nationalist writing proudly claims being 'fifth columnists' against the Allied armies. There are folk songs from the time, such as *Japan Gal La* or *Song of the Japanese War*. The somewhat giddily hopeful first verse, as I read in *Zale'n-gam*, and its 'free translation', goes like this:

> *Theilou koljang toni lep banna;*
> *Ging deng deng'e Japan lenna huilen kong;*
> *Peogo lhemlei saigin bang;*
> *Mao deng deng'e vanthamjol Japan lenna;*
> *Amao deng deng'e Japan lenna;*
> *Mongmo vailou kon sunsot selung hemtante,*
> *Atwi theikhong taa bang ging deng deng;*
> *Ging deng deng'e Japan lenna huilen konggin.*

Beyond the realms of Burma valley,
Floats the sweet note of the Japanese plane;
Like the musical notes of the harp,
Japanese planes hummed in the blue sky.
When the Japanese plane floats its sweet notes,
The hearts of depressed farmers will become glad

Like the sweet melody of the watermill,
The Japanese plane floats its sweet note.

As much as all these are placed as historical markers of the Kuki, nothing describes it as powerfully as the few years in the early 1990s, even as India itself was buffeted by the great changes wrought by the opening up of its economy in 1991, and another ongoing aftermath, that of the razing in 1992 of the Babri mosque in Ayodhya by Hindu nationalists. For the Kukis, it was the beginning of a military-style campaign by NSCN (I-M) to oust Kukis from what it perceived as its territory, by claiming the Kuki were not indigenous to the region, but were essentially transplanted—'first by the Meitei and then by the British', as relayed by a update in an UN-sponsored document—from what is present-day Myanmar and Bangladesh.

While land has always been an explosive issue in this region, a less disingenuous claim could be the territoriality displayed in several others ways. I-M pushed for taxes, demanding ₹100 a year from a household and ₹1,000 from each village. These were relatively small sums when compared to as much as ₹10,000 a month I-M was known to ask of truck operators—per busy truck, per month—and nearly a quarter of the salary it demanded from Naga citizens as contribution to the 'national' cause in addition to ₹100 a year many Nagas paid as 'ration tax' to support I-M cadre. The Kuki resisted payment of such taxes—partly because of the humiliation of paying to a militant adversary from another ethnic group altogether, and partly because it wasn't as if emergent Kuki militant groups did not have their own networks and systems of so-called contributions and donations. There was also fierce competition, as we have read, between I-M and various Kuki operators over the control of the narcotics pipeline between Manipur and Myanmar—primarily the Moreh pipeline. Control of timber and gold smuggling were other contentions. As was I-M's suspicion that Kuki groups were directly and indirectly aiding Indian security forces with whom conflict had escalated.

A retaliatory spiral of violence ensued. Escalating tensions in the Moreh area, a Kuki stronghold, had led to the Tangkhul Naga community in particular leaving town en masse in response to a quit-notice by the Kuki National Army in July 1992. In early October, news arrived of Kuki women being raped, mutilated and killed elsewhere in Chandel district. In October 1992, the United Naga Council issued a formal 'Quit Notice' to the Kuki community of Manipur. By end-November 1992 several hundred Kuki villagers had fled their homes.

A peace accord with UNC would be signed in June 1993, but it would prove to be meaningless. Backed by a contentious war of spin in which both communities blamed the other for hostilities, I-M unleashed its power. One among several incidents that would follow over the next few years took place at Zoupi—sometimes written as Joupi—in Tamenglong. Kukis of the village left on 13 September 1993 ahead of a 'quit' deadline of 15 September. The party was intercepted, 90 Kuki men separated from the group and then hacked to death. Later, 13 minors, all male and below the age of five, were hacked with machetes at a transit camp.

The butchery persisted through 1993. A Kuki officer of the Indian Administrative Service murdered in Dimapur. Men killed. Women raped and killed. Children burnt alive in a church. Children killed in transit camps. 1994. Several women raped and killed while out collecting herbs. Twenty-five men shot to death with automatic weapons after their hands were tied at the back. 1995. 1996. 1997. A continuing list of atrocities in brutal bursts that was reminiscent of the brutality unleashed on the Naga people by India's army in the 1950s. When détente of a sort arrived, marked by the absence of butchery more than the presence of peace, according to the Kuki telling they had been uprooted from 350 villages, and over 1,100 children, women and men had been killed. Every name, age, residence, and place of death is listed by the Kuki community and Kuki nationalists.

Records in the state archives of Manipur, as accessed by the researchers for a paper at the University of Bradford, placed the numbers of Kuki dead between 1992–1997 lower, at 473. This isn't unusual in conflict situations: a mix of inadvertent and deliberate under-reporting and over-reporting from every angle, every cynical actor in a conflict. Even so, the official numbers for both Kukis and Nagas are horrific. Besides the dead, 213 Kuki were listed as injured, and 2,909 Kuki houses and huts 'burned'.

In retaliatory violence, an indication that the Kuki tried to give back as good as they received in this supercharged ethno-political hell, 208 Nagas are listed as killed, 197 as being injured, and 2,576 homes burned down. The grisly statistics show that, while in 1992 the Kuki were caught off their guard, retaliation began in earnest in 1993. No quarter given, or expected. Not eye-for-an-eye or tooth-for-a-tooth, as I once heard the anti-establishment media person turned staunchly right-wing minister, Arun Shourie, describe the necessary approach to deal with Maoist rebels in Central India, when he addressed a security conference in 2007, in Chhattisgarh. 'For an eye, the entire face,' Shourie had expanded on the ancient Hammurabic principle. 'For a tooth, the entire jaw.'

The 13th of September, the day of the massacre at Zoupi, is marked by the Kuki community as Sahnit-Ni, Black Day.

And every day since that day, that year, and since 1997, has been spent by Kuki militant groups and various regional chapters of the Kuki Inpi, the community's apex group, in awaiting a formal apology from NSCN (I-M). Not the Nagas as a whole. Not a particular Naga tribe—even the Tangkhul, that has given so many leaders and cadres to NSCN and NSCN (I-M), and are—or were—neighbours to the Kuki in so many places. But specifically I-M, the organisation which the Kukis believe and a majority of the non-I-M version of the events of the time indicate, ran with the pogrom. Another indicator of I-M's primary culpability in the Kuki mind, as opposed to primary Naga culpability? The fact that Kuki rebels aligned with various other groups, including NSCN-K—a Naga group, and since 1988 I-M's staunchest foes within the Naga rebel construct.

Excerpt from the book, *Zale'n-gam*, by P.S. Haokip, Pres, KNO (pp 380–381), 1988, updated 2008:

The Kuki National Organisation maintains strategic alliances with Kachin Independent Organisation, National Socialist

Council of Nagaland—Khaplang, Shan State Army and Karenni National People's Party, Democratic Alliance of Burma, and particularly with Wa, Palung, and Lahu and Pa-oh peoples. In 2000, as a bulwark against the infiltration of alien groups into their areas, KNO initiated the formation of the Indigenous Peoples Revolutionary Army comprising of KNA, Zomi Revolutionary Army, Hmar People's Council and Kuki National front–Military Council.

KNO is also a member of the Federation of Ethnic Nationalities of Burma. FENB membership includes Palaung State Liberation Front, Wa National Organization, Lahu Democratic Front ...

'Why won't government of India protect Kukis?' Thangkosei Haokip asked me as the tea arrived. 'We are citizens too. Why treat us differently? Some Underground they demand, but Kuki Inpi we don't demand anything. We want justice for atrocities committed against Kukis. This is the stand of Kuki Inpi.'

It all came in a rush from the president of Kuki Inpi Manipur, a state chapter that also has the traditional Inpi, or apex tribal organisations, in Nagaland, Meghalaya, Myanmar—even a modern-day Delhi chapter in the manner of several community organisations from this region in India's capital.

Where do things go from here? I asked, given the history of the Kuki people, and their aspiration?

Haokip brushed aspiration aside to focus on the bloody history of the 1990s and to stake the claim of Kuki residency in the region from 'time immemorial', a favourite phrase in Manipur among all communities, ethnic and religious—even those who converted to a form of Hinduism in the 18th century or Islam not long after, or various denominations of Christianity from the 19th century onwards. Haokip compressed the history in a staccato manner. 'After the 1917 Kuki rebellion, you might have heard ... there are some things written ... after this we are living peacefully. India became independent, peace. Naga movement started under Phizo's leadership—there was peace.'

He cut to the chase. 'Then from 1992 atrocity started against Kukis. NSCN (I-M) started making incidents in Ukhrul, Tamenglong, here and there. Then we start taking up arms as a defence, like the village defence force. The result is now we have nearly 20 armed groups.'

He told me of how the Kuki Inpi as a whole had sent more than 60 memoranda to the government of India to settle various extant issues from that time, including that of a concrete resolution of conflict with the standing down and rehabilitation of Kuki rebels, protection of Kuki lands, and Kuki populations.

'And we have made another one,' Haokip said. 'Settle the Kuki problem before settling the Naga problem. Do justice to the victim before having negotiations with the murderer. We call it murderer.'

The Kuki leadership had also met Shambhu Singh, the joint secretary overseeing Northeast India in the home ministry, the same bureaucrat negotiating the maintenance of stall and status quo with the United Naga Council, headquartered in Senapati—about 60 kilometres and an universe north of where Haokip and I conversed. 'I asked him, tell us your stand,' the Kuki official continued—and shrugged as he described the bureaucrat's reaction: 'Laughing like anything.'

The government, Haokip insisted, is a 'silent spectator'. That inaction, and a sense of collective insecurity with the Naga and Meitei juggernauts, he said, is pushing 'Kuki-Chin-Mizo groups' to talk of alliances, join hands. 'This is in (the) pipeline. There is a feeling of alienation.'

Do you get a sense that the government wants to focus on diffusing the Naga issue and, in that context, keep the political conquest by the BJP of Manipur on its radar? That everything else, I asked Haokip, all other communities, even possible talks with Meitei rebels is secondary? If the government of India wanted it could reach out, work with state governments, talk peace with any set of rebels. After all, they have done it several times with various Naga groups since 1960—the creation of Nagaland state in 1963 with special constitutional protection was one major outcome; it signed another, the Shillong Accord in 1975;

signed the first Assam peace accord in 1985 and Mizoram peace accord in 1986; offered localised autonomy—imperfect and often corrupt as they turned out to be, and controlled by the Assam government—to Bodo, Dimasa and Karbi people in an attempt to conclude years-long rebellions in which they received active support from various factions of Naga and Meitei rebels.

Haokip reverted to the Kuki default position: 'But for more than two years during Kuki-Naga problem, when killing was going on, they'—the government—'were silent spectators.'

'We are not against the Naga issue,' he said next, 'but we say, treat every citizen equally.'

Coming to the Kuki issue, what is your sense of moving quickly from suspension to peace talks, and from peace talks to integration—well not integration, I quickly clarified, because that was a term of nationalist fervour and of government, but arrangement? Haokip laughed at this inadvertent reference to UNC's demand for the so-called alternative arrangement. Do you feel the governments of India and Manipur are more interested in managing the issues than trying to solve the issues?

'Even with NSCN, it has taken so long. Recently we saw in the papers they are going to have some talk with KNO, KNA ... (but) people now doubt the sincerity of Government of India also ... If you solve the Naga problem single-handedly'—he meant singly, in isolation—'you are inviting other problems also. Piecemeal solution won't do it.' He said the Kuki Inpi has three steps—'three pillars, we say': Be non-communal. Peaceful coexistence. Justice for all. 'All the problems are invited because of addressing only one ethnic group's interests.'

I shared my view gathered from several conversations, that things like suspension of operations with Kuki groups and others groups which are termed 'non-state actors' in security jargon were being driven more by the intelligence community and the military-security establishment than the larger policy community. The security establishment thinks in terms of attrition. When this is matched with political management, what you get is stall and status quo; incremental, make-believe progress with staged photo-ops and media statements in the hope that adversaries won't have the staying power that the government establishment can carry so much more easily.

'India is playing, the government is playing,' Haokip said as his colleague nodded and then brought us all another cup of tea. 'Managing. That's different from solution. In Manipur, Meitei are in the Valley, tribals in the hill. If you want to solve the hill problem, Kuki and Naga have to sit together. Focusing on one ethnic group will not solve the problem. In every district we live together. How can you separate it?'

Indeed, but if this is the case, had the Kuki Inpi suggested an approach with all communities? The situation in Manipur is different from Nagaland, but there—I shared with Haokip what he already knew—several church organisations worked with tribal and non-governmental organisations in an attempt to bring various Naga rebel groups to begin talks with each other. It didn't go very far, but every attempt was better than a slide. What about Manipur?

In Manipur the main problem is Kuki-Naga, Haokip insisted. Others, he said, 'are small issues'. I remained quiet, not advancing the point that both Nagas and Meiteis would certainly have something to say about that assertion—of the general Naga disdain for the Kuki position, and the Meitei position of Meitei centrality in everything to do with Manipur—even if Haokip restricted himself for this part of the conversation to matters of the hills, not the plains. 'I've been here three terms, going to complete nine years,' he spoke of his tenure as president of Kuki Inpi Manipur. 'In my first term I took the initiative to invite UNC for talk: "It's not good, let's close the chapter of the madness of the Nineties." I took initiative, personally. We talked in Senapati, in Kangpokpi also'—a Kuki redoubt between Imphal and Senapati. 'I asked them, "What do you want? Since you people started it you have to say sorry. Then we will do the same, also say sorry."' He paused significantly and to relay the key message with a smile. 'Message from top: armed group not agree.'

Haokip related an incident from 2010, the year he said he was invited for a 'Naga festival' to Ukhrul by UNC. The chief guest was Keviletuo Kiewhuo, who was at the time president of the Naga Hoho, the apex tribal organisation for Nagas in Nagaland. 'I began my speech—I was the first speaker.'

Here Haokip assumed an erect posture, as if at a podium, pride-upfront, placing his community's most dignified, unafraid face and spoke to the distance. The playback, as it were, was somewhat rambling, and tangentially sarcastic in the manner points are sometimes made in far-eastern India.

'Sorry to say but members of your community began the Nineties problem. What's the crux of the problem? The crux of the problem is that in 1949 Maharaja Bodhchandra signed the merger agreement [between Manipur and India]. That time not a single tribal was involved in the agreement. But we have a problem. Someone goes to Geneva, Thailand, everywhere ... they have all the manpower, all the resources.' Haokip lathered in the sarcasm, referring to the various favourite expatriate homes of I-M's senior officials and negotiators; he didn't mention Amsterdam, another I-M expat-hotspot. 'Yes, we have problem. In my humble opinion, if we don't sit together solution will never come. *Pin* drop silence was there. Solution is not in Geneva or Delhi. Solution is with us only.'

The function and festival soon concluded, and then, Haokip said, the Naga Hoho president came by to exclaim: '"Oooh *direct* to the point."' Haokip laughed out loud.

'Thing is, UGs are diverting everything,' he said more soberly, as to the source of there being no rapprochement. 'I-M leaders. It's the mindset. Of course, we never meet.'

And to think that, for a while, there was slim talk of rapprochement. During a visit to Ukhrul in 2009, as a part of my research for *Highway 39*, I spoke to several Tangkhul activists with ties to I-M and human rights groups who suggested common cause as a stepping stone for reconciliation. They spoke of a concerted effort among a section of Nagas in Manipur to work an alliance with Kuki and Hmar groups as a working coalition of tribal 'hill people' against the administrative stranglehold of Imphal.

An outreach of sorts would also come from Muivah—perhaps a part of the same outreach that brought Haokip an invitation to Ukhrul in

2010. In March that year, just a few weeks after arriving in India for talks, and a month before our meeting in New Delhi, Muivah made public statements and held a series of meetings over several days at Hebron, I-M's ceasefire HQ.

The occasion was 21 March, celebrated as the 30th Republic Day for I-M as marked from 1980, the year the undivided NSCN was formed. Muivah enforced religious fasting for all his kilonsers, or ministers, and senior staff who were called to Hebron. Wags had gone to town, insisting it was Muivah's Christian message to the kilonsers and I-M fat cats to 'shape up'—although some of the wags spoke more privately that the fattest cats could be found within his nepotistic inner circle.

Muivah also received visitors from several Naga tribes, members of the Forum for Naga Reconciliation, a visiting team of Quakers—along with Baptists, long-time Christian evangelists-turned-interventionists for Nagas. And he had made a show of meeting the Kuki Tribal Union, a Nagaland-based organisation with a history of fighting with early Naga rebels and, lately, as an ally and adjunct of I-M and its government.

In a few months, the president of the Union would send a message to the Kuki Students' Orgnisation of Nagaland. 'Our people who are living in the so-called Manipur state are still siding with the non-Christian Meiteis and fight against our brother Nagas,' L.H. Paohao declared in a statement that chose venom over grammar. 'Nagas and Kukis have two common things though we are from different community. Firstly, we are Christians, and secondly we are hill people. What do we have common things with the Meiteis? They are Hindus and plain people.'

'Funny things are happening in Manipur with our Kuki brothers,' the statement added. 'Many Kuki militant groups who are claiming to be the fighters of Kuki homeland are openly declared that they would stand firmly for the territorial integrity of Manipur before even having a single round of talk when arriving at an agreement—SoO (Suspension of Operation) with the Government of Manipur. Where will they establish Kuki homeland? Inside the Kangla? The whole world is laughing at us.' It ended with some slogans. 'Long live KSO! Long live NSCN! Long live Kuki-Naga brotherhood! Kuknalim!'

Kuknalim is a conflation words from two Naga languages—though some scholars maintain its provenance as being entirely Ao: from joining takok, na and lima—means 'victory to the land'.

Even so, as Muivah—whose faction proclaims 'Nagalim', or land of the Nagas—met his Kuki adjuncts, I-M released a note of Muivah's assurance to Kukis at large. It announced that 'Nagas and Kukis were living together and will live together as our fathers had worked in NNC time,' implying that the wedge had since been imposed between the two communities—neighbours in the hills of Nagaland and more so in Manipur—by vested interests. There wasn't, however, any direct word about peace-making with Kukis in Manipur. That would evidently be the function of those lower down the I-M ladder, and community elders, and even those like Gen. Varah, the quiet rebel leader who had spoken to me of the possible destruction of Manipur if the peace process went south.

Varah told me that he had travelled in Manipur several times for such outreach after the embers of the 1990s had cooled somewhat; indeed, even to ensure that the uneasy peace held. He told me he had visited Kuki villages, spoken to the headmen and other elders, and that he was treated 'politely' when they 'could have hurt me.' He claimed that he had also spoken to the Kuki Students' Union to help calm the situation.

And it was all now back on the burner as the push of negotiations for the Naga peace process came to shove.

The bachelors were doing well—I complimented the two Kuki Inpi colleagues for the steady supply of tea. The laughter done, Haokip returned to business.

'As KI our first step is to close the people's grievances. India has a justice system. Accordingly do justice, that's all.'

What does the government of Manipur say?

'The Assembly seats are 20:40,' Haokip mentioned the hills-to-plains ratio in Manipur's Assembly. Kukis, he said, like other hill people 'as a whole' have been demanding autonomous councils under the 6th Schedule of the Constitution—a position repeatedly articulated by the

UNC too. But the government? 'They say "no, no, no, no, no".'

No dilution of administrative control by Imphal. It's a position frequently and strongly articulated by Meitei interest groups. I'm told of a meeting in Shillong at which Haokip was present, and so were representatives of United Committee Manipur and AMUCO—All Manipur United Clubs' Organisation—two influential organisations whose motto could be said to be 'territorial integrity of Manipur' given the frequency of such statements at every hint of a peace deal with I-M and of course the instance of the ultimately abortive extension of the ceasefire with I-M beyond Nagaland. 'They said: "No, no, no, no, no".'

'I told them: whatever tribals demand, you say "no". Now Kukis demand Kuki state, Nagas demand Naga state … Manipur government is more or less majority command, na?' he spoke of the Meitei overhang. 'So, tribal alienation started. Then Kuki-Naga problem started. Beginning is negligence of state government also, initially.'

It usually is. State governments across this region have been remiss in providing governance for decades before problems erupted. Manipur has experienced it. So has Tripura. Giant Assam was once the copybook instance of how-not-to, a massive state that had administrative control over present-day Mizoram and present-day Meghalaya until they were hived off as separate administrative entities—and by then, rebellion and ethnic unrest had spilled over into bloodletting. I have always maintained that, rebellions in the Karbi Anglong and Dima Hasao regions of Assam were targeted against the apathy of Assam's government, not the government of India. Similarly, in the northern part of West Bengal, the Kamtapuri agitation and the explosive Gorkha political movement in the Darjeeling hills were first a reaction to poor governance by West Bengal than poor governance by India. Entire states in India have been born as a result of this sort of federal snafu: Jharkhand from Bihar, Chhattisgarh from Madhya Pradesh, Uttarakhand from Uttar Pradesh. And there will certainly be more.

It was a mix of a deliberate lack of development, myopic administration, arrogant administration, and an ineffective criminal justice system that repeatedly spawned unrest and anger in Northeast India as much as it has spawned and perpetuated, say, the Maoist rebellion in central, eastern and southern India. It's what Ajai Sahni, a New Delhi-based security analyst with one of the sharpest minds in the business, liked to term 'privileging violence'.

From a localised unrest, matters have so often escalated when people took to arms. And, just like that, the matter graduates from a local issue to taking to arms against the Republic of India. From complaining against a state, to becoming an enemy of the State.

In the context of my conversation with Haokip, there was also the matter of Myanmar besides dealing with the governments of Manipur and India. The Kuki people, like the Naga, have people across the border in quite large numbers; indigenous to that area and separated by lines drawn by the colonial British. But that's a near-impossibility at present, I suggested. No country in the region is about to permit a hiving away of territory for an integrated ethnic homeland. Not in the foreseeable future anyway.

'India and Burma, they (will) never agree,' Haokip readily agreed. Then he added with a laugh, 'It's not impossible also.'

Indeed. Maps change. South Asia's map has changed since 1947 to create India, Pakistan and Bangladesh. Maps within these countries have changed to create new provinces, states and districts. Border maps are under constant negotiation and occasional conflict for control, variously between India and China, Pakistan, Bangladesh, Myanmar and Nepal. India absorbed independent Sikkim in 1975. China eyes parts of Bhutan.

I was nudged into such reflection not too long before this conversation with Haokip, during an extended online conversation with the readers of the 'Northeast'-focused journal *thethumbprintmag. com*. A social-sector professional and activist from Assam, Banamallika Choudhury, had prodded me with her observation. 'Apart from the state, many Indians too—although they have never been here or do not know much about it—carry a proprietorial feeling towards the Northeast,' she suggested. 'A mutual separation followed by a mature neighbourly relationship seems out of the question, and concept.'

What you say is largely true, I had replied. And that is a major part of the problem: both the establishment and many even seemingly progressive Indians accept this Livingstonian construct as far as Northeast India—indeed, any part of what is declared and claimed as India—is concerned. To them, India's integrity is non-negotiable.

I have for long held a different view. India's integrity is not about being watertight with a map, a paranoid 'barbarians at the gate' approach, but about India's integrity being morally sound and politically sound—as it should be in a democracy. India became what it is on account of a highly contentious Partition, with several 'princely states' and ethnic groups choosing to, or not—or compelled—to be a part of the Indian Union. If a people wished for autonomy then and wish for such a thing now, then it is incumbent upon India to hear them out and work out a practicable solution rather than destroy people and their legitimate criticism and aspiration back to the Stone Age.

Who could have thought East Timor would gain independence, first from Portugal in 1975 and again from Indonesia in 2002? Eastern Africa is going through its own continuous, violent, re-birthing. Not too long ago who gave Namibia a chance? Or thought that Soviet Union would turn into CIS and the 'Stans'? In policy white papers I have written for think-tanks, I have openly considered the possibility of various options of a Naga nation; and the theoretical possibility of Manipur—specifically, Imphal Valley and parts of Manipur that wish to be with such a political construct—even requesting status as a United Nations protectorate as a precursor to autonomy or independence. And, of demographic and political changes totally transforming the present-day construct of North-East India and its internal and external boundaries—on account of climate change and migration, for instance, aspects we will discuss a little later.

'People can dream,' says Haokip, and showed me a map of Zale'n-gam and another that showed a composite of the homelands of the Zo peoples issued by the Zomi Reunification Organisation. Both homelands stretched across the India-Myanmar-Bangladesh trijunction.

'The 1917 war is not finished yet. Small, small issues not settled. Nobody has believed that the suspension of operations is a success in terms of a solution. Government of India engages in dialogue, not solution—how long will they dialogue-dialogue? Ten, twenty years? Then cadres will be disappointed. Another movement will start. So ...'

So.

6. The Problem of Intelligence

The intense ethno-political churn brings me to the residence of a ranking official of the Intelligence Bureau in Imphal. It's in a walled compound not far from the CRPF camp, west of the capital's Chingmeirong neighbourhood. We're seated in the lawns for drinks and conversation. The early-August sky is uncharacteristically clear and awash with stars. Unlike the setting, the conversation is anything but idyllic. While waiting for a senior police officer to join us—my host says he's a 'batchmate' of his from their days at India's premier officers' training institute for the police—we discuss issues that snarl community relationships in Manipur, and the massive umbilical of the Naga question that is irrevocably tied to this state and irrevocably affects the region.

There is a lot of talk in New Delhi and Northeast India about something big about to break in the Naga peace process, a move designed to take things from ceasefire to a solution. It could take a year, or five, or ten, because the interlocking problems that vexes my host this evening, the person responsible for sending intelligence updates and analyses for the national security apparatus in Delhi to frame policy, is essentially future-continuous.

He states the inescapable: 'Here, it all boils down to the issue of land.'

'The Nagas feel all the land in the hills actually belong to the Nagas, and Kukis were vagabonds who came and settled there. So, there is a land issue between Naga and Kuki. And the Meiteis feel the entire state actually belongs to them.'

The position has steadily hardened over several decades. Will there be much headway with any attempts of coming to the table without all participants willing to give-to-take? I ask the IB officer. Indeed, is there any point to come to the table without adequate groundwork, an isolated deal without collective confidence and understanding?

'There's no point.'

He elaborates: If the Nagas of Manipur are given concessions beyond autonomous district councils the government of Manipur won't accept it. The Kuki won't accept it either. The Meitei certainly won't. 'The Meiteis feel the entire state actually belongs to them—it was a part of their old kingdom. Now they have been confined to this limited area in the Valley, they are not allowed to buy land in the hills. So I feel until and unless this major issue of land gets resolved'—he uses 'land' interchangeably with 'territory'—'between the three major communities we are not going to head anywhere.'

And all the drumbeating by UNC and the response of the governments of India and Manipur to the Alternative Arrangement is essentially a dead-end, as I have for long surmised, of death-by-committee.

'Even the UNC now realises it's nothing but time-pass,' my host says. 'Go for these talks, come out with something, like the latest is a high-powered committee or a one-man commission to look into the issues. That just gives it a kind of a face-saving thing for the UNC.'

In any case all this just delays it for another year or two, or more.

'Absolutely.'

Nothing beyond what already exists.

'Nothing beyond what already exists ... well, maybe a little more empowered ADCs'—he refers to autonomous district councils and stresses the possibility of marginal giveaway with that polite phrase in colloquial Hindi, 'thoda bahut'—literally, little-lots. 'Now they don't have any powers apart from management of some schools. ADCs are practically non-functional. Most of the members are located in Imphal and you know what happened to those who disagree with I-M.' He refers to the Finch Corner shooting of Ukhrul's ADC member, widely perceived as only the most recent example of that temperament.

Meanwhile, there is the Kuki leadership which, as a countervailing pressure tactic insist on Zale'n-gam, the Kuki nation. The United Peoples' Front coalition of Kuki rebels pitch for a 'hill state' under provisions similar to Article 244A of India's Constitution, which permitted Parliament the power to create autonomous regions within Assam. The Kuki National Organisation conglomerate wants a separate state with an overlay of Article 38 which guarantees 360-degree welfare to citizens through 'social, economic and political' justice and equal opportunity. In 2012 a front, the Kuki State Demand Committee released a map of the 'Kuki state' which in Manipur covered Churachandpur district, the large Kuki-dominated Sadar Hills area of Senapati district and parts of Chandel, Ukhrul and Tamenglong districts. During the media conference at which the map was released the committee's general secretary made it a point to specify that map contained 350 Kuki villages from which occupants were evicted during 'the NSCN (IM)-led Kuki genocide of the 1990s'.

The committee followed through with a blockade of highways and major roads that passed through Kuki homelands—in effect, all of Manipur's significant arteries bar one. A week after that media conference, on 22 November, the committee decided to withdraw the blockade upon being assured by Gaikhangam Gangmei, Manipur's deputy chief minister, that his government would do all it could to begin a political dialogue with various Kuki rebel groups. The UPF and KNO agglomerates were under what the security establishment termed SoO, or suspension of operations.

But, of course, in reality whatever noises the government of Manipur made, no political dialogue, indeed nothing at all, would move without a stamp of approval from India's security establishment. For instance, several Kuki groups entered into a ceasefire in 2005 with the Directorate General of Military Intelligence of the India army. When the army called this truce—SoO—with KNO and its armed wing, Kuki National Army, it was at a press conference in the Moreh area. The government of Manipur wasn't informed. Manipur's government came into the picture only in August 2008 when it formally signed on to a tripartite agreement. Various Kuki armed groups were parked in designated camps and SoO was renewed each year. In this, Kuki civilian groups and the government of Manipur were mere spectators, pro-forma signatories. The go or no-go move for renewal was decided by India's ministry of home affairs and the army. It was a replay of the Naga peace process—in which the state government of Nagaland wasn't involved at all. The Indian army's ceasefire monitoring cell worked closely with its own chain of command as well as intelligence agencies. The government's designated interlocutor technically answered to the home ministry but in reality also to the national security advisor and the prime minister's office—leading to complications in case of satrapy-wars. These interlocutors dealt directly with the organisations of I-M, K and the Unification faction.

So, any political dialogue without a genuine desire for dialogue, reconciliation and rehabilitation would simply be more of death-by-committee, exactly as applied to UNC and the Naga situation in Manipur, and of course the overall Naga peace process, merely a continuation of managing conflict. It was a condition that the New York- and Guwahati-based political scientist Sanjib Baruah terms 'durable disorder', a description he applied to much of Northeast India. As far as I was concerned, none of it—peace talks with Naga, Meitei, Kuki and Hmar rebels—made any sense without the involvement of all communities in a theatre of conflict.

The officer from the Intelligence Bureau nodded in agreement. 'When these people [Kukis] raise their demands it will not be acceptable to either the Nagas or Meiteis.'

So, it's all locked in. Locked out, actually. Not that it's going to be easy in Nagaland either, I joke. A Tangkhul won't become chief minister of Nagaland. It's not going to happen. But if it does, I'll bring you and my Tangkhul friends and friends from Nagaland much Goan sausage as an apology.

He laughs. 'The mosquitoes bothering you?'

'No, I'm feeling at home. Just enjoying the grass under my feet and the general outdoorsy feel of the evening. But I do have an issue with all the divide-and-rule stuff.'

He's a little taken aback. But I push on, making a general point about India's standard security doctrine of what is commonly called Chanakya Niti, or upāya or Chanakya's principle, the legendary pre-Machiavellian pundit's way of sām, dām, dand, bhéd.

Stripped to the basics in this context: Suggest, offer advice. Offer to buy out. Put pressure or punish. Cause divisions, dissent.

This Four-Fold Path of command and control at any cost has been liberally and variously applied to several situations in Northeast India—our context that takes in rebellions by Assamese, Bodo, Garo, Khasi, Dimasa, Karbi, Kamtapuri, Mizo, Hmar and Tripuri groups, besides Meitei and Kuki groups of course—and quite spectacularly with the Naga rebellion from the 1950s onwards. In particular, splits with the polity and rebel groups have also been triggered by tribal equations, egos, even greed, but Mother India—the gentleman-spook smiles at my use of the phrase 'Bharat Mata'—has exploited and engineered quite a few, locally as well as regionally.

Ref 'Highway 39' notebooks. In late 2009, some senior functionaries of NSCN-U, specifically from the faction that had violently broken away from I-M and subsequently allied with Khaplang—and part of the core group that in private had spoken to me of the political aspect of Naga reconciliation being a case of 'winner takes all'—established contact with officials at MHA. From what I gathered, the ministry (P. Chidambaram was then the minister) reciprocated. The implication from the government perspective was easy enough to understand: try and minimise the reality, even with declaration of indefinite ceasefire and ongoing talks of groups reconciling, that I-M is still overwhelmingly the largest group in play; and continue to initiate flanking manoeuvres to weaken it as it would try to weaken any other significant faction, like K—which was for that moment allied with U!

This splitting and weakening was designed to aid the Indian position in any future negotiation, while it encouraged the ego- and turf-led jockeying for position among factions.

As it happened, some of those who reached out to the home ministry shortly broke with Unification and decamped to the main Khaplang faction in Myanmar. And, in short order, news reached me, via Naga insiders, of dissent brewing in that camp!

But now there are way too many splinters, I continue. Ironically, so many splinters that government agencies might have created are now unmanageable in a scenario of reconciliation. The perennial Indian approach of containing conflict within manageable levels is now unmanageable from the point of view of bringing peace to the interlocked histories and territories of Nagaland and Manipur. You can't split an organisation for leverage and then have nothing to offer the new splittees, as it were, or you will create resentment and a backlash. It's now adding to the problem. It's no longer a part of the solution …

'No longer part of the solution,' my host agrees, if only to stop my rant. 'What you're saying is true of the Nagas, I agree, but if you look at the Kukis—what do you have? There are 26-odd Kuki groups in Manipur—we've had very limited role to play in terms of dividing them, creating rival groups, or whatever. It's more or less happened on its own.'

But the government of Manipur …

'Maybe, but you can create two groups or 10 groups, but 26? Twenty-six *known* groups!' he chortles. 'There will be disgruntled elements and they will say "That clan has accepted that but we as another clan will not, so let's raise another group." This area's been disturbed for far too long and everyone is now quite comfortable with these groups, everyone is used to this kind of life. So now it's almost a natural process …'

I cut in here with a disagreement about how out of control it can get; it's an attempt to tone down his facetiousness even though I understood the reasoning. Public memory is short, but even so, surely, citizens of Manipur—especially Kuki citizens of Manipur—cannot forget the instance from 2012 when local media reported disturbing news as to how some Kuki rebel factions were extorting those who had been compensated for giving up land for the Integrated Check Post in Moreh, one of the showcases of India's cross-border outreach and a lynchpin of Indo-Myanmar border trade.

In mid-March that year, at a meeting at Manipur Press Club in Imphal, Hoikhotin Haokip and Veichin Lhungdim, in the presence of their husbands, spoke of how they feared reprisal from KNA cadres.

They had left Moreh to seek refuge in Imphal. The reason: they had gone public with their concern about KNA cadres insisting on a cut from the amount of compensation they were to receive from the government of Manipur; and now KNA might come after them.

Matters escalated in the beginning of April, in a manner that can without exaggeration be called the Manipur Model.

'The Integrated Check Post (ICP) Joint Action Committee disclosed that they were threatened by president of Hill Tribal Council (HTC) Jangmang Haokip,' the conflict-watch aggregator *satp.org* reported, quoting Manipur media sources. 'The ICP Joint Action Committee (JAC) questioned the inaction of the Chandel District Administration in the face of open threat. The JAC asked whether the Chandel District Collector has any secret understanding with the HTC president regarding ICP compensation. All the extortion at Moreh was carried out by the KNA through HTC, alleged the JAC. Asserting that the Chandel District Collector is well aware of all these facts, the JAC demanded that distribution/payment of compensation should be delayed until the KNA is driven out from Moreh and Chandel district permanently. In case the Government is not in a position to drive out the KNA, the land owners should be shifted to a suitable place under an arrangement by the Government, it added.'

I paraphrased all this for the gentleman-spook. He nodded, and brought our conversation back to the Naga issue.

'The moment you have some kind of settlement with I-M also, there's a possibility that there might be a split. Once these two gentlemen are no longer there'—he means Swu and Muivah—'there might be a splinter group that might come out of I-M itself—leave aside K and others.' Indeed, K—Khaplang—we acknowledge, is also quite aged, and his passing would inevitably trigger a free-for-all.

For a while now I had been hearing about a power struggle in the second tier of I-M in several conversations and exchange of communications with various rebel conduits, and various politicians and bureaucrats in Nagaland with access to rebel circles, besides conflict watchers in New Delhi. I-M's former army chief V.S. Atem was the name most often mentioned along with his successor, Phungthing

Shimrang. Rh Raising, the kilo kilonser or home minister, and of the Tangkhul tribe like Atem and Phungthing, was also mentioned as a contender to head a post-Muivah I-M.

'There we really do not have any role to play,' the intelligence officer smiles.

Then he gets serious. 'Things have got so complicated that I really don't know where we can begin in Nagaland and Manipur. We have to really think out of the box now. Frankly, between us—I mean the officers—we really do not know where to head and what to do. I mean, what kind of solution are you going to talk about and with whom are you going to talk about it?'

It's a startling, revealing confession. 'What I think is,' he resumes after a pause, after our drinks are refilled and fresh, steaming pakoras brought as accompaniment, 'some kind of Track Two dialogue is required between the three communities here in Manipur.'

Three? I tell him. There are dozens beyond Meitei-Naga-Kuki to other ethnicities, tribal sub-groups and clans, religious schisms, those affected by depredations of the state. In Northeast India, there will need to be years of patience and healing to deal with decades of hurt and horror.

The way to the offices of the United NGOs Mission-Manipur in Imphal is past Jesus Christ Photo & Video Studio, a small jewellery store and a car service station. UNMM is a coalition of organisations with all communities in Manipur & functions from healthcare to human rights, represented.

A small room next to meeting room has stacks of rolled up posters from a conflict resolution workshop. Input/ Output of various breakaway groups from a seminar. One such is headlined 'Naga Groups'. Action points read like something out of a human resource department-designed 'off-site' gig, but this case is a little more complex than corporate bonding because they haven't literally killed each other with office memos:

'To have common meetings of Kukis & Nagas Apex bodies at the District Level. To come with positive sides of the other communities.'

'To have UNC, KIM, Muslims & Meitei organisations meet with positive side of other communities.'

'To resolve any problem as far as possible together.'

Big circled message below: 'Relationship Building.'

Another seminar group (listed as Group-2) suggests approach with that term beloved of NGOs: stakeholders. Come by the phrase 'organic intellectuals' here. Writer seems to be a seasoned seminarist with stacks of frequent flyer miles! Seriously though, points, even if idealistic, make eminent sense. Chipping away required. Stakes high here—life or death:

'Coalition group (civil society, women orgs, church leader & organic intellectuals) should pursue continuously to the major U.G. to stop factional fighting.'

'To pursue govt stop to form any small arms group as part of counter insurgency measures OR Appeal for Immediate Action should be taken by govt against any illegal or antisocial activities done by any group.'

Separately, there are suggestions to assuage the perennial sores: unaddressed histories, disrespected identities, unreconciled aspirations. Understanding that history would be necessary to bring things up to speed with present-day political economy + understanding rationale of pol & armed groups, both who want 'IHL' or independent homeland + those who're 'armed gangsters'. And the third aspect: 'Militarisation & Divide & Rule'. That present would then morph via a 'movement for transparent, accountable governance' to a future which would need to factor several influences and ingresses, 'globalisation, Asian HW, trade'. There's the need to 'control resources'. The conclusion is stark: 'Sink together or Sail together'.

Before that, more ground to be covered—another set of suggestions offer. Sorting out land & resources. Raising awareness. Network, network, network.

Most of all, reparation—the need for justice, the need for the justice to be seen—across communities with histories of conflict:

'Goal: Restore dignity of victims. Provide means for future life.'

'Important: Responsibility for violations of rights is acknowledged.'

'Reparations: Individual + Collective, Material + Symbolic.'

Means nothing without addressing the aspect of human rights violation of women by state, security forces, Indian army—suggests another group: 'Context: Rape & Murder' the header chillingly states. 'Reparation Mechanisms: Official apology from Army to the Women of Manipur, Erecting Memorial Stones &

Monuments, Trauma Counselling, Official Commission, Common Monuments of all the Victims, Sustainable Livelihood Support Prog., Honouring them by Inviting Family Members to the Event.'

Very noble pursuits. Fat chance in current enviro. Will take years ++. But worth every damned effort, every doomed effort.

Peace is worth it.

7. Making War, Making Peace

There's the sound of a car, a short toot of the horn to request the gate be opened. It's my host's other guest, his 'batchmate' the senior police officer. He's glad to be taking the evening off. After some chit-chat about university years and careers, with a vodka and Sprite in hand, he gets into the groove.

'You've come for…?'

I've come to drink your liquor and pick your brains, I reply. The best conversations in Imphal-like places happen once the curtains are drawn and the doors are closed, I continue through the laughter. Unless you're in a place where they don't care what they say because either they are too powerful or too fatalistic. More laughter. But it's lovely this evening. There's grass under our feet, clear air, slight chill. A spook, a cop and a writer. Perfect. So—cheers! Confusion to enemies and clarity to friends.

'You've been nursing your drink for far too long,' my host says. 'I'll have to doctor your drink!'

Touché.

'Where are you put up?' the police officer asks solicitously.

Imphal Hotel, just for a few days on this visit before I travel elsewhere in Manipur, and to Tripura and Nagaland. There's a huge change from when I first stayed in 2008. Nothing worked. The toilet was mossy. Windows were broken, window screens torn. Sleep was about fighting off mosquitoes the size of pterodactyls—as ever, with wild swipes and Godzilla brand mosquito repellent from Myanmar. Hardly any electricity. No food. But leasing to a hospitality group appears to have helped. The electricity supply is still erratic but the rooms are clean, there's adequate food, the best coffee in town, excellent service. I give a brief review of all the hotels I have stayed at in Imphal, from fleabag to fancy.

Surreal Imphal. Conflict? Where's the conflict?

'Very good question!' the police officer, the head of one of Manipur's police 'zones' says. 'But the longer you stay the more you realize that there is this current … this undercurrent.'

'No, no, he's quite aware of the issues here,' my host intervenes.

I've been trying to pick your friend's brains about work, I tell the police officer. How about yours? There's an awkward pause at the ambush.

'So we were talking about what could be a possible solution to the issues in Manipur,' my host, the intelligence officer, allowed. 'I told him that beyond a point one doesn't know what solution one is looking at—issues are so complex and they have got intertwined in such a fashion, especially between the three main communities … it's very difficult to take out one and address that community's issues and then get down to the other two.'

And other groups and sub-groups, I again remind him. But even with the complicated ethno-political patchwork, surely the patching up must begin somewhere? It can't continue like this. The domino effect of conflict must somehow change to the domino effect of conflict resolution. Just before you arrived we were talking about the necessity to get a Track 2-Track 3—whatever track—to get communities across the table, to at least begin talking. There are NGOs from every community that could facilitate this …

'… Because until the three main communities here sort out their differences there is no point having a dialogue with the GoI on anything,' my host cut in.

'There is also a lot mutual distrust between the three communities, na?' The ranking policeman should know; unlike the spook he's from Manipur, this is home, one of the 'three major communities' that's so much a part of our conversation is one to which he belongs. 'They are always calculating, how to gain over the other. There isn't really anything that makes them say: "OK, let's do this together." That thing hasn't really come up at all.'

'There is hardly anything that all three demand together as Manipuris,' our host says. 'Your demands are either as a Naga or Meitei or Kuki. I have not come across a single demand from a Manipuri.'

Perhaps only the Meitei, I offer, for whom Manipur, 'the jewelled land' or 'land like a jewel', is today in name and spirit a part of their origin story—a name that followed ancient Kangleipak—and a part of their history and now part of the ethno-national rhetoric. And there is the occasional and creative application of history too for political reasons, right from calling the Tangkhul 'Elder Brother'. The application of the term 'Elder Brother' by many Meitei intellectuals in media and public discourse is wistful of a once-unified past that describes them as coming down from the hills in the times before written history to set up home in the less-topographically daunting Imphal Valley. But that sentimental ingress does not preclude the natural, ongoing suspicion between the 'hill' and 'plains' people, now also separated by religion— the Tangkhul and other tribes are overwhelmingly Baptist besides being overwhelmingly Christian, the Meitei largely Hindu-Vaishnav— language and specific ethnic identities. Indeed, much more so now with increasing identification by many of the 'Hindu' nature of Manipur as a direct and overt push by agencies of the Rashtriya Swayamsevak Sangh and only marginally less overtly by its major political arm, BJP. Whatever the reasons, the Meitei lead in claiming the 'Manipuri' tag with depth and conviction.

Our host nods. 'That has been a criticism or commentary, if you want to call it that: "We are the only ones who think of Manipur as a state."'

But history and history-making must surely go with present-day ethno-political realities, I offer—and here I begin to feel that I'm close to being irritated. I mean, I-M apart, why the hell would the Nagas go on about the hill districts as they do if there was proper development in the hill districts? If there was actually proper development the Naga argument wouldn't have a leg to stand on. You want to defang the Tangkhul? Give them better facilities, dignity. It goes beyond I-M. Accord the same dignity to other tribes. Sorry, I say, I get a bit emotional about these things. Because I try and talk to all communities, all groups, Meitei, Meitei-Pangal, various tribes among the Naga, Kuki, Zomi. Even among Nagas the Zeliangrong people tolerate the UNC and I-M for the greater Naga cause but they are very clear about their own identity and sense of insecurity and are very concerned about being subsumed by the Tangkhul and the post-conflict avatar of I-M. Now it's like a zero-sum game, you know?

'I know,' our host chuckles.

I gave an example of how I was in Guwahati earlier in the year to give a talk about the region and its dynamics with New Delhi and the region's geostrategic periphery. Besides several questions someone in the audience, a retired bureaucrat, asked me about the cause of unrest in the Karbi Anglong area in southeast Assam, with Karbi people—and the birth of some rebellions, however corrupted they may have become later. I said, for my money the Karbi issue was not against the government of India, it was against the lack of empathy and lack of development for which the responsibility lay directly with the government of Assam. Will the successive governments of Manipur accept the responsibility of misgovernance or non-governance that, besides the massive footprint of the government of India with its resources and security overload, led to Manipur being messed up? Because the issue of non-delivery of governance by the government of Manipur is much more than exclusively a Government of India issue ...

'I know,' he says again.

You folks know everything. That brings a laugh. I try to lighten things up a little with an anecdote or two and a joke I cracked a month earlier at a gathering of political young-Turks in Kohima.

Notes: July 2014

Tap, tap. Who's there? Pretty much the whole world and your Uncle.

This cynical PJ fetched a few laughs at a Kohima party. Jokes nearly always need to cut to the bone in NE. Tapping routine here. Been warned of tapping & tracking on a/c of my travel/research in Maoist zones. Will never forget that midnight call during trip in Delhi from an angel in MHA (some exist!) saying change all your PWs because formal request received from Chhattisgarh and he would have to pass on. I queried, which PW? He named all my accounts.

All. Says courtesy of retiring home secy. Another time, senior contact in CRPF
calls me as am stepping onto jetway to board flight in Hyderabad at the end
of a trip/transit no one seemingly knows of, ticket literally bought last-minute
after arriving in H'bad using a circuitous series of bus-train-no-receipt-rental
car. So, he says, you're in Hyderabad? Security must have flagged the passenger
manifest, flagged my name. Or snagged my phone. Show off! Probably tracked
me all the way out of Dantewada.

First time NE tracking claim during 2012 visit to give talk on internal
security at Army War College, Mhow. A colonel of military intel was my
host & liaison during visit. After my talk & intense Q&A (great interaction &
experience), over drinks & kababs at his place he tells me he's met me before.
Thought drink talking. No, he says, and shows off his Nagamese to prove a
point. Then, grinning, says he first 'met' me '3–4 years ago' during a mobile
chat between two I-M officers. They'd been discussing my request to visit
Hebron Camp & request to interview top officials including 'Uncle'—M. Then
he & his buddy, another MI Col, fall about laughing. Cheap thrills. Point made.

Child's play in today's environment of smart phones and smarter malware.

The intelligence officer and the police officer are very relaxed. Maybe
it's all the drink and just cutting loose on some downtime from the
madness all around.

'In a way,' allows the police officer, going back to our earlier thread,
a bit sombre now. 'The thing is with some or many of the points you
have raised I cannot either fully agree or disagree. What's going on
around here is so difficult to say. Every organisation, every group, every
community would like to emphasise the fact that they are correct, in
their own way they feel they have a legitimate claim, that they have been
wronged, that they have been neglected—but the fact of the matter is
that none of them can deny they are in one state!' He laughs. 'I mean,
if there was an easy solution then a long time back something would
have happened, na?'

There is a bit of silence, clearing of throats all around. Like the
reality around us we've hit a tricky patch.

'The Naga solution should have happened in the 1980s,' the police officer wistfully remarks.

I would say, the 1950s but perhaps India was still too busy building itself to respect any claim of autonomy within its Partition-mandated territory. And several times later. But those past generations either exacerbated the issues with arrogance, cussedness or lack of foresight—or all three—or simply moved on with that classic approach of conflict resolution: let future generations clean up. At least peace did break out in Mizoram, with the rebellion that sparked in the late-1960s formally ending with an accord in 1986—a peace that has since held with a collective sense of maturity. A peace that came because the political will and geopolitical situation in the neighbourhood was just right: India and Mizo rebels—and Mizoram's long-battered citizens—could break bread with mutual dignity just two decades after the grossest human rights violations by India's security forces and the strafing and bombing by the country's Air Force of its own territory and people India claimed by democratic right. A rebellion that began with the gross mishandling of a famine by the government—fresh kindling ready to burn along with all the stored kindling of neglect. The local government that worked directly under the government of Assam at the time—Mizo Hills District, as Mizoram was called at the time—was an administrative unit of Assam as much as this region bordering Myanmar to its east and East Pakistan to its west and south was an administrative responsibility of the government of India.

It was our host's turn to be wistful. 'I also feel that the political front of these UGs, for instance the UNC—were it to be in power and did not have to follow the diktat of I-M, or the UPF the diktat of the Kuki groups that form a part of UPF, then perhaps something could be worked out. You have to separate the two. The UGs have their own perspective, they've done their bit, had their conflict with the government of India, now they have come on to the negotiating table, so they should take a back seat, let civilians and civil society take it ahead. If we can work out something there and empower these bodies … because for example, if UNC goes for negotiations with government of India they know that when they come back they have to answer to

I-M … And I-M has its own agenda, it looks at issues very differently. So, you're not talking to the people who dictate terms, you are talking to the people who understand your problems and yet they cannot come to a solution because they have to go back and answer to their masters. Once this separation happens—if it is possible—then maybe something can come out of negotiations. Otherwise, it's not possible.'

In Nagaland, civil society groups have actually been very vocal and quite effective in bringing peace to the forefront, I submit. They have even taken on various factions of Naga rebels because in the eyes of many, whatever their issues with the government of India and its entire security apparatus and Nagaland's own horrific history of conflict with such state-run forces given free rein by the government of India, rebels have largely been discredited by their own actions.

'That's in Nagaland. And I don't know if there would be takers for this greater Nagaland thing—there or here.'

Many with whom I talk to, say: Look, we love the idea but we're realistic about it.

'It's not going to happen.'

Not-going-to-happen is the hallmark of this infernal knot with a history of over a hundred years.

8. Simon Come, Simon Go

The root causes of much of the latter-day troubles with claiming and re-claiming of lands, homelands, jurisdiction, control and independence is laid at the door of the British colonial government in India. From the Naga Club to the Republic of India, nearly all points of view for autonomy, independence, rebellion and state imprimatur have traced their logic to such documents and the colonial conventional wisdom of the time.

There were two key schools of thought among the British about how to interact with—deal with—the Nagas. The first, of forceful yet productive and 'civilising' engagement, the second to ensure the protection of non-Naga people by enforcing a protective boundary because engaging these tribes weren't worth the trouble and they were better off when left alone.

Naga nationalists have for long claimed this dictum of 'leave well alone' as proof of their autonomy. The Indian establishment, including anthropological and political communicators of Jawaharlal Nehru's policies, such as Verrier Elwin, have interpreted it as being exactly the opposite: 'leave well alone' was merely a school of thought, not active British colonial policy. (In some ways it isn't surprising that some of the colonial wisdom translated into unwise policies and depredations by post-colonial India—but more of that shortly.)

Here's how both colonial interpretations played out.

All through the 19th century, greater British colonial ingress into Northeast India—first as the East India Company in conjunction with the Crown government and, after 1857, the Crown government in full jurisdictional regalia—led to interaction and conflict with several tribes in the Naga Hills and beyond. There were regular raids by Naga tribes on the plains of Assam in search of plunder and as a mark of authority. Alongside, there were regular instances of head-taking as a matter of practice—for warrior pride and glory. Retaliation was equally brutal— and the colonial government also retaliated occasionally on behalf of attacked Naga villages, essentially believing the entire territory and its people to be subject to British colonial laws and behaviour.

British colonial records show a president in council in India recommending 'most stringent and decisive measures in regard to these barbarous tribes'. Troops were used to make an example in various ways: destroy an entire 'offending' village and kill inhabitants indiscriminately. Sometimes, on account of an error, 'innocent' villages were destroyed. Standing crops and granaries were destroyed. Elwin writes of this Empire pushback in his book, *Nagaland*, published in 1961—the year by which the Naga rebellion and the Naga people were steamrolled for a while but not won over—in these instances, against the Angami tribe:

'In 1866 a village called Razepemah, which had cut up a neighbouring Mikir village, was, in the words of the chronicler, "levelled to the ground; Its lands declared barren and desolate for ever; and its people were distributed throughout other communities." Other forfeits took the form of fines of grain and cash and forced unpaid labour.'

In 1879, the Angami village of Khonoma, a few ranges southwest of Kohima—about 20 kilometres away by road, half that distance as the hornbill flies—fought back against a British expedition, the same as they had in 1850 during which three dozen government troops had been killed in a spray of rocks and spears that rained down from a fort. By then the Angamis and other tribes had been fighting back against the British for several decades. But this time the Nagas of Khonoma attacked the party of the first British deputy commissioner of the Naga Hills, G.H. Damant. He along with 35 accompanying troopers were killed. The government's response was severe.

'In 1880 the village of Khonoma had its wonderful terraced cultivation confiscated and its clans were dispersed among other villages,' Elwin relates. 'The result was that the dispossessed villagers found themselves not only deprived of their homes, but, by the confiscation of their settled cultivation, they were during a whole year reduced to the condition of homeless wanderers, dependent to a great extent on the charity of their neighbours and living in temporary huts in the jungles. The result was widespread sickness and mortality.'

One point of view was that, except for occasional military 'promenades' in the hills, as Elwin put it, the people should be left entirely alone—the 'museum specimen' theory, as Elwin dismissively elaborates, which was conflated with the 'too much trouble' and 'too expensive' theories.

Cecil Beadon, the lieutenant governor of Bengal from 1862 to 1866 was a proponent of the other school of thought and practice, the so-called Forward Policy of firm engagement to control Naga tribes 'unable to exercise any general self-control'.

'The only course left us consistently with the duty we owe to the inhabitants of the adjoining frontier districts as well as to the Angami Nagas themselves ... is to re-assert our authority over them, and bring them under a system of administration suited to their circumstances, and gradually to reclaim them from habits of lawlessness to those of order and civilization.'

Beadon then wrote what later became the point of colonial command-and-control: 'These Angami Nagas are frequently mentioned in the correspondence of late years as independent Nagas, and a distinction is made between the tract they inhabit and British territory, as if the former was not included in the latter. But for this distinction there is no real ground. The treaties with Burma and Manipur recognize the Patkoi [Patkai] and Burrail [Barail] ranges of hills running in a continuous line from the sources of the Dehing in the extreme east of Assam to those of the Dhunsiri in North Cachar as the boundary between those countries and British India. There is no intermediate independent territory, and while the wild tribes who inhabit the southern slopes of those ranges are subject to Burma and Manipur, those who inhabit the northern slopes are subject to the British Government. These latter, including the Angami Nagas, are independent only in the sense that the British Government has refrained from reducing them to practical subjection, and has left them, except at occasional Intervals, entirely to themselves; but they have never enjoyed or acquired political or territorial independence; and it is clearly open to ... British Government in point of right, as it is incumbent on it in good policy, to exercise its sovereign power by giving them the benefit of a settled administration.'

This approach of presumption married to active engagement received precedence. Interactions increased. Roads between the plains and the hills were constructed. A system of messengers and interpreters was established. 'Peaceful commerce' increased.

In 1881 the Naga Hills except for the region of the Tuensang ranges formally became a district of British India, administered by way of Assam—in 1874 Assam had been hived out of the administrative province of Bengal and given the status of a Chief Commissioner's Province. (Kolkata was at the time the capital of Britain's Indian empire.) Kohima became the district headquarters. In 1888, what was called a sub-centre came up in Mokokchung, in the Ao homelands.

Even as the Naga Hills gradually came into British administration—although not British norms beyond the increasing acceptance of Christianity on account of the evangelical push by missionaries—the Tuensang area to the north and east of the territory remained demarcated as an 'Excluded Area'. Within British colonial ambit but, to quote an earlier assertion, 'too much trouble'.

As an aside, a further complication of territorial command-and-control, with great implications for the future, arose with the relationship of some Naga tribes with the kingdom of Manipur. There were some shows of strength.

For instance, we learn that in the winter months of 1832–1833, the 'cold season', Raja Gambhir Singh travelled through Naga territory on a march from Imphal to the Cachar area of Assam. This was about a year before his death. Kohima was among the villages that was compelled to submit to this king. There was evidently a stone placed in the village with Gambhir Singh's 'footprints ... sculptured on it in token of conquest,' Elwin relates. James Johnstone, who was the political agent for the Crown government between 1877–1886 and wrote a book about his time there—wrote that 'the Nagas greatly respected this stone and cleaned it from time to time. They opened a large trade with Manipur, and whenever a Manipuri visited a Naga village he was treated as an honoured guest.'

The British viewed Gambhir Singh as ambitious and with the ambition to conquer the Naga Hills—indeed, he appeared to match their ambition. But for lack of resources and logistics at the time, the British had to acquiesce to the reality that Manipur held 'some of sort of authority' in the southern Naga Hills. To counter Naga raids in North Cachar, two years later in 1835 the British government—at the time, Company government—gave over the responsibility of managing these raids to a local chieftain and the Manipur State, at the time run by the raja, Nara Singh. (The Company Raj had appointed a political agent to Manipur the previous year, in 1834, to keep an eye on Nara Singh.) This policy didn't find favour with the Commissioner of Assam at the time, Francis Jenkins, because the ferocious Manipur troops basically lived off the land—through plunder.

The Company and Crown evidently preferred a more organised loot, through the mechanics of government. Random living off the land was bad for politics and public relations.

Alexander Mackenzie, the colonial administrator-chronicler who published *History of the Relations of the Government with the Hill tribes of the North-East Frontier of Bengal* in 1884, felt that the government of the day in those Company Raj years was generally driven to accept the Manipur kingdom and its agencies as the de facto 'masters' of the hills; and only sent along a European officer with some Company troops to prevent 'needless outrages'. This Company policy of ceding control, which was frowned upon both by local officials and the Court of Directors of the East India Company at Leadenhall Street in London, was reversed in as little as two or three years.

India sought to seamlessly take over British administrative rules, regulations and practices of the colonial era. Along with all of

Northeastern India with the exception of Manipur and Tripura—that, as we have read, took until 1949 for formal transfer—in 1947 the entity marked as Naga Hills and the formerly 'Excluded Area' of Tuensang passed on paper to India's administration.

It was all a gargantuan, bewildering, shape-shifting, administrative jigsaw puzzle.

The government of India's narrative—and Elwin's narrative—took things way back to the beginning of the 20th century to buttress their claim of 'Excluded Area' being an administrative description. In this telling 'Excluded Areas' were very much 'included'—an extension of the Beadon principle, as it were. In 1902—I read in his book, *Nagaland*—under the provisions of a special Order-in-Council, the Tuensang villages were administered by the Governor-General of India through the Governor of Assam as his Agent and 'he was authorized to apply any British Indian Law to them'.

The Government of India Act of 1935 continued this arrangement, and Tuensang was defined as a 'tribal area' within India. 'There was no change in its status at Independence,' Elwin wrote, 'the Indian Independence Act of 1947 and the Extra-Provincial Jurisdiction Act of the same year authorized the Government of India to continue its administration.'

Indeed, there were other 'excluded' areas, also inherited from British colonial practice. From 1 April 1937, the Naga Hills District, the entire North-East Frontier Tract, the Lushai Hills and the North Cachar Hills became 'Excluded Areas' within Assam and were 'thenceforth administered by the Governor of Assam acting in his discretion, though the executive authority of the Province extended to them.' This meant, as Elwin explained, 'that no Act of the Central or Provincial Legislature could apply to the Naga Hills District unless the Governor so directed and he was empowered to make regulations for its peace and good government …With the coming of Independence in 1947 the same arrangement continued, except that the discretionary powers of the Governor were withdrawn and henceforth he acted on the advice of his Ministers.'

Just before India's independence, even the so-called excluded area was demarcated into 'controlled' and 'unadministered' areas.

Elwin invoked the romance of the Orientalist to describe Tuensang as 'beautiful and romantic' and that it was by 'no means entirely neglected' even in colonial times. He quoted an early 20th century official as noting: 'Let the inhabitants clearly understand that they are British subjects, and as such they may look to Government for redress in return for the obligations we impose on them as regards raiding.' Between 1910 and 1940 these raids ostensibly aimed at reducing the practice of head-taking. Indeed, he alluded to such incursions also ultimately creating the path for the Austrian ethnographer Christoph von Fürer-Haimendorf to travel to this region 'to spend a year in research, one result of which was the well-known book *The Naked Nagas*'.

This orientalist flush ended with Elwin's own assertion about India inheriting pre-Independence protocols: 'In June 1947 I toured for over a month in this part of the hills in the company of Mr W. G. Archer, a member of the I.C.S., who was in charge of Mokokchung. I saw how Tuensang was then divided into what were called "controlled" and "unadministered" areas, but how his writ did, in practice, extend over the whole area.'

Elwin devoted several pages to describe how, especially in the Tuensang area, post-1947 was a welcome era. Villagers in the area appreciated the government's help in lessening and, ultimately, stalling attacks between villages and tribes, killings, taking of heads and burning of homes. Sometimes the issue could be a dispute over something as seemingly simple as fishing rights, such as the one between Phomching and Urangkong villages in December 1949, which spiralled into retaliatory violence for several months. Or the example of Noklak village which, over two raids by Burma-based Naga tribes in May 1951 lost nearly a hundred dead, most with their heads taken, and with more than half the dead being women. These tribes also imposed taxes and demands for cattle and money on Nagas that were now on the Indian side. The government opened an 'administrative centre' in Mon in 1951 to prevent such incidents and one the same year in Kiphire so that, like the Konyak in Mon, the Samtang people in Kiphire could be protected from raids from across the border. Indian government officials sat down with their Burmese counterparts and discussed the matter with a view to a solution.

'As a result of the joint intervention of the Burmese and Indian Governments, the Indian Naga villages were freed of this burden,' according to Elwin, 'and in 1953 when the Political Officer of Tuensang visited the area they gave him a warm welcome and expressed their gratitude, declaring that "they felt confident about the future as the Government had come to their land."'

In 1948, the district's history tells us, for the first time an administrative centre was established at Tuensang. In 1954 the area, including the present Mon, Longleng and Kiphire districts, was brought under the North East Frontier Agency, or NEFA—the evolved form of NEFT, the British-era North East Frontier Tract—as the Tuensang Frontier Division. This was distinct from the Naga Hills, the governance of which lay with the then-vast province of Assam.

In 1957, this so-called frontier division was merged with the Naga Hills District of Assam to form an administrative unit called the Naga Hills-Tuensang Area, or NHTA. The food chain was bizarre—an adjective this book is frequently compelled to use. While NHTA on paper answered to the governor of Assam, its control lay with India's foreign ministry. (It would all segue to the collective entity of the state of Nagaland in 1963.)

Ergo: the Indian assertion that excluded areas were actually very much included areas. It was a figure of speech, not fact; and a crucial telling about Tuensang and the Naga Hills was necessary in the saga of claims about 'Nagaland'.

Indeed, such external interactions and interventions had transformed the Nagas, people of 'exceptional toughness of fibre and physical strength'. Over time, fear and animosity turned to acceptance of the other. They fought the Ahoms in the plains, but it brought a 'first glimpse of a wider civilization'. The 'slow encroachment' in British colonial times of the tea-planter, traders and police on land 'which, if not their's, was at least their's to exploit', upset the Nagas and triggered raids, violence, but over time brought mutually beneficial trade. And, even as the Nagas fought each other and took heads, but the British, who 'often punished them', also helped to banish such 'fear', banish ignorance; and missionaries 'brought an ideal of gentleness and forgiveness'.

'After Independence the new concept of a welfare state came to the Nagas, and the free Indian people took their tribal brethren everywhere to their hearts.'

Elwin continued this fairy tale—part fair, part tale—imbibing India's generosity that now carried the British torch to continue to bring light to deepest, darkest NH, then TA and then NHTA.

'The years went by; wonderful roads began to urge their way through the hills; the jungle was tamed and conquered; the masses of people experienced the essential sorrows and delights of all mankind; they tilled the forest clearings, they fished and hunted, they learnt new ways of doing things. Their sons and daughters went to school and the cleverest of them studied in India's universities and even abroad.'

The point at the time of Elwin's publication in 1961 was to underscore India's justification for everything that had happened in the Naga territories since 1947. A primary purpose was the government of India's alleged legitimacy of claim and the alleged illegitimacy of the claims of Naga rebels—and the adverse publicity of butchery in the Naga areas that the government of India was attempting to supress through intimidation and law.

After all, the immunity- and impunity-driven Armed Forces Act was already a reality, having been legislated in 1958.

Meanwhile, away from this narrative of administrative inheritance, the political reality was fraught and fearsome, depending on who was at which receiving end. Dominoes kept falling at regular intervals. The extended bloodbath that would drag history kicking and screaming to the present-day in India's far-east, was just a few short years away.

The continued demand for Naga autonomy was a strain on post-British India. Indeed, the strain had begun to show in the immediate years before Independence. In some ways the root lay in the statement of a group of elders of the Naga Club who had made a representation to members of the Simon Commission in 1929—the Naga Club was formed in 1918, a mix of officials and village headmen who visited

Kohima and Mokokchung—for continued protection of the hills from the plains. There was a fear the political reforms proposed for the Subcontinent by the Simon Commission would overwhelm the Naga Hills.

There's a fascinating recounting of the incident by Elwin—but evidently presented not for the purpose of accepting the Naga claim for autonomy and independence but for buttressing the post-independence government of India's claims of having done no wrong by the Nagas in continuing with British practices and, indeed, actually strengthening the position with Constitutional provisions. Here's how Elwin says it went:

'When the Simon Commission visited Kohima in January 1929, members of the Naga Club submitted a memorandum to it demanding that the Nagas should be excluded from the proposed reforms and kept under direct administration to save them from being overwhelmed by the people of the plains. Their leader made the point that: "You are the only people who have ever conquered us and, when you go we should be as we were." The Nagas recall that Mr Attlee and the Hon. Mr E. Cadogan, who visited Kohima, smiled when they heard this.

'It will be interesting to quote Mr Cadogan's recollections of this visit to Kohima which he gave in a speech on the Government of India Bill before the special Committee in the House of Commons in May 1935. "I suppose," he said, "I am one of the few hon. Members of this House who have had conversation with the head-hunters of Kohima in their own jungle. These little head-hunters met us and had a palaver. Presumably the District Commissioner had informed the tribal chieftain that my head was of no intrinsic value as he evinced no disposition to transfer it from my shoulders to his head-hunter's basket which was slung over his back and was, I think, the only garment he affected. I am telling this to the Committee in order to prove that these little tribesmen are more sophisticated in their own particular way than perhaps the Committee may imagine. They have a very shrewd suspicion that something is being done to take away from them their immemorial rights and customs. This is the way they put it to me, They said, "We hear that a black king is going to come to rule over India. If that is so, for goodness sake"—or whatever corresponds to the expression goodness sake—"do not let it be a Bengali." They ended by saying that they much preferred Queen Victoria.'

This mincingly Orientalist and deeply racist observation was interpreted by the government of India as the Naga Hills being very much part of continued dominion as one ruler—white or black, but definitely not Bengali—handed over control to the other.

9. 'That There Should Be No Bloodshed Is Recognized'

In April 1945 the quasi-casual nature of the Naga Club evolved to the Naga Hills District Tribal Council, a government-sanctioned voice and, in some ways, a precursor to several similar councils in independent India. The Naga National Council, or NNC, evolved from this in March 1946, when, at a meeting in Wokha—in the homeland of the Lotha tribe—the council opted to rename itself NNC with the objective of voicing Naga aspirations and with a political objective of autonomy.

NNC aimed at negotiating the Naga future at a time of intense negotiations for the Subcontinent's future. Representations were first made for autonomy and then for inclusion of the Naga Hills into Assam over Bengal—but with the proviso for autonomy overlayed with a demand for a separate electorate. Nehru disapproved of this and formally made it known to the Council the following year in June—by then Nehru had been leader of India's interim government for several months and well on course to shortly become independent India's first prime minister.

Although he disagreed with the idea of a separate electorate, in 1946, Nehru was on record not disagreeing with the Naga need for autonomy—the demand hadn't yet escalated to independence.

'The whole Naga territory should go together and should be controlled in a large measure by an elected Naga National Council. [...] I agree entirely with your decision that the Naga Hills should constitutionally be included in an autonomous Assam in a free India, with local autonomy and due safeguards for the interest of the Nagas,' Nehru had replied in August 1946 to NNC leader T. Sakhrie's letter seeking autonomy and a separate electorate, as I read in an essay by the academician Sajal Nag; the passage is quoted more extensively in Elwin's book. '[…] I see no reason whatever why an extraneous judicial system should be enforced upon the Naga Hills. They should have perfect freedom to continue their village panchayats, tribal courts, etc, according to their own wishes …'

Through 1946 and 1947 negotiations continued between NNC and the prime minister of the vast Assam province, Gopinath Bordoloi and his associate, Bimala Prasad Chaliha—both huge figures in pre- and post-Partition Assam as those who helped to create the state as well govern it as chief ministers. Meanwhile, factions within NNC were jostling for perspective and power, with a drift towards a harder line.

Then, over 26–28 June 1947, two months shy of India's independence NNC—now debating internally between autonomy to outright independence to being a British protectorate—reached an accord with Assam's governor, Sir Mohammed Saleh Akbar Hydari. This 'Nine Point Agreement' which is still included in briefing papers and backgrounders for MLAs in Nagaland, spelled out several specifics.

The preamble to the Memorandum stated: 'That the right of the Nagas to develop themselves according to their freely expressed wishes is recognized.'

All judicial matters were to be resolved according to Naga customary law—shades here of the future Article 371A of India's Constitution—except for appeal to the governor for death penalties and 'transportation'. Senior bureaucrats in the districts would share responsibility and accountability at various set levels and functions and matters of agriculture and public works would remain with the Council—which also undertook to pay and control all matters of education and forestry. No central or provincial government laws that impinged on the agreement or 'religious practices of the Nagas' would have 'legal force in the Naga Hills without the consent of the Naga Council.'

Land was of course sacrosanct: 'That land with all its resources in the Naga Hills should not be alienated to a non-Naga without the consent of the Naga Council.' The Council would be responsible for all matters related to taxation.

Item 6 was 'Boundaries' and in that lay the seeds of future sabotage—at least from the perspective of Naga nationalists and rebels who remained livid at the formation of the state of Nagaland in 1963. 'That present administrative divisions should be modified,' the item on boundaries read, 'so as (1) to bring back into the Naga Hills District all the forests transferred to the Sibsagar and Nowgong Districts in the past, and (2) to bring under one unified administrative unit as far as possible all Nagas. All the areas so included would be within the scope of the present proposed agreement. No areas should be transferred out of the Naga Hills without the consent of the Naga Council.'

Some colonial regulations such as the Bengal Eastern Frontier Regulations of 1873, which issued the Inner Line Permit, or ILP, to manage entry of non-Nagas into the Naga hills, would remain in force—and remains in force till the present day. (Before digital applications became widely accepted as a result of Covid-19 restrictions, the ILP form would insist on pro-forma grovelling: 'Sir, I have the honour to state that I am in need of ILP for short stay …')

To continue to the Hydari Agreement: Point 9, 'Period of Agreement', was a political plum for NNC. 'The Governor of Assam as the Agent of the Government of the Indian Union will have special responsibility for a period of 10 years to ensure the due observance of this agreement, and at the end of the period the Naga National Council will be asked whether they require the above agreement to be extended for a further period or a new agreement regarding the future of the Naga people arrived at.'

The post-Independence government of India reneged on the deal, pushing instead for an agreement for the right to self-determination, not self-determination itself—essentially, negotiations for degrees of autonomy, not independence. Consultations began to draft and implement what would become the Sixth Schedule.

Hydari, like his legacy of the so-called Hydari Plan, soon faded. His grave lies in Kangla Fort. The governor of Assam died at Waikhong while on a visit to Manipur in December 1948.

Meanwhile, the hard-liners within NNC continued to move harder to the right.

NNC leaders claimed there was a meeting with Mohandas Gandhi in Delhi's Bhangi Colony on 19 July 1947, less than a month before India's independence and just months from his assassination in January 1948. It is claimed Gandhi heard the pitch for Naga freedom, and declared that he would be 'the first to be shot before any Naga is killed'.

The version I've read quotes Gandhi a little differently. It's a conversation that Phizo would purportedly have in June 1977 with Prime Minister Morarji Desai, in London. I read of it in *My Journey in the Nagaland Freedom Movement* by Biseto Medom Keyho. Phizo was at the time living in self-exile in Bromley, Kent; the life of a gentleman-rebel dressed in tweed. Desai, riding high after the Janata Party's astounding defeat of Indira Gandhi-led Congress in the general elections earlier that year, had agreed to meet upon being requested by Phizo's niece, Rano Iralu, and on the condition that Nagaland would be off the table. The Gandhi aspect of the conversation reportedly went like this:

Phizo: I have come to meet the prime minister of India because my people have been suffering for a very long time. And you have become the prime minister of India for only about three months. I am not blaming you for our sufferings—that I want you to understand, but I thought we could find a way to bring about an end on the matter.

Desai: The Nagas are not suffering. And if you talk about Nagaland, I shall not talk with you. I told your niece Rano that I am prepared to meet you as a person but not about Nagaland.

Phizo: In 1947 when the British were about to leave their Empire a Naga delegation went to Delhi to meet Mahatma Gandhi because our situation may not have been understood by the Indians. And we explained to Mahatma Gandhi that the Nagas are not Indians and Nagaland is not Indian territory. We submitted the points of discussion to Mahatma Gandhi earlier as his secretary asked us to do so. I think his secretary was Mr Pyarelal. We asked Gandhi if India will attack Nagaland when it became free. Mahatma Gandhi said, 'If you say that Nagas are not Indians and Nagaland is not Indian territory then the matter must stop there. We also do not want the British and they are going. India will not attack you. She has no right to do so and I will sacrifice my life for you before any Naga (is) shot.'

Desai: From where the meeting took place?

Phizo: In Delhi at Bhangi Colony. Mahatma Gandhi was assassinated soon after. If he had lived a few months longer the Naga problem would not have arisen but if we do what Mahatma Gandhi would have said were he alive there will be no difficulty.

Desai: Why have you brought up Mahatma Gandhi's name? I know him better than you. I will not follow him. I will do everything what I consider to be right. Now, what more do you want to say?

It ended poorly. Desai kept insisting there weren't any problems. Indeed, that matters had been resolved twice over, with the peace deal of 1960, formation of Nagaland in 1963 and the Shillong Accord of 1975—which we shall read about shortly—all of which had granted Nagas numerous benefits, Constitutional and customary. Phizo kept pushing, bringing Nagaland and Naga aspirations and the still ongoing conflict into the conversation, even though his own organisation, NNC, was much faded and in three years there would be a resurgence of rebellion with the formation of NSCN—as yet-undivided NSCN.

Phizo: Will the prime minister of India exterminate the Nagas?

Desai: Yes, I will exterminate all the Naga rebels. There will be no mercy.

Phizo: Is not that horrible?

Desai: We are protecting our citizens. Only a few Nagas are giving trouble, harassing the people in the villages—that we cannot allow. We must protect our citizens. And I will exterminate all. There will be no mercy.

Phizo: Whether we are few or many I thought we could go into the matter deeper.

Desai: I told you I shall not discuss Nagaland and if you want to talk about Nagaland, this is the end of the meeting. What more do you want to say? …

Khodao Yanthan [Naga leader accompanying Phizo]: When you were elected prime minister, because all through your life you fought, the Nagas thought you will be the man for the final settlement of the Naga problem.

Desai: What is there to settle? ... I will have absolutely no leniency on rebels. If you want to persist on [sic] independence I will have nothing to talk ... I will certainly exterminate the Naga rebels. I have no compunction in that.

Phizo: Mr Prime Minister, will there be further opportunity for discussions?

Desai: What discussion? There will be no discussion.

There would be, 20 years in the future. But for the moment, much blood would flow and Nehru's dictum of India's unity at any cost had now passed seamlessly to the man who came to rule the empire of India after his daughter, Indira.

And that, alas, was only the bloodbath from 1970s on. The inexorable journey towards the Great Naga Killings continued to gather momentum in the late-1940s. Each decade from the 1950s to early decades of the new millennium would demand blood sacrifices from the Nagas; and a retaliatory trail that drew the blood of India's armies and paramilitaries—all in the name of the loving, caring embrace and preservation of India's professedly democratic republic, pitched across the world at every opportunity as the land of peace, the land of the Buddha and the Mahatma.

On 14 August 1947, the same day as Pakistan formally declared independence and a day earlier than the formal Indian announcement of its own Independence, hard line Naga leaders announced the independence of Nagas.

Some intense back-channel negotiations followed over the next three years, through India's desperate attempt to stitch together a country with alliances and the acquiescence of several hundred 'princely' states. Then, the hard-line element within NNC, the organisation chaired by Phizo since end-1949, resolutely moved towards a show of greater independence. A plebiscite was held on 16 May 1951, several months before independent India's first parliamentary elections which would be entirely boycotted by the Nagas. The result of the plebiscite, extrapolated to interpret the views of all Nagas, claimed that almost the entire Naga population bar .01 per cent had voted to break from India. Even pro-government commentators admitted that all Naga villages had been reached for the plebiscite. (And there was a brief confluence of interests—or, at any rate, empathy—with non-Naga people of the region. Naga nationalists like Phizo and his colleagues had been regularly in touch with several tribes in far-eastern India and also with leading Manipuri—Meitei—nationalists like Hijam Irabot. I had once been told in Imphal that the ballots for the plebiscite had been printed there.)

The government of India and the provincial government of Assam naturally dismissed the results of the plebiscite. To them it smacked of manipulation and they badmouthed it in the manner they had criticised it since the announcement of the plebiscite in 1950. Efforts to diminish the issue was poised on a precipice. Nehru met Phizo and Naga delegations a few times over 1951–1952, including once with Phizo when Nehru was campaigning for elections in Assam. Records show he promised Phizo autonomy for the Nagas, but not independence. Civil disobedience as a matter of protest had meanwhile begun to increase in the Naga Hills.

Nehru had for some years maintained the unviability of an independent Naga nation from the perspective of its politics and economy, let alone geopolitics. A meeting with a Naga delegation led by Phizo on 11 March 1952 and their continued insistence on independence, finally got to him: '… even if heaven falls or India went to pieces, Nagas would not be granted independence'. In his essay, Nag mentions that Nehru repeated his logic in August 1956 during a speech in the Lok Sabha during the debate on the Naga Hills situation, a time when the Naga Hills were already aflame: '…it is no good talking to me about independence for that area. I consider it fantastic for that little corner between China, Burma and India to be called an independent state. I was not prepared to discuss independence … I should be glad to meet them [the Naga delegation] provided they made it clear that they did not demand independence.'

But, impractical or not, that's what they wanted—at least the Naga Council and several of the tribal chiefs did. And here history may not be as kind to Phizo even within the Naga construct, even with his iconic status—not only on account of the mysterious orders that would in a few short years lead to the death of senior colleagues in NNC, like the arrest, torture and killing of the relatively liberal T. Sakhrie, but also because if Nehru would soon have the blood of the Naga people on his hands, so would Phizo and his hard-line colleagues who dismissed repeated offers of autonomy.

But perhaps they had been angry at being sold short, that India's constitutional provisions were inadequate to the needs and ambitions of the Naga people. Elwin offers a revealing comment in this context:

'The Sixth Schedule, therefore, does give the tribal people of the hill areas of Assam a considerable control of their own affairs and protection of their land and customs. Had it been introduced in other parts of India, where the tribesmen do not enjoy anything comparable, it would have been welcomed enthusiastically. In Assam, however, the Nagas as well as the other hill people were already thinking in terms of a special State, for which, they felt, the Sixth Schedule was an unsatisfactory substitute. They wanted a Legislature and Ministers. What they got was a District Council.'

Matters escalated in early 1953. Nehru and U Nu, the first premier of independent Burma—it had gained independence in January 1948—met to discuss border issues. Although the border with the Naga Hills and Tuensang Area was about a fifth of the eventual agreement on the north-to-south border of 1,643 kilometres, it set Naga leaders and people on edge, as it was seen as a bid to divide Naga homelands. When the two premiers visited Kohima for a public function on 30 March 1953, NNC took umbrage as they were disallowed from meeting Nehru. Tribal chiefs too felt insulted. Several of those assembled walked out. Apocryphal telling has some Naga chiefs raising their traditional handloom lower garments and flashing their posteriors at the premiers—they mooned Nehru, to use a colourful Americanism.

On 31 March 1953 the news even made it as far as *The New York Times*, in a Page 3 article by Robert Trumbull to which headline writers provided an exotic twist:

BOOING TRIBESMEN WALK OUT ON NEHRU;
Naga Headhunters Quit Rally in Bid for Independence—
Burma Chief Sees Snub

The embarrassment of government was quickly followed by the irritation and anger of government. NNC leaders began to be arrested. Villagers began to be raided to target weapons caches. That summer, the precursor to the legislations of immunity and impunity that would follow in the next few years, *The Assam Maintenance of Public Order (Autonomous Districts) Act, 1953*, was quickly passed by Assam's Assembly, received the assent of the governor on 26 May, was published in the official *Gazette* on 3 June. It came into play in the Naga Hills.

Arrests and protests became routine. Minor skirmishing began, escalating to major skirmishes. The Naga Hills was declared a 'Disturbed Area' in January 1956. The Indian Army took control—but full-scale operations by security forces had already begun in 1955. In two months, on 22 March 1956, Phizo and his colleagues declared a free Naga government. The flag of the Federal Government of Nagaland, what over time came to be better known by its acronym, FGN, was raised in Phensinyu, in the Rengma Naga homelands between Kohima and Wokha.

'Nagaland is a people's sovereign republic,' the Yehzabo, or Constitution, of FGN declared. 'This has been so from time immemorial. There shall be a Parliament with a strength of 109 Tatars [MPs]. The President will be elected by the people and his Cabinet will consist of fifteen Kilonsers [Ministers] ...

'Nagaland will maintain permanent military neutrality. There will be no standing army for the maintenance of law and order. There will be a Department of Home Guards headed by a Chief to function in the dual capacity of police and patriot soldiers ...'

Every tribe was earmarked a division of 500 men of all ranks. A major-general would command each division. Ranks equivalent to that of the Indian Army made up the remainder of the pyramid. Awards were instituted, from the Victoria Cross to the Military Cross and Military Medal. Home Guards were paid, but pay was irregular and ultimately became a need-based emolument—future Naga rebels would streamline this aspect in the course of building financially viable conglomerates through donations and extortion. In these early years, weapons and ammunition was sourced from caches created after WWII from abandoned, captured or retained weapons courtesy of the fleeing Japanese and resurgent Allies alike. Some were looted from raids on security forces. Indian officials noted attempts to buy weapon supplies from Manipur and Assam. Konyak Nagas, well-known for making guns, now switched their expertise to fashioning mortars. 'When Japanese supplies ran short,' goes an Indian account, 'the rifles were rebored to take .303 ammunition.'

Indian authorities disparaged the signatory of the document, a Mr Hongkhin. They ridiculed the head of government as an elderly figurehead of a Naga who was dressed up in a European suit, a pipe stuck in his mouth and a suitably sombre photograph taken. The rebels were 'tactless enough' to ask him to return the suit after the photo-op—so went a version of this tale.

But Indian authorities and the neighbourhood heard of the intent in the Yehzabo, which in several ways remains a blueprint of the Naga rebels' organizational structure and intent in the present day.

'All forms of trade, business, industry, transport and other public utility will be free and will be in the hands of private enterprise. Education will be in the hands of the people. Religion will be free ...'

'In Nagaland, land belongs to the people and it will remain so. There will be no land-tax, and other forms of taxation will be formulated by different administrative units ... Each Naga village is a republic in its own right. Each Naga family or tribe occupies its own distinct region, and shall continue as before to exercise full authority over its own affairs, including land, community organizations, social and religious practices and customs ... Men and women, above 22 years of age, will have equal rights of voting. There will be equal wages for equal work, irrespective of sex.'

There were to be governors for each tribal area and an administrative chain extended down the line to the village. There was a system of courts, ultimately answerable to the Federal High Court. Terms that are used till today in Naga rebel structures were coined then, drawing from different Naga languages. Kedahge, or President, came from the Rengma language. Kilonser is a Yimchünger word. Tatar, or Representatives, was derived from Ao.

Women were an integral part of the administrative and rebel supply chain, conducting various functions from being field nurses, to cooks, tailors, in-charge of supplying rations to rebels and be part of the information and courier system. There were no lack of volunteers.

This was also the time of a religious push, which led to the practice prevalent at least in the early 1960s of several churches in Nagaland displaying the 'Nagaland for Christ' sign against India's 'Hindu government'. In 1956, orders were issued for pastors to accompany groups of rebels.

Phizo would flee in December 1956 after slipping into East Pakistan, helped by a well-known Baptist missionary, Michael Scott, and the cooperation of Pakistan's government.

Evidently, Bimala Prasad Chaliha tried his best for rapprochement. He had led several delegations for talks with Naga Council leaders in 1953. Chaliha was at the time president of Assam Pradesh Congress Committee. In mid-September-1953, he wrote a report—which came to be called the 'Chaliha Report'—for his colleagues about what should be done in the Naga Hills.

'THAT THERE SHOULD BE NO BLOODSHED IS RECOGNIZED,' the Chaliha report urged in capital letters. The report, which also forms a part of the Bishnuram Medhi Papers at New Delhi's Nehru Memorial Museum and Library, continued:

'1. That the present impasse in Nagaland should be resolved.

2. That the differences should be settled amicably and peacefully by negotiations.

3. It being understood that the negotiations will take place if the Congress party accepts to discuss the Naga Independence Issue...'

His colleagues and Nehru disagreed.

Indeed, Nehru wrote a note to Medhi, Assam's chief minister at the time, in mid-May 1956, when the army's war in the Naga Hills was in full flow. The note was evidently written after a meeting with top Cabinet ministers, officials from the external affairs and defence ministries, and chief of army staff, Gen. S.M. Sriganesh. Among other things, it prepared the ground for further action by invoking things beyond the core Naga question and extending to the realm of geopolitics—'...much more to it than the mere military approach', as Nehru put it. 'These Naga troubles and revolts have a larger significance for us in the international sphere and they give a handle to our opponents everywhere. More particularly, of course, Pakistan takes advantage of them.'

Nehru was still friendly with China at the time. The escape of the Dalai Lama to India in 1959, the freeze in India-China relations and the 1962 war were still some years in the future. Chairman Mao's China was several years from offering training and logistics support to Naga rebels. But a geopolitical foreshadowing and Nehru's own firm views of the Naga construct led him to take a firm stand.

'There can be no doubt that an armed revolt has to be met by force and suppressed,' I read further in a reproduction of Nehru's note to Chief Minister Medhi. 'There are no two opinions about that and we shall set about it as efficiently and effectively as possible. But our whole past and present outlook is based on force by itself being no remedy ... Much more must we remember this when dealing with our own countrymen who have to be won over and not merely suppressed ... It may be that the present is no time for the political approach, because it may be construed as a sign of weakness. But anyhow our minds should be clear that and even now onwards we should do nothing which will come in the way of that political approach and we should let it be known that we want to be friends with the Nagas unless they revolt against us.'

The Naga people, driven between the government of India and Federal Government of Nagaland—both entities who claimed to speak on behalf of the Nagas and both of which would be increasingly armed and dangerous—were about to spectacularly become what the lexicon of conflict chillingly terms 'collateral damage'.

Within the years, from January 1955 to July 1957 ... 79,794 houses have been burnt down and also 26,550,000 maunds of paddy rice have been burnt down and destroyed by the Indian armed forces ... 960,000,000 rupees worth of things have been lost through this fire destruction in six hundred twelve villages out of eight hundred fifty two Naga villages, approximately...

'1) The ladies are very often intended [taken or villagers asked to supply] from all Naga villages. The elders are shot to death when refused to supply them with intended ladies...

4) The Naga women and girls are made naked and raped publicly every day.

5) Young girls with young men are arrested together, and their shameful covers [clothing that cover the genitals] are taken off and forced them to make intercourse publicly in the Church buildings.

6) The Naga virgins, aged between ten and fifteen years are raped to death by the Punjab Regiment...

8) The glory of the mighty forces of India is to commit sodomy by making unusual sex with the Naga boys through the rectum...

13) The daily practice of the mighty forces of India is to pierce the Naga victims with red-hot iron, even to their shames...

14) Shave off the Naga victim's hair and the chilly powders are applied all over their bodies. Forced them to eat one-fourth seer of chilly powders at the point of bayonets...

15) The innocent villagers are arrested everyday, and are ordered to dig out their own pits of six feet deep ... they are put with heads upside down in their respective pits ... For instance, the terrible drama was made to the twenty two unfortunate victims at Mukhami village border by 9th Gurkha Regiment, on January 7, 1957...

19) ... one Naga Home Guard Videlhoulie, Kohima Village, was shot at Kohima village wet cultivation on July 12, 1957. When the victim was

*beheaded, his own sister named Duonilhouü was forced to carry the head up
to the Kohima police thana...*

*21) The Naga victims' legs, hands, fingers and even their testicles are
broken and grinded everyday, everywhere in Nagaland...*

*25) The indigenous Nagas ... have been living now from hand to mouth.
Their wealth has totally been lost ... The nations of the world should not turn
a deaf ear to these entreaties of ours today...*

—From a letter dated 3 August 1957 to the United Nations Organisation
signed by Khrisanisa Seyietsu, Kedaghe (President), 'Government of
Nagaland'. Excerpted from *Nagaland and India: The Blood and the Tears*
by Kaka D. Iralu.

'... When disturbances broke out in the Naga areas, it was obviously
necessary for Government to regulate the entry of visitors to ensure
their own safety. Even so, in some cases foreign missionaries and others
have been enabled to visit the hills from time to time and have received
a warm welcome from both officials and the people. Responsible
journalists visited the Naga area even in 1957; at the height of the
troubles, a body of them toured Tuensang ...'

' ... Progress was hindered, peace impaired for a time when a group
of politicians revived the suspicion and fear that had almost gone. But
that peace and security is on its way back now, and in any case we must
beware of estimating a people's history and the quality of its life by its
dramatic and publicised incidents ...'

—From *Nagaland* by Verrier Elwin.

The white-washing of India's Nagaland ingress continued years after
Nehru's death—and long after the death of his minister colleagues
and senior bureaucrats who oversaw the savagery of the 1950s in the
Naga Hills.

A first day cover issued by the Department of Posts in December 1967 shows, on a stamp worth 15 paise, a likeness of Nehru in his usual garb of white kurta and churidar and 'Nehru' jacket, holding a Naga spear and wearing a Naga headdress complete with its accoutrement of bison horn and hornbill feather. He is shown striding ahead of a group of Naga warriors in full ethnic finery. The artwork suggests the compact Nehru as a tall, slim man, much taller through the technique of foreshortening—certainly much taller than the Naga warriors following him. It's as if Nehru is showing them the way. The legend is benign: 'Nehru and Nagaland.'

10. Interlude: 'Urra Uvie'

Khonoma, a sometime bastion of resistance to the British, Japanese and India, remains a spiritual holdout to the Naga rebellion. There's a sign on the way to Khonoma from Kohima, to the right of the twisting, often-muddy road:

'Nagas are not Indian: their territory is not a part of the Indian Union. We shall uphold and defend the unique truth at all costs and always.'

The quote is ascribed to Khrisanisa Seyietsu, who held office from July 1956 to February 1959 as the president of the rebel Federal Government of Nagaland—and evidently the successor to the mysterious Mr Hongkhin who signed FGN's Constitution. The Reverend V.K. Nuh, general secretary of the Council of Nagaland Baptist Churches at the time, formally unveiled the commemorative plaque in February 2007.

In picture-postcard Khonoma, by the tiny grocery that caters to visitors and locals alike, a large block of basalt hosts the flag of free Nagaland and a memorial decorated with wreaths of flower and pinecone. Placed in 1997, it remembers 46 people from Khonoma who died fighting India between 1956 and 1992. The text is stark: 'These men and women of Khonoma gave their lives for the vision of a free Naga nation. We remember and salute them and still hold fast to their vision.'

Then there is that marker—Phizo's grave and memorial—by the gate of Nagaland's Secretariat.

At the base of the memorial, 'commissioned by Funeral Organisation Committee on behalf of the Nagas', is a statement from Phizo, first in Angami, then in English.

Urra Uvie
Urra kha mia tsülie
Lho
Ungumvümia sü
Upecütsie zo

Our land is our
Heritage.
To none shall it be surrendered:
As whetstone our opponents sharpen
Us.

Nobody except the most foolish would dare to remove these markers. Physical wounds often heal. But to desecrate these markers would be to destroy peace. In any case, here India will at worst remain an entity of compulsive power; at best, an entity of convenience.

That much and no more.

11. To the Hall of Mirrors

Notes: 30/08/2014: Varah (and most of us) got it wrong. Ajit Lal wasn't appointed interlocutor for Naga peace talks. R.N. Ravi was, on 29/08/14. He'll hold concurrent charge of chair of Joint Intelligence Committee to which he was appointed 4 days earlier! Pulled in by new NSA Ajit Doval.

Interesting, as Ravi's a curious piece of work. Isn't known to be heavy-handed. Polite to a default! If previous approach holds, he will begin in the Naga scene by attempting to gain the trust of I-M & others, pols & CSOs and play Delhi's game at the same time. Tagged him back in 2009 for being unusual. Among the rare few serving government officials to have highlighted how AFSPA was counterproductive. Ravi was addl. director with IB in Shillong & backed the statement of R.S. Mooshahary, the governor of Meghalaya—who had earlier headed the elite National Security Guard and the Border Security Force!—when gov spoke at a conf of police chiefs of NE (incl. Sikkim) and West Bengal in Shillong. AFSPA would 'continue to be misused' he said. Said if act is removed situation 'will improve' ... AFSPA has made people 'vulnerable.' Suggested doing away with AFSPA or at least modify it. Ravi as serving officer stood to lose way more than Mooshahary by going against the grain of conventional wisdom but he backed him. [From 2009 notes]: 'We have every reason to do away with the Act and we believe that our police force can tackle the law and order situation.'

Ravi stuck to position after retirement as IB special director in 2012. Wrote and spoke on jettisoning AFSPA and adopting a hearts-and-minds approach. Views refreshingly dovish, widely disseminated. But just heard from a mutual acquaintance with whom Ravi shared a sentiment: 'I have a job to do.'

Expect part dove, part hawk, all establishment.

February 2015 > Note prep for columns > Something big about to happen with Naga peace process. Several indicators.

Turf war beginning. Actually, began right after K broke ceasefire in Jan 2015. Ref text exchange with 'Kohima' on 08/02/2015 about J, major with K (former U, former I-M):

Kohima: Hi! J was shot yesterday by K! He is shifted to Guwahati.

Me: F*#k. Why? How is he doing?

Kohima: He will live! The sad thing is his family was also in the car and he was driving but luckily they all escaped unhurt.

Me: Good to hear. What's the reason? Is it about internal tension in local K/U after ceasefire break? I-M settling old scores? Shall call you tonight...

Kohima: Kindly use 2nd number

Notes: April 2015: Spectacular pulling out of peace process in late-March by NSCN-K. Taga HQ in NW Myanmar intact but leaders & cadres immediately exited designated ceasefire camps in Nagaland—home since a ceasefire with K in 2001—engaged in sporadic attacks on security forces before exiting India. Significantly, Khaplang fired two key pro-ceasefire, pro-talk negotiators before pulling out. Indian security establishment's going to town with new fav phrase: 'abrogated the ceasefire' adding to old fav phrase 'must abjure violence', both of which home ministry/PMO media faithfuls reproduce.

My reading (also conf by Kohima & J) is that Khaplang accepts at this time there's little benefit from weakening hold over his patch of Naga nationalism, idealism + bankrolling by biz & citizens in Nagaland & Arunachal. He would rather nurture turf in MY, protect ceasefire deal with MY junta signed in 2012 in exchange for being left alone.

Tricky stuff for India as K, at least as long as Khaplang lives, likely to continue providing sanctuary—for a consideration of course—to ULFA-I (Paresh Baruah still thick with K + evolved to moving weapons), NDFB factions & CorCom. Alliance still strong. Expedient mix of funds, weapons & narcotics. Can crack only if MY govt & all-powerful Tatmadaw agree to flush out anti-India rebels as Bhutan & Bangladesh did, but GoI quid pro quo with MY not yet at that tipping point.

Ergo: That leaves the negotiating future primarily to I-M even if it doesn't speak for all rebels, let alone all Nagas. I-M's numerical/operational/financial heft will count. I-M will be helped by civil soc push to maintain peace.

But just because K is out of peace/reconc equation for now doesn't mean any settlement can ignore smaller rebel factions like NSCN-KK which broke away from K after Khaplang fired them. KK = Khole Konyak & Kitovi Zhimomi. More alphabet soup but necessary ingredients to any peace process.

Challenges: 1) Honourably carve out integrated future not only for rebel leaders, but also cadres 2) Addn complications re ethnicity = territory. Muivah + many key leaders + bulk of I-M cadres from Ukhrul, Senapati, Tamenglong in Manipur. 3) Old issue: how to find 'honourable alternative' in these homelands without upsetting Manipur's ethnic applecart?

UNC's massive uptick of demand & protest for Alternative Arrangement ever more logical to No. 1 & 3. Reiterate: Naga settlement CANNOT come about without adjustments in I-M's pocket boroughs in Manipur. Mention new input from New Delhi & Imphal (further chk root source: NSA/PMO + Sangh thinktanks or just NSA/PMO?): given to understand that one such adjustment involves giving AA wing with UNC control over finance, admin & dev, but allow Manipur govt control of police. Constitutional provisions to check absolute powers of all. Many balancing acts for this complicated deal to go through—with biggest being grand gestures to Meiteis/Valley, Kukis, Zo ...

Modi has announced sports univ for Manipur. Meiteis/Valley won't be bought that cheaply. To begin/end, Modi/team need to ensure that, at very least, territorial integrity of Manipur is seen to be preserved. Sure-fire buy-in would be withdrawal of AFSPA, Manipur's most explosive emotional trigger after territory. AFSPA now removed from municipal limits of Imphal. Several laws besides AFSPA permit search, seizure and combat against enemies of the state so the removal can easily be extended without any loss of control. If security hawks are wary, AFSPA could remain along Indo-Myanmar border. That porous membrane anyway needs check with narc + weapons + smuggling food chain.

Getting feedback that recent low-key visits by senior army officers to Manipur being interpreted as evaluation of poss give-and-take. Context: one visitor, army chief Dalbir Singh, uniquely placed. Commanded RR Btn in Nagaland + 3 Corps in Rangapahar (due north of Hebron) + Eastern Command in Cal/Kol. Full NE op-footprint experience.

More issues: Reconciliation between I-M & Kukis. Kuki Inpi Manipur + all KI in other states insist on formal apology. Seems like a small price for peace and recon but will I-M manage ego climbdown? Trade loss of face for greater good? BJP plans also major issue. Senior Manipur bureaucrats reconfirm earlier stands—BJP wary of any move that extends Congress/Ibobi govt in Feb/March 2017 Assembly elections. BJP of course targeting 40-seat 2/3 heft of Meitei-majority Valley. Plus, fat cats in pol, establishment, rebels live off economy of conflict. Offer econ/peace opportunity or they will likely sabotage/ delay for status quo benefits.

Notes: 10/06/2015: K really laying it on thick post-ceasefire break. Massive attack with suspected PLA + KYKL on 6 Dogra Regiment between Tengnoupal & New Samtal on morning of 04/06/2015. K & CorCom alliance alive and kicking. 20 troopers dead. Attack with IED, RPGs, assault rifles. Big response on 09/06 by army. Paras & other target K & KYKL camps in Myanmar in cross-border op. Claim camps destroyed + 70 rebels killed. Mynamar govt reportedly in loop. Change in equation? Manipuri rebel groups usually supplement perimeter security when Myanmar army brass visit places in bordering Sagaing Administrative Region! Op coordinated by 3 Corp in Dimapur, GOC Lt Gen. Bipin Rawat.

K clearly out for now. I-M clearly in—for now.

Reiterate: Peace deal/accommodations is make-or-break for Look/Act East + pivot to counter China. Policy without factoring people is poor policy.

Book Two

MIRRORS

12. Agreements and the Fibre of Optics

The delegation from NSCN (I-M) was already in a room at 7RCR—the moniker given the prime minister's residential complex of several bungalows in the heart of Lutyens' Delhi—when Modi walked in, followed by the home minister, Rajnath Singh. Both walked to the slightly raised dais, like the floor made of rich wood. Modi and then Rajnath shook hands with a smiling Muivah, who was flanked by Doval and Ravi—the three dressed in smart suits in contrast to Modi's summer kurta and Rajnath's starched politician's white kurta-pyjama and an elegant 'Nehru' jacket. They took their seats together, Modi at the centre, Rajnath to his right and Muivah to his left. To the left of Muivah were Doval and Ravi. There was no Isak Swu; gravely ill, he was in a New Delhi hospital.

As this cosy photo-op family looked on, the emcee began a drone, largely in Hindi, of a remarkable introduction. He spoke of an 'historic agreement' about to be signed on that day, 3 August 2015. He spoke of how India had been dealing with this 'continuous conflict' between government forces and the Nagas, how thousands of lives and several generations were lost. Now, 18 years since 1997 we had arrived at the stage where Nagaland would begin its journey on the path of peace and development ('Nagaland shanti aur vikas ke path par chal parega …'). The gentleman then invited Ravi ('on behalf of government of India') followed by Muivah ('on behalf of NSCN') to take their places for the signing ceremony.

Ravi scratched his nose once as Muivah slowly settled in. Rajnath coughed briefly. First Ravi and then Muivah signed. Muivah put his pen back in the top pocket of his jacket, Ravi in the pocket of his shirt. Modi, seated, led the applause. Then Muivah and Ravi walked towards each other, and exchanged folders which had their signatures on a page of ceremonial, heavy-grammage paper that would soon be referred to as the 'Framework Agreement'. Muivah walked to Modi and he got up, shaking his hand and then Ravi's. Then they all sat, before Muivah was invited to present his remarks.

That led to a delay of a minute or so, as an official shuffled up to Muivah and bent low to speak to him and Muivah searched about for his statement, printed in large type on a couple of sheets of paper. Doval briefly held his arm as Muivah walked slowly to the podium. His breathing was heavy and audible to everyone in the modest-sized room. He showed the weight of his 81 eventful years.

'I thank God for this momentous occasion,' Muivah began his deliberately paced speech, speaking slowly. 'On behalf of the Chairman Mr Isak Chishi Swu and the Naga people kindly allow me to begin by saying that Naga people have great respect for Mahatma Gandhi because he understood and respected the Nagas when the Naga delegation met him for the first time in 1947. Unfortunately, after his demise, the Indian state resorted to military might to crush the Nagas. Armed confrontation followed inflicting heavy losses on both the parties.'

Muivah praised Prime Minister Narasimha Rao's 'courage to admit that it is political issue and should be solved through political negotiations'. The ceasefire agreement followed in 1997 and with it a beginning of 'political negotiation'. He spoke of the commitment of 'NSCN' to 'leave no stone unturned' to find a 'negotiated amicable settlement between the two parties'.

He ignored the two premiers who followed Rao, Deve Gowda and Gujral, during whose tenures the ceasefire agreement was finally negotiated and signed and jumped to praise their successor, of his 'recognition' of the 'unique history and situation of Nagas' in 2002. 'We Nagas appreciated the statesmanship of Mr Atal Behari Vajpayee and we gave our commitment that if the Government of India would understand the reality of the Nagas, the Nagas will appreciate the reality of India even ten times more and we never back-track from our commitments.'

Then came praise for Modi and his 'wisdom' to work out 'a new relationship between the two parties on the basis of this uniqueness'.

'Beginning from now the challenges will be great so also the responsibilities. The obligations to meet the needs of the people shall be paramount for both the parties to make this historic Endeavour more meaningful. Let me also assure you that Nagas can still come closer if their rights are respected. On behalf of the Naga people allow me to assure you once again that Nagas can be trustworthy and take into your confidence for any policy in the Northeast and beyond the frontiers.'

Muivah ended with, 'Kuknalim.' May the land be free.

Modi, by now in a Tangkhul jacket and draped in a large traditional shawl, then spoke for several minutes. The audience included Atem, the former chief of NSCN and then NSCN (I-M)'s army and India's army chief, Gen. Dalbir Singh Suhag, seated next to each other in the front row. An interesting tableau, as Suhag had commanded both the Eastern Command from Kolkata and III Corp. based in Rangapahar, southwest of Dimapur, all Naga factions and Hebron, I-M's headquarters, firmly in his sight.

Modi began in English by mispronouncing Muivah as 'Mahua', a beautiful tree that grew beautiful flowers that brewed a fragrant, potent spirit, but smoothly recovered, reading from teleprompters to praise Swu's role in the process: 'I wish that Shri Isak Swu, who played a leading role in reaching this agreement, was present today. He could not be here because of poor health. I wish him speedy recovery. Just as his contribution to this agreement has been huge, his guidance will remain crucial in the times ahead.'

'I have the deepest admiration for the great Naga people for their extraordinary support to the peace efforts,' he continued. 'I compliment the National Socialist Council of Nagaland for maintaining the ceasefire agreement for nearly two decades, with a sense of honour that defines the great Naga people.'

Then followed tropes about his 'relationship' with the 'North East' being 'deep', and how the 'rich and diverse culture and the unique way of life of the Naga people' make India and the world a more beautiful place'.

'Unfortunately, the Naga problem has taken so long to resolve because we did not understand each other,' Modi added. 'It is a legacy of the British Rule. The colonial rulers had, by design, kept the Nagas isolated and insulated. They propagated terrible myths about Nagas in the rest of the country. They deliberately suppressed the reality that the Nagas were an extremely evolved society. They also spread negative ideas about the rest of India amongst Naga people. This was part of the well-known policy of divide and rule of the colonial rulers ... It is one of the tragedies of Independent India that we have lived with this legacy.'

He spoke of 'the prism of false perceptions and old prejudices,' the resultant 'weak ... connectivity,' 'modest' development and 'elusive' peace. He spoke of how 'peace, security and economic transformation of North East' has for him been a top priority, and at the 'heart' of 'my foreign policy, especially the "Act East" Policy'.

'Soon after entering office, I appointed an interlocutor for talks with the Naga leaders,' here Modi referred to Ravi, 'who not only understood the Naga people as also their aspirations and expectations, but has great affection and respect for them.'

'Today, we mark not merely the end of a problem, but the beginning of a new future. Today, to the leaders and the people of Nagaland, I say this: You will not only build a bright future for Nagaland, but your talents, traditions and efforts will also contribute to making the nation stronger, more secure, more inclusive and more prosperous. You are also the guardians of our eastern frontiers and our gateway to the world beyond ... Equally, the rest of the nation will join you in shaping a future of dignity, opportunity and prosperity for the Naga people.' He spoke of a 'new future'.

Then Modi, following his proven predilection for the dramatic, went off-script for several minutes as he switched to Hindi. After repeating some of the background as he had in English, he rambled on in a mix of Hindi and Urdu.

'Muivah, Swu ... aur sabhi Naga groupon ko saath le kar ke jo bhumika ada ki hain, jo aane wale dino mein Nagaland ki bhavishya ko swarnim banane mein kaaran banne wali hai ... Bahut hi jald is accord ke anukul sari vyavayastha ko hum vikasit karenge aur ek bahut badi shakti, NSCN ki, raj ke vikas ka hissa banegi ... hamare apne Nagaland ko nayi uchayi par le jayen ... Mere pyare Naga bhaiyon, aapne jitna hum par vishwas kiya hai, main usse bhi zyada takat se prayass karta rahoonga … Is mainstream mein aane ke liye unka hruday se swagat karta hoon … NSCN desh ke un logon ke liye bhi margdarshak banega… jo galat raaste se nikal karke sahi raaste par ana chahte honge …'

As his speech ended with applause, Modi led Muivah off the dais.

A few things stood out in the half hour or so of ceremony.

The emcee's repeated use of 'Nagaland' to mean the homeland of the Naga people—a common enough misconception or more precisely, incomplete understanding—but tone-deaf for such a scripted occasion for nuance.

Muivah's unsurprising appropriation of NSCN's mantle and the mantle of the Naga people (… 'Let me also assure you that Nagas can still come closer if their rights are respected … On behalf of the Naga people allow me to assure you once again that Nagas can be trustworthy …' and so on) as if there was no history beyond that of NSCN in general and NSCN (I-M) in particular. And, with Swu's illness, it would essentially be Muivah's path.

Modi's tom-tomming of his own initiative by ignoring that of every predecessor or administration and smoothly equating himself with Mohandas Gandhi was expected. Although at his level of discourse it was surprising to hear the regular conflation of all Nagas with Nagaland, and as if the agreement would only effect and help this 'Nagaland'; and a tone, as if 'NSCN' signified all NSCNs and all Naga rebels. As we have seen, both positions were horribly exposed in 2001, when the extension of the ceasefire with I-M was extended beyond 'territorial limits'—effectively, beyond the boundaries of Nagaland—and the massive non-Naga pushback in Manipur and to a lesser extent in Arunachal Pradesh and Assam led to the rescinding of that extension. To have that error of nuance carried over 14 years later and repeated by a prime minister of India in the presence of the government's architects and executors of security, displayed either the ignorance or the arrogance of the government. For my money, both.

Besides Modi's obvious fallacy-with-a-flourish, all Nagas, and certainly all Naga rebel groups, would also slowly unpack his extempore journey after his initial remarks, which would appear to be somewhat condescending and insulting to them, about his inference in Hindi about how they had now left the 'wrong path' to walk the 'correct' or 'right' path.

Taken individually and collectively, it all made matters far from clear, and left everything open to interpretation, conjecture, confusion and misunderstanding—especially as both the government of India and I-M declined to share the content of the Framework Agreement. Indeed, an agreement to come to an agreement.

I wrote at the time of how a deal with I-M was only a half-way house. To ensure the Framework Agreement wasn't rendered meaningless required an intricate balancing act. All major interest groups would have to be in on the peace deal, I had written in a commentary on 7 August, or the flimsy deal would quickly die. This included taking on board the states, Manipur, Arunachal Pradesh and Assam, as I had stressed for more than a year: all three states peremptorily resist ceding territory for autonomous Naga homelands, let alone an integrated Naga homeland.

In the immediate aftermath of the agreement, hype among India's pro-government media almost completely ignored the fact that the Framework Agreement was only a memorandum of understanding for peace and reconciliation with I-M. It naturally didn't take on board NSCN-K, which remained an unmitigated threat at the time. Indeed, the necessity of making it an I-M-plus exercise became rapidly evident when I learned that some doughty members of Naga civil society groups, including several indomitable ladies of the Naga Mothers' Association, were planning a trek to Myanmar to meet faction chief Khaplang and try to convince him to de-escalate violence and give lasting peace for the Nagas a chance.

Smaller groups with which government enacted ceasefires, such as K breakaways NSCN (Khole-Kitovi) and NSCN (Reformation), meanwhile distanced themselves from the government's I-M project. Even Adinno Phizo, the sidelined expatriate daughter of rebel icon Angami Zapu Phizo, issued a statement on 4 August assuming guardianship of Nagaland and reiterating a hoary claim: 'Nagas are not Indians and Nagaland is not Indian territory.'

Such sabre-rattling apart, there was the matter of mainstreaming I-M by absorption into Naga polity—let alone Indian polity—and productive society. 'In comparison,' I had written at the time, 'the government and NSCN (I-M) may find the disarming of rebels and possible absorption of some cadres into policing or paramilitary units easier to achieve.'

This left much of I-M's leadership and cadre to consolidate their hold in Manipur. A settlement with I-M could not come about without adjustments in its pocket borough.

A misstep would light a fire, claim lives and livelihoods.

In the meantime, a strange ceasefire had morphed into a strange agreement.

On 14 August, a day before India celebrates Independence Day and barely 11 days after signing the Framework Agreement, Naga rebel armies—all factions, whether in ceasefire or not—celebrated Naga independence, first declared by a council of leaders in 1947. In Camp Hebron, headquarters of I-M near Dimapur, the flag of an intended sovereign Nagaland was unfurled and raised.

Naga women and men in combat gear marched past a grandstand. Muivah, present with most of his senior colleagues, had his right hand raised in salute.

It was all so strange that I suggested something that would only appear as strange in comparison—although with far greater emotional impact than anything the government of India had done to the Nagas since butchering them as a matter of state policy and utterly squeezing people in Mizoram, Manipur and elsewhere:

If only India's strongman was strong enough, individually and as a part of a collective leadership, to have the courage to apologise for its past mistakes. Surely a strong Indian leader—and Prime Minister Narendra Modi was certainly politically stronger than his predecessor—would not display weakness, but confidence, generosity and respect for renewal, to apologise for the terrible policies of alienation and mandated atrocities in north-east India? He could so easily go beyond the mention of the 'tragedy' of 'divide and rule' and 'false promises and old prejudices' at his post-signing speech on 3 August. This would help to clean decades of bad blood, show the way to the peoples of Nagaland, Manipur and elsewhere to sort things out, clean up their own decades of bad blood with each other with an attempt at truth and reconciliation. They had attempted it in Nepal. They had done it in Rwanda. They had …

It was good to dream.

13. Interlude:
Shooting Monks for Development

Notes: 02/05/2016

Police shot at hundreds-strong crowd of protesters, including Buddhist nuns and monks, in Tawang, a town in the northwestern corner of Arunachal near the border with Bhutan and Tibet AR. At least two protesters died (some unconfirmed reports claim four, even six). Several others were injured, including monks. The protesters had been demanding the release of a Buddhist monk, Lobsang Gyatso.

It seemed like a karmic relationship between development and death, that hydropower plum with more than 40,000 MW worth in some stage of planning and implementation in Arunachal Pradesh—accounting for about two-thirds of such projects in India's far-east.

But shooting monks and nuns? For this geopolitical sweet spot— China's territorial ambition plus India's maps of security and energy security—the situation was more like 'Deafcon 3' on a scale of 5 being minimum and 1 maximum. It was my yardstick for loosely measuring the admixture of heavy-handed application of policy, itchy palms and twitchy trigger-fingers leading to a threatening situation. (This scale is of course inspired by Defcon, or defence readiness condition 5 to 1 as practiced by the United States military establishment.)

While the administration and police ran for cover, New Delhi quickly came into play. Besides security implications it is also the home turf of minister of state for home affairs at the time, Kiren Rijiju. By 4 May, the fracas had become a topic in parliament, two top officials, Tawang's deputy commissioner and superintendent of police, were among those suspended and a government-led inquiry initiated.

As always, there was a back story. Lama Lobsang was a vocal critic of hydropower projects, both small and large, in the area. The activist Lama was also general secretary of Save Mon Region Federation, which spearheaded such protest on behalf of the area's Mon-pa people. Just a few days earlier, on 26 April he led a group of villagers from Gongkhar to protest the allegedly shabby work on the spillway of the 6 MW Mukto Shakangchu micro 'hydel' project. Micro projects were generally more welcome in Arunachal than massive ones, such as the protest inundated Dibang and Lower Subansiri projects, the first a little less than 3,000 MW and the second at 2,000 MW. Lama Lobsang, according to activists, was engaged in protesting about 7,000 MW worth of medium and large projects in Tawang district.

The Lama was arrested for disturbing the peace. Though Lama Lobsang was quickly released, he was rearrested on 28 April after he evidently mouthed off against Tulku Rinpoche, the abbot of Tawang's famous monastery, asking the guru to back off and alleging he had little appreciation of the concerns of the Mon-pa. A meeting by local panchayat officials was called that day, which ended up trash-talking the lama for his earlier comments about the venerated abbot and some officials filed a police complaint against Lama Lobsang. He was hauled off to jail. Then the gathering on 2 May to demand his release, the shooting, the killings.

It quickly became a twisted take on peace and prosperity when chief minister Kalikho Pul meanwhile headed off to New Delhi. On 3 May, just one day after the outrage he was chief guest at a conference, 'Hydropower@Crossroads', organised by The Associated Chambers of Commerce and Industry of India, or Assocham. Pul offered both state- and private sector players single window clearance 'for installing and commissioning' of hydropower plants. He spoke of fast-tracking such projects and promised to 'ensure that there are no barriers to investors'.

It seemed somewhat Nero-like in the context of the eruption in his state, and underscored yet again the administration's willingness to override people's consent for projects. In a way it seemed like another re-run of 2012, when in April of that year the government violently dispersed protesters who had gathered to protest against the private sector-led 2,700MW Lower Siang Hydro Electric Project. At the time I had written that worse would follow. It regularly had: suppression of such protests has become routinely violent.

And now, Tawang. Warring lamas may be perversely amusing to some. And Government-led damage control is as much optics as law and order. But the root cause of it all remained: the resentment of several local communities about a hydropower policy that has been repeatedly been rammed by New Delhi down the gullet of Arunachal Pradesh, often freely aided by local, loyalist satraps of the Indian government of the day. Arunachal would remain a battleground where the dream of more power for India met the state's increasingly vocal citizens—alongside the on-again-off-again battleground it already is for India and China.

It also remained a battleground for Naga rebel groups and for the continuing tussle between such groups and India's security establishment—on account of the ceasefire with I-M being limited to the boundaries of Nagaland, Framework Agreement or not.

14. Après Swu, Le Déluge

28/06/2016

Expected, but still seismic in many ways for the Naga peace process. Isak Chishi Swu, I in I-M, died of multiple organ failure at 12:40 hrs, Fortis Hospital, south Delhi. 87 yrs old. He'd been admitted to Fortis on 05/07/15, exactly a month before signing of FA, for major kidney & urinary tract problems. Weeklong mourning declared by I-M.

What's happens now to FA? In any case uneasy year since FA signed. Uneasy year piled on uneasy ceasefire.

There will be a new Yaruiwo after appropriate interval, but nobody with Swu's stature. More a cipher or engineered plant—plantation specialists all around! The I in I-M is part of a brand—no new initial will change it; if at all it will have to be a new splinter/offshoot for renaming. Muivah will remain power centre & puppet master. I-M will continue to recruit, train, arm on basis of ceasefire rules & until final peace agreement signed. No demobilising before that. Everything will continue. All govt can do is pressure directly & indirectly for I-M to come to terms & scale back its tax/ donation/ extortion + parallel admin for I-M, the same applies to other groups. Nudge I-M—more precisely, M—to the 'path'.

But M has for long walked I-M down his own path. Swu increasingly focused on prayer, Muivah focused on organisation & appointing loyalists to key posts. Now with estimated 5,000 armed cadres (earlier estimate 7K–8K but at any rate there will be aggressive recruitment with an eye on negotiating leverage), with some numbers in camps in Myanmar—preparatory ground in case FA heads south. Because FA could, & not only on account of there being others in the game. Peace cannot come only with I-M on board. Hollow FA. No substance, no 360-degree approach to peace. Still an agreement to decide what to agree on! As reiterated in col for HT: 'The framework agreement remains for all practical purposes an inside job between the signatories. The public and *other players remain in the dark. In effect, there is little beyond two signatures and stated intentions to move forward.'*

Stand validated by 'big reveal' of FA: Ravi's statement to Vijaita Singh of Hindu on 28/06, day of I's passing: 'Swu played a historic role in the framework agreement. It was his idea. His departure is a big loss. For the last several months he has not been actively participating in the talks as he was in hospital. Sometime in March–April, he said now that we have a fundamental understanding on core issues, why don't we sign the agreement?'

This also validates information about Swu wanting to have an agreement in place before his death, which he knew would only be a matter of time. A matter of legacy. But what of Muivah's legacy? Will he carry the flag for his colleague?

Leaders of all groups, even Khaplang, have eulogised Swu, spoken of the nobility of the Naga cause but how can there be lasting Naga solution without reconciliation among Naga factions? Or until they are neutralised by govt (IND & MY) so as to be made toothless.

Leaders and cadres of these rebel groups also need to be 'mainstreamed' within the Naga structure: in politics, admin, paramilitaries, others pensioned off or provided seed money to fund businesses, younger cadres provided retraining or education. The Nepal template + Mizoram template for reconciliation & rehabilitation.

A huge gesture made on 15/06/2016, some days before Swu's death. All 60 MLAs of Nagaland (CM: T.R. Zeliang) offered to resign en masse to pave that way. They resolved to 'put pressure' on GoI & I-M to speed up the process. It harked back to Mizoram's Congress chief minister Lal Thanhawla stepping aside to accommodate rebel leader Laldenga of Mizo National Front as CM after the peace deal in 1986. Nagaland MLAs made similar statement in 2012 (CM: Neiphiu Rio), when they adopted a resolution to give up their positions to accommodate rebels to aid the process of peace and reconciliation.

Beyond the political acquisitiveness & bling they've been pushing it for a while, trying to nudge groups together, work a channel. Need to acknowledge unanimous resolution adopted by Nagaland Assembly even earlier, in November 2009. Pushed by then-CM Rio. All, including Opposition Congress MLAs, acknowledged that UG movement had 'selflessly worked, fought and sacrificed for the aspirations and the rights of the Nagas, and also to those who continue to follow the tradition of selfless sacrifices for the common cause of Nagas'.

But will that 'sacrifice' for mainstreaming rebels into Naga/Indian construct work? Eyewash? How many Tangkhul, Mao, Zeme will Nagaland Assembly absorb—let alone accept? Meaningless without similar accommodation in Manipur. Also, this is not a homogenous ethno-political situation like Mizoram in 1986 when Congress chief minister Lal Thanhawla stepped down. Muivah CM of Nagaland? Forget it. He anyway sees himself as bigger than CM. Needs another structure. Also, as talk is cheap, will Nagaland MLAs actually resign to make way for others, or in the end just push to expand house?

Dynamics further complicated by inevitable leadership struggles in all rebel groups. E.g., Muivah is 82. Power play within I-M has been the talk for at least two years. Disarray may provide plum pickings for GoI, but if a next-gen leader perceives greater power & influence in a state of continuing conflict, he will choose status quo.

Nagaland's future and that of much of its neighbourhood depends on this rubble-strewn road where all travellers will need to behave like saints. Amen.

And suddenly, Nagalim, or Greater Nagaland, was back with a bang in the optics of negotiations as players of conflict and peace continued to jostle for space.

As Swu's body lay in state at New Delhi's Nagaland House on 29 June, attended by his family, comrades, senior politicians, media and, notably, India's national security adviser Ajit Doval and R.N. Ravi, interlocutor for talks with I-M, the loudest statement was the flag draping Swu's coffin. As we have read earlier, it is common to Naga rebel factions and is of a light-blue background with three ribbons of red, yellow and green. A white six-pointed star of Bethlehem is at the top left corner of the flag that highlights at least one rebel slogan: 'Nagaland for Christ'.

In a mourning period that lasted till 4 July—two days after Swu was interred in his home village of Chishilimi in Nagaland's Zunheboto district, homeland of his tribe, the Sema—all such flags flew at half-mast 'throughout Nagalim', according to an I-M communiqué.

In a speech in Senapati town of Manipur on 29 June, Shürhozelie Liezietsu, president of Naga People's Front, a canny political party that had for the moment tripped up its former strongman Rio, spoke of Naga integration. This conflated with an item of negotiation between the government and I-M. It also strengthened the stand of UNC to administratively delink from Manipur—for long seen by Nagas in Manipur as a way to overcome majoritarian-Meitei interests. The statement, capitalising on Swu's death, was also transparent in its intent of leverage in the run-up to elections to Manipur's Assembly in early 2017.

The second gesture of importance was articulated by Swu's family at the memorial service in New Delhi on the same day. Even as the Yaruiwo, or chairman, was publicly mourned by his long-time comrade Muivah—the real power centre of this faction—one of Swu's sons announced that now that they had lost their father, they would look to Muivah, the prime minister, as a father figure and source of guidance.

In Naga-rebel dynamics and Naga ethnic dynamics, this carried significance. At the very least it spoke to how Swu would be portrayed as a bridge—a claim to an over-arching Naga future that Muivah and I-M were aspiring to. This could not be underscored enough. Muivah, a Tangkhul, numerically the second largest Naga tribe, and with its homeland in Ukhrul district of Manipur, continued to be seen as an outsider by many in Nagaland. Besides tribal borders, it was rooted in the fait acommpli of Nagaland's statehood in 1963, which birthed a set of leaders with affiliation to tribe and state within the political and territorial construct of Nagaland, while other Naga peoples were left to their own devices in Manipur, Arunachal and Assam.

This dynamic was also seen as again spurring UNC's stand of administrative separation, considered by many in Manipur as a ploy to carve out post-conflict territory for I-M's leadership and cadres, overwhelmingly Tangkhul. Swu provided legitimacy, however slim, for Muivah and many of his Tangkhul colleagues who dominated I-M's leadership. Swu's son extended that legitimacy, at least in the matter of optics, at a crucial juncture. But with Muivah at 82, the futures were confounding, variable.

In a rare gesture of conciliation, all Naga groups—even the NSCN faction led by S.S. Khaplang, who broke away in 1988 with a massacre of cadres loyal to Isak and Muivah, and broke away from a ceasefire with India in March 2015—condoled Swu's death. All reiterated Naga nationalism and a future of unity and peace for Nagas. This lip service would need to translate into comradeship for the future, coming a full circle from 1988—or a comprehensive Naga peace process would be rendered meaningless.

There was also the dynamic of divide and rule.

For all of Modi's talk in August 2015 of nearly apologising for the aspect of divide-and-rule, for a cabal of India's security officials, for all the public showing, cold calculations for ending the Naga rebellion had, besides combat, long extended to the waiting for the demise of the ageing leaders of NSCN's biggest factions, I-M. The same principle applied to I-M's arch-foe, Khaplang and the K faction. Should the factions splinter thereafter in turf wars among the next level of rebel leadership, the exercise would be reduced to a mopping-up operation.

Less than three months after the signing of the Framework Agreement, Doval and Ravi headed to Myanmar's capital, on 15 October, as special invitees of the government of Myanmar at the signing of treaties with eight rebel groups—significantly, not K against which the Tatmadaw had already resumed operations just hours earlier. Doval met Myanmar's president Thein Sein and other senior officials during the 24-hour visit. I read in a newspaper report of the visit: 'With India committed to stabilising the Northeast, Doval had discussions with the Myanmarese junta to ensure the weapons supply line from Ruili in China's Yunan province is snapped by the Myanmar army and anti-India insurgents do not get refuge or patronage.'

Meanwhile, work would continue to pressure major tribal and political accommodations in Nagaland as well as Naga homelands in Manipur, Arunachal Pradesh and Assam. Because, as several insiders in the peace process maintained, whatever the divide-and-rule plays so beloved of India's security apparatus, there was no alternative to the parallel project of rebel leaders being absorbed in the political arena with a combination of meaningful positions and face-saving sinecures; leaders and cadres being 'mainstreamed' in administration and paramilitaries; others pensioned off or provided seed money to fund businesses; and younger cadres provided temporary allowances to transition into the mainstream and provided retraining, or their education underwritten.

If this complex to-do panned out, it would help diminish other I-M demands expressed over the years. Though I-M scaled back its once cast-in-stone demand of absolute sovereignty for the Naga people more than a decade earlier several other matters remained on the table besides the sticking point of integrated Naga homelands—'Nagalim'. These have included the joint defence of Nagaland; its internal security; consultation for foreign affairs issues of direct interest to the Nagas; and a separate flag for Nagaland alongside the Indian.

Meanwhile, I-M continued to train, recruit, arm and maintain a several thousand-strong army from its headquarters at Camp Hebron. I-M's adjacent training area of Mt Gilead was for real. Its 'Town Commands' across Naga areas continued to impose parallel administration. Its Alee (or overseas) Command stationed troops in areas of Myanmar adjacent to Manipur's Ukhrul district. Provided Myanmar's government couldn't be prevailed upon by India's government to attack, this would provide escape routes and sanctuary for I-M's leadership and cadres if the peace process collapsed; or even, provide sanctuary for some next-gen leaders, should they disagree with the realpolitik of succession after Muivah.

But Muivah, stubborn in his own way, was holding his ground. A Naga political insider told me after Swu's death: 'Muivah would like to see this through.'

It would be a stunning legacy for which Muivah clearly needed more time as much as determination and broader outlook on his side.

For the peace process to be convincing, it would also need to be a comprehensively Naga agenda and have on board all Naga rebel factions for any peace and reconciliation process to be meaningful. Smaller factions were already, proactively jockeying in this space—and there was talk of a broad front of smaller Naga rebel factions coalescing.

But a major thorn in I-M's—and India's—side continued to be

Khaplang, 76 at the time of Swu's passing. Ironically, K had for long been seen by I-M as an Indian lever to keep it at bay, but that game had been suspended with K breaking away from a ceasefire in March 2015.

For a while it had seemed as if Muivah finally realised he needed friends more than foes. Just short of a year before Swu's death, Muivah had set a conciliatory tone upon his arrival in Dimapur from New Delhi on 12 August 2015, just days after signing the Framework Agreement. At a civic reception at the airport attended by representatives of influential tribal organisations, or Hoho, and the Naga Students' Federation, Muivah spoke of 'peaceful coexistence' with India and a future in which Nagas would not be 'under' India and yet not 'totally separated'.

He also reached out to other Naga rebel factions and groups—with which I-M still aggressively jostled for personnel, territory and revenue. '… No matter what, the past is past,' Muivah had announced. 'Before god and before man, we will forgive each other.'

Like other faction chiefs, Khaplang too had condoled Swu's death. But like Muivah's statement his gesture was exploratory. It wasn't yet a firm flutter of an olive branch.

Meanwhile, a year into signing the Framework Agreement with I-M, some conciliatory gestures began to be made by the government of India to demonstrate that it was walking its talk.

Absalom Raman, also known as Absalom Rockwang Tangkhul, I-M's long-time hammer in the Arunachal-Assam-Nagaland tri-junction area, was released. As a buck lieutenant-colonel, he had led the group's ingress into the Arunachal districts of Tirap and Changlang in 2002–2003, strong-arming influence away from arch-rivals K. In 2003, he was widely suspected of being behind the abduction of a businessman in Assam's Dibrugarh who had refused to pay 'taxes'. Absalom also fronted political negotiations in Arunachal's chaotic 1999–2007 period that saw five shape-shifting governments, including those led by the Congress and BJP. In 2012, now a brigadier, Absalom was arrested at a village along the border of Arunachal and Assam.

Anthony Ningkhan Shimray, I-M's key arms procurer until his arrest in late-2010 in Kathmandu—I-M maintains it was abduction, Indians and Nepali authorities maintain Shimray was in Kathmandu to work a grey-market arms deal with a Chinese supplier—was released from New Delhi's Tihar Jail in August 2016.

Amazingly perhaps for anyone except those acquainted with the blurred underground-overground among Nagas, Shimray was within days fêted by the Delhi chapter of the Naga Students' Union—and in general by every major Naga student group, besides Naga human rights organisations and church groups. The felicitation took place at Nagaland House in New Delhi. Nagaland House is the official representation of the government of Nagaland, where legislators, officials and their families and hangers-on often stay when they visit Delhi.

Shimray, who was described as an 'activist' spoke about being 'faithful to the vision of God'. He added, alongside praising the government for his release for the sake of the Naga peace process: 'I am just a follower, and I am not the leader. I want to be a faithful follower till the end of my life.'

It seemed like more a LinkedIn pitch to Muivah and his core team—the real core team—than to peace. Events would soon show it.

And Absalom, whose name means 'father of peace' in Hebrew and was named after a son of a Biblical king, David, went back to his old business in Arunachal Pradesh: playing enforcer and cementing his place, literally, as chief of operations. Events would soon show that too.

These gestures made to I-M were par for the reconciliatory course. Indeed, it wasn't the first time such a gesture had been made. ULFA chairman Arabinda Rajkhowa—who was born Rajib Rajkonwar—was released on bail in early January 2011 from Guwahati jail, after the state prosecutor declined to contest the bail application. Rajkhowa had been jailed for more than a year after being arrested by Bangladesh authorities and handed over to the government of India.

As part of an imminent peace process, Rajkhowa asked for the release of several jailed colleagues in both India and Bangladesh. This included ideologues and even Raju Baruah, ULFA's deputy military chief—who together came to form the so-called pro-talks faction of ULFA even as the organisation's former military chief, Paresh Baruah, among several co-founders of ULFA along with Rajkhowa way back in 1979 in Assam's Sibsagar district, remained aloof. (He formalised the split in 2012 and assumed leadership of ULFA (I), or independent.)

The gesture was made in an attempt to bring to an end one of eastern India's most violent and embedded insurgencies and had the full backing of the Congress-led governments of the time in both Assam and New Delhi. And, while on the surface it might seem odd that Rajkhowa was putting on a show of bravado when, as a leader of a cornered, even partly discredited group he ought to have been on the defensive, it demonstrated the complicated nature of peace and conflict. The peace overture was a significant acknowledgment that, while issues of underdevelopment and fear of the Assamese identity being swamped, which birthed ULFA in the first place, were yet to be resolved, the Assamese wished to sort it out to their own satisfaction.

Indeed, developments such as the release of key Naga rebels and some among ULFA turned the spotlight on some key rebel leaders from Northeast India still in jail. For instance, Raj Kuman Meghen, the chairman of a leading Meitei organisation, UNLF.

Meghen, also known by his nom de guerre, Sana Yaima, was in India's custody even as Rajkhowa was released from an Indian jail; Meghen was arrested in end-2010. Like the arrests of several key ULFA, Bodo and Naga rebels, it was all quite cloak-and-dagger. Meghen suddenly appeared in Indian government custody after several decades underground. The *BBC* sourced information from senior Indian military and intelligence officials to claim Meghen was flown out from Dhaka in an Indian aircraft, a courtesy of the friendly government of Prime Minister Sheikh Hasina. Indian government officials at first denied it, but after several weeks put out that Meghen was arrested by a team from the National Investigation Agency while crossing over to Bihar from Nepal.

A top Bodo rebel leader, Ranjan Daimary too was handed over to India by Bangladeshi authorities in 2010. As with his colleague from UNLF, Daimary's release would have to wait for an opportune moment.

In the face of government-led euphoria and the undeniable relief of many citizens, it is usually prudent to inject some caution into these matters. The grinding down of rebels and rebel operations range from scaled up anti-rebel operations; to rebels falling prey to the rigour of maintaining operations at high pitch, to losing initial idealism; to an India-friendly government such as the one led by Skeikh Hasina in Bangladesh denying anti-India rebels sanctuary and even helping in the arrest of several; and the signing of several suspension-of-operations agreements such as the ones Kuki rebel groups signed with the governments of Manipur and agencies of the government of India.

In no instance have any of these peace deals or arrangements come about on account of better development, the diminishing of kleptocracies in northeastern India and within various agencies of the Indian government active in this region, and the acknowledgement by Government of India—and various political formations that run it—that regional and sub-regional identities in 'Northeast India' have needs and minds of their own.

The reasons that led to the region's discontentedness and a myriad of rebellions continue to exist—peace, intended peace, or not. Moreover, along with many other chroniclers and analysts I too have heard from several bureaucrats and police officers tasked with administering Government of India's will and testament at the grassroots in this region that, more often than not, those 'in-charge' of the 'Northeast' in New Delhi whether in the home or defence ministries—the key satrapies—are either disinterested or clueless about the complexities in this region beyond keep-China-out and Delhi-knows-best. Like Mainland China, Mainland India continues to claim to know what is best for all its citizens. The other driving imperative is that of an economy of conflict—a treasure-trove of siphoned government funds and unfulfilled projects. The civic wrecks that are Guwahati, Dimapur, Kohima, Imphal, Shillong, offer only a passing, though significant, feel of the malaise.

15. Interlude: Going by the Bookkeeper

Sept. 2016: Interesting memo copy arrived as a msg. Major news in some Naga circles. Underscores again the axiom: A rebel needs a cause—and a budget.

From letterhead, GPRN wt N = Nagaland, not 'Nagalim', seems like NSCN-KK budget, not I-M, but amounts are quite large, so ...

Always a confusion as all use National Socialist Council of Nagaland & Government of the Peoples' Republic of Nagaland for admin arm. Usually I-M uses Nagalim. All use Naga Army for armed wing.

Very different approach to Maoists. Regionally disparate cause & nature of Maoist rebellion + playbook of organise-as-you-go. Revenue source can range from a tiny bag of rice to taxing ore-carrying trucks. Some sectors organised, some not. NSCN, irrespective of faction, do things literally by the book, or bookkeeper. Evolved since birth in 1980, carried on thru splits from 1988 on, with I-M arguably the most organised. Admin acumen of I-M is legendary—other Naga factions and rebel groups in NE strive to mirror it.

These budget papers for FY ending March 2017, so 2016–2017, accounting year reflecting Indian standard. Two-part budget presented to 'Collective leadership'. Ministry of Chaplee Affairs, finance arm, presented budget for ₹51.29 cr (precisely ₹512,975,310), with income and expenditure balancing out at that figure. Naga Army presented a budget for a little over ₹117 cr (₹1.17 bn). That's nearly ₹170 cr (₹1.7 bn) for a group in ceasefire.

Different heads for expected revenue:

'Salaries': ₹12.5 cr (₹125 mn)—that's from salaries of Nagas, even in Nagaland where citizens are exempt from paying income tax as special GoI dispensation.

'Commercial' & 'Shop Tax': ₹17 cr (₹170 mn)

Tax on vehicles: ₹1.5 cr (₹15 mn)

'Excise duty': ₹2 cr (₹20 mn)

'Non-plan' income: ₹3.5 cr (₹35 mn)—freewheeling income?

Smaller amounts from several heads like 'Ration tax', 'House Tax & live soul census' & 'Court Fee/fines'—evidently from those hauled up for 'justice'.

Expenses for GPRN much fuzzier. ₹20 cr (₹200 mn) marked for Naga Army though it has its own budget. 'National project' & 'National Contingency Fund' each take up ₹10 cr (₹100 mn)—evidently, don't ask, don't tell. Various ministries & depts get ₹8 cr (₹80 mn). ₹1 cr (₹10 mn) kept for expenses for 'Collective Leaders' & same amt for 'Ration'.

Naga Army exp the biggie. Four biggest heads as follows:

'Arms & Ammunition Procurement': ₹15 cr (₹150 mn)

'Command, Operation, Tour & Duty': ₹13.1 cr (₹131 mn)

'Military Operation': ₹6 cr (₹60 mn)

'Basic Military Training': ₹5 cr (₹50 mn)

'Military Intelligence': ₹3 cr (₹30 mn)

'Research & Development': ₹6 cr (₹60 mn), but for an outfit that buys arms and ammunition off SE Asia's open black market, this could be a slush fund within a slush fund. Maybe tech?

'Signal & Communication Department': ₹6 cr (₹60 mn)

'Procurement: Vehicle & Office Property': ₹6 cr (₹60 mn)

Other big heads: 'Stipend', at ₹15 cr + (₹150 mn +); 'Food Stuff': abt ₹13 crore (₹130 mn); ₹2 cr + (₹20 mn +) for uniforms. Evidently also a caring organisation, as amounts set aside for 'Medicine & Medical Treatment', 'Leave & Transfer & Domestic problems', 'Maternity', 'Marriage', and 'Obituary & Casualty'.

As with GPRN, Naga Army has special tax collectors. Army's collectors are usually those who hold rank of captain & collect Army Tax. The azha (orders) these collectors enforce is sinister pressure alike for citizens or a corp. prospecting for oil & natural gas in Manipur and Nagaland.

Naturally, process is hardly public for all factions. I-M media handlers shared only how a March 2016 meeting at Hebron had offered the guidance of the very ill Isak Swu. Swu urged 'ethical revenue collection and judicious spending'—according to report in Nagaland Post— all conducted with 'highest standards of "revolutionary patriotism, sincerity and transparency"' while executing this '"financial matter".'

Heh.

16. Palaces of (Stolen) Straw

Too-clever-by-half policy application and bullheadedness over several decades by India's security apparatus have contributed to political and security quagmires in far-eastern India. Nagaland and Manipur are not exceptions. As elsewhere in the region, politicians and administrators of these two conflict-linked states—following the template of Mainland India that is so often reviled in these parts, and along with their compatriots from the remaining 'sisters' as it were: Assam, Arunachal Pradesh, Meghalaya, Mizoram, Tripura and Sikkim—undermine development and, therefore, the all-round security of citizens. To put it in another way, they steal the futures of their own people through corruption and ineptitude.

Such scandalous myopia is usually buried under the expedience of conflict and its eager corollary: the economy of conflict that sees no evil and wouldn't hear of any, while feathering nests funded overwhelmingly by central government budgetary support and grants in aid—90 per cent of the total expenditure and more in some instances. Even the nests of 'national workers' and 'patriots', the grandiose euphemism that rebel leaders with vast real estate holdings in the region and in Southeast Asia, even major Indian cities, ascribe to themselves. Several former chief ministers, even serving chief ministers, own and control vast estates and businesses. As I have repeatedly written, in a book and in numerous columns and essays, the wealthy also count among them rebels who are now landed gentry—several of them with large homes and leisure-and-business properties. I have visited some in the course of conducting interviews and while attending various events and functions.

Contractors to government have patrons in the bureaucracy, politics and among rebel groups—often these patrons are themselves contractors, through close family and operations that use that charming Indic word: bénāmi. No-name. Not in their name.

(You've read the joke I shared earlier about such places, Beverly Hills—exclusive suburbs and residential patches in and around Dimapur and Kohima and the 'farms' near Imphal.)

Such wealth is steadily accrued in small and big ways and even the instances that are officially outed, as it were, showcase the greatest arrogance and disregard for accountability. The report of the Comptroller and Auditor General (CAG) of India on social, economic, revenue and general sectors for the government of Nagaland for the financial year-ended March 2014, the latest as we stared at pivotal regional elections and a pivotal peace deal, detailed numerous examples of misappropriation and mismanagement running into hundreds of crores—tens of billions—of rupees. Loss to public good increased when inefficiency was factored in.

The report mentioned, for instance, how between 2009 to 2014—the period during which Neiphiu Rio was chief minister—Nagaland's department of power permitted margins of 'up to 763% to the suppliers in respect of eight major works'. During the same period, the department didn't bill for over 40 per cent of energy it distributed, and didn't collect for a third of the bills it did raise.

In its audit, CAG found that in Nagaland's irrigation department, 'utilisation certificates were not based on the actual funds expended'; and that the department lacked basic information about irrigated areas and intensity of cropping.

An executive engineer of the public works department in Nagaland's Atoizu division drew ₹78.51 lakh or ₹7.85 million as 'pay and allowances' against non-existent employees. The director of land records and survey department drew ₹1.24 crore (₹12.4 million) meant for modernizing land records by forging receipts in the name of three of his colleagues. The Nagaland State Mineral Development Corp. Ltd, besides executing ₹22.75 crore (₹227.5 million) of works not on its approved agenda, also paid out ₹6.14 crore (₹61.4 million) against 'unexecuted items of work'. Consultants were hired elsewhere 'on recommendation of VVIP', resulting in extra payout; and works awarded without inviting tenders. According to CAG, the health department 'provided undue benefit' of ₹10.25 crore (₹102.5 million) to a 'local contractor' to place a magnetic resonance imaging machine at Naga Hospital in Kohima; and more than ₹11 crore (₹110 million) was 'diverted' by a division as salary and furnishings—without supporting vouchers. The report listed numerous instances of such brazen corruption.

(In a conversation with me, an MLA from Nagaland justified such theft as 'It's okay, it's Indian money'. No, I countered during this truly bizarre exchange, it is money given by the government of India—and, by extension, the people of India—for the people of Nagaland, several of whom are your constituents. He diverted the conversation by politely asking after my family.)

Even accounting for the cash-and-carry nature of elections and the unholy wink-and-nudge over election funding and practices by most political parties, it was difficult to discount the 2013 general elections to Nagaland's Assembly and, perhaps for the first time, the visible snagging of big fish.

There was great public outcry for clean elections in the run-up to polling on 23 February. As with a growing cry for reconciliation among rebel groups and a conclusive and honourable peace deal to act as emotional closure, it was a decisive and positive landmark at a time of several cynical negatives.

But there was also that persistent cry all along the political-electoral food chain, only half-jokingly conveyed to me to in a text message by a political insider: Kiman poysha dibi? In Nagamese: How much money will you give?

And the unsaid, as I texted back to that acquaintance in Kohima using 'honey' as the usual handy colloquialism: Modhu bi dibi, deh? Any liquor on the side?

That became evident when the vehicle in which Nagaland's home minister Imkong L. Imchen was travelling on 18 February drove into a search-and-seizure bust by personnel of Assam Rifles near Longsa village, in Wokha district. Imchen was travelling from Kohima to Koridang, his constituency in northwestern Mokokchung district, a route that runs through Wokha. It was around six in the morning.

That is typical for driving in this eastern edge of far-eastern India. People prefer to leave as early in the morning as possible. Indian Standard Time, an unitary application across the country, compels it. Bangladesh, to Nagaland's west, is a half-hour ahead of IST. Myanmar, to the east of Nagaland, clocks one hour ahead of IST at GMT +6.30. But Nagaland—and Manipur, Arunachal Pradesh, Tripura, Mizoram, Assam, in a Bangladesh-to-Mynmar longitudinal time warp—have to hold to IST and its golden mean of twisting the workday that dictates 'early' onset of daybreak and dark. Campaigns by several groups and individuals, including, notably, one by the Assamese filmmaker Jahnu Baruah to have for this region a second time zone, have thus far come to nothing.

Anyhow, the troopers found in Imchen's car ₹1.10 crore (₹11 million) in cash, two old .303 rifles with 100 rounds of ammunition, five 7.65 mm handguns with 80 rounds of ammunition, and a case of liquor. It was formally announced the same day by R. Vyasan, Wokha's young deputy commissioner and the designated 'returning officer' for the elections. (Vyasan had clearly been seasoned by reality since the days I first met him in Wokha in 2009, when he was a freshly-minted officer of the Indian Administrative Service.) Perhaps Imchen believed in his immunity and impunity as home minister, but the bust of this influential member of the incumbent Naga People's Front party and government pointed yet again to murky realities of politics here walking hand-in-glove with misappropriation of public funds with a parallel lack of an income tax regime; and, of course, the all-to-easy access to weapons. Perhaps he was just cut from the don't-give-damn-cloth with which so many politicians and bureaucrats in far-eastern India suit themselves.

And, perhaps, the memory of being detained at Kathmandu airport three years earlier had dimmed. A check found Imchen carrying a large amount of cash in ₹500 and ₹1,000 notes, denominations long banned by Nepal authorities upon India's request, primarily as a way to reduce the circulation of counterfeit currency of which Nepal had become a conduit, and as a corollary, control unaccounted cash with which numerous Indian travellers typically binged on the plentiful shopping, entertainment and the casinos of Kathmandu.

Imchen was detained under the Arms Act, not law related to disproportionate assets or unaccounted funds. It was the same penal code that applied in the case of ₹1 crore recovered two days before Imchen's arrest, on 16 February, from a helicopter used by a NPF candidate in northern Longleng district. Nyemli Phom had shown a sense of entitlement with as much flourish as his colleague. His chartered chopper landed at Assam Rifles' helipad at Longleng without permission or information. When security personnel queried him and searched the aircraft, Phom displayed an authorisation letter from his party's treasurer—which evidently certified that Phom was carrying the cash for election expenses.

The twisted nature of politics in Nagaland became even more evident when NPF, instead of apologising, opened a broadside against its significant local rival at the time, Congress—which had 18 seats to NPF's 35 in the 60-member outgoing assembly. NPF accused the Congress of deliberate attack and favouritism. A formal party statement accused the Congress of applying 'illegal force and the power of its high command to suppress the voice of the Nagas'.

This twitsed offence-as-defence stemmed from the search-seizure performed by security forces on a Congress candidate from central Wokha district, Y. Sulanthung H. Lotha, on the same days as Imchen's bust. Lotha was found with ₹3.7 lakh (₹370,000) in cash and a weapon. NPF's charge was that Lotha was quickly released on bail, unlike Imchen, who made bail only two days after his arrest.

For its part, the Congress ignored Lotha's faux pas and exhorted voters to 'wake up from their slumber and think rationally' to vote for a 'better government and better Nagaland'. Union home minister Sushilkumar Shinde, a cabinet minister in the Congress-led central government of the time, was also conveniently at hand to offer glib talk of the need to negate terror and corruption.

Conspiracy theories swirled in media, social media and the grotesque and often hate-filled rumour mill of what has over the years come to be known as Whatsapp University. To have a contingent of Assam Rifles detain the Nagaland home minister's car could not have happened without the active involvement of 'New Delhi' and India's security apparatus. A Congress candidate was trapped only to present to the world an instance of equal opportunity, but it was actually a deliberate sacrifice of a pawn to encircle the enemy's king: NPF leader and incumbent chief minister Neiphiu Rio.

That gentleman, who has for some decades carried his slickly groomed person with two-tone panache—a jet black fringe on his head with a beard that's pure-white royale—is the patriarch of his family's major businesses and real estate holdings. A tiny sampler: A grand villa in Dimapur and two major resorts in the outskirts which I've visited. The lesser one, when I first visited it in 2009 even has a public-funded waterway, part of an irrigation project, running through it and a motor launch to take visitors sightseeing. His older residence on Bayavü Hill in Kohima was transformed into a plush hotel—at which my publisher at the time, HarperCollins, arranged a reading of *Highway 39*; it was all duly paid for and receipt provided. Across the valley is a newer hotel owned by his family where I have also stayed in the course of subsequent research trips. Indeed, at the time, some friends and acquaintances in Kohima joked, not without irony, that I should share custom with Rio's political rival, T.R. Zeliang, whose family too has vast business interests, including hospitality, real estate and media—and who wished very much to be chief minister.

Away from the conspiracy theories, the detention of senior Naga politicians appeared to also be a signal to Naga rebel groups, which had lately adopted a holier-than-thou posture of publicly declaiming a distance from exerting electoral influence—a spin with negligible purchase—that the central government could play hardball as it worked to convert lengthy ceasefires into formal peace talks.

Whatever the claims and counter-claims, they all again served to underscore the terrible structural and moral vulnerabilities of the place. Something was rotten in the state of Nagaland.

In Manipur, about a third bigger than its northern neighbour Nagaland, and with a population approaching three million, the situation of waste was—is—similarly lamentable and abundant, the situation of skim depressingly similar and abundant.

The CAG report for Manipur for the year ended March 2013—the latest available in the period of run-up to the pivotal elections of 2017 and only one among many such reports during Chief Minister Okram Ibobi Singh's three consecutive terms since 2002—listed several horror stories in the area of HIV/AIDS, a core concern and literally a cash point in this state. Elsewhere, too, were wretched stories of petty and grand theft.

The youth affairs and sports department, a vaunted Manipur construct, was also evidently a gravy train. In nine sampled field offices, CAG listed nearly ₹15 crore (₹150 million) unaccounted in cash books. Two district sports complexes were listed as 35 per cent completed and more than ₹6 crore or ₹60 million paid out, but 'spot verification' found 'no physical structures'. Elsewhere, contractors' profit was included in cost estimates. The agency tasked with developing sports complexes couldn't provide tender documents, agreements with contractors, and detailed vouchers for more than ₹250 crore (₹2.5 billion) worth of projects.

Several thousand pre-school kits for the anganwadi, or village crèche programme, lay undistributed for more than two years. Bridge and road works routinely listed agreed tender amounts far in excess of estimated cost—in one instance, an excess of 146 per cent. Payments were also made for 'fictitious work'. Besides such outright corruption in the books, inept road works—deliberate or by default—led to 'unfruitful' expenditure totalling several billion rupees. Manipur's tourism department was marked for excess payment to contractors.

As with its Nagaland audits, CAG urged the government of Manipur to, in turn, urge officials to respond. Usually, nobody bothers to reply, or they reply years later rendering the entire exercise meaningless. With deliberate obfuscation, delays and indifference to accountability by governments it's usually left to media, or stray political opposition, to publicize such matters to citizens. Generally, it matters little that such realities are as much violations of rights and constitutional guarantees as any that civil society in Manipur and Nagaland place at the doors of government of India and its executors of security and political affairs. But there's usually nobody to bell the fat cats.

For anything at all.

17. Of Some Encounters in Manipur

In some ways Okram Ibobi Singh's legacy came home to roost at the end of January 2016, penetrating the government's complacency with what, in human rights parlance, is termed extra-judicial killing. In India, 'fake encounter' is a more colloquial cousin; 'staged encounter' a more elegant one. All descriptions are devoid of the very real life-and-death outcomes.

And, in Manipur during Ibobi's tenure, they became the calling card to deal with all manner of threats, perceived and real, walking hand-in-glove with the government's wink and the impunity provided by AFSPA. It was—and remains—Manipur's foulest open-secret.

A policeman confessed to conducting a staged encounter killing in 2009. On the morning of 23 July that year, Chungkham Sanjit was shot dead inside a pharmacy in central Imphal. Thounaojam Herojit, a constable with the Manipur Police, told media—recorded in a stunning newsbreak by *Imphal Free Press* and given countrywide prominence by *Indian Express*—that he killed the youngster in cold blood on orders from a superior, Akoijam Jhalajhit. At that time of the incident, Jhalajhit was additional superintendent of police of Imphal West district. At the time of this exposure, Jhalajhit was its superintendent of police.

Jhalajhit issued a denial within days of the newsbreak on 27 January 2016. It was expected. And a quick check of his superiors in a chain of command at the time of the incident revealed that Manipur's director general of police was Yumnam Joykumar Singh, and Ibobi, who at the time also held the home affairs portfolio.

Joykumar was the state's longest serving director general of police in recent times, serving two stints, one from March 2007 to January 2012, and again from June of that year until his retirement in August 2013. In government as well as non-government circles he was widely regarded to be Ibobi's enforcer during that time. The Joykumar years have long been considered as troubling by several human rights organisations, for transforming Manipur Police—and, in particular the elite Manipur Police Commandos—into a near-private army that, even as it worked to stanch crime and insurgency, it did as it pleased. Indeed, those years saw increased depredations by the Manipur Police and Manipur Police commandos, which appeared to outpace the unlovely human rights record in Manipur of Assam Rifles and various paramilitaries that answered to the central government. (Although Manipur Police ran its own trigger-happy operations, these agencies and Manipur Police often worked in tandem.)

Sanjit was shot dead inside Maimu Pharmacy not far from the entrance to Kangla Fort as Manipur's capital went about its business. His self-confessed killer, under suspension for some years along with other colleagues, told the media that his nerves cracked after recent indications that he was being isolated. He feared that he could be 'disappeared' by his own police colleagues.

Nobody, not even his family, denies Sanjit had once been associated with the rebel People's Liberation Army. Twice arrested and freed, he was, his family insists, detached from his former comrades and had since 2006 worked at a private hospital as an attendant.

The police insisted he had tried to flee; he had a Mauser 9 mm pistol which he threw away. So, they had no option but to shoot and kill Sanjit. The truth—now Herojit's truth too—appears to be that Sanjit's presence was convenient. Several bullets were pumped into his torso after the pharmacy's staff was asked to clear out.

Tehelka magazine published horrific photographs of the cold-blooded, point-blank killing of Sanjit by the Manipur Police commandos. The article was headlined, 'Murder in Plain Sight'. I possess a few more images that did not make it to the *Tehelka* article, perhaps for reasons of space, perhaps for reasons of propriety. These images showed a bloodied and dead Sanjit sprawled on his back across some old cartons and medical junk at the far end of Maimu Pharmacy.

Within days, the Sanjit Joint Action Committee, comprising

citizens from his neighbourhood and other nearby areas, was pressing for accountability and justice. Within weeks, members of the committee began to be harassed. In September, jeeploads of police commandos came looking for its convener, Thongatabam Anita Devi. She managed to escape. A lawyer associated with the committee told me they suspected Sanjit was killed because 'some police officers wanted gallantry awards'. Meanwhile, a top officer told a court of inquiry that photographs of the killing were faked. The matter dragged on in a local court.

Sanjit's was not the only unusual death in Imphal that July morning in 2009. Several minutes earlier, not far from where he was killed, Thockchom Rabina and her unborn child were shot dead while shopping. She had been buying bananas at the time. With Rabina was her two-and-a-half-year-old son Russel.

The only reasonable explanation—if ever it can be called reasonable—was that Manipur Police personnel had fired shots to cover a staged encounter taking place nearby, to make it appear there was an exchange of fire while the police were under attack and a shot hit Rabina. A police version claimed she was accidentally killed when the police fired at a 'fleeing youth'. That was Sanjit. He wasn't fleeing anywhere. In his delayed confession, Herojit maintained Sanjit offered no resistance whatsoever; he just seemed to stoically accept that he was about to be killed.

Sanjit's stunned family, whom I met some months after his killing, unsurprisingly did not receive any gesture of contrition from the government. Neither did Rabina's devastated family. Her father-in-law Damu told me when I visited the family's home in a suburb west of Imphal: 'There has been no clarification from the government. No clarification, so no apology.'

Over the space of some of those Ibobi-Joykumar years I saw numerous instances of government over-reach—and an insistent public pushback that literally refused to lie down and die.

Theatre has for long been the cultural lifeforce in Manipur and brilliant plays showed the wrenching hurt of a people caught in a crossfire of cynical ambition backstopped by lawless laws, cuttingly showed the corruption and, literally, bloody-mindedness of the government. One such play referred to Loktak Lake, a leading jewel of Manipur's ecological treasure trove and its achingly beautiful landscape, as being the preferred staging area for encounters and a dumping ground of the 'disappeared'. As body after body, of men and women and, occasionally, of youngsters barely of voting age showed, it was a case of art imitating life. Photo exhibitions and protest meetings against the state's depredations weren't rare. What a muted media could not always record, colleagues in the arts, academia and in the fraught space of human rights did.

It was a time of anything-goes. Among the many incidents of over-reach, one that gutted me at a personal level was the instance of Manipur Police and Assam Rifles on the morning of 14 August 2009 abducting and subsequent detaining Vidyarani Chanu. It was an attempt to smoke out of hiding her rebel-affiliated parents. At the time Vidyrani was eleven years-old.

Vidyarani was traumatised beyond belief when I met her a month later at Immanuel Grace Academy, a tiny, modest thatch-and-tin-roof residential school near her home in Nongmaikhong Mayai Leikai, deep in the rural hinterlands south of Loktak Lake.

Her parents gave themselves up. Vidyarani lived. If one could call that life in a place terror could visit so suddenly, seamlessly.

Shall never forget the image. Vidyarani sits, head lowered. Straight, lustrous black hair covers her face. Wrings her hands. When she doesn't do that, hands cover her face. Her grandfather Salam Ningthemba strokes her hair, tries to calm her as Basanta & Ranjeeta from Human Rights Alert prepare to question her. But Vidyarani's hands never stop moving. She's terrified.

Watching Vidyarani is a wrenching experience. She is the same age as my daughter. The same height. Same class, 6. But my daughter has thus far not been abducted by police & detained illegally because the state is upset with her parents.

Basanta is done for now, after a few minutes of taking her through a section titled 'Arrest and Detention'. Her grandfather & school principal Memcha did most of the talking. You have any questions? Basanta asks.

Yes, many. But first please tell her that I've a daughter who is as old as she. When I go back home, I'll tell my daughter about meeting Vidyarani. And then I begin the chronicler's horrible task of taking her to the dark place where her mind now lives.

When she was in custody, what was she doing? What was she thinking? Did she pray to God? Did she pray for her parents? What did she tell herself to keep her strength going?

'I wanted to see my parents,' Vidyarani whispers. Her restless composure begins to crack.

'Tell, nothing will happen,' Memcha gently urges.

'I was very scared.' Pause. 'I sometimes thought that the police will go to my house when I am not there. I thought if my parents got arrested they would be tortured. I was afraid for my two younger brothers. I was scared the police would arrest them.'

Do you remember where you were kept? Did it look like a jail, with bars, or was it just a room?

'A room.'

Were you alone?

Basanta now explains: her two grandmothers were with her. They came to ask for her release, but when that didn't work, they asked to remain with Vidyarani. She was preparing to cook, Basanta says while consulting his notes, when she heard police commandos arriving. She was very scared. One of the commandos pointed his automatic rifle at her and at the grandmother. Since they could not find her parents, suspected of associating with PLA, they took Vidyarani.

Vidyarani is crying. Grandfather Ningthemba gently wipes her eyes with a hand, then gives her a large light-blue handkerchief. The little girl clutches the piece of cloth. She suddenly gets up and rushes out of the hut. The young lady who brought her in rushes after her. Memcha says something. Basanta translates the Meiteilon. 'She feels like vomiting.'

'She worries that if she speaks the truth something bad will happen to her parents. They are still in custody. So she is afraid to speak.'

18. Interlude: Sharmila Is Free!

09/08/2016 (Tuesday): Irom Sharmila breaks her 16-year fast. It's all a bit giddy.

Comment prep + interview notes:

This is a person afflicted with Malaise de Manipur, the underrated sibling of Malaise de Kashmir and unkempt child of Malaise de India—some say illegitimate child, though in these modern times, tender constitutional love and developmental care can still paper over old-fashioned repression/domination.

The birth in 1949 didn't go so well. It rarely does, with squabbling parents fresh from a shotgun wedding, the certificate of marriage to the Indian union still contested after 67 years. Then there is Manipur's lot of seeing its own children being beaten, raped, murdered and legally ill-treated as non-citizens, the good cop of India's Constitution diminished by the bad cops led by AFSPA ... A decades-long run of error and terror from state and non-state actors alike. Here PTSD = Permanent Traumatic Stress Disorder.

Sharmila update/notes/comment-prep:

Freed on a personal bond. Undertaking to give up her fast brought about this roundabout acquittal from a morally decrepit case for the prosecution that kept her jailed all these years on a charge of trying to commit suicide. She cast herself as a protester after the November 2000 massacre of ten civilians by troopers of 8 Assam Rifles, in reprisal for being attacked by Manipur rebels. The governments of India and Manipur then recast Sharmila as what I have repeatedly described as a living martyr.

Sharmila remained a living martyr even after her release.

Elders of a locality in Imphal, Manipur's capital, denied Sharmila permission to live among them. She who fought for them for their return to liberty and equality, a productive future, and against abdication by the Indian and Manipuri governments to offer governance and development. In a turn of the greatest irony, on 10 August, a day after her formal release from jail, she returned to her ward—her jail and home these past years—at the Jawaharlal Nehru Institute of Medical Sciences. The local chapter of Indian Red Cross offered her a home.

Rebel groups of the majority Meitei community, Sharmila's own community, have always kept her at arms' length, unnerved by a competing moral stand. Sharmila out of jail is seemingly for them a pariah with a Gandhian death wish: to lead with peace. Morally righteous voices are already being conveyed to media, hypocritically damning Sharmila for selling out to the highest bidder—not India's intelligence agencies but, as it happens, the dictates of her own life choices. Rebels will light this path for many elders of Manipur, among them some entrenched activists of Manipur—a few of whom openly take ideological cues from rebels. They were enraged, as they cannot control her.

And if agents of the governments of India and Manipur and various political parties, rejoiced in Sharmila's decision to end her fast, to integrate with the Indian electoral system to contest assembly elections in early 2017, they too perpetuated the error of their ways. Sharmila wasn't theirs to run either.

Sharmila freed would not reduce the human rights overhang for any government. And it would matter little if this bedraggled eccentric, this lady of courage beyond belief was unable to make a transition into an Aung San Suu Kyi that many now expected her to. It matters little if she wins or loses the elections—even the lofty post of chief minister she declared that she aspired to.

Because, as martyr or living martyr, younger Manipuris will embrace the idea of Sharmila. As a candidate, or a T-shirt, or campaign button, Sharmila will be the face of the youth, their fortitude, hope in a future. If she lost, as she inevitably would in a cynical system that thrives on funds of which she possesses little, younger Manipuris, no less scarred than their elders but with greater urge to attain escape velocity from the morass of the present, would carry the idea of Sharmila, the politics of Sharmila, even as the elders so easily reject her, so easily mocked her when she—again, so spectacularly— showed a mind of her own.

Many elders saw betrayal. The younger see a future. Unlike their elders, they don't believe in miracle cures for collective madness. They believe in the curative principle of public opinion for prosperity, for peace.

Notes: 15/06/2016

Sharmila now has a bank account, with State Bank of India. After 16 yrs of being jailed and fed through a nasal drip for demanding the removal of AFSPA from Manipur, she has for the past month tried to sort out her post-incarceration life and purpose. Nandita T, who cooks for her, brings her food, tells me she's eating light, nutritious, it's a different non-intubated world.

Sharmila also reaching out to a wide range of people. The displaced in the Loktak lake area to the south of Imphal. Visiting NGOs that stood up for her and against extra-judicial killings in Manipur. Professionals visit her at the retreat she now calls home in the Imphal suburb of Langol. Last week she visited the mother of Luingamla, a Tangkhul Naga girl who was shot in 1986 by an army lieutenant for resisting rape. Luingamla was 14. She is today a protest icon for Tangkhul women. There's even a shawl named after her, a memory of her courage: the Luingamla kashan.

The state's major political parties would pay hugely for Sharmila's facility and credibility. Ibobi reached out to her, Sharmila turned him down. Ditto BJP—which has already begun to attract large-scale defection from Congress.

Sharmila or not, political success will hinge on several distinct bouquets. The Meitei, egged on by Meitei rebel groups, want a permit system like ILP to control the entry, residency and work of non-Manipuris. The non-Meitei are resolutely against the permit system in the shape it was introduced in 2015 in the assembly (it subsequently did not receive presidential assent) and which led to massive violence and government blowback. A new draft is being eagerly watched. At any rate, it will be a major election issue.

And all communities are keeping a hawk's eye on the Naga peace process—more precisely, with NSCN (I-M) that many Meiteis believe could involve a trade-off: ceding administrative control of Naga areas in Manipur. The Kuki-Chin-Zo trust neither the Meitei nor the Naga.

Already, election diktats are in. On 27 July, the administrative arm of I-M, issued a warning in one of its areas of influence, the 'Khurmi Region' in Chandel district, '... that until and unless election notification is served by the Indian government, election campaign in the region is strictly prohibited/not allowed'.

The notice, oddly phrased and spelled but clear, was signed by the 'C.A.O'—central administrative officer—'and Care taker' of the region, issued on a letterhead marked with the seal, Nagaland for Christ. 'Failing to comply with this general circulation, the culprit (s) shall be awarded arrest order and award stern punishment will be taken to the culprit (s) by the GPRN.' The notice ominously added: 'No complaints shall be entertaint.'

It's a typical taint. In Manipur complaints have a history of rarely being entertained.

19. 'There Is a Way That Seems Right to a Man, But ...'

On one of my visits to Churachandpur, the charming diminution of which is CC'Pur, I saw a sign by a church just outside the eponymous district headquarter town in southern Manipur. 'There is a way that seems right to a man, but in the end it leads to death.'

This Americanised version of Proverbs 14:12 could well be paraphrased as: There is a way that seems right to the government of Manipur—but in the end such presumption can lead to chaos.

And both chaos and death visited CC'Pur after Manipur's legislature passed the Protection of Manipur People Bill, 2015 on 31 August that year. In this concentration of the Zomi, which the government simplifies into the Kuki-Chin-Mizo group, a call for closure given by three tribal students' bodies to protest against this bill and related amendments to two Acts—one regulating land ownership and the other, establishments—spiralled out of control.

Police overreacted. Rage spilled over and police and politicians' residences—these belonged to leaders of Zomi ethnicity—were attacked. Retaliation by government killed nine protesters and injured several dozen. Local students' groups and other organisations representing tribal groups demanded the resignation of the MLAs of each such tribe elected during the last general elections to Manipur's Assembly, held in 2012.

Residents were upset that the bill, which sought to regulate the entry, stay and work for outsiders similar to inner line permit systems operational in Nagaland, Mizoram and Arunachal Pradesh, and the amendments, were formulated without any consultation with the tribal people of Manipur. There was concern that such legislation would lead to unsettling tribal folk in Manipur's hill districts and encroachment there by the people of the plains—mostly non-tribal Meitei. There was also concern, voiced less directly, that a template which decided who exactly was a long-term resident of Manipur—and, therefore, out of ILP's purview—would literally unsettle some residents in the hill districts that shared borders with Mizoram, Assam and Nagaland and even Myanmar.

Though some of the fears were unfounded—tribal land here is protected by India's Constitution—it was based on that often-expressed and often-ignored reality in Manipur: governance typically favoured the plains and downplayed the hills. Among several of Manipur's flaws, this attitude was one which, without addressing it and fixing, there couldn't ever be a political cure in Manipur.

The movement for ILP and concerns expressed against it wasn't new. During several visits to Manipur in 2014 I witnessed the initial peaking of the movement. It then settled down until mid-2015, when news arrived of an imminent peace deal between the government of India and the NSCN (I-M). As integrationists feared that a settlement with this pre-eminent Naga rebel group could spark a merging of Naga tribal homelands in Manipur with Naga homelands in Nagaland, Arunachal Pradesh and Assam, the ILP movement in Manipur renewed its energy. After local police shot a student protester on 8 July, the movement flamed on across Imphal Valley—but significantly, not in the hill districts; and, not far beyond the Meitei community.

The signing of the Framework Agreement between the government of India and I-M on 3 August ensured momentum and pressure, leading to the panic passing of the ILP bill by Manipur's legislature on 31 August. It was partly designed to assuage concerns among the Meitei, mostly resident in Imphal Valley, that if there was indeed any actual ceding of administrative control in the Naga homelands, the use of ILP—that sought to protect the rights and livelihoods of particularly the non-tribal, plains-residing Manipuri—would also act as a balance. Of course, in that case massive development input in would also be required in Manipur and emotional sops such as repealing or scaling back AFSPA, but ILP was at the forefront of applying such balms.

But there were deeper issues along with deep ironies in this complex matrix of Manipur.

One such was the irony that non-tribal Manipuri nationalists and rebels, almost exclusively Meitei, insisted on autonomy or independence from India citing uniqueness of race, history and purpose. Yet, when it came to Manipur, using a template of imperfection perfected by the government of India, they—along with the government of Manipur—preached integration from the perspective of the Meitei community. A frequently used phrase in nationalistic Manipuri rhetoric and varnished truth was that, from 'time immemorial' people of the plains and the hills, Meitei and non-Meitei, have lived in harmony.

Besides being simplistic, such reading of history ignored aspirations and concerns of the hill people. It whitewashed the underdevelopment of the hill districts compared with Imphal valley. The chaos also highlighted the fact that autonomous councils in the hill districts had for decades been starved of funds and the most basic administrative autonomy—hiring staff, purchasing supplies—by the government of Manipur. It was, as we have read, a matter that leaders of the United Naga Council and leaders of other communities discussed in detail with me. It was also reflected in the allocation of funds—Valley versus Hills—according to the Manipur government's own documents.

Nagas and Kukis, of course, weren't the only ones with feelings of such discomfort.

'In this society, we have no future,' M.C. Chin Min Thang, vice-chairman of the Zomi Council, told me during a meeting in CC'Pur, in the town's convenient meeting place: the improbably named and spelled Fat Jame's Restaurant. 'Manipur government... will be taking over our lives.'

As a response, he added, 'We (Zomis) demanded an autonomous hill state. Kukis want a hill state. Nagas, they demand Alternative Arrangement'—by which Nagas hope to interact directly with New Delhi, jettisoning Imphal.

Amidst growing chaos, it became clear that it was now up to the government of Manipur to regain the faith it has lost through action, presumption and miscommunication, as much with the Nagas as with non-Naga residents of the hills.

Ibobi Singh's government had other ideas.

This sense was reinforced in an article in *Hindustan Times* headlined 'Imphal's "conspiracy" theory: Delhi behind tribal unity, unrest.' The article dated 9 September 2015 highlighted the surprise of a Congress legislator from Manipur and a local, politically-inclined human rights activist, that people of the hills of Manipur, home to the Naga, Kuki and Zomi tribes, had seemingly come together against the Meitei-dominated plains.

Particularly the Naga and Kuki communities, by virtue of Kuki leaders maintaining a studied silence since I-M signed a framework peace agreement with the government of India on 3 August. That was unusual as the Kuki community hadn't formally forgiven I-M for the genocide it accused I-M of triggering against Kukis in Manipur in the early 1990s.

But now, had the bills provided just such an impetus, unlikely as it was? I recalled a visit to Ukhrul in 2009 when I was told by a young Tangkhul ideologue with ties to I-M's leadership of how he and his colleagues were reaching out to the Kuki-Chin-Zo people of Manipur. 'The hills have a common future,' he had told me. He claimed it was part of a concerted effort by a group of Nagas in Manipur to engineer a coalition of tribal hill people against the administrative stranglehold of Imphal.

At any rate, 'Conspiracy', and 'New Delhi' and its 'Chanakyas' were, according to the article, behind escalating tensions in the hills since three bills—for ILP, and amendments to land ownership norms and registration of businesses—were passed by Manipur's legislature on 1 September.

The ideologues of the movement and of similar sentiments as displayed in the article appeared to have ignored a blinding irony: there were plenty of Chanakyas right there in Imphal Valley.

As ever, optics replaced solutions.

There was a remarkable photo-op on 27 October in Imphal. That day, in the middle of Kangla Fort, a potent nationalistic symbol for the majority Meitei people—indeed, the repository of Meitei origin and soul—deputy chief minister Gaikhangam Gangmei and another legislator, Irengbam Ibohalbi Singh, exchanged gifts.

Gaikhangam, a Rongmei Naga from the western hill-constituency of Nungba, looked dapper in a white kurta and dhoti; the splitting image of a Meitei gentleman. Ibohalbi, a Meitei representing Oinam in the heart of Imphal Valley, had a Naga shawl draped over his shoulders. Smiling, they stood between the giant statues of two mythical beasts, the Kangla-Sha. The occasion was the celebration of Mera Houchongba, which traditionally marks unity among various communities in Manipur.

It has remained a symbol of respectful interaction, if not exactly unity, between the plains and the hills. The tradition predates the accession of the kingdom of Manipur to the India union in 1949—rationale, as we have read, for Meitei nationalists and rebels who feel the signing over of Manipur was done under duress; and a fact that security nabobs in New Delhi often ignore.

The two politicians met even as strikes and road blockades in homelands of Naga, Kuki and Zo people continued to massively squeezed supplies of food and fuel in Imphal Valley and turned life there hyper-inflationary. They met even as a Kuki organisation announced a 20-day economic blockade from 3 November to protest the recent killing by police of two Kuki men.

Gaikhangam, a staunch ally of Congress strongman Ibobi Singh, had by that time attracted much venom, being seen as a key traitor to the tribal cause in general and Naga cause in particular. For his part, Gaikhangam consistently fronted Ibobi to issue several appeals to all tribal groups to begin discussions with Manipur's government over the three contentious legislations which awaited the formal assent of India's president—without which these couldn't become law—at the time of the photo-op. Along with several Meitei politicians—including those of All India Trinamool Congress with which the state government had butted heads, triggering suspension of some MLAs by the speaker and, consequently, by-elections that November—Gaikhangam also pitched for harmony among communities. The much-publicised ceremony at Kangla was consistent with that approach; even the choreography of being photographed with Ibohalbi, elected MLA in 2012 on a Trinamool ticket.

But matters continued in stalemate. Meanwhile, rebel groups of every ethnic and political hue, in ceasefire with government or outright combat, turned on the pressure either for settlement or as battle statement. On the day of the photo-op, UNLF, Manipur's oldest rebel group, issued a media statement owning up to two attacks on Assam Rifles personnel just two days earlier. *Imphal Free Press* reported UNLF's assertion 'to regain the lost sovereignty of Manipur', and that UNLF 'vowed to continue their fight until they liberate Manipur'.

Photo-ops were little more than partial remedy. But Manipur's elected leaders were for the time beyond listening. They hadn't listened for several months.

June 2016:

Protests demanding ILP continue to rage in Manipur. State at standstill for several weeks. Stall with UNC continues. Status quo situation in CC'Pur, elections due in Feb–March 2017. Us Vs. Them is already the election platform.

But ILP protests have come around to the roll of Meitei dice. Leaders and managers are largely absent from protest lines, as ever the pawns remain the citizenry, driven by a collective hysteria accumulated by years of repression by the Indian security establishment, a corrupt local political establishment, an economy in shambles, and paranoia over the Naga peace settlement territorially tearing Manipur apart.

Schoolchildren have been shanghaied into the frontlines of protest and, when they are taken away by Manipur Police—not central paramilitaries or the army—in police vans, when they are countered by water cannons, it makes for iconic protest imagery. It whips up more anger and hysteria. UNLF has for long been suspected as being part of a conglomerate sponsoring the ILP movement. The viral circulation of a photograph earlier this week showing an ILP leader taking an oath of loyalty touching the UNLF flag has only reinforced the idea.

The leveraging of the crying game is also a move for concession, to pressure the consent of the president of India to The Protection of Manipur People Bill, 2015. It still lies with him, undergoing dissection by a committee, and some BJP legislators I have spoken with suggest it may continue to do so—by procedural manipulation of the BJP government in New Delhi—to make the incumbent Congress government in Manipur look weaker and more ineffectual than it already is.

It's a card for the BJP's election play in a state firmly on its win-radar. As the party is also in talks with Naga rebels and is reaching out to Kuki and Zomi groups, it would like to straddle all horses. On the other hand, with its back to the wall, the Congress could cynically pull out all tactical stops.

Meanwhile, bodies of protesters killed in firing in CC'Pur on 31/08/2015 and 01/09/2015 by Manipur Police still lie in the local makeshift morgue— unclaimed by their families as a continuing mark of protest. A ghoulish memo to withdraw the bills that still haven't received assent of the president of India.

Manipur's fires have barely begun.

20. Ibobi & I-M: Shake, Rattle & Roll

Who would want to shoot at Ibobi Singh?

The answer might fill a large black-book, but the government of Manipur pointed the finger at NSCN (I-M). As with so many things with Manipur and the Naga peace process, paranoia, insecurities and intrigues plagued this chessboard at the bleeding edge of India's so-called Act East policy, but I-M's involvement was not improbable given Ibobi's recent history with the hills and his destination.

On the morning of 24 October 2016 Ibobi and his colleagues choppered up to the district headquarter town of Ukhrul. He was to inaugurate an unfinished hospital here, a local development office and two electricity sub-stations. Shots were fired—it isn't clear by whom—after he arrived. Two police vehicles were set on fire by protesters, two Manipur Police personnel injured.

Ibobi left without fulfilling any agenda except that of reconfirming the divide between the hills and plains of Manipur.

Ukhrul was already locked down on account of a boycott called by the Tangkhul Naga Long, the apex body of the Tangkhul for whom Ukhrul district, as we have read, is the tribal homeland. Like other tribes in Manipur they have for long accused government of stacking job opportunities against tribals, of skewing development projects in the interest of the plains. Such as a major dam—the Mapithel dam—in the most recent instance that submerged several tribal villages and displaced their population, a 'collateral' cost to bringing water to Imphal and irrigate the surrounding valley even though it was nearly inevitable the project would be either delayed, or delayed to extinction with inflated costs and likely siphoning of funds, for some as precious a stream as water. It was just how things worked.

Tangkhul Naga Long had warned against Ibobi's visit. The haste to inaugurate the projects was seen as being politically motivated, timed to soothe tempers and curry favour before elections. The protests in the hills certainly were politically motivated.

To be fair to Ibobi, his administration had since 2002 had been ethno-agnostic—because it also impacted the Meitei. His government and Manipur's police had been censured by the Supreme Court for human rights violations in Imphal Valley. Manipur was—remains—impoverished. Infrastructure was in a shambles. Government was so corrupt that the Comptroller and Auditor General's reports about Manipur, as we have read, carried a despondent tone.

Equally, anti-Ibobi and anti-Meitei narratives weren't the only twists.

Nothing moved in much of Ukhrul, from development projects to the death of a political target, without the say-so of I-M, a ruthless organisation with a long reach. Since the signing of the Framework Agreement the organisation actually had a freer run.

As if in reflection, central government forces, especially Assam Rifles, omnipresent and heavy-handed in Manipur, and with a major presence and extended history of conflict in Ukhrul, lay low in the aftermath of the shooting incident with Ibobi. Local politics played out with local players and local police. It was as if the BJP and the superstructure of the Sangh, whose strategy was to aggressively stitch together a broad-spectrum alliance for imminent elections to Manipur's Assembly and balance the Naga peace process at the same time, were letting Ibobi run with an even longer rope. It was an incendiary, high-stakes game. And, although few in Manipur would cry for Ibobi, it appeared that Manipur wasn't done with tears.

Ibobi appeared to be determined to drag the shaky relationship between the hills and the plains—and between the non-Meitei and Meitei—to a new low, because in a twisted way he hoped to leverage it to resurrect his political fortune. Many Meitei, even if they reviled Ibobi, now saw him as a protector of Meitei interests and a person who would not compromise Manipur's territory. Moreover, there was as yet, just months before Assembly elections, simply no alternative to Ibobi in Congress or outside it. It appeared that Ibobi was back at playing winner-takes-all, his signature move.

He spectacularly attempted to claw back advantage of the narrative.

On 25 November, Manipur Police commandos arrested the president and information secretary of UNC. Ibobi didn't blink when protests broke out in Naga areas, and blockades and violence escalated. He called the bluff by ordering security forces to escort convoys of trucks into the valley.

On 9 December Ibobi announced the formation of seven new districts, adding to the existing nine. Of these, four were earlier a part of Naga-majority districts. Noney was carved out of Tamenglong, Kangpokpi from Senapati, Kamjong from Ukhrul and Tengnoupal, a pivot on the route to Moreh and the highway to Myanmar, from Chandel. This effectively cut largely non-Naga areas from the districts and subtly played into misgivings that even some Naga tribes and clans have towards either the domination of I-M or those from the 'northern' Tangkhul areas, even in the Tangkhul redoubt of Ukhrul. And, in effect, it administratively cauterised several largely non-Naga areas from a Naga push.

Naga rebels subsequently attacked police and paramilitaries, but Ibobi didn't budge. He was playing at saviour.

I-M was left looking silly. The UNC was emasculated. The government of India and the BJP in particular, were left looking inept, too-clever-by-half. Ibobi had made his ultimate play for a fourth term— at the cost of toxic Manipur.

December 2016. Assembly elections due Feb–March 2017. But Manipur, touted as gateway to SE Asia is in lockdown, with curfew in central districts & arson/ attacks fuelled by ethnic violence. Possibility of President's Rule especially with BJP govt in Centre, but Ibobi knows that would play to his narrative, make him look like more of a saviour/ martyr.

So, a battle of attrition over political futures. Congress & Ibobi (Ibobi even more than Cong?) want 4th term. Boosted position by taking on old foes: IM + UNC.

Ergo: Ibobi again projected as protector of majoritarian interests, of Manipur's heart & soul. To him it appears to matter little that three tenures has seen a great slide in ethnic relations & urban + rural infra. Corruption limited only by the funds at hand. Human rights violations never as rampant, at least since the 1980s.

Of course Ibobi knows the game, he's played it before. In 2010 he barred Muivah's entry into Manipur. It led to rioting & Naga deaths but bought Ibobi the halo of Manipur/ Meitei protector. Congress won 2012 assembly elections in a landslide. Cong: 42 (hills + plains), Trinamool: 7, Manipur State Cong: 5, NPF: 4, NCP (Sharad Pawar's lot): 1, Lok Janshakti Party: 1. This time BJP will try to whittle away at Cong despite hell/ high-water + capitalizing on NPF, NPP being in its coalition in Centre. Tough play.

Meanwhile, emotions at fever-pitch. Through December 2016 Meitei neighbourhoods in Valley imposed counter-blockades on trucks/ buses/ cars travelling to Naga areas. Mid-Dec onwards enraged Meitei crowds torched vehicles & destroyed goods heading up to Naga areas. Grim payback. Like 2001, 2010. Getting calls/texts from Naga contacts in Valley saying they're holed up in Imphal's Naga enclaves (mostly around Chingmeirong/ Khumman Lampak stadium) and some managed to slip thru to Ukhrul, Chandel, T'long. Meitei contacts angry. Naga + Meitei friends horrified & frozen. They say they're trying peacemaking but nobody listens to reason when anger is engineered to this point.

Manipur on edge. Works for Ibobi, who's a master of working that edge to gain edge. Tension works for him. Repeat: Possibility of President's Rule unlikely to deter him. Nothing seems to stick to him. Ibobi, the Teflon king of Manipur.

On 22 December 2016, I had remarked in my 'Root Cause' column in *Mint*: 'The Bharatiya Janata party's next big project in north-east India, the claiming of Manipur from the Congress, has probably flamed out.' The assertion was based on Ibobi's last-ditch attempt to secure for himself a fourth term from the goodwill he aimed to earn in Imphal Valley with the creation of new districts. Between a stranglehold on the

40 plains-seats in the Assembly, besides a number of non-Naga seats among the 20 hill seats, he expected to be over the majority count of 31.

But a flurry of defections from Congress to the BJP took place from December onwards, including an Ibobi protégé, Nongthombam Biren Singh, who quickly emerged as the party's spokesperson in Manipur. BJP's election campaign was primarily fronted by Modi, his political adjutant Amit Shah and other senior BJP officials, who made showy, high-profile speeches promising everything from peace to prosperity. There were hardly any significant speeches by local BJP leaders. And, expectedly, BJP's political alliances such as those with the Naga People's Front and National People's Party in Parliament translated to alliances in Manipur.

Meanwhile, the three bills which had caused so much unpleasantness and bloodshed, lapsed, unsigned by the President. I was told of a gentle nudge by security mandarins and BJP leaders.

The bodies of the nine killed in those protests still lay unclaimed in a make-shift morgue at Churachandpur. The families of the dead and the community looked to them as martyrs, searched for an apology that never arrived.

And, just like that, Ibobi began to look a bit shaky.

Year-end Notes: 28/12/2016

The ongoing fracas in Manipur raises a query: Is the Naga peace process, which prime minister Narendra Modi revived in mid-2015 with fanfare, dead? Or stalled?

Nobody will of course admit this. There is simply too much loss of face involved, but the process has a default bug of failure. It's just too darn complicated, this chess game of lives and futures. I'll repeat: The Framework Agreement of 03/08/2015 is the flimsiest of deals. As I wrote last week, the agreement has no content except strengthening positions from which to negotiate.

The government and I-M have deflected calls to make the agreement public, while throwing in key words like 'shared future' and 'honourable' settlement.

Meanwhile, Modi got to project himself as peacemaker. And I-M raised its profile, claiming pre-eminence. By extension both became deciding factors in the future of the Naga people, whose homelands extend beyond Nagaland to contiguous areas of Manipur, Arunachal Pradesh and Assam.

I-M's aggression in general and in Manipur in particular has earned the irritation of Ravi and certainly the irritation of NSA Doval who, as one Naga insider told me, is 'really irritated with I-M'.

Join the club, gentlemen. Irritation is an old script for these parts. After all, many Nagas have been irritated since 1947. And many in Manipur have remained irritated since 1949, when it formally joined India, and quickly discovered that India's talk of mutual respect, peace and prosperity was only talk. That, all the political poison and creeping juggernaut of corruption that afflicted the 'Mainland' transferred seamlessly to nearly every corner of NE.

Happy New Year.

21. Interlude: Of Uncles (and Aunts)

As 2017 broke, only one thing was clear: the BJP, backed by the heft of it running India's government, was going to go all out to win Manipur. For nearly three years the party had its eyes on ending the government of incumbent chief minister Ibobi Singh, a three-term reign of error and terror.

In the wake of central paramilitary forces escorting a few convoys of trucks carrying fuel and other supplies after several months of central government stall, in the fourth week of January a giant Indian Air Force C-17 Globemaster transport aircraft ferried several fuel tankers from Guwahati to Imphal. It was an extravagant gesture for a central government that, thus far, had been content to let Manipur's Congress government stew in its own rancid juice, repeatedly claiming with technical, constitutional correctness that law-and-order was a 'state subject'.

The die was cast with the announcement of general elections to Manipur's Assembly, over two days, 4 and 8 March.

And that, essentially, also put the Naga peace process on hold, as it was intricately tied to Manipur.

Meanwhile, an important sideshow played out in Nagaland, which, even if it was couched in intense political rivalry, actually exposed just how misogynistic Nagaland's political system really was. Whatever the post-conflict future, for now it appeared that little would be won politically for Naga women in the firm grip of patriarchy.

As ever, it had to do with some 'Uncles'.

On 22 February 2017, Shürhozelie Liezietsu, an 81-year-old on the verge of retirement from active politics, was sworn in as chief minister, replacing his Naga Peoples Front (NPF) colleague T.R. Zeliang, who resigned on 19 February in the wake of massive socio-political unrest across Nagaland.

Trouble had begun to brew in late December when the state's election commission notified elections to urban local bodies, with 33 per cent reservation for women. Key tribal organisations—Nagaland has 16 major tribes—began to protest saying it went against customary law and against special privileges granted to Nagaland under Article 371A of India's Constitution which protects such law, although it contradicts other provisions that offer reservation and equality to women.

Statistics spoke true. A handful of Naga village councils have female members. Nagaland assembly hasn't had a female legislator since the state was formed in 1963. Women are largely restricted to tribal women's organisations subservient to a particular tribe's council, or the Naga Mothers' Association, a feisty outfit of immensely brave and tough women that has taken up issues such as HIV-AIDS and drug abuse. Indeed, NMA has even sent representatives to Naga rebel strongholds in Myanmar—specifically the Khaplang faction's headquarters in Taga, a tortuous trek of several weeks—to urge peace and reconciliation.

The election commission was following up on an order of Gauhati High Court buttressed by the Supreme Court, based on a petition by women applicants who challenged the government's refusal to hold municipal elections though Nagaland's Assembly had enacted a law in 2006 reserving a third of the seats for women in such urban entities.

Protests began to snowball even as women offered candidacy. Pushed to the brink by mounting protests from tribal and students' organisations—another den of misogynists—the government called a truce on 30 January by announcing the postponement of elections by two months. It reversed the decision the next day, again urged by courts. Crowds erupted. Two youngsters—male—died in police firing in Dimapur.

On 1 February, elections were held in 12 of the 32 urban councils. The very next day these were annulled after Dimapur and Kohima witnessed widespread protests and rioting. The demand grew for Zeliang and his council of ministers to quit. That took till 19 February.

While Nagaland's unlovely cross of institutionalised misogyny got heavier, to claim that Congress and the Church brought down Zeliang was glib.

Church groups are involved in every aspect of Naga life—far more than rebel groups which impose parallel administrations. Many church groups also impose ultra-conservative and regressive practices, but detrimental mixing of 'church' and state wasn't unknown elsewhere in India, including, quite spectacularly by the BJP-led central government that had taken office in May 2014.

To some observers Shürhozelie's appointment appeared to be a compromise to stave off Zeliang's arch enemy, former chief minister and NPF strongman, Neiphiu Rio. If one were to consider conspiracy theories, Rio versus Zeliang topped the chart, a bitter rivalry played out over the shoulders of a state combusting on somewhat ludicrous, and dangerous, male outrage.

Rio won for NPF the 2013 assembly elections and took office as a third-term chief minister. He contested Lok Sabha elections in 2014, won, and travelled to New Delhi as MP in the hope that NPF's political allies, the BJP-led National Democratic Alliance would elevate him. Perhaps he would become a senior minister—an elder statesman representing not just Nagaland but Northeast India. With it could arrive the plums of responsibilities related to the Ministry for the Development of the North-East Region, or Doner. The other tantalising doner kebab, to employ a brazen pun involving that fetching Anatolian rotisserie, could be some sway over the fattened cow of the Shillong-based North East Council. NEC, like Doner, controlled large sums for various projects.

He was instead put to pasture, denied any portfolio, while Zeliang competitively filled his space in Nagaland. Zeliang also assiduously courted influential BJP general secretaries. The previous May, NPF—indeed, with Shürhozelie as president—suspended Rio from the party. Zeliang was seen as being close to BJP functionaries tasked with handling northeast India.

Cut to the present chase. The BJP, an NPF ally, had for several weeks had proxies in right wing media vehicles and public affairs decry the alleged role of the Congress and massively influential church entities in Nagaland, in the fracas over municipal elections. But the electoral math didn't add up.

After all, NPF, a NDA ally, had 46 MLAs, of whom eight switched en masse from Congress in 2015, in a 60-member house. NPF led the Democratic Alliance of Nagaland (DAN) government with four BJP MLAs—of whom three switched from the Nationalist Congress Party in 2014, the year after assembly elections were last held—and a lone member of Janata Dal (United). It was a bit rich for BJP to accuse the Congress of manipulation.

The biggest medium-term gainer in the fracas appeared to be Rio and his cabal, who would certainly plot a return: all it would take was a party with a new name and old faces and a leveraging of alliances in Nagaland and New Delhi, the payback being new quid pro quo wine in new bottles.

Bereft of governance for years, the biggest loser would remain Nagaland.

And its women.

It took me back to a public meeting in 2013, in a well-known Kohima café. Among the speakers was Rosemary Dzuvichu, an academician and a passionate communicator, whom I have heard men describe as being eccentric. Evidently, Dr Dzuvichu didn't give a damn.

The professor of English spoke of discrimination against Naga women, about how they took the burden of so much, only to be repeatedly, pointedly set aside; the village democracy and egalitarianism of the Nagas was a hoax when it came to women and it travelled up the chain all the way to Kohima, suffused every aspect of public life. I listened, enthralled and horrified in turn—and as several Naga men in the audience shifted uncomfortably—as she described instances of punishments for molesting and raping women being handed out by village councils. Occasionally, a temporary excommunication or banishment from the village. Sometimes, application of the slope rule, if you will. How large was the woman? Had she been attacked on the downslope of the track or the upslope? How could a scrawny man drag a robust lady up a slope? And so on, with figurative nudges and winks as such justice was dispensed.

A senior Catholic priest seated at the same table as me smirked, dismissively shook his head and murmured, 'She goes on too much.' The discomfort appeared to be non-denominational. A senior Baptist pastor seated a few tables away had his face carved as if in stone.

After Dr Dzuvichu was done, I milled about for a while. A young man came up and introduced himself as Yanpvuo Kikon. He was administrator of the trendy new Naga Blog on Facebook and an infotech specialist who had come home after working for some years in Pune, to start something at home. Brave New Nagaland, he hoped. We had been in touch through a public discussion on *thumbprintmag.com*, a Northeast-focused digital media forum that had invited me to interact with its readers, and discussed matters related to identity and racism—of mainland Indians towards those from far-eastern India.

As we chatted, I couldn't resist complimenting the professor. 'She's amazing,' I said, pointing my head towards Dr Dzuvichu, in complete awe at the courage and determination it took to speak as she did, literally in the Naga capital of misogyny. 'You know, right, that women will bring peace and prosperity? They have sense. They are the past, present and future.'

Yanpvuo smiled broadly. The priest moved away. The pastor had in any case left as soon as the event ended.

22. The Mahabharat Man

Nongthombam Biren Singh became chief minister of Manipur on 15 March 2017, ending the three-term run of Okram Ibobi Singh of the Congress. A protégé of Ibobi, Biren switched sides in late-2016, when the campaign for assembly elections was in full flow. He quickly went from local BJP spokesperson to the party's chief ministerial choice after BJP managed to cobble together a coalition by mid-March 2017.

Ibobi's desperate gambit to win Manipur for the fourth consecutive time for the Congress—and for himself as chief minister—didn't pay off. In the absence of allies, the 28 seats the Congress won fell short of the 31 required for majority in the 60-member house. A spectacular burst of defections from Congress added to a late campaign surge by the BJP (that fetched it a count of 21, from zero previously). The support of four allies from the Nationalist People's Party and the finessing of an independent MLA from Jiribam took the coalition to a slim majority—but enough to prove majority in the Assembly after the BJP was invited to form the government by a BJP-appointed governor, Najma Heptullah.

With a slim majority, the BJP combine would of course be vulnerable to jettisoning by fair-weather allies, defection being as high an art in Manipur as elsewhere in India.

A peculiarity of this electoral outcome was that, for the first time in decades, there would be a substantial Opposition. Even if the BJP consolidated its hold, it would have the Congress at its heels.

And, ironically, this would be to find fault in the BJP's delivery of its election promises—peace, infrastructure, connectivity, prosperity, accountability—that Manipur sorely needed and what Ibobi had been unable to provide. Moreover, Prime Minister Modi and his senior BJP colleagues had publicly placed their names to it all.

For some local analysts Biren immediately assumed the role of the state's great white knight. Relatively young at 56 to Ibobi's 69 years. Not bogged down by the past administration's corruption and abysmal record of development and infrastructure. Untainted by the fracture of relations between Manipur's various ethnic groups. Not singularly driven by the majoritarianism of his own Meïtei roots. Not darkened by massive human rights crises and violations during Ibobi's 15-year run.

Although it escaped such analysts that Biren and several of his colleagues were an integral part of the previous Manipur administration and Congress structure, and driven by the zeal of a new convert to another political party and one with massive financial and political heft, Biren went about his early days as his new role model Narendra Modi might. It was reminiscent of the prime minister's outreach to neighbouring countries in the early weeks of his first term in the summer of 2014, a blitz of inclusive and positive, if triumphalist, optics and promises and rhetoric to last a generation.

Within weeks of his appointment as chief minister, Biren travelled in a motorcade to Ukhrul—practically enemy country for his predecessor— for the warmest welcome in 15 years accorded to that office. It was a daylong visit. It of course helped that the Nagaland People's Front joined the BJP-led coalition in Manipur. It had marked the second successive time the Nagaland-based party had won four seats in the hills and, significantly, in I-M's area of influence. It helped too that the local BJP was still riding on the coattails of the Framework Agreement between I-M and the BJP-led central government. The détente caused by the agreement was already fraying and the Valley and 'non-Naga' hill regions of Manipur were on edge with speculation about post-Agreement territoriality, but there was still enough traction to offer Biren an opportunity to make a gesture.

At a gathering on 11 April in Ukhrul town, Biren was effusive after receiving a red-carpet welcome. 'My political mission is without boundary,' he announced. 'I will try my best level'—level best, but best level does have a loftier ring—'to bring equal development of the hill and valley'. To buttress that claim he announced a ₹201 crore (₹2 billion) 'package' for development in Ukhrul district. It was a bonafide overture of respect, quite different from the abortive attempt by Ibobi to announce a similar package a few months earlier, which was attempted in a bid to patch things up after creating the seven new districts and to mollify UNC and its key players into calling off a blockade that had choked Imphal Valley. Biren's announcement that capped the visit came with great political mileage.

But the visit and genuine welcome also came with riders from his hosts that Biren couldn't possibly acquiesce to without utterly losing his core constituency of the Meitei and that other counterbalance to the Nagas of Manipur: everyone else. The newly-minted chief minister was presented with several demands, nearly all politically charged. Indeed, incendiary. Among these was the request that his government acknowledge the 'legitimate right' of Nagas to integrate contiguous Naga homelands; rescind the new districts created at the end of Ibobi's tenure; and unequivocally support the Framework Agreement.

The wish list appeared to mirror several demands that I-M would stick in the maw of Indian negotiators from time to time. And, much like the Framework Agreement, it was practically dead on arrival, just leverage for one negotiating party with which to beat the other negotiating party over the head.

For the moment, he had an easier run to Churachandpur to reach Kuki and Zomi hearts and minds and to wash away bad blood from police firing in 2015. In early May, he did the seemingly impossible: he got communities in Churachandpur to believe, as part of a written undertaking, that his government would consult all groups before legislating matters related to residency and the Inner Line Permit.

And, in turn, he received assurance from community members that they would claim and bury their nine dead by 24 May.

It seemed like the closure of old and new wounds.

But Biren's command-and-control spots began to emerge shortly, during the whirligig honeymoon months this sometime journalist and footballer's run as the photo-op prince of Manipur, inaugurating yet another project, advising officials at yet another site, present for cutting every reasonably thick PR ribbon. It was as if Biren had taken after Rio, his current counterpart in Nagaland, than his own predecessor and mentor Ibobi, who was occasionally content to let other colleagues steal the limelight in a bid to retain his flock. The spots that combined privilege and power in an unsavoury mix began to show in the unlikeliest manner for a man in the middle of a love-fest with large swathes of this conflict-weary, deliberately impoverished state and, certainly, with local media that legitimately offered him the benefit of early doubt. It's quite a story.

In 2011, Biren's son, Nongthombam Ajay Meetei, stood accused of killing a student in a case of road rage. Irom Roger wouldn't permit the political princeling in a SUV to overtake. Ajay shot Roger, who died on the way to the hospital.

Biren was then a minister in Ibobi's second-term government and among his favourites. After initial attempts at playing things down, public furore compelled the government to hand over the investigation to the Central Bureau of Investigation (CBI). To his credit, Biren handed over his son to the custody of CBI investigators.

On 7 January 2017, a time Biren had emerged as the energetic spokesperson for BJP in Manipur, a local court in Imphal announced a verdict against Ajay, holding him guilty of a relatively watered-down verdict of 'homicide not amounting to murder'. Ajay was sentenced to five years of 'rigorous' imprisonment. There was briefly talk then of Ibobi's heavy hand influencing matters—especially as the well-connected in Manipur usually, and quite literally, were used to getting away with murder. It seemed like an opportune moment for a former mentor—who was still chief minister with all the powers of state that had as a matter of record slowed the process of local justice and civil rights for over a decade—to pull the plug on a renegade.

At any rate it hardly dented Biren's political fortunes. He publicly retained the moral high ground gained from his visible actions of cooperating with the investigation. He managed to retain Heingang, his constituency in Imphal East district, for the fourth successive time in the assembly elections declared in early-March—with the slimmest majority since he had first won Heingang way back in 2002. Biren was chosen in mid-March to lead BJP in Manipur. And there he was, Congress rebel to BJP chief minister in five months flat.

As it happened, Roger's mother thought her son's killer had got away with too little. She wanted more punishment for Ajay. She began to explore ways and, through local rights activists managed to finally engage a New Delhi-based lawyer, Utsav Singh Bains, to escalate the matter to Manipur High Court, to appeal the case and to file a petition in the Supreme Court.

In the second week of May, Bains claimed he had received threatening WhatsApp calls from several people asking him to back off—he claimed this first happened in late-March after he returned to New Delhi from Imphal. He maintained the callers identified themselves as speaking on behalf of PLA, the major 'Meitei' rebel group. Police reportedly agreed that the call originated in Myanmar where, as we have read, PLA, the armed wing of Revolutionary People's Front, and several other major rebel groups in Manipur maintain refuge for leaders and cadres.

Over the following weekend Binalakshmi Nepram, a media-savvy rights activist who had meanwhile taken interest in the matter of helping Roger's mother with counsel, alleged that Manipur police personnel visited her family home in Imphal on the afternoon of 12 May and intimidated her aged parents upon not finding Nepram. They allegedly did the same at the home of a candidate who contested against Biren in the assembly elections. The police version in some media reports was quite vanilla: that they were merely following up on Bains's accusations, and the visits were merely that of investigation to learn more from people who were familiar with Bains and the matter of judicial review.

While controversy raged over whether it was procedure, intimidation or over-reaction, it did take the shine off Biren, besides underscoring several axioms about Manipur. A primary one being: the intimate and opportune relations that politicians of Manipur—in varying degrees much like politicians in several other states in the region—maintain with rebels of various shades in an arrangement of mutual benefit that has for decades married local ethno-nationalist sentiments to pure survival.

As to Biren: Had this studiously humble and affable candidate, before, during and just after elections, now grown fangs and claws two months into his job as chief minister of a BJP-led government? Had he begun to believe in the infallibility of image? With near-absolute power and the pinnacle of ambition, had his skin become thinner? The answers came quickly.

Biren often projected himself being a part of what is colloquially known as the Sangh Parivar. The right-wing Hindu nationalist conglomerate has the BJP as its most public political face and the RSS its selectively public motivational face. RSS is the primary fuel to the Sangh's engine of growth that powers several hundred political, religious and non-governmental organisations whose activities range from scripting foreign and economic policies to an attempt to bring India's indigenous populations—nature-worshippers, animists and Christians alike—into the fold of a firmly paternalistic Hinduism. Like his colleagues in Assam and Tripura—the first electorally won by BJP in 2016 and the latter in early-2018—Biren went with New Delhi's diktat of accepting a political advisor with close links to the Sangh in general and a BJP general secretary, Ram Madhav, in particular. Madhav, an old RSS hand, at the time had responsibility of northeast Indian affairs for his party and alma mater and picked such advisors associated with a New Delhi-based think-tank he controlled.

Among Biren's newer affectations was to wear the 'Modi jacket', essentially the 'Nehru jacket' relabelled since 2014 by fans of India's brash new prime minister, who eschewed the jackets Nehru preferred, plainer fabrics and a mix of beige, off-white and blacks, to include loud monochromes. Besides matching peacock colours, Biren also began to voice Indian-nationalistic rhetoric, travelling quite the distance from Meitei traditionalists and Meitei nationalists and their harking to religious practices such as the firmly nature-oriented Sanamahi and looking to staunchly Manipuri origin stories, by instead equating heroes of India's anti-colonial fight with one of his key mentors in New Delhi.

For instance, in late-December 2018, Biren publicly announced he would not tolerate the 'humiliation of his leaders' and 'national heroes like Rani of Jhansi and Prime Minister Modi'.

He was walking his talk, taking the cue both from mentors in Delhi and his predecessor in Manipur to stretch law to an unlovely extent. One cycle began soon after the official celebration on 19 November that year of the birth anniversary of the queen of Jhansi who famously took on forces of the British East India Company during the so-called Sepoy Mutiny of 1857 and subsequent wars. An Imphal-based journalist, Kishorechand Wangkhem, aired an intemperate video on Facebook criticizing the celebration of that anniversary as going against Manipur's history of resistance against both the British and India. As we have seen, the Anglo-Manipuri wars of the 1890s, which led to British dominion over the kingdom of Manipur and a controversial accession to India in 1949 by Manipur's king, widely regarded in Manipur as being coerced by a resolutely unitary India, continue to be emotionally incendiary. As is the subsequent Meitei nationalist movement from the 1960s on that tipped over to militancy in the 1980s, aimed at gaining autonomy, even freedom, from India. Simply put: The birth of Meitei nationalism was predicated on what was—and is—perceived as Indian colonialism.

Wangkhem maintained that the celebrations insulted Manipur's resistance icons by linking the Rani's fightback against the British during the mutiny of 1857 to Manipur's freedom movement and generally pandering to the Hindu-right's nationalistic project. 'Your knowledge is null and f——d up,' Kishorechand ranted in apparent reference to Biren and, as reported by local media, called him a puppet of 'the Centre' and Modi, whom Wangkhem described as 'a chaiwala with no knowledge of history'. This last was a reference to Modi's often-repeated and disputed claim that in his younger days he sold tea at a railway station in his home state of Gujarat; a claim—like several that placed Modi at opportune and expedient moments in Indian and global history—that was amped up by public relations in the run-up to general elections to parliament in 2014 that propelled Modi to prime ministership.

Biren went ballistic at the insult. Wangkhem was fired from his job as anchor at the local television channel, ISTV. Within two days he was arrested by local police on a charge of sedition, released on bail after four days and rearrested a couple of days later by the National Investigation Agency under the National Security Act. The latter charge could keep Wangkhem in jail for as long as a year, no questions asked. Manipur's governor Najma Heptullah backed the move.

During the time Wangkhem was incarcerated, I asked a senior human rights practitioner from the region about the incident. We discussed how an imputation by government officials and government agencies that the abusive journalist encouraged present-day rebels with this outburst, was humbug. The practitioner mentioned that he had reached out to Biren to request Wangkhem's release. How can I? was the relayed response; he used the 'F word'. (Wangkhem was released after the Manipur High Court on 8 April 2019 revoked the charges against him.)

While this demonstrated Biren's relatively thin skin overlaying a certain political sycophancy, another incident demonstrated a relatively thick one—but to similar ends. In early 2018, he announced at a political rally in Gujarat's Madhavpura village that, in the time of Lord Krishna, North-East India was a single entity. That Lord Krishna 'made them part of India' by marrying the princess Rukmini, whom he alluded was from Arunachal Pradesh. A video of the speech was widely circulated on social media. Many local nationalists accused him of selling Manipur's soul, based on a myth and the need to curry favour. Raghu Ningthoujam, a scientist with Indian Space Research Organisation wrote a detailed essay in the popular Manipur-centric portal *e-pao.net*, attempting to dismiss Biren's statement with a scientific, if sarcastic, approach that separated myth from political marketing.

Biren appeared to be tone deaf to a key aspect of proven history. Hinduism was foisted upon the Meitei by diktat—an uncontested assertion—in the early 1700s. Meidingu Pamheiba, the king who did so, and persecuted practitioners of Sanamahi, the traditional religion of the Meitei, is reviled by many Meitei nationalists and intellectuals. The monarch mandated Hinduism as the state religion—that was in 1720. 'And he had to punish the conscientious objectors of that religion,' the historian and theatre director Arambam Lokendra told me during an extended conversation at his Imphal residence. 'Then, in the 1730s, Tantrik priests came from Sylhet [in present day Bangladesh] and said, "Oh your great land is the land of Shiva, the land of Mahabharata, let us name your place Manipur."'

Mahabharat myths, as it were, flourished and persisted after the culture of forced conversions set in. And so did a discourse by early converts, said Professor Lokendra, that Manipur was part of the Mahabharat. It was an essential component of new mythology.

Biren's line followed Hindu-right myths rooted in the epic *Mahabharat*, and several myths that found wing during a period of an aggressive pro-Hindu campaign in the 1930s. It was led by one of the earliest civil society movements in Manipur, the Nikhil Hindu Manipuri Mahasabha, in 1934. The organisation encouraged prizes for writing such history. One such myth the Mahasabha encouraged was that the Pandav warrior and ace-archer Arjun had a son, Babruvahan, by marrying the princess Chitrangada from 'Manipur'.

More than one critic—including the ISRO scientist—have pushed back by suggesting that the Manipur of Chitrangada was possibly Manipura or Manikapatnam, in Odisha. Indeed, decades earlier, as far back as the 1930s push for Hindu-mythological validation by the Mahasabha, Meitei radicals and Sanamahi practitioners—often the same—went to Odisha to photograph and document a village called Manipur, which records a legend, a tradition of Arjuna's visit. Religious resistance grew, leading to a revival of the Sanamahi movement in the 1930s. A form of communism merged with nationalism would soon follow, later riding the tiger of armed rebellion.

And, as Biren ought to know, mythology can cut both ways.

The Hindu-push isn't unusual. I've read in Hindu-pride texts that Ulupi, the serpent princess who married the philandering archer, has a connect with Ukhrul district in Manipur, the homeland of the Tangkhul Naga tribe. The same as the 'U' in Ulupi has no etymological link with Ukhrul, the Nag in Naga, formal Sanskrit for snake, has little to do with those of the Tangkhul or any of the Naga tribes.

But Northeast India remains a feverish project in the Sangh's imagination and construct.

Whatever his personal predilections, for the sake of BJP—a party that kept a close advisory watch on Biren with its cohorts of Sangh organisations, think-tanks and policy-lackeys—he was for all practical purposes, and for the moment, projecting himself as Inclusive Biren.

Alongside, since forming the government Biren presided over a steady changing of loyalties of Congress functionaries and even members of the legislative assembly over to BJP—a political procurement helped by laying out the promise of a new order with a new outlook. Biren also quite blatantly reached out to local media in a manner quite disturbingly common across India by offering sops in the hope of PR quid pro quo. He offered them insurance. Literally, insurance.

Did Biren prove to be opportunistic? Certainly—what politician is not?

A majoritarian? He would have to be, inclusive optics or not, to assuage fears of the Meitei community alongside the interests of his majoritarian political masters of the moment in mainland India.

Was Biren really Ibobi II? While to some observers that might be a work-in-regress, his skin-type was evidently thinner, which could prove to be a challenge for a Manipur desperate for a new-gen tomorrow. Because Biren wasn't necessarily of a new generation, just a relatively new leader from a wolfpack of old leaders, a new chief ministerial face tied to old thinking—tied to the legacy of which he was an integral part for more than a decade.

23. The Lawless Law

Just months into Biren's rule, an interesting update arrived on an ongoing case in the Supreme Court case about extra-judicial killings in Manipur. Indeed, 1,528 such alleged killings, which included several instances of staged or 'fake' encounters. It was among the most significant human rights marquees in India in recent years—perhaps on par, if there can ever be a par for such matters, as the petition that led to the formal acknowledgment in the Supreme Court in 2011 of extra-judicial overreach in Chhattisgarh related to the Maoist rebellion; and the formal disbanding of the Salwa Judum vigilante group.

It was being played as much in Manipur as it was in the Supreme Court—which has pursued the matter, based on a 'public interest litigation', or PIL, by the Extra-judicial Execution Victim Families Association, Manipur, an organisation representing the families of victims. Its partner in the PIL was Imphal-based Human Rights Alert, a watchdog. As with the Salwa Judum case, the process itself was setting benchmarks for the response and culpability of the state and India's shaky human rights cause-and-effect template. It had certainly rattled Manipur's fractious and incestuous political structure.

News arrived in early August 2017 of the Central Bureau of Investigation constituting a five-person team to examine 97 instances of alleged extra-judicial killings between 2000 and 2011, although the PIL recorded cases all the way back to 1980. CBI's move followed a Supreme Court order only weeks earlier, on 14 July, that CBI conclude such investigation into 'fake encounters or use of excessive or retaliatory force' by the end of 2017—also the deadline for filing cases. The Court declared that it would review progress and CBI's compliance in January 2018.

The focus of the CBI investigation would involve the Indian army, Assam Rifles, central paramilitary forces and even Manipur Police, which, like the paramilitaries, has for long piggybacked on the impunity and immunity offered to army personnel under AFSPA to conduct their own campaigns of interdiction and intimidation. Pradip Phanjoubam, the editor of *Imphal Free Press* at the time, would soon make an important point in the newspaper, with which I was in agreement—indeed, had been advocating for some years. It is a fact that police piggyback on the regime of impunity provided by AFSPA even though AFSPA wasn't designed to protect the police. This proved particularly true in Manipur.

The police, as Phanjoubam suggested, were aware, on account of judicial intervention and media investigations, that they can be charged for excesses and overreach under the laws of the land. And that process was under way in the Supreme Court.

In evident recognition of the practice of piggybacking, in an earlier hearing in April 2017, the Supreme Court bench directed that cases of the army and Assam Rifles and those of the police be segregated for investigation and judicial process. The bench also dismissed a plea that internal inquiry and investigation on several incidents by the army was adequate from the perspective of human rights. Both were significant developments.

During the hearings in July 2017 the Supreme Court bench was also harsh on central government representatives claiming that compensation had been paid to families of the victims. While it was an admission of wrongdoing, the court observed that compensation was hardly the preferred avenue else 'all heinous crimes' would be settled that way, over-riding the law of the land.

It was dulcet compared to a cutting observation of the Court as early into the hearings as 2015: 'Now it's like you kill 10 people, pay compensation and the matter ends there.'

It was also dulcet compared to the scathing indictment of AFSPA by the same bench, of Justices Madan Bhimrao Lokur and Uday Umesh Lalit in July 2016:

'It does not matter whether the victim was a common person or a militant or a terrorist, nor does it matter whether the aggressor was a common person or the state. The law is the same for both and is equally applicable to both,' the bench stated in its 85-page judgement, adding, 'This is the requirement of a democracy and the requirement of preservation of the rule of law and the preservation of individual liberties.'

Meanwhile, reportage by local media in Manipur revealed as false several instances in which the state government—the responsibility for whose defence in court and in the public domain had now passed from Ibobi to Biren—claimed to have paid compensation.

AFSPA was born in the hazy, paranoid days of post-Partition chaos. A series of ordinances that emphasised 'Special Powers of Armed Forces' were issued in 1947 to cover Bengal, Punjab, Assam and the United Provinces of the time. These were coalesced under one umbrella legislation the following year.

Some years later arrived the war against Naga rebels. In 1958, the home minister at the time, Govind Ballabh Pant, 'declared that "certain misguided sections" of the Nagas were involved in "arson, murder, loot, dacoity, etc."'. He added—as I read in a government report to review AFSPA: 'So, it has become necessary to adopt effective measures for the protection of the people in those areas … In order to enable the armed forces to handle the situation effectively whenever such problem arises hereafter, it has been considered necessary to introduce this bill.'

Pant, under the guidance of prime minister Nehru, steered the bill that initially became the Armed Forces (Assam and Manipur) Special Powers Act, 1958. Significantly, some MPs opposed the bill. One of them was Laisram Achaw Singh of Manipur, a former academician and a long-time socialist. In debates in the Lok Sabha, Laisram described provisions of bill-soon-to-become-law as 'unnecessary … an anti-democratic measure … a lawless law.'

The MP from Manipur, who has by far the best description of AFSPA and, by extension, every heavy-handed cousin—'a lawless law'—was prescient. The fig-leaf that AFSPA provided the army and paramilitary led to arguably the most shameful application of force and disregard for human rights and 'collateral damage' in independent India's history, the strongest application began in Nagaland and the Naga homelands in Manipur.

(Manipur police records speak of the time: 'In 1961 Ukhrul, Mao-Maram and Tamenglong Sub-Division were declared disturbed areas under Section 3 of the Armed Forces (Assam & Manipur) Special Powers Act 1958, and army took over the control of operations in these areas … The West Bengal Security Act was also brought into force in June 1961. These measures combined with the arrest of some important leaders of the hostiles proved very effective in maintaining law & order. One of the results was the surrender of a large number of hostiles with weapons.')

AFSPA was in the mid-1960s extended to Mizoram (and, since September 1980, in Imphal Valley—and, in short order, all Manipur). Over the years, amendments led to the replacing of 'Assam and Manipur' with 'Special Powers'. An expansion saw it applied to all far-eastern states and territories with the exception of Sikkim, which had not been annexed by India at the time of the last amendment of AFSPA in 1972.

AFSPA is sprawling in its insurance of immunity and impunity:

'Any commissioned officer, warrant officer, non-commissioned officer or any other person of equivalent rank in the armed forces may, in a disturbed area,

'(a) if he is of opinion that it is necessary so to do for the maintenance of public order, after giving such due warning as he may consider necessary, fire upon or otherwise use force, even to the causing of death, against any person who is acting in contravention of any law and order for the time being in force in the disturbed area prohibiting the assembly of five or more persons or the carrying of weapons or of things capable of being used as weapons or of fire-arms, ammunition or explosive substances;

'(b) if he is of opinion that it is necessary to do so, destroy any arms dump, prepared or fortified position or shelter from which armed attacks are made or are likely to be made, or any structure used as a training camp for armed volunteers or utilized as a hideout by armed gangs or absconders wanted for any offence;

'(c) arrest, without warrant, any person who has committed a cognizable offence or against whom a reasonable suspicion exists that he has committed or is about to commit a cognizable offence and may use such force as may be necessary to effect the arrest;

'(d) enter and search without warrant any premises to make any such arrest as aforesaid or to recover any person believed to be wrongfully restrained or confined or any property reasonably suspected to be stolen property or any arms, ammunition or explosive substances believed to be unlawfully kept in such premises, and may for that purpose use such force as may be necessary.'

There is a procedure subsequent to any arrest:

'Any person arrested and taken into custody under this Act shall be made over to the officer in charge of the nearest police station with the least possible delay, together with a report of the circumstances occasioning the arrest.' The interpretation of least-possible-delay has come to be 24 hours: as a clause in Article 22 of the Constitution provides—that 'every person who is arrested and detained in custody shall be produced before the nearest Magistrate within a period of 24 hours excluding the time taken for journey from the place of arrest to the nearest court of the Magistrate.'

As I have written earlier, if this seems reasonable, the point that follows immediately after is not and it is the one that is nearly always used to justify torture, molestation, rape and even the killing of innocents—though such events have been written off as nuances of conflict. The following paragraph has protected rage, revenge and near-genocide in the Naga areas and Mizoram through the 1950s, 1960s, and later, relatively more isolated but no less numerous cases in both the hills and plains areas of Manipur and Assam—and in faraway Kashmir through a similar legislation enacted in 1990:

'No prosecution, suit or other legal proceeding shall be instituted, except with the previous sanction of the Central Government, against any person in respect of anything done or purported to be done in exercise of the powers conferred by this Act.'

Suggestions to repeal or soften AFSPA have consistently fallen on deaf ears.

It required the death of Thangjam Manorama Devi on 11 July 2004 and the consequent protest in Manipur for Government of India to even set up a committee to review the Act.

That year Manipur burnt more than usual for that horrific decade, after Assam Rifles personnel abducted, raped and killed Manorama, whom they suspected to be a member of PLA. It triggered a firestorm of protest, even self-immolation. The most searing image from the time, besides the corpse of Manorama, was of ten middle-aged women marching to Kangla Fort in the centre of Imphal—a historical and spiritual hub for the Meitei as well as a residence co-opted by Assam Rifles. The ladies stopped at the gates, disrobed and, naked, screamed in a paroxysm of grief and anger at Assam Rifles in particular and the Indian Army in general to rape them as they did their 'daughter', Manorama.

It bears repetition that the women carried a banner with a message in large capital letters: 'Indian Army Rape Us.'

In the wake of what became a cascading citizens' protest, a delegation comprising representatives from 32 civil society conglomerates travelled to New Delhi to meet Prime Minister Manmohan Singh. Nine among the delegation met the prime minister to hand over a 15-point memorandum, the main pitch being the removal of AFSPA.

There were several significant outcomes of that visit.

On 20 November 2004 Singh issued an inclusive statement that went farther than any statement by a head of government on such matters, before or since. In several ways it was a huge—and entirely overdue—gesture and made after he travelled to Imphal. He addressed a gathering after Kangla Fort was formally given over to the 'People of Manipur'—in this case via chief minister Okram Ibobi Singh—by Lt Gen. Bhupinder Singh, the director general of Assam Rifles at the time.

'Our government is committed to addressing the concerns and grievances of the people of Manipur,' Prime Minister Singh announced. 'I met representatives of some organisations of Manipur in Delhi. I sympathised with the pain and sorrow of the mothers who lost their children. Having given my assurance that we will try to redress legitimate grievances on the Armed Forces Special Powers Act, we have set up a committee to review the provisions of the Act. The Committee will suggest checks and balances in the Act or replacing it with a more humane law which takes into account your legitimate aspirations and national security concerns. It will complete its work in six months. I hope the work of this committee will result in lasting peace and harmony.'

He added: 'The progress and development of Manipur will be advanced if peace and order prevails. We must today resolve to eschew all violent methods of settling grievances and join the constitutional process to find solutions.'

'I have already said we want to improve Manipur's connectivity to the region around. We would like to invest in modern infrastructure to enable this. However, for this to happen, we need peace, security and political stability.'

A result of this admittedly noble pursuit was the establishment of what came to be known as the Justice Jeevan Reddy Committee, to review AFSPA.

It was chaired by B.P. Jeevan Reddy, a former judge of the Supreme Court. It had four other members: S.B. Nakade, an academician and jurist; P. Shrivastav, a retired bureaucrat and a former special secretary at the home ministry; Lt Gen. V.R. Raghavan, who earlier held the post of director general of military operations; and commentator and analyst Sanjoy Hazarika.

The committee's terms of reference were straightforward enough:

'Keeping in view the legitimate concerns of the people of the North Eastern Region, the need to foster Human Rights, keeping in perspective the imperatives of security and maintenance of public order to review the provisions of the Armed Forces (Special Powers) Act, 1958, as amended in 1972 and to advise Government of India whether—

'(a) To amend the provisions of the Act to bring them in consonance with the obligations of the Govt. towards protection of Human Rights; or

'(b) To replace the Act by a more humane Act.'

Over five months, the committee held 13 meetings and conducted 17 public hearings across the far-east and New Delhi. They met nearly 200 people ranging from the general public, relatives of victims of excess by security forces, lawyers, activists, students and tribal leaders; to senior bureaucrats and senior officials from the Indian Army, Assam Rifles, CRPF and the Border Security Force and received written representations from some state governments.

The security establishment unanimously recommended the continuation of AFSPA in its current form. Significantly, so did the Ministry of Home Affairs in a presentation to the committee, even though it had technically set up the committee to make AFSPA more 'humane' in the first place. This gave away the game. The governments of Assam and Arunachal Pradesh recommended retaining AFSPA in certain parts of the states, as did Meghalaya, where AFSPA was enforced in a 20-kilometre strip along its border with Assam. Mizoram, where rebels had signed a peace deal in 1986, requested that AFSPA no longer be applied to the state. A letter to the committee from Mizoram's home secretary, C. Ropianga mentioned: 'For the people of Mizoram, the Armed Forces (Assam and Manipur) Special Powers Act, 1958, leaves a scar on their minds, and all sections of people regardless of political parties to which they belong are against this particular Act.'

Manipur, Tripura and Nagaland did not send an official response; though the committee recorded representations by senior bureaucrats and police officials of Nagaland that the 'Act should be replaced with a more humane legislation since it had generated suspicion between the Nagas and others'.

Citizens and civil groups without exception recommended that AFSPA should immediately be repealed. Equally, there was telling commentary about the need for the presence of Indian Army and paramilitaries to remain in the region. The reason was two-fold. One was to watch over the vast international borders in this region—with

China, Myanmar, Bangladesh, Bhutan and Nepal. The other was to keep watch over, and stall 'non-state armed groups' many of which simply preyed on the very citizens on behalf of whom they claimed to be fighting a just war.

The committee took in all this, absorbed Constitutional provisions of freedoms, quoted Article 14 in Part III of the Constitution, which 'ensures to its citizens equality before law and equal protection of laws'; and invoked Article 21, which 'expressly declares that no person shall be deprived of his life or personal liberty except in accordance with the procedure established by law'. Besides, the committee cited several existing constitutional provisions and laws of parliament, the Indian Penal Code and the Code of Criminal Procedure that gave vast powers to the armed forces and the police to intervene in several situations, and various existing laws that the central and state governments had at their disposal to deal with armed rebellion and terrorist threats. There was adequate central and federal oversight. Indeed, the committee reasoned in a bid to offset the iron-handed and often arbitrarily applied law that often seemed like a wayward cousin of the so-called sedition laws, the Unlawful Activities (Prevention) Act, 1967, as amended in 2004 was adequate. The Act, the committee noted in its report, 'defines "terrorism" in terms which encompass and cover the activities of the nature carried on by several militant/insurgents … is applicable across India, it would also not be seen as discriminatory, unlike AFSPA, which is selectively applied to a few states'. AFSPA, as the committee bluntly describes in its report, 'has become a symbol of oppression, an object of hate and an instrument of discrimination and high-handedness'.

The Justice Jeevan Reddy Committee formally handed over its recommendation to the home ministry on 6 June 2005: AFSPA should be repealed.

The ministry buried it.

Two years later, in 2007, the Administrative Reforms Commission headed by veteran Congress party member Veerappa Moily also suggested the repeal of AFSPA; in its place bolstering the Unlawful Activities (Prevention) Act with provisions to enable the armed forces to operate in the charged climate of Northeast India.

The government ignored it.

Successive home ministers during this phase—Shivraj Patil, P. Chidambaram and Sushilkumar Shinde—occasionally discussed AFSPA, but didn't go against the establishment grain beyond a point.

Prime Minister Singh's claim from November 2004 remained as hollow as the prospect of a dignified peace and closure for the region.

But criticism of AFSPA kept arriving, sometimes from unlikely sources. The governor of Meghalaya at the time, Ranjit Shekhar Mooshahary, a former director of the elite National Security Guards, and director general of Border Security Force had on 1 November 2009 spoken of the need to remove AFSPA from Northeast India in general and Manipur in particular. In this he was joined by an additional director of the Intelligence Bureau, R.N. Ravi—the future government interlocutor of peace talks with NSCN (I-M). It made headlines.

'The Act which has been in use for a long time is ineffective and there is need to revisit it,' media quoted Mooshahary as saying at the closing session of the Conference of Police Chiefs of the North-East, Sikkim and West Bengal in Shillong. 'If the Act is removed, I think the situation would not worsen. In fact it will improve ... The Act has made the people vulnerable. The Centre could think of doing away with the Act or applying it in a modified way.'

In January 2010, Mooshahary would go farther. Speaking at a conference of the North-East Region Commonwealth Parliamentary Association, also in Shillong, he tore into AFSPA. 'We cannot contain insurgency-related violence by alienating the citizens. We can do so more effectively by involving them ... This Act has alienated the civil society more and more with the passage of time ... and has lost its relevance in view of the emerging role of the civil society in violence-prone areas ... I do not subscribe to the view that we need to continue fighting insurgency and terrorism with the help of the Armed Forces [Special Powers] Act.'

Ravi, the serving intelligence officer, who stood to lose more than Mooshahary, told the media: 'We have every reason to do away with the Act and we believe that our police force can tackle the law and order situation.'

Some, like M.K. Das who was appointed Manipur's director general of police, gained voice at the end of his career—but this is meant as praise, not criticism, as just raising the issue of AFSPA is a leap of faith for a government employee, past or present. 'If we do not have the Army Act, inconvenience caused to the public will be less,' Das remarked to media persons in end-November 2013, in Imphal, a day before demitting office. He stressed that the army or AFSPA should not be employed for an 'internal matter'. The army should be used 'only for external aggression'.

The Congress party-led United Progressive Alliance government repeatedly ignored such advice. Prime Minister Manmohan Singh backed down on his promise in end-2004 to replace AFSPA with a more 'humane' law—a step that would have assuaged both public anger and the overstated insecurity of the army in such matters. Singh and his colleagues reneged on the one big, dramatic gesture that would have helped to erase several emotional scars that are built on real scars and still-festering wounds.

(Indeed, just months after Das's suggestion, the human right circus played out at the month-long United Nations Human Rights Council meeting in Geneva that began on 3 March 2014. As with any reference to human rights violations, Indian diplomats at the UN worked diligently to protect AFSPA's application. In 2013, they had also dismissed accusations of human rights violations as the imagination of fevered non-governmental organisations. Besides denials, there was downplaying of conflicts by using bureaucratese on the lines of 'disturbances of internal order which necessitates the presence of the military', as a government committee once put it.)

That government, and every government since the time of AFSPA's enactment in 1958, failed to realise—or, at least, failed to realise with enough momentum to overturn the pushback from the Army and security establishment—that AFSPA has never stopped rebellion. It instead bred resentment against India by protecting prejudices and atrocities. Because good cred, if you will, isn't earned by traumatising those India calls its own, but by acknowledging they are citizens first, with Constitutional rights. Indeed, reverses for several key insurgencies in India's far-east have not happened on account of AFSPA, but a combination of effective policing and coordinated combat operations. Effective and ongoing Indian diplomacy and changing political realities in countries like Bangladesh, Bhutan and Myanmar—which at one time or another harboured 'Indian' rebels—have underscored that active peace-making, governance, development, accountability and ethno-regional respect are the surest guarantors of India's internal security.

Not long after the two-term Congress-led UPA government gave way to the first term of the BJP-led government of Narendra Modi in May 2014, there was another public fracas over AFSPA. In particular, The Armed Forces (Jammu and Kashmir) Special Powers Act, 1990, more or less a template of AFSPA-1958 applied to this region after a Pakistan-backed insurgency broke out in 1989. (Pakistan's prime minister at the time, Benazir Bhutto, signed off on it. Indeed, she would admit that supporting of terrorism in India as state policy began during her term. She mentioned this in late-2003 at a global conference I blueprinted for a major media house in New Delhi—but that's another story.)

In this fracas a senior Congress leader, P. Chidambaram, took centre-stage. No slouch when it came to controversy and a heavy hand during his multiple tenures as cabinet minister in Congress and non-Congress governments, in mid-November 2014 Chidambaram criticised the Kashmir version of AFSPA as 'obnoxious' and as having 'no place in a modern, civilized country'.

Chidambaram's remarks came in the wake of army personnel being sentenced for staging an encounter in Jammu and Kashmir in 2010; and other army men shooting young Kashmiri boys in a case of mistaken identity earlier in November 2014—and being prosecuted in a rare blaze of publicity. Expectedly, ministers of the BJP-led government tore into Chidambaram, accusing him of leveraging security matters for political gain. After all phased assembly elections in Jammu and Kashmir were to begin on 25 November 2014.

To be fair to Chidambaram, it wasn't the first time he had voiced such an opinion. For instance, he chided the army's opposition to making AFSPA more humane during a talk in February 2013 at the

Institute for Defence Studies and Analyses, a New Delhi-based think-tank underwritten by the ministry of defence. At the time, Chidambaram was a cabinet minister in-charge of finance in the Congress-led government; just prior to that, between November 2008 and July 2012 he had been minister for home affairs.

28/05/2015

The most significant recent security-related development this week has to be the decision by Tripura's cabinet on 27 May to remove AFSPA, after consultations with central government agencies and the armed forces.

Those outside NE rarely understand the effect AFSPA has on the emotions and politics of the region. Worth every repetition: It permits the state to brutalise the people it so dearly claims as its own—collateral damage in the name of peace—and offers fear, torture and death when dialogue would do.

Tripura's action must be mirrored across the region. NE has a new heft in New Delhi because of China's over-arching interest in the area; the promise of energy, trade and communication links with Myanmar; and similar impetus with Bangladesh, with the added socio-political pressure of immigration from that country. AFSPA is no substitute for development or diplomacy; even less a formula for national integrity with the resentment it spawns.

Tripura's action comes nearly 10 years to the day when on 06/06/ 2005, Justice Reddy Committee recommended be repealed. MHA buried the report. That mistake must be reversed. There's every reason.

Tripura's decision to remove AFSPA—applied primarily in the tribal areas of the state—is not altruistic. It is practical; integrationist even. The state's rebellions, like most rebellions in NE, were and are a direct consequence of political and administrative apathy. In Tripura's case, many disgruntled tribal folk saw a conspiracy of domination by a constructed majority: several waves of mostly Hindu/Bengali immigrants. Resentment erupted into armed violence in the 1970s and peaked in the 1990s, when AFSPA was extended to Tripura.

Brutal policing, deft politics, some development and aggressive border controls, especially with Bangladesh, which envelops Tripura on three sides, have since reduced insurgency to a trickle. Over the years the state—its economics, politics and administration controlled by the majority Bengali population—has also seen itself as a regional player. While Tripura's hydrocarbon reserves will fuel it, the state's improving infrastructure and locational advantage in relation to Bangladesh's modernising waterways, port and rail networks will sustain it. Bangladesh is already pitching to create a hinterland of investment, manufacturing and services in Tripura and, if possible, all NE. Makes sense. Bangladesh has NE to its north, east and south-east.

AFSPA detracts from such a future.

Tripura government's decision to remove AFSPA is a leap of faith, even though insurgency still occasionally troubles it, and a salve for the state's human rights record that is far from lily-white. But—hugely significant—for Tripura, this is a 'manageable' insurgency for which the army is no longer required.

By itself and as imagined pieces in India's Look-East jigsaw, NE wants to move ahead, ditch the economy of conflict and embrace the economy of peace. Even Manipur—on paper the state with most active rebel groups, mostly resident in Myanmar, and with a flourishing narcotics food chain linking security personnel, politicians, administrators and rebels—wants to break free.

AFSPA has been lifted from the municipal limits of Manipur's capital Imphal. Top practitioners in India's security establishment have maintained that removing AFSPA from the rest of the state—or everywhere, barring a slim strip along the border with Myanmar—wouldn't harm the security situation.

As to removing AFSPA entirely from everywhere, it's a no-brainer.

In any case AFSPA is so last century.

There was another brief liberal burst, in the Congress's election manifesto for the 2019 general elections to the Lok Sabha. Even allowing for the caveat of talk-is-cheap and that some promises keep hot air balloons afloat for at least five years until the next elections, it was significant, and took the route via Jammu & Kashmir. The manifesto suggested an overhaul of India's policy in Jammu & Kashmir without compromising in any way India's territory and security. 'Congress promises to review the deployment of armed forces, move more troops to the border to stop infiltration completely, reduce the presence of the Army and CAPFs

[Central Armed Police Forces, or paramilitaries] in the Kashmir Valley, and entrust more responsibility to the J&K police for maintaining law and order.'

The offer of 'talks without preconditions' actually took a leaf from the BJP's briefly-practiced playbook, when in late-2017 it appointed a former Intelligence Bureau director as interlocutor in Jammu & Kashmir. He had offered this undertaking: 'For a substantive dialogue, I will need to talk to everybody.' That was a brief bloom since the steady downhill roll since 2016 (including the matter of being unable to prevent attacks by militants, besides the policy and political reverses that the promise of axing Articles 370 and 35A of the Constitution triggered).

The Congress manifesto was a copybook hearts-and-minds play. As was the suggestion that, to 'omit' Section 124A of the Indian Penal Code, the so-called sedition law, wouldn't be an act of weakness. It remains among the most misused laws in India. It has also gratuitously drawn in thousands of farmers, fisherfolk, tribal folk and forest dwellers across the country fighting their displacement for industrial projects, among other depredations.

And, there was a promise to review Jammu & Kashmir's version of AFSPA enacted in 1990 and the Disturbed Areas Act that the Kashmir version and its parent, AFSPA, legislated for the east in 1958, rides on. For application or continuation of AFSPA, a particular area must first be declared 'disturbed' by the local government, a nuance that is often missed: a local government is entirely complicit in the application of AFSPA. At any rate, the promised review of AFSPA by the Congress held huge significance—even if only for the merit of a public debate—for Jammu & Kashmir, and, of course, India's far-east.

Indeed, the Kashmir version of AFSPA was even more permissive in reach than its eastern parent in a few micro-detailed parameters— even though troops in the east acted thus in any case. Kashmir's AFSPA permitted troops to 'stop, search and seize any vehicle or vessel reasonably suspected to be carrying any person, who is a proclaimed offender, or any person who has committed a non-cognizable offence, or against whom a reasonable suspicion exists that he has committed, or is about to commit, a non-cognizable offence...'

Another micro-detail for the Kashmir version permitted the 'power of search to include powers to break open locks, etc.—every person making a search under this Act shall have the power to break open the lock of any door, almirah, safe, box, cupboard, drawer, package or other thing, if the key thereof is withheld'.

In the same way they rubbished Chidambaram's public intervention on AFSPA in end-2014, senior BJP leaders tore into the manifesto, termed these aspects as 'positively dangerous', as harbouring an 'agenda of Balkanization', and a blueprint that would compromise national security. BJP's own manifesto, promising a 'determined and strong' India, offered quite the opposite—and carried it through in letter and undemocratic spirit.

In all this grey, sometimes the army's view could be refreshingly black and white—even if one disagreed with it. During one of my talks on internal security at the Army War College in Mhow, Madhya Pradesh, in the early-2010s, my host, a senior general, capped a lively discussion on AFSPA by saying: 'If you don't want AFSPA, then don't deploy the army.'

It was an important point from the army's perspective: if you want us to do a job because politicians and bureaucrats have messed up, and can't handle it, and neither can the police, then give us protection from judicial scrutiny to do so.

Whatever the arguments and counter-arguments, I have for several years held out the slogan in my writing and talks: repeal AFSPA to regain India.

I still believe it has more than a dove's chance with a hawk.

In the middle of all this arrived in mid-August 2017 a curious article in *The Hindu*, which quoted an unnamed home ministry official as saying that the ministry had 'decided to rescind the power to invoke' AFSPA in Manipur and Assam.

But the validating bureaucratese—words like 'rescind' and 'abjure' were the lifeblood of government—required interpretation.

While revocation of such powers would be excellent, it could not be misconstrued as the revocation or repeal of AFSPA itself. Indeed, with all the drum-beating since end-2004, nothing whatsoever had softened AFSPA and, three years into a BJP-led central government it was abundantly clear that any central government would be reluctant to repeal AFSPA. The piece of legislation was simply too attractive a device of command and control.

The mention of Manipur and Assam was interesting as the BJP was in the government in both the states and for all practical purpose, a straight line of security diktat extended from New Delhi to Imphal and Dispur, Assam's administrative capital.

However, for the central government to devolve the power completely to states, AFSPA would need to be amended by Parliament.

To apply AFSPA, as we have read, a particular area has to first be declared 'disturbed'.

Section 3 of the Act defines the 'powers' to declare it so, if the area 'is in such a disturbed or dangerous condition that the use of armed forces in aid of the civil power is necessary, the governor of that state or the administrator of that Union territory or the Central government, as the case may be, may by notification in the Official Gazette, declare the whole or such part of such state or Union territory to be a disturbed area'.

To technically 'rescind' its power, the words 'Central government' mentioned twice in that particular section, would have to go. And, even if it did, would state governments really be free to extend, limit or jettison AFSPA as they wished?

Indeed, BJP chief minister Biren Singh chaired a cabinet meeting in late May 2017, a little over two months after taking office, and extended the state's 'disturbed area' status quo by another six months—the time limit for periodic review. As AFSPA was already in force, it became a procedural matter for a bureaucrat to issue an order of extension.

But the decision was, in reality, taken by the chief minister in consultation with his cabinet colleagues and administrative, police and intelligence officials; and not infrequently in consultations with the commanding general or senior officer of the local armed forces garrison. That travelled up the food chain to New Delhi, and back.

The security establishment and the army called the shots here. It was unlikely they would 'rescind' that power in the near future, despite a liberal leak or two in the home ministry's plumbing.

Meanwhile, the political theatre was on in earnest. The usual tragicomedy.

The former director-general of police, Joykumar, was now deputy chief minister in Biren's government. He held the important portfolio of finance and several related departments, and, alongside, the responsibility for science and technology and civil aviation. Besides, Joykumar wasn't shy about sharing his chief ministerial ambition in private, had won on a ticket of the Nationalist People's Party, or NPP, an enterprise the leadership of which Meghalaya's youthful chief minister Conrad Sangma inherited after his father's passing in 2016. NPP had offered support to the BJP-led central government since 2014 and, with its four seats in the same elections that had catapulted Biren to the forefront, had proved crucial for the BJP-led coalition taking office in Manipur.

An ironical twist in the plot was offered by instances of human rights violations and extra-judicial killings during that time prepared for the Supreme Court by Babloo Loitongbam, who headed Human Rights Alert. Babloo was also Joykumar's nephew—and had also battled the state during his uncle's tenure as chief of police appointed during the extended run of a Congress government.

Would Biren jettison Joykumar, a person who was vastly more powerful than Biren during Biren's years as protégé of Ibobi, and who saw himself as chief minister? Could he jettison Joykumar, considering the support of NPP remained crucial for the survival of the BJP-led government in Manipur? Would CBI's investigation proceed unhampered, seeing that the leading political party in India and Manipur were the same? Would its investigation be held as leverage for Joykumar's continued good behaviour as an ally of government?

Would justice be served?

The answers were in the wind.

On 16 January 2018, the Supreme Court bench expressed displeasure at the speed of CBI's investigation and compliance of deadline and urged the agency's director to step up and personally take charge. The judicial ticking off mentioned a hearing in less than a month on 12 February, with the promise of more legal fire and brimstone.

In half-a-year since the judicial—and, perhaps, judicious—dressing down of the defendants, all the that had become certain was that the government would drag, or be made to drag, its feet. And, that the Army would fight the process tooth and nail; it would also fight to retain AFSPA and continue to contend that any action its personnel were accused of in the period being monitored by the Supreme Court was done under AFSPA's protective umbrella. Indeed, on 28 January Gen. Bipin Rawat, India's chief of army staff, was quoted as saying in a report by Press Trust of India that time wasn't right 'to even rethink on AFSPA'.

The backroom plays and delays were made abundantly clear on 27 July 2018 when the two-judge bench of the apex court again pulled up CBI for delays in its investigation and filing of charges. Three days later Supreme Court Justices Lokur and Lalit hammered home the point when they summoned CBI director Alok Verma. The judges became impatient when CBI's representatives and counsel cited procedure and again when Verma mentioned that, meanwhile, 14 people had been charged for their alleged roles in extra-judicial killings.

There was reason for the court's impatience. Investigation for the more than fifteen hundred allegations in the public interest litigation had been whittled down by a CBI undertaking to investigate ninety-seven instances; and only 14 instances, by the CBI's own admission, for which it claims readiness to file charges.

CBI was plainly stalling. But even that stall was an indication that the human rights hornet's nest was well and truly stirred by the PIL and the Supreme Court. And, even with stall, with the little that it did, related cases and petitions were arriving at Court in remarkable ways.

AFSPA loomed again. The army's chief was back in damage control mode. This time—in the greatest of ironies—the 'collateral damage' of the PIL on extra-judicial killings was the army itself. And it was put into a spot by CBI.

In early August, CBI had filed charges against Major Vijay Singh Balhara for allegedly causing the extra-judicial death in Manipur of a 12-year-old boy, Azad Khan. A commission of enquiry by retired Supreme Court judge Santosh Hegde had earlier identified the incident—from six that he chose at random to investigate from a basket of over 1,500 cases in Manipur alone—as an extra-judicial killing by the major and his colleagues. The major had at the time been on secondment to Assam Rifles. Justice Hegde had questioned evidence that, among other things, accused the boy of being a member of a militant group.

In this most curious of cases, Gen. Rawat criticised the action of his colleagues in public. On 2 September, during an interaction with senior officers and their spouses in New Delhi, Gen. Rawat questioned the need for about 380 officers and other ranks to take a plea a day earlier to the Supreme Court, pleading against any possible dilution in AFSPA. Nearly 360 army personnel had earlier filed a similar petition, triggered by the charges brought against Major Balhara.

The Indian Express, which was among several publications to report the interaction, quoted a source as saying that Gen. Rawat was scathing in his censuring of personnel in the office of the army's judge advocate general—head of the legal branch of the army—and that, they had 'misled' the petitioners.

As we have read, Gen. Rawat was far from being a proponent of diluting AFSPA. But his recent irritation was understandable. What the army personnel had done in their apparent defence of a fellow officer was merely highlight AFSPA in general, and an officer's case and the situation in Manipur in particular.

The fresh petition and the general's response spotlighted AFSPA when all the army wanted was for the law to remain but lawlessness attributed to it buried. It opened up for the army the awkward possibility, as Gen. Rawat himself hinted at during his interaction on 2 September, of the Supreme Court suggesting a review or dilution of AFSPA. His position was made more awkward in the third week of September when a serving major general, Rajeeva Kumar, joined the 740 petitioners.

Far from diminishing interest in AFSPA, it continued to arc-light AFSPA.

The arc lights also brought back to focus an additional embarrassment that, barely reported by national media at the time, had already arrived a few weeks that very July. It was in the form of an affidavit in Manipur High Court. It maintained that a serving lieutenant colonel, Dharamvir Singh of the Para Commandos, had complained in 2016 to higher authorities about corruption—and several custodial deaths of Manipuris in the headquarters of 3 Corp in Dimapur in Nagaland; besides allegations of several killings of non-combatants by the army in Manipur. The colonel's wife filed the affidavit maintaining that Singh was arrested by his colleagues to stanch such leaks. It didn't take much to figure out the pressure: some of India's top generals had commanded 3 Corp around the time of the lieutenant colonel's complaint and arrest.

The thing was, even with all the ire and attempt at justice brought to bear by two judges of the Supreme Court, AFSPA could change its character only through legislation in India's parliament where it was born. The government's own scathing reviews of AFSPA since 2005—or, more precisely, by government-appointed committees—hadn't had any effect in the face of massive pushback by the army and policy hawks. So, an adverse Supreme Court decision would only raise the patriotic pitch that was any government's go-to policy in times of political adversity and imminent general elections to parliament. The Court knew this. Naturally the Army and the government knew this too.

But they all also knew that the ongoing saga in the Supreme Court will have raised several tricky, sticky questions. The more the matter stayed in the limelight, the more awkward it would be.

So, the Army and government tried to push back again. The collective of army petitioners pushed for recusal of the Supreme Court bench of Justices Lokur and Lalit. The plea was based on a development on 30 July, when the two-judge bench had criticised CBI director Alok Verma for going slow on investigation and filing cases and charges against several accused of extra-judicial killings. The bench suggested that 'murderers' were meanwhile roaming free in Manipur. The petitioners quickly latched on to this statement as proof of the judges being biased and demanded their recusal.

In end-September 2018, India's attorney general at the time, K.K.

Venugopal, underscored this collective plea for recusal by telling the bench of Justices of Lokur and Lalit that he had 'instructions from the Union of India that we are supporting these petitions'. Former attorney general and senior lawyer, Mukul Rohatgi, told the bench of 'genuine apprehension' among petitioners that they wouldn't receive a fair trial. Both suggested security forces were demoralised on this account.

On 12 November, Justices Lokur and Lalit dismissed the plea and the apprehension. They said it should be 'clear' to all that security personnel 'are made of much sterner stuff than is sought to be projected … It is unfortunate that a bogey of demoralization of the Indian Army, paramilitary forces and the State Police is being raised …'

All the Army and government received was the Court sticking its judicious pins into the voodoo doll of the army and government's own making—and making it all a matter of judicial record that would continue to be leveraged by human rights petitioners, activists and judges who could rise above stupendous establishment pressure. And India's army chief Bipin Rawat could now say to several hundred of his officers and men: I told you so; it was a bad idea to go to court in the first place. The embarrassment also extended to Manipur police personnel who continued to be discomfited by a Supreme Court mandated investigation being conducted by CBI into extra-judicial deaths in Manipur.

The muck simply wouldn't go away.

24. Optical Illusion:
'Safe and Productive' Manipur

Meanwhile, as 2018 journeyed to 2019, Nongthombam Biren Singh continued the game of optics.

He announced to a visiting Myanmarese delegation on 11 June that Manipur remained 'safe and productive' for business and investment. It was in the capital Imphal at a conference titled 'Connecting India's Northeast with North West Region of Myanmar: Roadmap for all-round Prosperity.'

It was co-organised by the government of Manipur, the ministry of external affairs and the New Delhi-based alt-right think-tank, India Foundation, with close ties to the hawkish spectrum of policy and security, besides what is commonly called the Sangh Parivar. (The biography of the Foundation's leading light and a member of the board of governors, Ram Madhav, described him as 'Member, National Executive, Rashtriya Swayamsewak Sangh (RSS)'. Another member of the board of governors was Shaurya Doval, who headed Zeus Caps, an investment firm, and National Security Advisor Ajit Doval's son. A clutch of BJP ideologues and legislators populated the board.)

Biren's upbeat pitch projected one of the weakest economies in the region, with appalling infrastructure, corruption, and an immense concentration of army and paramilitary to offset Naga, Meitei, Kuki and Zomi rebels. A state to which AFSPA is applied except for some areas of Imphal—but which is routinely 'sanitised' with Kashmir-like checks before the visit of 'VVIPs' and before every Republic Day and Independence Day. In Manipur, a place for me of frequent visits and which, like all of far-eastern India, occupies a special place in my heart and mind, checkpoints are legion and rough handling of citizens routine—especially along the highway that leads from Imphal to Myanmar.

In some ways it was reminiscent of the time India's Congress tourism minister, H.K.L. Bhagat, ensconced by anti-terrorist commandos wielding state-of-the-art assault weapons, assured a group of British tour operators in New Delhi in January 1986 that India was safe. I had attended the event; I was then few months into my first job in media, at the South Asia bureau of *The Asian Wall Street Journal*. Or the time Jammu & Kashmir's chief minster, Mufti Mohammad Sayeed, similarly ensconced, invited businesspersons and a few analysts over Christmas in 2003 to assure us all was well. I counted a dozen army checkpoints on the drive up to snow-covered Gulmarg from Srinagar, besides numerous heavily armed patrols and army outposts.

Biren had similar security accoutrements.

To be fair, from the perspective of agenda, the conference was an indicator worth highlighting. Manipur remained in several ways a live project for an eastward push for both national politics and national business, with a pitch of shared prosperity offered to the state's multi-ethnic, multi-religious people who harbour a very strong sense of ethnic identity and sense of nation—their individual nations. After all, in the same way Assam was electorally won by pressing the case for the demographic security of the majority Hindu population allied to development, the underpinning of logic in Manipur has since 2017 been a hammering away at potential benefits of the Act East Policy, with Manipur, as we have read earlier, as the overland bridgehead to Myanmar and beyond. Better infrastructure remained a wishful blueprint, and the subject of numerous promises made by several senior BJP officials—from the prime minister, party president and home minister downwards—during election stump speeches for general elections to both the Assembly and Parliament.

Both public and private sector organisations have eyed Manipur for its potential hydrocarbon reserves and other minerals. A few companies also conducted prospecting exercises but abandoned them in the face of extortion by rebel groups.

I had tracked a few cases across Manipur and Nagaland. It was a web of politics and business—overground and underground.

I-M had for some time controlled access to chromium deposits in Ukhrul, but a plum for the overground-underground also lay in hydrocarbons. In July 2014, I-M nixed an exploration project in Nagaland. The group's civilian arm, the Government of the People's Republic of Nagalim, through its ministry of mines and minerals wrote to an entity called Metropolitan Oil and Gas Pvt. Ltd, rejecting the firm's prospecting licence. The permit was issued by the government of Nagaland. Work stopped.

Metropolitan Oil was at the time in the eye of a controversy in Nagaland. Documents circulated by activists to a few policymakers, media persons and analysts (a set reached me) questioned antecedents and credibility of the company's promoters and accused them of making false claims of expertise and solvency. A little digging showed the company had no experience in that field—it was just an expedient corporate entity. Local media meanwhile speculated about the proximity of politicians of the Zeliang tribes to Metropolitan Oil. The Zeliangrong tribal homelands in Nagaland's southwest was a key exploration area, and in any case customary law about land ownership made the whole matter murkier.

It also went beyond constitutionally mandated rights in Nagaland that permits the state primacy in mineral rights. The right is sometimes conflated to ownership of land by a particular tribe—individually and in community trust—and, therefore, the extent of negotiable benefits that would accrue from mineral exploration. Indeed, this overlapping aspect had provided activists of the Lotha tribe, for instance, the leverage to prevent exploration and extraction of oil by Oil and Natural Gas Corp. Ltd in Wokha district of Nagaland.

I-M's censure was based on such allegations but of course there was that aspect which wouldn't go away: what on earth was I-M doing throwing around diktats in the first place? Because they could. And because it was hardly altruistic. The group's record with businesses in general and also the episode with a major New Delhi-based energy arm of a conglomerate, which pulled out of hydrocarbon exploration in Tamenglong, intimidated by the demand for a massive 'donation' to I-M, proved it. (A senior executive of the company and government insiders in both Nagaland and Manipur separately spoke to me of it.)

I-M wasn't the only one in the game, but it was the biggest player. The chaplee, or finance ministries of NSCN-K and other factions too attempted to extract 'taxes' and 'donations' from individuals—even politicians and bureaucrats—and businesses, of which more a little later. In July 2014, the time of the Metropolitan fracas, Nagaland-based newspapers carried an announcement by K, that an 'official with the following phone numbers has been appointed to oversee financial affairs pertaining to the Southern Zone—9862567272, 9436111777'.

The same as in Nagaland and elsewhere in the region, a 'productive' Manipur, therefore, was predicated on a 'safe', 'conflict-free' Manipur.

Optics wouldn't cut it.

And, meanwhile, there was the matter of the eastern gate and the people who lived near it, and were concerned about where the tides of the future would take them.

Day at Aimol Tampak vill. near Pallel, SE edge of Imphal Valley & the plains gateway to Moreh. 'Model' village and justifiably so: not a speck of trash, neat lanes, neat houses and yards, gardens irrespective of relatively wealthy or modest. Bins placed along lanes. The Aimol like many comms are in throes of that favourite activity and phrase of NGOs: 'capacity building!' Tagging along with folks from Imphal NGO, CORE, to see how this 'capacity building' for handling future interaction with throughput of people + trade along AH 1 is coming along.

Abel Lanu shows us around. The idea is for children to learn after school what they are not taught at school. Thrice a week, 3 to 4 pm. Mon: traditional customs & culture of Aimol tribe, Tue: briefing on govt schemes for employment & adult education, schools for Class 9 & 10 students under Manipur tribal affirmative action schemes Fri: health/ hygiene, sanitation, 'moral science'. All by 'local scholar' & NGO/govt health worker ... All at the small, neat Interactive Learning Centre, a hut with walls of packed mud, thatch and bamboo, skylights of latticed bamboo strips, tin roof. Deep into the village, very quiet, east of NH 102/ AH 1.

Notice on the wall outside of solar power under Jawaharlal Nehru National Solar Mission via a supplier in Kolkata: 'Happy News! Home Lighting! Light, capacity of 12 hours a day. Mobile chargeable. Solar plate chargeable. Electric power chargeable. Just take home and test it, Enjoy the benefit of Light, Overcome darkness, make happy family with plenty of light. Students for whole night study.' Environment-friendly & evidently aware of Manipur's appalling power situation!

Inside, clear area in the middle, racks of books ('Library Box'), books in Aimol-Roman, schoolbooks, mags, encyclopaedias, GK in English on one side, posters made by children of implements: dao (machete), bamboo fishing and carrying baskets, reed and dried-gourd 'kusem', like a bagpipe. Children learn to play drums, sing folksongs. Encouraged to wear traditional headdress, wraps, sarongs. See/ hear demo.

As guests, treated by children to the most charming and healthy snack: on a beautifully folded platter of banana leaf, a small slice of locally grown watermelon, pineapple, cucumber, a little pomegranate laid out like a flower. See hopeful message on learning centre wall as I leave: 'Coming together is a beginning. Keeping together is progress. Working together is success.'

Good for preserving for tribal/ethnic identity in a small village. Will it survive? Integrated or bypassed by future + open, regional/ international highway? Revisit in 5–10 years. Likely: status quo as conflict/ border situation still iffy, with chaotic politics in Manipur & Myanmar. But who can tell?

25. A 'Nation' and Its 'Workers': A Calling to Account

Spontaneous sympathy and empathy towards rebel groups have steadily leached away of its own accord, the result of a mix of rebel arrogance, overt corruption, and being out of step with a people who aim to realise their aspirations without overhangs and relics of the past.

Nagaland offers several such indicators.

Better-connected and better-empowered citizens of Nagaland have simply stopped paying tax to any rebel group irrespective of tribal connections. For example, I know of several such entrepreneurs and professionals in Kohima, Dimapur and elsewhere and they—from different Naga tribes and tribe clusters, Ao, Angami, Lotha, Rengma, Zeliangrong, Chakesang, to name a few—readily declare so in private conversations. Until peace and demobilisation and, more importantly, disarming of rebels arrive, most remain reluctant to declare so publicly.

It was a distinct shift—and it had become more pronounced since the signing of the Framework Agreement in August 2015. Much like fellow Nagas, none of them dismiss, disregard or in any way disrespect the Naga peoples' movements and various cycles of rebellions since the 1950s. A majority have family histories of immense suffering, including torture and death at the hands of Indian security forces given a free reign by obtuse, callous governments who saw no contradiction in variously arresting, beating, raping, torturing, shooting and burning alive Naga children, women and men to demonstrate the inclusive nature of India's Constitution and democracy, hurt others through generations of overkill in order to claim and reclaim Nagas as citizens of India. And they carry these histories—preserve these histories, oral and increasingly written, raw and eloquent—with immense sadness and great dignity even as they journey with their children to as peaceful and productive a future as possible through opportunity underwritten by both government policy and individual enterprise.

Rebel cause is to them noble. Rebel business is to them reprehensible.

Then there was ACAUT. I liked to joke that this collective is a cut above the rest, but the organisation became demonstrably more than an opportunity for a weak pun.

The oddly-named but resolute Against Corruption and Unabated Taxation, which took wing in May 2013, consistently displayed courage above and beyond normal in a state with immensely corrupt state machinery and with several active, heavily armed rebel groups that, as we have seen, imposed parallel administrations and an organised system of revenue collection literally at the barrel of a gun.

I first came across ACAUT as a round sticker on the back of a privately-owned minivan I was travelling in from Kohima to Imphal in 2014. That sign of defiance and desire for accountability by the owner of the van, a mid-level government employee moonlighting for extra income over a weekend, transformed Nagaland in ways unimaginable not too long ago.

ACAUT quickly faced rebel ire. It held an anti-taxation rally against rebels on 31 October, 2013, in Dimapur. Several thousand attended the rally that received extensive pre- and -post event coverage in local media. The rally drew an outraged, even stunned response from I-M in a media statement five days later. I-M claimed that 'with the full backing of the Indian armed forces' some among Dimapur's Naga Council had created a Frankenstein's monster 'out of a rat'. The rebel group even invoked 'our Lord Jesus Christ', a frequent rebel trope in this deeply Christian region, to warn away ACAUT.

Bluster and outsourced humility didn't work. Even accounting for the possibility that ACAUT was encouraged by India's security apparatus, it had clearly touched a raw spot. Protests intensified.

In August 2014, ACAUT riled another faction, NSCN (Khole-Kitovi), or KK, that as we have read was formed after breaking away from the Khaplang or K faction. ACAUT's secretary Solomon Awomi was released after being held for several days in that group's headquarter at

Kehoi Camp, east of Dimapur. KK was compelled to give in as ACAUT and its support base of citizens, far too numerous to be wished away as stooges of the Indian security establishment and its canny intelligence annexe, stood firm.

It also stood by its remarkable 'Open Letter' of April that year to senior government officials to stop giving nearly a quarter of the pay of government employees to rebel groups—which added to the provocation that contributed to the kidnapping of its secretary by KK and threats in general by all groups.

As ACAUT spread its wings it also questioned the government on numerous malpractices, and exposed numerous 'scams', from recruitment to various government posts and misutilisation and siphoning of central government funds, to bogus voter rolls. In early 2015, ACAUT, openly urged by letters in Nagaland's media and other forums, extended its key result area to corruption. In August that year, through media and its Facebook page ACAUT published a list of what it termed 'backdoor appointments' between 2005 and 2015 in Nagaland's Health and Family Welfare Department and followed it up with an exposé of examination fiddles in the State Council of Educational Research and Training. The same year, it published photos of injuries inflicted by a rebel group on a Naga person for refusing to pay tax.

The group became a force, whether the rebels, Nagaland's government, or those not from Nagaland who dip freely into that state's well of wealth liked it or not. In a conversation with me, a critic of ACAUT, a senior official of BJP, dismissed it as being run 'by a bunch of disgruntled Congressmen'—in Nagaland this can be interpreted as being pro-India but it was rich coming from a legislator of the BJP, which had seamlessly appropriated nationalistic agenda and would soon adopt every ill of governance and arrogance in the entire Northeast from a much-diminished Congress. In any case, the politician's slur was a discourtesy. ACAUT had indeed touched a public nerve and placed rebel groups and the government alike on the defensive. Even its critics agreed.

In 2016, several months after the Framework Agreement had been signed, the organisation again earned I-M's wrath when it raised matters of extortion. What is this 'nuisance called ACAUT'? I-M shot back, adding with a sentimental twist that didn't carry well: 'No Naga organisation or party had ever mobilised Naga public support to reject the "absolute sovereign rights" of the nationalist government to impose and collect taxation.'

Clearly, some citizens disagreed with this arrogance—and this dissonance was at the root of a collective, comprising community leaders, students, even a handful of former bureaucrats, to form ACAUT. It began to ask hard questions—questions that hadn't been effectively asked for decades in Nagaland's lamentable complicity of silence.

On 18 June 2017, the watchdog again took on I-M, and quite spectacularly. A few days earlier, the rebel group was widely regarded as having stopped road-widening work on a stretch of the Dimapur-Kohima national highway, demanding a cut of the fee. Local media reported or-else threats to burn down machinery of the project's contractors.

ACAUT waded in. It released to media a 'three-day ultimatum' for I-M to come clean. Had the group 'demanded tax'? If so, was it the group's policy to 'stop all developmental works' in Nagaland till a settlement was arrived at with the Indian government? If not, would the group's leadership contemplate 'action' against 'rogue' cadres and expose such rogue elements 'with their complete identity and designations, so that people of Nagaland know who these anti-people are'?

Alongside, the watchdog urged contractors to deliver quality work, and asked the state government to not sit idle as Nagaland was yet again held literally to ransom.

I-M's response was splutteringly livid, but ACAUT simply didn't give a damn.

Another stunning incident, just before Christmas in 2013, had significantly begun to tip the scales away from whatever moral high ground that rebels retained among Naga citizens. The disquieting episode had nothing to do with ACAUT and everything to do with impunity that carrying weapons can bring even to the most righteous rebel. And so, it came to I-M, which mixes Christianity and power more effectively, brazenly, than any other Naga rebel faction.

On 21 December, cadres of I-M from one of the faction's designated ceasefire camps in Mukalimi, in Zunheboto district stopped a taxi, roughed up several passengers and allegedly molested two missionaries. These two ladies were of the Sümi, or Sema, tribe. It was an outrage anywhere; more so in the tribe's homeland.

Locals grew restive in the belligerent absence of an apology. Matters escalated within days. Several hundred civilians, many armed with machetes—dao—and guns converged on the Mukalimi camp. Sporadic firefights ensued. A civilian was killed and a few were injured.

On 30 December, the camp was overrun. Cadres—'national workers'—fled. For I-M it was a staggering loss of face.

I-M initially attempted damage control by accusing its arch foes—besides paramilitaries and the Indian Army, the Khaplang faction—of conspiring to incite civilians and even firing from their shoulders. It didn't work.

'Have the Naga people lost (their) faith in the present Naga National Workers?' prompted a 30 December administrator's post on the popular We The Nagas group on Facebook, a social media lightning rod like another Facebook group, The Naga Blog. The responses cut across tribal lines and ranged from insults to lessons. 'They r more interested in making money then fighting for the Nagas, Only few R dre who z fighting for Real,' declared one post. Another suggested: '… Feel the pulse of the common men … If the National Workers try to continue to play the role of Pigs and Dogs in George Orwell's ANIMAL FARM, someday they shall be overrun by the considered inferior animals.'

Alongside such reflection by the younger generation with which many in the ageing leadership of the rebel groups appeared to be out of touch, major tribal and influential church institutions in Nagaland united in condemnation of the attack in particular and behaviour of rebel groups in general.

Eventually the leadership of I-M held a court martial at Hebron. A sergeant of the outfit, of the Tangkhul Naga tribe, was awarded capital punishment by a tribunal. Two others charged with the 21 December assault were cashiered.

After decades of conflict for what was—and, to a great extent, is—overwhelmingly seen as a just cause, the warriors, the so-called national workers, now themselves seemed like a lost cause.

By the time of its confrontation with I-M in June 2017 over the group's alleged demand for a cut from roadworks, ACAUT had marked a substantial presence across several social network forums. At that time, it recorded a robust presence on Facebook, with just shy of 51,000 members, not shabby for a state with a population of less than three million with several hundred thousand who live in relatively remote areas with poor digital connectivity. Numerous students and professionals from Nagaland who live in the larger cities and university towns of India, and expatriates sprinkled largely across Western Europe and North America had signed on, and frequently cheered ACAUT. It had become a symbol for accountability in a region where there was—is—so little of it, and a model to follow for outraged citizens anywhere. (Indeed, it surprised me as to why such a movement was absent in Manipur, which has always remained vocal—even violent—about transgressions and insults by the government of India and its agencies, but remarkably somnolent about demanding accountability of its myriad rebel groups and a state government machinery and public servants repeatedly exposed as corrupt and inept.)

The citizens' movement continued to escalate matters. In mid-August of 2017 ACAUT filed a public interest litigation or PIL at the Kohima Bench of Gauhati High Court, in the hope of cleaning up bogus voters in electoral rolls—after proving through a Right to Information disclosure that in as many as 23 constituencies there were several polling stations where registered voters exceeded the population of entire villages.

On 25 August, at an impressive rally in Dimapur, it unveiled its 'Battle to Reclaim Nagaland.' These include a suggestion to involve all

Naga rebel groups in the ongoing peace talks between Government of India and I-M.

There was a call for the state government to do away with posts of advisors and parliamentary secretaries to government, a way to reward members of legislative assembly who are not directly given ministerial berths. Nagaland has a 60-member assembly. The chief minister at the time, T.R. Zeliang, had at the end of July appointed nine advisors with cabinet rank, 26 parliamentary secretaries, besides the dozen cabinet ministers, including Zeliang. This bloated bandwagon rewarded an astounding 47 out of 60 legislators, including BJP legislators who were at the time members of the National People's Front-led coalition government. ACAUT also demanded appointment of a Lokayukta, or ombudsman for Nagaland; termination of all 'backdoor appointments'; better roads using the funds already with government; and central government investigation into siphoning of funds.

All of this nearly eclipsed another stunning event in early August 2017. Before raising its latest battle-cry against corruption and sloth in government, ACAUT's leadership had met I-M's leadership. It actually drew out the outfit's general secretary Muivah, who warned the watchdog that it had become 'political and serious', and that his organisation was the 'right government to collect tax from the Nagas'. He even threatened ACAUT that it could of its own volition face 'unwanted incidents' in future.

Muivah didn't gain face with this, coming off exactly as ACAUT had been projecting: a petty, bloody-minded mob boss of a petty, bloody-minded organisation.

On the other hand, ACAUT gained immense face. It capped four years of demanding accountability on behalf of citizens sickened by conflict, corruption and stasis. When I next checked the group's Facebook membership, in September that year, it had gained nearly 40,000 members in less than four months.

At one level ACAUT and its well-wishers appeared to be out on a limb, considering that cleansing Nagaland could take several decades, and a blowback could easily arrive from influential groups of citizens fattened on entitlements and corruption, let alone rebels who still carried weapons—and some would continue to carry weapons even if a formal peace and reconciliation took wing. But it was as easy to believe—and hope—that the watchdog's growing public appeal showed that the time for blowback against status quo may well and truly have arrived in Nagaland.

26. Relative Values of Attrition: K After I But Before M

Notes: 06/06/2017

Stall in so-called Naga peace deal, but now it has a fresh twist.

From what I have been able to gather from those, Naga and not, who have intimate knowledge about the negotiations, is that onus of the stall is now being placed on the wider leadership of I-M.

This is for a curious—and obvious—reason: reluctance to part with the perks of ceasefire. There is too much influence, revenue and lifestyle to lose. The stress here is on the wider leadership—not the wider cadre, several thousand strong, who would find integration with society an easier prospect.

All rebel factions have fattened since ceasefire, especially the leadership. Because while there's no 'battle' except battle for turf/ revenue, it's now the business of rebellion. Relatives of some rebel leaders have business and real estate investments in Northeast India and even the National Capital Region (I've walked past a plush shop or two!) and across Southeast Asia.

Now comes the tricky part of reconciliation and integration, and this goes beyond the government's efforts that have revolved around grinding down the opposition, inducing implosions in factions, and so on.

Muivah is old and ailing. Swu, his colleague in I-M, died in 2016. Phungthing Shimrang, I-M's army chief is a contender for 'next-gen' leadership, along with another power centre, V.S. Atem, a widely respected former army chief. There could be more factions after Muivah.

While such potential implosion would appear to be perfect for the government, there is now the aspect of stall from the rebel side.

'Mainstreaming' rebels by absorbing some cadres into policing functions, or paramilitary functions such as an industrial security force, or special police battalion in the manner, say, that Nepal achieved with its former Maoist rebels—some of whom were also inducted into the army—would be relatively

easier. It would prove more difficult with rebel leadership.

While Muivah could be offered a largely ceremonial post of elder statesman in the Naga construct, most of his senior colleagues have little or no base in the political establishment of Nagaland. Even if some were to be accommodated in newly-designed political and administrative structures in Manipur—owing to their tribal ties there—it would be a limp version of the heft they now exhibit in great influence and implicit threat provided by the weight of weaponry. Then there's robust revenue. In a twisted way it would amount to giving up the good life, become shadows of their current avatars.

Update from sources: Doval and Ravi continue to be intensely irritated.

My take: Doval/establishment opted for showy optics. So if there's now a stall, tough. Both sides have to think differently. I-M have made their play quite plain. Waiting for GoI to show its hand.

And within days, the peace project had another dimension added to it—likely a matter of some glee in the governments of India and Myanmar, glee among some in I-M and consternation among various rebel groups that depended on a rebel leader's sanctuary and logistics for their continued existence. On 9 June 2017, S.S. Khaplang died.

Besides the Taga region of northwest Myanmar where it was headquartered, the Khaplang or K faction was also influential in northern and eastern Nagaland and several Naga-majority districts of Arunachal Pradesh. Besides speculation about his successors, Khaplang's death threw open speculation of the faction's active patronage of numerous rebel groups operating in Northeast India, especially Manipur and parts of Assam; and the possibility of the faction returning to ceasefire with the government of India nearly two-and-a-half years after Khaplang spectacularly, violently jettisoned a ceasefire in place since 2001.

As far as a successor went, from what I had been able to gather in the immediate aftermath was this. One likelihood would be to elevate a Naga of the Konyak tribe to a ceremonial elder statesman position of chairman—to balance the large number of Konyak Nagas who formed part of the faction's estimated 1,000-plus band, and retain a Hemi

Naga—from among Khaplang's people, and hosts to the faction's headquarters in Taga—as chief operating officer. Leading the run for chairman appeared to be Khango Konyak, who was earlier elevated to vice-chairman by Khaplang. But he could be undercut by other Konyak colleagues trusted with the rebel army's supervisory functions and Hemi Nagas who wouldn't stand control of an 'outsider'. As ever, Naga ethnic politics would continue to confound—and, in this case, possibly cause chaos and splinters.

Focus also turned to Niki Sumi, formally the military advisor of the faction and Khaplang's trusted arm for carrying out operations. Sumi was of the Sümi, or Sema tribe of Nagaland. General Niki, as he liked to be called, was present during Khaplang's funeral rites on 12 June, saluting his former boss. The flamboyant Sumi was dressed in a trademark beret, worn at a rakish angle. A thick gold chain around his neck flashed as he saluted, the top buttons of the tunic of his combat fatigues undone. It wasn't clear yet with whom Sumi would throw in his lot, which power-centre he would gauge as his greatest insurance—or even, if he would bide his time to make his play for leadership, lead a faction as a warlord, or create leverage to return to India.

All this would become clearer over the following weeks, including a possibility the faction might implode into one or more breakaways. There was a school of thought that suggested this would not happen: as the relatively small numerical strength of such splintered groups and internecine skirmishing would be counter-productive to the ceasefire in Myanmar the Khaplang faction has enjoyed since 2012, including autonomy to administer its territory.

Certainly, this last option would benefit the several rebel groups that made up Corcom, and ULFA-I and Bodo splinters to whom Khaplang provided refuge and patronage, and banded them together with his faction to form the grandly titled United National Liberation Front of Western South East Asia, in April 2015. Much like Sumi, they would be gauging post-Khaplang winds.

Such hopeful unity wouldn't, however, please the government of India, which would benefit from the breakup of the alliance, as it would then force the belligerent conglomerate to a place of relative insecurity.

(Although conversely, India could also benefit somewhat from the post-Khaplang faction staying together as it could then reach the new leadership for ceasefire, reverting to the 2001 status quo; all the while working to detach other Northeast Indian rebels from the post-Khaplang K. As the saying went: whatever works.)

About the only group that was likely to be entirely upset with the post-Khaplang faction's possible unity were their arch-enemies, I-M—which had since played hardball to ensure they remained the primary voice for a post-conflict Naga future. It was an increasingly contentious position.

Much was being made of Muivah's condolence message for Khaplang. 'Based on the declaration made by our former chairman late Isak Chishi Swu on forgiveness and reconciliation,' Muivah announced through I-M's communication channels, 'we have forgiven S.S. Khaplang of all the political mistakes and crimes he had committed, however grave they might be, in the precious name of our Lord and Saviour Jesus Christ.'

If this churlish message amounted to forgiveness, it was an entirely new definition. While Swu was relatively softer on Khaplang and—reportedly—repeatedly encouraged reconciliation, Muivah and several of his colleagues had not been able forgive Khaplang for bloodily breaking away from the undivided NSCN in 1988 and killing numerous cadres in the process of so doing. Indeed, Muivah and Swu and other leaders of I-M had very close calls at that time. During an attack in 1989 by K cadres, a wounded Muivah, and his wife, barely managed to escape with their lives from a hideout in the borderlands of northwest Myanmar.

Muivah's message appeared to be more like payback to the one Khaplang delivered after Swu's death the previous year, which was open in its respect for Swu and thinly veiled in its derision for Muivah. Khaplang had said Swu was a 'true Shepherd amid the wolves, a Gospel among the revolutionaries and a revolutionary among the Gospels' and 'the only ray of hope' among 'the contemporary Naga world torn with deception, suspicion and disunity'.

Now with Khaplang's passing, I-M remained the crucial link in the process of power-playing to peace. In that respect the news wasn't pacific.

Rebel insiders also pointed to I-M stockpiling weapons and ammunition in the Somra tract in north-western Sagaing Division of Myanmar, directly across from Ukhrul district of Manipur, both homes to the Tangkhul tribe. Should hostilities resume with India it would form a refuge for the mostly Tangkhul senior leadership of I-M and loyal cadres, give some among the senior leadership breathing room before heading to other, less stressed points of the compass in Asia and Europe. And that would naturally throw all equations that involved the government of two countries, four Indian states, and at least a dozen rebel groups, into greater flux.

There was only one certainty in all the uncertainty in this Pandemonium Box which had opened and wouldn't now be shut— couldn't be shut for some years. The government of India would now turn the screws. Hard. It was just a matter of some months, if not weeks.

As ever, the only play in the government's playbook would be derived from the near-mythical Chanakya's ancient and extensive library. The divide and rule that Prime Minister Modi accused his predecessors of practicing would be back. Indeed, it had never been away.

Notes: 12/09/2017

A small skirmish that could impact bigger events.

Today I-M killed five allies of K. Three of those killed in the skirmish are reportedly from PLA—a part of the CorCom umbrella. Significantly, two others are believed to be Tangkhul tribesmen of Manipur Naga People's Front—backed by another CorCom member, UNLF.

As significantly, the incident took place in Kamjong district, which was in December 2016 carved out of Ukhrul district in a bid by the state government to rein in I-M/UNC/Nagas. (Manipur now has a BJP-led government, but they are hardly likely to reverse this strategic move by the man/party they replaced: Ibobi/ Congress.)

This, like MNPF, leveraged disquiet that some Naga tribes and even some Tangkhul clans, such as in the 'southern' Tangkhul region of Kamjong have towards domineering I-M, and by extension the 'northern' Tangkhul.

If this seems confounding, that's because it is, but buried in this event is a series of implications that will impact peace talks with I-M.

One is of course the mission-creep that has led I-M's enemies among Manipur's rebel groups to mount an attack on an area the former considers its turf. Kamjong is way too close to Ukhrul for I-M to take such an incursion without immediate and violent reprisal. Besides loss of face, not doing so would encourage more such incursions—blessed by K and CorCom.

The second factor: I-M can't be seen to be weak, not when it could affect its negotiating position with the Indian government.

India's security establishment could sit back and let a bunch of rival rebel groups kill each other off, but the downside—and there are several—could be a surge in bloodletting that in a worst case could jump from rebel warfare to killing of non-combatants on the basis of ethnicity and geography. This could set off a firestorm in ethnically fragile Manipur. It's happened before.

More such skirmishing could even lead, in another worst-case, to I-M hardliners pulling out of peace talks to go underground, for all practical purposes become warlords and regroup to create, if possible, another burst of rebellion. Because—and here, assume the peace deal goes through—what security will former I-M leaders and some heavy-handed cadres enjoy in Manipur—or Tangkhul homelands, for that matter—without the clout of weapons they now have, with which they earn both fear and favour to fund the group and themselves? Without this clout or acceptable reconciliation, their enemies will descend on them, try to exact revenge. Payback time.

There is a push to hammer out the peace deal by December 2017, well in time to make a big impact on Nagaland's Assembly elections due by March 2018. The biggest gainer in that case will likely be BJP, which expects to increase its seat count from the current four in the 60-member assembly. Or, at least, be better placed with an alliance to influence government formation in a Zeliang-Rio face-off. But Rio is a comeback man. Could turn tables completely. BJP will in any case back the winning horse, the more generous horse.

Political flux. War during peace. Blood chess. Horse trading. Pick any adjective. The usual.

Game on.

Representatives of six rebel groups and factions journeyed to New Delhi on 26 September 2017, to meet R.N. Ravi, the government's interlocutor for the Naga peace process. The meeting took place a day later. I-M wasn't a part of this.

Thus far, these six groups had been united in little but their opposition to government of India-led talks aimed at formally bringing peace with I-M—which had thus far excluded all other factions and even the Naga people at every level.

I-M had since crowed about being true representatives of Naga aspirations and its 'national workers' being the true inheritors of a rebellion that began in the 1950s. But it was clear to some observers that an agreement between one rebel group of a few thousand cannot speak on behalf of nearly three million people. As I had repeatedly stressed in my writing and talks since 3 August 2015, the day of the signing of the Framework Agreement between the government of India and I-M, not when there exist other groups and factions also in ceasefire. Not when the second largest Naga rebel outfit, K, was still around. Not when there exists an elected government of Nagaland and elected officials in Naga homelands in contiguous areas of Manipur, Arunachal Pradesh and Assam.

The arrival in New Delhi of representatives of the six groups, of which two were factions of NSCN and the remaining four vestiges of the original Naga National Council, signalled a new phase in this convoluted game of peace-chess. It was both official recognition that deals had to be cut with all groups to effect true peace—as well as an encircling manoeuvre against I-M.

There were other persistent pressures.

Ravi, for his part, continued to express his irritation over I-M's stolid stand which, as we have discussed, appeared to be driven by the group's reluctance to give up the perks of ceasefire—which permitted recruiting, arming, training of cadres and, the government's turning its expediently blind eye to a parallel administration and great wealth for some leaders—and reduced influence in a civilian afterlife.

ACAUT, the increasingly popular group pushing accountability for rebels and the local government alike, continued to express its disappointment with all rebel groups, with I-M at the apex. On 27 September, the day of the meeting with the six groups, the Forum for Naga Reconciliation (FNR), the church and civil society led initiative that has since 2008 worked to bring all rebel groups to a common platform of peace and unity—with admittedly patchy results—issued a strong statement:

'Currently Naga institutions are collapsing even as more fragmentations are occurring and there is a growing economic inequality even as the common person is burdened by taxation. Furthermore, there is alarming increase of social ills and the nexus between Naga National Groups and vested individuals and parties are strengthening the culture of impunity.'

'All these have added to a situation of confusion and anxiety among the Naga public, as well as the Naga National Groups,' FNR's statement added. 'There is now a lack of clarity and purpose on the direction Nagas are heading towards. The loss of accountability, transparency, trust and respect for each other has made the process murky.'

When Ravi arrived in Dimapur a little shy of a month later, on 23 October, he was accorded a grand civic reception at Dimapur airport by several tribal organisations.

He later drove to Chümoukedima to the south of Dimapur. At the Rhododendron Hall of the Police Officers' Mess he held an hours-long discussion with the 'working committee' of the grouping that had come to be called NNPGs—Naga National Political Groups. There he described the Naga peace process as 'inclusive'—a matter widely reported by local and national media. And he fully established that the prime minister's office is now running the show—with visibly invisible hands, if you will, of the office of the national security advisor. 'Ravi said the first major change in the peace talks was to bring out the Naga peace process from Home Ministry and put it under the Prime Minister's Office (PMO) since the issue was magnanimous in nature with so many issues and ministries involved which was too tedious a task for a single ministry to handle,' *Nagaland Post* reported in a front-page news agency-based article the following day. 'Besides, he added, things move faster in the PMO which was one important aspect for the issue as it needed to be resolved at the earliest.'

Symbolically, it was the first time that Ravi had held a 'peace' meeting in Nagaland. And, along with the reiteration of the power shift from the home ministry to the PMO, another unmistakable message informally went out to I-M with this flanking manoeuvre: I-M might be the biggest game in town, but it certainly wasn't the only game in town.

27. Game On ++

25/10/2017: Game on ++

On the day of Ravi meeting with NNPGs, 24/10, NIA issues media release saying it has seized nearly INR 28 lakh in Dimapur from Shelly, wife of NSCN-K general Niki Sumi, the mastermind of several attacks against Indian troops.

29/10/2017: NIA announces it has proof of four Nagaland govt officials channeling INR 20-25 crore of extorted funds to K from 2012-16. Names them with designation: Vilepral Aja, addn. director with dept of agriculture; Kekhriesatuo Tep, superintendent of dept of fisheries; K. Hutoi Sema, exec engineer of dept of irrigation and flood control; Purakhu Angami, former director with dept of tourism. Claims arrests were done on 13/10/2017. NIA claims handwriting matches those in slips and registers maintained by the four.

Classic power play with signals going out loud and clear. For several years now combat in this sphere has generally kept away from families of combatants on every side. The government publicly tagging the wife of a senior K officer is a back-off gambit. It's also seen as a move to create fissure in K by exposing Niki's vulnerability, though whether that will actually happen as part of a continuing play to get K or a substantial section of it back to the talks-table, including Niki, is as yet wide open.

The game extends to signalling China, which India's security apparatus has long believed is the puppeteer behind K and its allies.

08/11/2017: Myanmar quid pro quo for India's Rakhine/ Rohingya deadpanning.

Mizzima, the respected Myanmar news organization, quoted Maj. Gen. Phone Myat saying, 'We will not allow our soil to be used against India.' The general was speaking at the India-Myanmar regional border committee meeting in Imphal on 1–3 November. Significant, as Gen. Myat is commander of

Tatmadaw's North West Command that oversees the Sagaing Division where K and all other 'Northeast' rebels base/ operate.

18-member delegation from Myanmar for the meeting hosted by 'Spear Corps'—3 Corps—based in Rangapahar, not far from I-M's Camp Hebron. Indian delegation headed by Lt Gen. Anil Chauhan, GOC of 3 Corps. Gen. Chauhan was a brigadier and CO of 59 Mountain Brigade in Senapati when I interviewed him for 'Highway 39'. He took over 3 Corp in January 2017.

News report adds: 'Myanmar army has not been able to concentrate on these anti-Indian rebels because of their diverse counter insurgency commitments, but apparently India's strong support to Myanmar on the Rakhine issue is now been reciprocated by the Tatmadaw.'

'Rakhine issue' is like blood money: Rohingya lives for quid pro quo against rebels.

But all this, Ravi/ Doval's arm-twisting, this play with Myanmar, will it bring it all to boil, bring K in one form or another to the table alongside efforts by Naga citizens' groups to reach out for peace and reconciliation? In any case, watch for more 'Chanakya' cracks in the mirror.

How the wheels churn. Gen. Phungthing is out as longvibu—army chief—of I-M. Anthony Ningkhan Shimray is in. On 28 November 2017, I-M's leadership announced Shimray's appointment; he would formally assume his command in a week.

It signalled more than an appointment. My conversations with some insiders pointed to seismic shifts and churn within the rebel structure. And that immediately took the development beyond the dynamic of I-M, because significant moves within a rebel construct were basically prevailing winds through which the peace process would navigate. At least for government negotiators this looked like another move in an extended endgame.

By this time, the jostling within I-M, of which I had been writing about in media for some time, had become abundantly visible. The government of India wasn't the only entity positioning for a post-

Muivah future. With Swu gone and Muivah infirm but resolutely holding on, internal and conflict resolution dynamics had for some time involved the Tier 2 creamy layer of leadership. In that jostling two former longvibu, V.S. Atem, and his successor, Phungthing, were in play.

For some years they had been placed alongside Muivah's nephew Grinder, seen by many as the leader's heir apparent and the keeper of his and I-M's golden keys. Grinder's less visible role was as a conduit, as we have read, between I-M and the government. This was an action for which he earned the privilege of live-and-let-live from the government. Grinder flourished as a businessman in the National Capital Region with few queries as to corpus and capital infusion—not entirely unknown among a class of Nagas.

But Grinder had died in April 2016. The mantle of heir-apparent now passed to other relatives, primarily, another of Muivah's nephews, Apam—who was said to hold the golden keys, even if he was not generally accepted as Muivah's heir.

For now, Anthony Shimray sat better with this succession than Phungthing. Perhaps Shimray's public declaration after his release from prison the previous year, of being a lifelong follower, had helped.

Meanwhile, my sources in Nagaland informed me that Phungthing, despite official paeans, was being privately painted as a fall guy for having become somewhat ineffectual while pursuing the good life. That was true irony. Naga rebel leadership, indeed, much of rebel leadership in far-eastern India hasn't exactly been known for frugality after initial years of ideologically-led battle. Essentially, the word was: Phungthing had become something of a liability, too headstrong for even a group of headstrong people.

It was a fall from grace, from being the person who kept the pace of recruitment, arming, and generally being the enforcer of a parallel administration in Naga homelands. Like Atem, Phungthing was a hardened man, but more recently given—as I was told by I-M insiders—with carrying on some policies and operations which were not always approved of by what is known as the collective leadership.

For all his talk of Christ and His glory Shimray too was a hardened man, with intimate knowledge of the group's weapons pipeline and an equally intimate experience of handling operations of the overseas or Allee command, in Bangladesh for instance. Word from the inside was that, Shimray was expected to carry through Phungthing's unfinished agenda of preparing ground in Naga homelands and in sanctuaries in Myanmar in case the peace deal didn't work out to I-M's advantage; even as he remained a bulwark right here at home to ensure it did.

But the peace deal was not only about a deal with the government of India, or the various states of India that had Naga homelands. It was also about deals within the rebel structure.

And I-M was far from a family show.

20/02/2018

Nagaland Assembly elections on 27/02. Results: 3 March. Means nothing for the peace process, so far has it drifted from that dynamic. Nagaland's politics is very much its own bubble. I-M + NNPGs (+ K?—a matter of time) increasingly their own bubble.

Heads-up: 3rd anniversary of Framework Agreement with I-M coming up on 03/08.

But who cares about peace when there's politics to play? The expected has happened. The BJP has cut a deal with Rio over Zeliang. Negotiated an alliance with newly-formed Nationalist Democratic Progressive Party (NDPP), Rio's new outfit that will target Zeliang's NPF, a destination, like the BJP, for disgruntled legislators as well as those enchanted by various perquisites. It clearly works: Rio already elected unopposed from North Angami II constituency in the region of Kohima! Declared elected unopposed on 13/02 by chief electoral officer as Rio's NPF opponent—only opponent, his relative Chupfuo Angami—withdrew his candidature.

That's clout. Not sure what the BJP will do except play second fiddle to Rio in Nagaland. In its manifesto BJP has promised free travel to the Promised Land to the elderly. Congress, the same. A big deal in this 'Christian' state, but more purposeful Promised Land ought to be post-conflict, reconciliated, rehabilitated Nagaland. Glory be.

Seat sharing by the NDPP-BJP combine in a 40:20 split in the 60-seat assembly is designed to derail incumbent NPF—Rio's former home and BJP ally with which both Rio and BJP broke off in early 2018 when it became clear NPF strongman and incumbent CM Zeliang, was unwilling to share power with them.

Meanwhile, agitprop against BJP at high pitch. The influential Nagaland Baptist Church Council openly advocated that voters choose their future with 'Christian and Naga identity and to have allegiance towards one's faith, rather than by going with any communal party'. The Morung Express, a leading paper, published a somewhat bizarre appeal by The Ao Theological Association to 'not to let the slogan of development and good governance persuade the Naga Christians to deny the Cross of Jesus Christ'. Evidently, too much burden for the cross to bear a lotus.

But that's okay. Rio is Christian. So are all of Nagaland's incumbent and wannabe legislators. In Nagaland, BJP legislator or aspirant or key leader is Christian—even as the Sangh minority-bashes elsewhere. Politik, Politik über alles!

28. Interlude: Sharmila Has Moved On, But Malaise de Manipur?

On 14 May 2018, Irom Sharmila, Manipur's former protest icon cradled her new-born twin daughters, Nix Shakhi and Autumn Tara alongside her 'non-resident Indian' husband, Desmond Coutinho. The photograph taken in a Bengaluru hospital was far from the image she was known by for more than a decade: nasal drip that force-fed her, unkempt hair, tortured expression, fierce eyes.

If ever there was a living martyr, Sharmila was one. Her act of not putting food to her mouth for 16 years from 2000 was as potent as any protest against AFSPA that still covers most of Manipur.

Indeed, the Supreme Court has since 2017 repeatedly ordered the CBI to expedite investigations and filing of charge sheets in nearly a hundred alleged instances of extra judicial killings between 1980 and 2011. It was based on a public interest litigation.

The petition predated the ending of Sharmila's fast in August 2016. She had nothing to do with the petition. And that was precisely the incongruity about the chatter that attended Sharmila, including a decision to contest Manipur's assembly elections in March 2017. Because Sharmila never claimed to be greater than her cause. She was a symbol and she knew it. There had always been a wider world going about its business of justice and accountability as Sharmila went about it in her own way.

Her ending the fast was met with incredulity. Why had she given up when most of Manipur remained under AFSPA? She had taken to fasting with the promise she would persist until AFSPA was discontinued in Manipur.

I received requests from activists in Manipur to inquire into Coutinho's antecedents in Ireland and the UK. Why did he write letters to Sharmila in jail proclaiming his love for her? Why would she respond? Was Coutinho a trap by the government of India to distract Sharmila from her purpose?

The second decision, to fight elections, was well-meant but utterly naïve.

She stood against Congress Party's incumbent chief minister and strongman Ibobi Singh. Sharmila polled less than 100 votes.

Her electoral decimation surprised few besides herself and a core of diehard supporters. Sharmila was only a symbol of the political cleansing that many Manipuris hoped would galvanise voters, shake up the system, affect incumbents and warn those like an insistent BJP. As it happened, the BJP formed a coalition government with Biren Singh as chief minister.

A disheartened Sharmila soon left Manipur for Kodaikanal, to be with Coutinho. Meanwhile, questions continued about her remarkable decision to end her fast.

Few factored in the reality of a person who abused writers—including me—for simply writing about Sharmila, let alone hordes of well-meaning activists: of a man besotted with Sharmila. Or that she, whom few believed had a romantic bone in her body although her very act of defiance was born of extreme romanticism, could yearn for companionship in her years of solitude.

Now Sharmila had moved on. But causes endure in Manipur. As did AFSPA along with administrative arrogance. And the mantle of that unlovely legacy had passed seamlessly from the Congress to the BJP.

There was now no poster-girl to highlight it all. But there were still posers, posters and protests. They called for a cure to Malaise de Manipur.

Book Three

SMOKE & MIRRORS

29. Meanwhile, in Myanmar …

17/08/2018: NSCN-K update

At a peace conference with several armed groups representing ethnic nationalities that have a tense relationship with Myanmar's government, a government official said NSCN-K would remain outside the purview of the so-called Nationwide Ceasefire Agreement (NCA). That agreement was signed by eight such armed groups in 2015, during the term of the former military junta. Khaplang was alive then, and K kept away from the umbrella agreement. Post-Khaplang K has also kept away from an ongoing series of peace talks with ethnic groups pushed by the present Aung San Suu Kyi-led National League for Democracy government, which continues to use NCA as a pivot.

In part, K stayed away from NCA because it had signed a separate ceasefire with the junta as far back as 2012. But more so, because it has held on to its ostensible demand for sovereignty, an independent Naga homeland in Myanmar as well as across the border in India.

That's now untenable. In both Myanmar and India, what was seen in 2012 as a way to buy peace—more precisely, absence of conflict—with K, is now seen as a hurdle to conclusive peace.

This will put pressure on K and its current chief, Khango Konyak, who succeeded Khaplang. Unlike Khaplang, who was a Hemi Naga from Myanmar, Konyak is from the eponymous tribe largely located in Nagaland's northern Mon district.

Upshot: Expect both India and Myanmar to squeeze K via military ops and choking funds pipeline. In any case, India's game falls flat if K, united or splintered, doesn't come on board for a peace deal.

Meanwhile, guess who's playing saviour in Manipur? Biren Singh. On 16/07/2018 he announced in New Delhi that he and his colleagues would quit government if their 'consent' was not taken for the so-called Naga Accord, or if Manipur's territorial integrity was in any way threatened. What set him *off to briefly acquire an ethno-moralistic spine was clearly the renewed buzz for autonomy—even a watered-down version—in Manipur's Naga homelands.*

18/09/2018

This is a fast fracture even for post-Khaplang K!

Khango Konyak 'impeached' by a group led by Yung Aung, nephew of S.S. Khaplang—who died in June 2017. Effectively, Naga leadership of 'Indian' provenance ousted in this ethno-territorial coup by Nagas who have homelands in present-day Myanmar.

Inevitable question: Will Khango and officers and cadres loyal to him enter ceasefire negotiations with government of India and join in with NNPGs? Or would they ally with I-M because it's more powerful?

For Option One, there would need to be a cooling period for the rebels who just weeks ago were among India's bitterest foes.

Option Two: Conceivable that Khango would find room in I-M in the same way his tribesman Khole Konyak, who was expelled by the much smaller 'Unification' faction of NSCN in 2016, joined I-M. (In NSCN's bewildering unmusical chairs, Khole was earlier expelled from his post as army chief of NSCN-K in 2011 when Khaplang was the faction's supremo!) Theoretically, I-M would rather incorporate a potential foe than be undercut by yet another faction in peace negotiations, where I-M projects itself as the premier voice of Naga identity and aspiration.

In practice though, Option Two would be impractical for Khango. Unlike Khole, who is now a figurehead in I-M, Khango could bring with him large numbers of cadres, and end up being another semi-warlord with competing influence. Being an element of NNPG as chief of a faction would offer more leverage than jostling with I-M heavies as an underdog.

The same could apply to Niki Sumi, the mastermind of several attacks against India's army and paramilitaries since K broke away from a ceasefire in early 2015. In any case, Niki is badly leveraged, with the government interdicting his wife Shelly and choking a revenue pipeline that would buy him clout and legitimacy within K.

Either way, both Khango and Niki could join the queue for post-conflict integration, possibly gain sinecures as part of a final settlement. It's all a matter of realpolitik negotiation. The word was that K cadres and leaders who came away from Myanmar to India were likely to be relocated in what were called 'designated camps', like the current practice for all rebel groups in India which were in ceasefire or talks with government.

Meanwhile, I-M continues to mark territory. In June 2018 I-M issued notices to the effect that 'financial administration of Southern Nagaland'—a euphemism for Naga areas in Manipur was transferred from one kilonser or minister, to another. In mid-September, just days earlier, I-M's ministry for home affairs banned 'night clubs, gambling and any anti-social activities' around Dimapur.

Fat chance. For I-M those moral-majority days are done.

30. Interlude: A Short Christmas in Meghalaya

Over late-December 2018 and early 2019, one of Meghalaya's most open dirty secrets for decades—besides a deeply internalised racism and corruption—burst into media glare. 'Rat-hole' mining for coal. It yet again brought attention to its seething underbelly, usually hidden from public glare by the region's mesmerising natural beauty, an immensely empowering tradition of matrilineal society among many of its peoples and, in the giddy imagination of a 'national' media and a giddier internet, the celebration of Shillong, the capital, as India's capital of music—to some, the capital of rock.

Fifteen workers were trapped by the flooding of such a rat-hole coal mine on 13 December. A month later, into the new year, people were still waiting for word although to find any of them alive now would be miraculous. Meanwhile two more workers died at another coal mine on 6 January in the East Jaintia Hills which, along with areas in the Khasi Hills and Garo Hills, forms the state's coal belt. The coal feeds the state and parts of the region. I've also seen this coal dumped in vast mounds across the border from Dawki, in Bangladesh's Sylhet district, during a drive up from the teeming city that gives that district its name.

Many more miners would continue to die in this unregulated and exploitative industry that sustained livelihoods of the poor and sustains several of Meghalaya's millionaires—and the state's economy and politics. It was based on the poor entering slim openings in coal seams, and burrowing around for coal.

At one level, rathole mining lacked respect for the lives of the poor, as an excellent, outraged editorial in *Mint* pointed out on 8

January, one among several slapdowns and criticism in media about monumental callousness. *The Sentinel of Assam* wrote on 3 January of how Meghalaya's government came to a standstill for eleven days since 22 December over Christmas and New Year holidays.

Scroll.in reported the chaos that set in after a week of relatively tepid response: 'On December 24, the NDRF [National Disaster Response Force] turned off the two pumps at their disposal. "As everyone in the government celebrated Christmas, we stared at the shafts and at each other waiting for better pumps to arrive," said an NDRF official, who asked not to be identified.'

Additional chief Secretary P.W. Ingty, the official in charge of the mission, went on leave.

It was all very 'chill'. (Just how chill can it get? In July 2020 @MeghalayaPolice would tweet this: *'Weed like to inform the general public that, of all the Essential items permitted in the times of #Corona, Marijuana ain't one of them. Sorry for our bluntness, but that's just how we roll! Kudos to @RibhoiPolice for intercepting a Truck carrying 500 KGs of Marijuana.'*)

It has all remained perfectly chill with coal in particular and environmental and community issues in general. Like status quo ante chill.

In 2014, the National Green Tribunal (NGT) banned coal mining in Meghalaya. Despite an attempt in 2012 to introduce regulations through a mineral policy, it literally remained full of holes and, in practice, winks. NGT permitted the transportation of coal already mined in this organised-unorganised sector for which the state and several miners realised benefits. Meanwhile, the labour behind it remained a grey area of migrants from poorer districts of Assam, and from Bangladesh—from adjacent districts like Sylhet, Sunamganj, Netrokona and Mymensingh, among others.

In August 2018 an NGT bench upheld the 2014 order—which began with a public interest litigation filed by an Assam-based non-government organisation representing the Dimasa people, who complained of water bodies being poisoned on account of mining in upstream Meghalaya. The 2018 order also noted that illegal mining had continued in this extra-legal industry—this last definition is my phrasing.

In November 2018, two intrepid environmental and human rights activists from Meghalaya, Agnes Kharshiing and Anita Sangma, went to the East Jaintia Hills to investigate stories they heard of transportation of not just old stock, but new: meaning, illegal mining. They were attacked. Kharshiing was hospitalised for over a month. While some accused were rounded up, a key accused, Nidamon Chullet, a leader of the ruling National People's Party of Chief Minister Conrad Sangma, surrendered to police on 25 December. It is likely Chullet gave himself up to take the lesser rap of an attack on activists than run the risk of also finding himself rapped for the mining deaths.

For his part, chief minister Sangma, whose party is an ally of the BJP, soft-pedalled the issue. In a videotaped statement on 4 January he said that he didn't see the mining ban 'as a solution right now'.

Then he tied himself up in knots: 'Environment and safety of miners must be given a priority. The regulation must be as such that the economic condition should not be affected.' He also maintained it was difficult for 'the agencies and the police to keep a watch'. Conrad, an alum of Wharton and London's Imperial College, conceded little.

He also mirrored the protection offered rathole mining by his predecessor Mukul Sangma of the Congress, the mover of the 2012 mining legislation. Mukul's mining and geology minister, B.M.

Lanong, had maintained that the policy would permit regulation of mining. And he had said this: 'There will be war between the stakeholders, miners and the government if we do away with the rat-hole mining practices.'

At the time of the Christmas disaster, the mines and geology portfolios were the responsibility of Conrad.

31. A 'Re-imagining' in 2019: More Church, State, Chanakya

'Today, we need to re-imagine the Indo-Naga Peace Process with one that encompasses and complements the political exchanges in Delhi between the Government of India and the Naga political groups by raising Naga peoples' voices through inclusive participation and transparency,' the Forum for Naga Reconciliation (FNR) announced on 14 January.

The statement was a slap to Naga armed groups in general and, by extension, to the politics of peace process itself, which FNR correctly termed 'one dimensional'. FNR mentioned that it spoke up as it had a 'mandate from the Naga people'.

That was wishy-washy, because basically, FNR wished again to be counted. It had been ignored by all major factions of Naga rebels since 2012 or so, and thereafter kept at an arm's length by the Indian government. That apart, the call to 're-imagine' the process was spot on. Because the process, announced with fanfare by prime minister Narendra Modi in August 2015, was badly stuck three-and-a-half years later.

Despite public and political outreach since by government negotiator R.N. Ravi—the word 'interlocutor' appeared to be well past the expiry date—the process remained hazy. As we read, a much-delayed 'masterstroke' formally brought in six smaller rebel groups onto a parallel negotiating platform in September 2017, signalling to I-M they weren't the only game in town. A major split later the following year in the still at-war K faction, had also fortuitously brought an expelled leader, Khango Konyak, to talk peace and reconciliation. Khango, as expected, became a part of 'NNPGs'.

Splinters would assist the government's negotiating strength. But the peace deal has always remained not so much about honouring Naga history and struggles, which would in any case be addressed with suitable words and totems. And, in any case, the rights of people in most Naga homelands in India were in one way or another protected as to land ownership and customary laws.

It was always about what would happen to leaders of the various armed groups.

To recap: Cadres would be absorbed into society, police and various paramilitaries with relative ease. But would top leaders—especially in I-M—used to vast power and vast funds backed by weaponry, be content with being accommodated in autonomous regional councils across Manipur and Arunachal Pradesh, special rights in Assam, and a bicameral legislature in Nagaland? The idea of a bicameral legislature for Nagaland, which was being seriously considered, was a device to accommodate more 'rebel' legislators. Alongside, there was also discussion about a 'delimitation' exercise aimed at increasing the number of seats in Assemblies of Nagaland, Manipur, Arunachal and Assam. Ergo, greater political representation alongside greater political assimilation.

That was the word of accommodations being discussed in the negotiations with both I-M and the grouping of other factions. Such news filtered in from sources—both Naga and not, government and rebel—who were the eyes and ears of various negotiators.

For its part, I-M continued to act as if outwardly, nothing had changed. On 11 February, it appointed a new chairman and vice-chairman.

The new chairman, Qhehezu Tuccu, and vice-chairman, Tongmeth Wangnao Konyak, wouldn't anyhow be calling the shots. Muivah and his coterie retained that influence. Muivah sealed both appointments, and was present at Camp Hebron for the swearing in.

As we have seen, the last of Swu's gestures was urging the signing of the Framework Agreement. The ailing Swu died in June 2016. Khole Konyak was appointed vice-chairman in May 2016, just weeks before

Swu's passing the same year. But Khole had died of a stroke in December 2018. Both these deaths had created a ceremonial, even ceremonially ethnic, vacuum that needed to be filled.

That Tuccu was like Swu of the Sema or Sümi tribe, and Tongmeth Wangnao, like Khole of the Konyak tribe, was more form than function. (But form was as crucial as function in Naga society.)

Tuccu, popularly known as 'Q Tuccu' was not a towering personality like Swu, who was respected across the factions of NSCN, and across Naga homelands. But Tuccu was a homegrown I-M man. He was also from the commercially lucrative Dimapur region—a melting pot of Naga society that was carved away from Assam for giving Nagaland access to the plains and a train station and was now home to most Naga tribes—but the gesture would resonate in the Sema homelands. It would also signal to Semas in other factions that they continued to be welcome in a group that had large numbers, cadres and leaders—including Muivah and chief of I-M's army, Anthony Shimray—from the Tangkhul tribe.

Tongmeth Wangnao had broken with K to join I-M several years earlier. In that sense his appointment—a Konyak to replace a Konyak—provided a notional balance to that largest Naga tribe.

In the tortuously complicated world of Naga politics in general and Naga rebel politics in particular, all this was significant.

Besides, I-M continued to behave like it was the only group that still mattered, one that still had structure and ambition. Because K, or whatever remained of K, once I-M's most formidable opponent apart from the government of India, was in complete shambles.

The headquarters in Taga of Khaplang's nephew Yung Aung, who took control of K in August 2018, was over-run earlier in February 2019 by Myanmar's army.

Cadres and leaders of the 'anti-talks' factions of ULFA and the National Democratic Front of Bodoland, and the six Manipur groups under the umbrella of CorCom, who had all found sanctuary in K camps, were on the run.

(Indeed, the general of Tatmadaw, Myanmar's army, had evidently done such a good job of decimating the stronghold of the Yung Aung faction of K and other 'collaterals', that in end-May the high command would send this general to tackle the situation in the Rakhine state, where the rebels of Arakan Army were giving Myanmar's army a tough fight. This was the same general, Phone Myat, who attended the military conference in Imphal the previous November and announced that he wouldn't permit Myanmar's 'soil' to be used against India. The news service *irrawaddy.com* would write of it on 28 May, quoting a spokesperson of the Arakan Army: 'U Khine Thukha said he had heard that in February 2019, Maj-Gen. Phone Myat had successfully taken control of the headquarters of the National Socialist Council of Nagaland-Khaplang (NSCN-K), in the Naga Self-Administered Zone of Sagaing Region, without a single gunshot fired. "It seems they [the Myanmar military] want to test him for the Rakhine command," U Khine Thukha said.')

While all this could be termed as a victory for India's security establishment, it also helped I-M. It was now unquestionably the most influential Naga rebel group, both within the peace process and outside.

The announcement on 10 March of elections to India's parliament over April and May 2019 pretty much ensured the so-called Naga framework agreement for peace remains without solution for some time. I-M had earned breathing room by default: as soon as dates for the elections were announced the so-called Model Code of Conduct monitored by the Election Commission of India kicked in, and no major policy decisions or sops could now be implemented until after a new government took office. In any case, India's Machiavellian—or Chanakyan, if you will—political and peace-making machinery would now be entirely concentrated on the conduct of these general elections. The BJP-led central government and the BJP-Sangh superstructure wouldn't, like any incumbent government or political superstructure, leave anything to chance to ensure a second consecutive term to run India.

Besides, the blunt truth was that, there was nothing imminent about a peace deal in any case. My assessment was—and remained—based on unresolved issues. Recent interactions Ravi had with a joint legislators' forum and other interactions of the legislators had only served to reconfirm several of the points I had repeatedly been making since 2015.

A breakfast meeting on 27 February 2019 at the state banquet hall in Kohima, attended by Ravi and several members of the joint forum that included chief minister Neiphiu Rio, the deputy chief minister, speaker, and leader of the opposition T.R. Zeliang, had its share of blunt talk. Ravi provided an update of what he described as a 'situation of peace without a solution'—a catchy description—to the legislators, primarily from Rio's ruling NDPP, its coalition ally BJP and the opposition NPF.

It was interesting to receive news of what transpired. Ravi's first point was that, there can be no solution with just NSCN (I-M)—even though the Framework Agreement was signed with much flash and bang, with the prime minister, home minister and national security advisor present, only with that group; and, even though inclusion seemed to be the obvious route, a need for political grandstanding left out several factions. In fact, I continued to maintain that NSCN's Khaplang faction, for instance, broke ceasefire with government in early January 2015 as much on account of the internal dynamics of the Myanmar-based group as much as indications that the government would imminently strike a deal with its arch rivals. The governments of Nagaland, Manipur, Arunachal Pradesh and Assam were also left out of the loop. Naga citizenry were largely excluded.

To recap: That disastrous fallout was partially recouped when the government finally reached out to six other and smaller, rebel groups in 2017 and formally brought them onto a parallel negotiating platform in September that year. A major split in NSCN-K in 2018 had since brought an expelled leader, Khango Konyak, to talk peace and reconciliation. And, we have just read about the havoc wreaked on Yung Aung by Myanmar's army, which would lead to more rebel-arrivals to India.

The live debrief, if you will, that I received about Ravi's meeting with Nagaland legislators led me to dig deeper, which triggered another debrief—to use a cloak-and-dagger term.

At one time in the negotiations—so I was given to understand—I-M negotiators reportedly insisted they would 'deal' with other factions. Ravi reportedly pointed out that, a military option against other factions wasn't the answer for I-M to maintain its primacy in peace negotiations. Such a course, Ravi is believed to have conveyed to I-M, could be balanced by the government also using the military option. But that would be utterly regressive and lead to a downward spiral, and possibly reignite a conflict that nobody really wants anymore. There was a veiled threat held out here to all factions: A military option could as easily be used against the other factions, those a part of the 'NNPG' collective, as against I-M.

At this aggressive powwow Ravi pushed hard for 'civil society' to be brought on board. The inclusionary messaging to I-M was on the lines of: If you ignore the voice of the people, you may have an agreement, but Nagas will not have peace.

Another message that went out was—and this was an eminently logical one: as I-M could not be realistically expected to bring those factions on board after two decades of faction-fights, besides territorial and ego disputes with them, the government was the only entity that could reach out to every relevant group of rebels and citizens and work every possible track—direct, so-called Track 2, or Track Infinity, for that matter—of diplomacy and negotiation. Ravi pitched himself as the key talking-head for negotiations with all groups. As the government's interlocutor for all groups, he could weave in various strands.

And, such a push would soon emerge, of nudging I-M to share the peace and reconciliation platform with the others.

I was given to understand there was an in-principle agreement but no firm date for such a meeting between long-time antagonists.

26/03/2019

Ravi is at it, election-announcement or not! He returned on 25/03/2019 for a two-day visit to Dimapur during which he met key politicians, and I-M leaders. The meetings were held in Chümoukedima—'Chümu' to familiars.

There remains the necessary but vexed matter to get all Naga rebel groups on the same page, and to sign on it—especially as issues and rhetoric are by and large common, and the issues are mostly resolved.

The biggest question, of course, remains why a final peace deal to transform ceasefire to formal peace isn't being signed. During my discussions with some insiders earlier this month during a visit to Nagaland and in subsequent interactions elsewhere in NE and Delhi, a few things were made clear.

Foremost of these: the government will not negotiate on the matter of sovereignty and independence. That old stance has evolved to the more nuanced position of 'shared sovereignty'. And it remains there.

As a state since 1963 Nagaland has its own constitutionally mandated freedoms including an independent legislature, freedom from taxation— Nagaland's budget is massively supported by central funds: India's taxpayers [For 2021–2022 about 93% would be derived from central sources in one form or another]—and the freedom to practice customary laws including the ownership of land and resources. In several ways, the Naga people have moved on, within Nagaland and other contiguous Naga homelands in Manipur, Arunachal Pradesh and Assam.

Now the question of integrating Naga homelands remains ticklish. There is agreement that integration of the Naga people is a 'legitimate aspiration' but it cannot be brought about by decree or deal. The Naga political issue can't be resolved in isolation. There are neighbouring states, all with resolute positions on territoriality, in the equation. So, any integration will need to be approached as a natural democratic process, otherwise, as an insider put it, 'it will be disastrous'. There's a buy-in within I-M, because they see reality, but there's always the matter of 'face'.

Other aspects include I-M's insistence on a separate constitution and flag. As far as the constitution is concerned, for the government it's unworkable: such acquiescence could also open a Pandora's box in more restive parts of India. The BJP is determined to nix Article 370 in Jammu and Kashmir and subsume Kashmiri identity to 'Bharat'. It won't let a constitution-and-flag exercise take place in a less politically volatile and, in its scheme of expediency, less explosive geography—and have it blow back at them in J&K! In the BJP's scheme, J&K has infinitely more bang for the electoral/ political buck that Nagaland. I-M for them is just an organisation—a large rebel group, but just another rebel group.

As far as the Naga flag is concerned, talk is that it could be hoisted in the premises of a pan-Naga cultural body, an agency that, for all practical purposes, would be a symbol of emotional integration over the incendiary aspect of territorial integration.

These remains sticking points with I-M. Resolving these matters would serve the rebels' face-saving need for an 'honourable' solution.

The real sticking points lie elsewhere. One is of course to get all groups on board a common platform. At the very least, a common meeting as a first step.

Such a meeting would signal agreement on the future. Relatively young cadres could be rehabilitated in police or paramilitary units or provided funds and training for employment or entrepreneurship. Many leaders could 'retire' or become leading lights in several autonomous councils in various Naga homelands, practical for a society that largely lives and votes along tribal lines. Their place in future Naga politics would depend on their own acumen and application.

And what if key leaders disagree?

If they press for status quo, they run the risk of Naga society rejecting them. If rebel elements break away and seek refuge across the border, they will find former sanctuaries in Bangladesh and Myanmar have evaporated.

Fighting is no longer a viable option unless the situation in Bangladesh and Myanmar—or far-eastern India—change radically.

32. Who Killed Tirong Aboh?

21/05/2019: Arunachal Pradesh legislator Tirong Aboh, his son, and nine of his entourage including security personnel killed in an ambush. The incumbent MLA from National People's Party (NPP)—national president = Meghalaya CM Conrad Sangma = NDA ally—was attacked near Khonsa, HQ of Tirap district which he represents. NSCN hotspot for years, first K then after I-M push. Now I-M > K. Men in combat fatigues sprayed Aboh's motorcade with bullets. Elections to AP Assembly held on 11 April, alongside elections to the state's two parliamentary constituencies. Aboh's killing = Pandora's Box, Pandemonium Box, pick any name.

In the expected media clamour that followed, Indian media, in the country's far east as well as the 'Mainland', unequivocally blamed 'suspected' NSCN (I-M) rebels. Aboh wasn't known to have a pleasant relationship with I-M.

In contrast, media in Nagaland was careful to not immediately tag any particular faction of NSCN, papering over the incident with a general reference to 'NSCN'. Besides K and I-M, at the time of the killings there was also the Reformation or R faction, and the NK or Neopao Konyak-Kitovi Zhimomi faction—the latter two also in peace talks with the government. Moreover, as we have read, internal dissent led to the K faction's post-Khaplang chief Khango Konyak being removed in a coup in 2018, and his place claimed by Yung Aung, a nephew of S.S. Khaplang, the original K in the faction's name—and who died in 2017. After his ouster Khango Konyak moved to India with loyal cadres and sued for peace as the faction NSCN (K-Khango).

So, which alphabets in this alphabet soup killed Tirong Aboh?

K, the Yung Aung faction of K, that is, quickly denied any hand in the matter, although in the immediate aftermath of the hit there was slim speculation that it could be a fightback. After all K had over April and May been hammered in Myanmar by the Tatmadaw, and its bases in that country's northwest, not far from the border with India, overrun. The feedback from K sources matched the general perception in security and rebel circles: K believed it to be a squeeze induced by India's diplomatic overture to bring this at-war—India's security establishment prefers 'belligerent'—faction to heel, if not back to ceasefire and, in quick order, peace talks.

While such dynamics explained that faction's animosity towards India, it didn't explain the hit on Aboh. To turn the lens on I-M was easy on account of the faction's record of animosity with Aboh and its proven reputation for throwing its weight around in Naga homelands. This, as a quick reminder, includes Nagaland, contiguous Naga homelands in Manipur and Assam and the districts of Tirap and Changlang in Arunachal—which wrap around the eastern extremity of Assam. Both districts have Myanmar to their east and Assam to their west. Tirap has to its south the Nagaland district of Mon.

As in other regions, I-M has fought pitched battles with other Naga rebel groups to retain territory and influence in Tirap and Changlang. We have also discussed I-M-sanctioned assassinations, in Manipur, for instance—if not sanctioned by the group's individual or collective leadership, then certainly by a rogue general or two, answering to themselves and invoking proximity to Muivah for legitimacy, immunity and impunity. Besides, I-M's blessings were still counted in some areas as being a factor for a candidate's electoral chances as party affiliation and popular mandate. An I-M hit on Aboh would therefore be in character, especially with a record of bad blood between them.

An audio clip of a conversation between NPP worker Nokniyam Nokbi and a person who claimed to be speaking on behalf of I-M also buttressed that suspicion. In the clip, the 'suspected NSCN (IM) leader', as the news portal *eastmojo.com* described him, can be heard speaking in Nagamese, accusing and threatening Nokbi, from Laho village in Arunachal's Tirap district about going about his political business without sanction. The person tells Nokbi that the youngsters in several villages are marked: '… apni khan sob suspect list-e ahibole ase …' A threat is held out about a meeting evidently planned for the following day: it cannot go head. And if it did, they all would find out who would die and who would live: '… kun moribo, kun bachibo itu toh janibo apni-khan na …' The clip had been floating around on select social media circles since the call was reportedly made in March 2019, and some days later, on 29 March NPP worker Jaley Anna was beaten to death by 'suspected NSCN (IM) militants'.

These events played against the backdrop of intense political powerplays typical in Arunachal—as brutal as any practiced by rebels. A comfortably elected Congress government in 2014 had, by 2016, been transformed into a government led by the BJP. In those elections the Congress had won an absolute majority with 42 seats in the 60-seat Assembly; the BJP had won 11. Aboh, the assassinated MLA, had won as a candidate of the People's Party of Arunachal and at the time of his assassination had switched to BJP-ally NPP—a fledgling party which hadn't even contested the 2014 elections; but in 2019, it gained Aboh, its first-ever genuine, as it were, local legislator actually elected on its platform.

Adding a ghoulish touch to Arunachal's riotous politics, Aboh won posthumously. Results to Arunachal's 2019 Assembly elections were declared on 24 May, three days after his death. As it turned out, Aboh defeated Phawang Lowang, the BJP candidate in Khonsa West constituency. With Aboh's death, a by-election was merely one of the emerging byplays.

NPP president Conrad Sangma, chief minister of Meghalaya and an ally of the BJP in Arunachal, had since Aboh's assassination burned the phone lines to New Delhi. From all accounts, Sangma asked hard questions about Aboh's death. And his words had heft, as NPP was also an ally of the BJP-led National Democratic Alliance, and was in a crucial coalition with a BJP-led government in Manipur.

As the murkiness surrounding the incident grew, two things became clear. One was the crying need to repair Arunachal's utterly broken and brazen politics. And, of course, to force the pace of the Naga peace process, and de-weaponise trigger-happy rebels.

That impulse appeared to be even more urgent by June 2019.

All through that month, and especially in the third week of June, India's security establishment was abuzz after media carried news of co-ordinated operations by armies of India and Myanmar to flush out rebels of the Yung Aung faction of NSCN-K, or—to add to the bewildering count of factional initials—NSCN-K (YA) and several Manipuri and Assamese groups, among others. Yung Aung had evidently carried on the practice of his ousted predecessor, Khango, and his dead uncle, Khaplang, to provide sanctuary and logistics support to such groups, including the 'Independent' faction of ULFA, a Bodo splinter group, and the half-dozen Manipuri rebel groups under the umbrella of CorCom.

Called Operation Sunshine-2, the move against this rebel conglomerate was conducted by Myanmar's army from mid-May to the second week of June. It followed Sunshine-1, a brief burst of operations at the end of February.

There were some reports of joint operations with India, but this was quickly denied by Myanmar's army. On 18 June, an official of the bizarrely-named Tatmadaw True News Information Team clarified that there were no joint operations. Brigadier-General Zaw Min Tun told *The Irrawaddy* that matters extended only to coordinated action by the armies of Myanmar and India in their respective territories.

That appeared to be true. I'd received a few indications of the activity on the Indian side of the border. On 29 May, for instance, the ranking bureaucrat of Tobu sub-division in Mon district in Nagaland released an advisory on account of the 'prevailing law and order situation'. So that they wouldn't be mistaken as hostile by Indian forces, the advisory requested citizens:

'1) Not to venture out for hunting 2) Not to carry any kind of weapons 3) Avoid movement during the night 4) Not to wear camouflage clothes 5) To carry proper identity Card like the Aadhar, Epic [Electoral Photo ID Card], job card, etc …'

On the same day, I received news from sources in Nagaland of several cadres of NSCN-K's Yung Aung faction being in the 'general vicinity' of Monyakshu and Changlangshu villages—located along a ridge a few kilometres west of the border with Myanmar—and Yei, a couple of ridges away to the northwest. This specific information accompanied another nugget: Indian forces had employed unmanned aerial vehicles or UAVs to detect these rebels.

All this chimed with the Myanmar general's pointed denial of cross-border action of the sort attributed to the Indian army at least thrice since 2015. These were reported as having taken place across the border from Ukhrul district in Manipur—and which took much diplomatic outreach by India to smoothen.

At any rate, the denial hardly dampened the extended endgame India's security apparatus have been playing for some years—a mix of military action backed by understanding between India and Myanmar to flush out remaining rebels from north-eastern India who have camps in north-western Myanmar.

It was also another nudge to Niki Sumi, the flamboyant mastermind of several attacks against Indian troops and a warlord with the disarrayed YA faction—for the time, as I wrote in a commentary for an Indian publication—flagging the imminent likelihood of his departure from Myanmar. Besides pressure in Myanmar, General Niki could hardly ignore the steady pressure mounted on K in general and him in particular for several years—in particular after K walked out of the ceasefire agreement and began to attack Indian military and paramilitary personnel even as Indian forces clamp down on their operations, logistics, financial and otherwise, in India; and attempt to do so with K's bases and its headquarters in Myanmar. It was as if the signing of the Framework Agreement with I-M in August 2015 firmed up a distinction for the government: K were the bad guys and I-M the good bad-guys, as it were. What the Khaplang faction and others new to the talks table were penalised for, similar I-M practices continued unabated for the time being.

For instance, the National Investigation Agency had as early as August 2016 filed a chargesheet against a few K functionaries, including

Isak Sumi, whom it describes as the 'self-styled finance administrator of NSCN (K)'. Assam Rifles personnel 'apprehended' Isak in Dimapur that July, accusing him of 'extortion of money from the civil population in Kohima and Dimapur'.

Besides incriminating documents, he was also accused of possessing ammunition and drugs.

Pressure was upped after the death of Khaplang in June 2017. Besides combat operations, including, as we have read, a September 2017 hit by the army on some K strongholds across the border in Myanmar, in October 2017 a team from NIA seized nearly three million rupees in Dimapur from Shelly, the wife of Niki Sumi. NIA then announced it had proof of four Nagaland government officials passing between ₹20–25 crore (₹200–250 million) of extorted funds to NSCN-K from 2012 to 2016.

After shutting down this pipeline, on 25 March 2018 NIA arrested three senior government officials from Dimapur, Nagaland's commercial hub.

They were accused of diverting government funds to, among others, NSCN-K, the Reformation or R faction, and the Federal Government of Nagaland (FGN), the once grandiose but greatly diminished group that derives lineage from the father of the Naga rebel movement, Zapu Phizo. But there was precious little about diverting funds, government and otherwise, from businesses and the public, applied to I-M. Was it because they were in peace talks with the government of India? But so were NSCN-R and FGN. Was it a signal that nobody was untouchable, including I-M?

Even as undoubtedly many among Nagaland's extortion-weary, corruption-numbed citizens perhaps celebrated along with India's security mandarins, the disturbing fact was that the other cases and instances, involving other factions, which continued to have the run of revenue from similar sources as those NIA and other agencies had thus far interdicted and accused, continued uninterrupted.

'Thus far' was the operative phrase. Because, for Indian government agencies there appeared to be no climbdown whatsoever from the preparedness that kicked in during Sunshine-2. It was a microcosm of what would continue to play out in an attempt to roll up rebel networks—and also offer a warning to those in ceasefire, particularly those like I-M who were as yet far from defanged.

And I-M did lose some more teeth.

On 15 July 2019, even as the dust-ups in Myanmar and India with K and associated rebels groups hadn't quite settled, pressure was upped against I-M in Arunachal. Security forces arrested an I-M major in the tri-junction area of Assam, Nagaland and Arunachal Pradesh and recovered weapons and ammunition from his vehicle and, later, his home. This followed the buzz in security circles that Anok Wangsa, the major, acted on the orders of the I-M boss in the region, Major-General Absalom Tangkhul, to hit Aboh.

The I-M major Wangsa's arrest has opened up Pandora's Box a little wider to exhibit the sort of warlordism that lay at the core of politics in northeast India in general and Arunachal Pradesh, Nagaland, Manipur and Assam in particular. Delinking militancy-on-hire from expedient politics in Arunachal, Assam, Manipur and Nagaland and elsewhere in the region would surely be as crucial for peace as actually disarming rebels.

33. The Kashmir Conundrum and Other Stories

20/07/2019: R.N. Ravi appointed governor of Nagaland.

Leaves interesting possibilities on the chessboard that is the process of peace, formal reconciliation and rehabilitation of various Naga rebel groups, especially as Ravi remains the interlocutor for peace talks with I-M, the NNPGs who're now six + Khango breakaway from K. Unlikely Ravi will continue to hold the office of chair of Joint Intelligence Committee and deputy NSA to which he was appointed in 2018. Already, joint office of interlocutor + Nagaland governor is plenty.

Ravi the governor will remain Ravi the face of the Naga peace process. Thought: Ravi has probably brought the process as far as he can as an across-the-table negotiator. Another person appointed in his place can tick off the meeting-minutes as policy grinds to completion. As governor, Ravi will be well-placed for a statesman-like role unlike the BJP apparatchik he replaces (unless Ravi becomes active BJP/Sangh apparatchik himself—distinct possibility if he wants to retain more power than he's ever enjoyed. Track Ravi's appearances/participation in events of Sangh affiliates.)

Plus side: Ravi knows all sides. He's met nearly every major interest group across four states that form the loci of the Naga peace process. He also knows most of the moves.

As ever, the space to watch has become way more interesting (more akin, though, to the Chinese curse-as-compliment: 'May you live in interesting times').

05/08/2019: Okay, so Ravi's job just got harder—or easier, depending on the perspective. Huge development. Govt has abrogated Article 370 in J&K, plus, Article 35A stands revoked.

06/08/2019: Even bigger development. J&K to be split. State reorganisation bill passed in Lok Sabha. There goes I-M demand for flag, Constitution, the works. In BJP/Sangh construct, J&K is way more leverage in national politics than Naga settlement. The dice are thrown. From now it's a transparent game of pure attrition and take-it-or-leave-it for I-M and other groups.

In my media writing I had flagged the possibility of splitting of Jammu & Kashmir into union territories under the direct control of the central government in September 2016, after protests flared up after the killing of Kashmiri rebel Burhan Wani. And again, in June 2018, right after BJP withdrew support to the Mehbooba Mufti-led Peoples Democratic Party (PDP). Indeed, a little over a year after that break, with seismic developments over abrogating provisions of Article 370 of the Constitution, which provided special status to Jammu & Kashmir, and by that default also revoking Article 35A of the Constitution, which safeguarded special residency status and employment for citizens of that state, it seemed incredible that BJP had actually entered into an alliance with PDP after a fractured mandate in assembly elections in Jammu & Kashmir in 2014.

The BJP had overturned nearly seven decades of history literally overnight with an order signed by India's rubber-stamp president, and without consulting the citizens of J&K—a matter conveniently provided with the legislature in suspension and the application of Governor's Rule managed directly by the home ministry and the prime minister's office. There was little doubt that it wouldn't also follow through with its election promise of several years, including, most recently, parliamentary elections won in May 2019, of restoring what it saw as political balance in J&K by breaking it up into J&K & L—Ladakh—as the BJP-led government was pushing through in Parliament.

This, and the matter of abrogating constitutional provisions by fiat, not parliamentary debate, fed directly into the dynamics of Naga peace negotiations and rebellion's geography across four Indian states.

In particular, the matter of accommodating Naga interests in Manipur without upsetting non-Naga communities. And, in a cascading effect, ensuring the peace of mind of citizens and the volatile ethnic and political equations across all far-eastern states in which the BJP either had majoritarian religious cachet or wished to buy out popular support, as it were, with the promise of development and protection of livelihoods—exactly what it had taken away in much of J&K. All, of course, accompanied by the business it had excelled in since 2014, and what might be an elegantly put companion to that telling Chinese phrase, 'fragrant grease': the trading of horses. It also accompanied the viral information process used spectacularly by what had come to be known as the BJP-Sangh's 'IT Cell'. (I had heard an acolyte of BJP-RSS stalwart Ram Madhav proudly describe this anything-goes process at a literary gathering in Thiruvananthapuram, as 'total politics'.)

The plan for splitting J&K had been around for several decades. I first encountered it in the run-up to the J&K Assembly elections of 2002. The Jammu State Morcha, a coalition of small parties and independent candidates, was guided by the RSS to demand statehood for the Jammu region. Indresh Kumar, a senior RSS official I met in Jammu at the time, as a part of election coverage for *India Today*, the newsmagazine where I worked at the time, claimed it was an eminently logical move.

This logic had also existed beyond right-wing silos for several years. Essentially, it advocated trifurcation of Jammu and Kashmir. Kashmir Valley would be its own entity. So too Jammu. And Ladakh would be an Union Territory directly administered by New Delhi. It was driven by an attempt to strategically isolate Kashmir from Jammu and Ladakh. With the BJP's move in parliament, this has now translated into bifurcation—of Jammu & Kashmir as one Union Territory, the other being Ladakh.

Unsurprisingly, it received great support for the party from non-BJP nationalists and BJP hardliners and the 'Sangh' alike. The concern in the Northeast—far-eastern—India was immediately that, if the BJP-led central government could do this with J&K, one of the most watched geopolitical hotspots in the world, what would prevent it from strong-arming anything in the east, and, following the template since the 1950s of managing the disorder?

There were valid reasons for the concern. As far as special Constitutional provisions were concerned, the dissolution of Articles 370 and 35A, with the government arguing that these held back the social and economic development of the state, in effect also undermined special provisions it had defended in the east. Article 370 had accorded Jammu & Kashmir autonomy in several aspects, including law and order. Article 35A of the Constitution, among various provisions, granted special rights to permanent residents of Jammu & Kashmir for: '(i) employment under the State Government; (ii) acquisition of immovable property in the State; (iii) settlement in the State …' and, of course, defining who were such residents and who could, therefore, vote locally.

A point to consider here was that, development or the lack of it in J&K wasn't an exclusive aspect of Constitutional provisions, but also of intense militancy in particular since 1989, whether precipitated and fuelled by Pakistan; exacerbated by corruption and sloth within the local political and administrative structure; or sustained by awkward policies and people skills of successive governments of India.

The other point: The junked Article 35A most closely resembled special provisions for several far-eastern states.

For instance, Article 371A of India's Constitution permits for Nagaland primacy of 'religious or social practices of the Nagas', 'Naga customary law and procedure', 'administration of civil and criminal justice involving decisions according to Naga customary law', and 'ownership and transfer of land and its resources', besides preference for government jobs and other matters.

Article 371C provides for administrative safeguards for the tribal 'Hill Areas' of Manipur; while local laws safeguard the land and customary rights of tribal folk. Article 371G applicable to Mizoram is nearly a mirror of the provisions for Nagaland. Arunachal Pradesh restricts access, residency and ownership of property to outsiders. As we have read earlier, special provisions also govern the rights of tribal folk and forest dwellers in other north-eastern states such as Assam,

Meghalaya and Tripura under the Sixth Schedule of the Constitution. (Indeed, ownership of property is also reserved in Uttarakhand, Himachal Pradesh, and parts of Jharkhand and Chhattisgarh, among other states.)

In effect, the BJP in its manifesto and manifestly in the claims of its senior leaders, promised development and full assurance of special Constitutional provisions with such fetters, as it were, in vast geographies of India and, yet, claimed that Article 35A prevented the development of J&K.

So, if an aggressively nationalistic party could ride roughshod over one region of India to pander to its political ideology and political base, and disregard citizens' rights as collateral damage, then what would prevent it from effecting similar strategy as and when it was expedient in the country's far-east?

Notes: 08/2019: Had pointed this out in an article in 04/2019 when BJP's manifesto for Lok Sabha elections was released. Article ran and was within the hour yanked from the net. Web page prompt read 'site under maintenance'. But all other links on that page worked fine. Took screenshots. Enquiry fetched the obvious answer: apparently, orders from on high as it made party look awkward. Asked publication if it made a person look awkward too, as home minister & colleagues had been playing up J&K, 370 & 35A at election rallies but going pro-protection with special benefits in NE. Awkward silence. (Similar silence after an article was yanked after I wrote a J&K security heads-up after the rape of eight-year-old Asifa Bano in Jammu in Jan 2018, but that's another story. Gag orders for J&K were national. For NE, still comparatively 'local'. That will change with Assam as it keeps drifting further to the Hindu-right.)

Panic buttons began to be pressed in Nagaland as much over the fate the of peace deal as on account of a concern that protection accorded to it by Article 371A of the Constitution could be lost.

There was also some concern with the interlocutor of peace talks with Naga rebel groups, Ravi taking over as governor of Nagaland in early August. Moreover, there was the added push by Ravi who made several statements that the Naga peace deal had a deadline of three months—to be settled by October–November 2019, in a repeat of the pressure applied for a similar deadline the previous year. It was portrayed by I-M and its proponents in media—usually, by long-time friends, sometimes co-alums of some I-M leaders at university—as both downgrading of the talks and arm-twisting.

Comments to that effect were also attributed to Muivah. The August 2019 issue of *Nagalim Voice*, an I-M mouthpiece, described a meeting earlier in the year, before Ravi's appointment as governor: '… it became a matter of discomfort for NSCN negotiators led by Chief Negotiator Th. Muivah when the Government of India started turning capricious and bossy as reflected by the body language of Ravi.'

The complicated truth lay somewhere in between.

For the BJP it had become imperative—and expediently so—that public relations benefits of fulfilling its election promise of abrogating Article 370 and its companion, Article 35A, be contained within 'Mainland' India. The alternative, revoking special provisions under the Sixth Schedule and various sub-categories of Article 371 in the North-East would lead to massive protests across that region, irrevocably upset the Naga people and several dozen other ethnic groups, carried the potential to jeopardise peace talks with I-M and other Naga rebel groups and destroy any lingering trust towards the government of India.

Certainly, the spill-over of developments in Jammu and Kashmir onto the Naga peace process was likely to be a nixing of demands such as a separate flag for Nagaland—or Naga homelands—and what has sometimes been described as 'shared sovereignty'. Because, by agreeing to these in Nagaland or the Naga people would open Pandora's Box in Kashmir a little wider: If it was okay for the Naga people, why not for Kashmir? And so on, in a viciously circular argument.

And yet, the central government must offer a substantial, face-saving deal in Nagaland and for the Naga people, or risk having the Framework Agreement for Peace signed in August 2015 by Ravi and Muivah, in the presence of prime minister Narendra Modi, shown up yet again as an empty gesture.

While these were complications of the BJP-led NDA government's own making, I-M's position too was tricky, and some of it led by a delusion.

Muivah, I was given to understand, felt insulted by Ravi's appointment as governor. For him, Ravi being appointed governor and yet remaining interlocutor amounted to a perception of loss of face: Ravi downgraded from being the prime minister's envoy to a Constitutional figurehead and the peace process thereby downgraded from the prime minister's office to the beck and call of a home ministry lackey.

If true, that would be erroneous. In real terms Ravi, before and after his appointment as governor of Nagaland, remained an extension of India's national security apparatus, in which the prime minister, home minister and national security advisor formed the trinity.

I-M's drumbeaters in media also played up I-M as the sole voice of the Naga people. They cited the meeting with prime minister P.V. Narasimha Rao in Paris in 1995 to stake that claim.

While the meeting certainly took place, the interpretation was outright embellishment. I-M leaders did indeed meet Rao which, as we have seen, began the process of talks, climbdown and eventual ceasefire. But they also met prime minister H.D. Deve Gowda in Zurich in early 1997, which led directly to the ceasefire. And the ceasefire with I-M was signed in August 1997, when I.K. Gujral was premier. It took until Modi to convert that ceasefire to talks for a final settlement. It wasn't about one premier—unlike one Muivah—but a process.

It was also important to remember that NSCN's Khaplang faction signed a ceasefire in 2001, when Atal Behari Vajpayee was prime minister. As we have seen, that alone was acknowledgement by the government of India and, by extension, the Naga people, of at least one other major party also being a claimant to representing aspirations of the Naga people. That ceasefire broke in 2015, but by now breakaway factions of K were in ceasefire as well as ongoing peace talks, alongside six other Naga rebel groups—and Ravi was the government's interlocutor for it all.

In all this jostling for advantage a key point remained glossed over. The Naga people as a whole were the main claimants and beneficiaries of a lasting solution. But it was as if both the government and the rebels had yet again lost sight that political capital ultimately rests with the people.

34. Interlude: Free Trade = Freely Traded

29/07/2019 (AR Facebook page)

'ASSAM RIFLES SEIZES AIR RIFLE SCOPES WORTH APPROX RS 50 LAKHS SEIZED IN MIZORAM

ASSAM RIFLES, in a search operation on 29 July, recovered huge qty of illegal Air Rifle scopes of foreign origin to include Bushnell, Leupold and Marcool, worth approx Rs 50 Lakhs from general area Zokhawthar in Champhai district.'

Pic shows plaque with list: Bushnell: 400 Nos.; Leupold & Marcool: 50 of each.

Ref screenshot of indiamart.com page that popped up while searching for related news:

Under the options 'Compass, Telescopes & Survey Tools' it has this helpful offer: 'Tell us what you need, and we'll help you get quotes.' Bushnell scopes from ₹7,990, Leupold scopes from ₹19,900. Marcool not on offer but plenty of other options, from low to high: Gamo, Pronghorn, Discovery ...

Someday, as weapons move from dark web to light :) rifles and ammo too? Meanwhile, what's AR/Mizoram Police going to charge them with? Not paying import duty? Exactly! AR announced that 'The recovered items were handed over to Customs Department for further investigations.'

Narc of course remains a big ticket here. Ref that drug bust in Oct 2015 in Mizoram which snagged 100K+ meth tablets (local price INR 300 each = INR 30 mn+ haul). Three Myanmar nationals arrested. Border between Mizoram and Myanmar a little over 400 km. Mizoram Police worked the bust with help of volunteers from Supply Reduction Service—now there's a name!—anti-narc offshoot of Young Mizo Association.

Besides arms/ammo & weapons accessories & narc, AR's hauled quite a lot of other items on this smuggling route. Ref similar monetary value haul from 03/07/2018 by Sercchip Btn of AR & Mizoram Police of 15 kg pangolin scales & 610 kg ginseng.

Manipur, Mizoram, Nagaland ... Pick a border, any border. The Eastern Gate is wide open!

35. Flag, Constitution, and a Push That Came to Shove

10/09/2019

From all accounts, Uncle M is still upset. In the matter of rebellions and fractious peace processes, it's always good to be able to tell friend from foe. The Naga peace process is already throwing up some interesting parameters and possibilities.

On 09/09/2019 Ravi met Muivah at the Nagaland Police complex in Chümu. Feedback is that of a long sulk. Muivah evidently upset that it has all moved beyond him—and that the peace process is now demonstrably greater than him. Word came back of a near-confrontation. More than flag and Constitution—now exposed as negotiating fig leafs—it was a matter of deals. Immunity. Various accommodations. And, most importantly: Face.

Where will Muivah fit in? What indemnities will he, his family and senior colleagues enjoy?

To reiterate: it boils down to the post-conflict status of the leadership of I-M, and Muivah in relation to all other groups. Indeed, all Nagaland and the Nagasphere, as it were. Flag and constitution provide I-M's leadership with an exit line.

Flag and constitution were not a done-deal part of the framework agreement, but the can-neither-confirm-nor-deny aspect has muddied the waters and still provides I-M a free run with agitprop. It's clever because it's emotive, in a situation of great expectation of lasting, honourable peace and nervousness about renewed conflict. And, ironically, it comes against a BJP government that has repeatedly displayed its mastery of using emotion to gloss over a range of problems, including lynching, remonetisation and its effects, and a faltering economy.

The flag is the flag of 'Nagalim'. Interpreted through I-M's lens, the Yehzabo would accord the chief of the organisation, in this case the prime minister, or *Ato Kilonser, Muivah*—not I-M's figurehead of a chairman, or *Yaruiwo, Qhehezu Tuccu*—the role of de-facto chief of a pan-Naga organization. Through this, Muivah would still hope to control the polity and politics of the Naga people—the Nagasphere. This would upend existing political structures—and that is making others nervous.

In September, I came by a complete copy of I-M's Yehzabo; I-M's Constitution was articulated first in the unified NSCN's manifesto in January 1980, before the first split in 1988 into I-M & K and was loosely based on Yehzabo announced by the Naga National Council in the mid-1950s—of which we read earlier. It was re-endorsed at an I-M meet on 6 April 1996 and later released for publication—the document was marked 'Dated Oking, 22nd August 1996'. It was yet again endorsed by I-M in 2006.

The 'Preamble' announced acceptance of the 'truth of popular sovereignty'. They were good words to begin with, but like quite a lot in India's Constitution that's all they amounted to in application. Just words.

This 'amended' Yehzabo urged the formation of a complicated and contradictory entity: an 'Independent Sovereign Christian Socialist Democratic Republic'. Basically, it amounted to something on the lines of Nagaland for Christ but Glory Be to Our Godless Communist Brothers & Sisters in China Who Inspired and Motivated our Cause from the 1960s. At this stage, keeping in mind just how far Nagaland and the Naga people had come in their aspiration in a range from livelihoods to gender parity, it was difficult to not be facetious.

The Yehzabo ran to 12 pages and was divided into five parts. Part I was titled: Nagaland: Territory and Jurisdiction. Part II: Council and Government. Part III: Legislature and Executive. Part IV: Judiciary. Part V came in in three sections: A) Economic System B) Religious Organizations C) State Official Language. No surprises here: English would be the link language as in present-day Nagaland.

From a detailed reading, this root-Yehzabo of I-M appeared to be behind the times for application into any modern Constitution that sought to protect and nurture modern society and polity. It espoused a classic unitary approach and carried the seed of a dictatorial command and control structure, along with a degree of rhetorical flailing. It seemed to be prudent for I-M to have kept this historical Yehzabo vague, and to share no details of a future 'Constitution'—how much would it be based on its own roots, or would it be just a souped up Article 371 (A) with a Naga name—except to score pressure points with during negotiations with the government of India and for public consumption. In a Naga society that had moved on from 1963, the NSCN root-Yehzabo would likely draw massive criticism. It was all in the document.

Part I: Article 1 stated, 'The territory of Nagaland shall comprise of all the territories inhabited by the Naga and such as other territories the council may, by law, admit on such terms and conditions as it deems fit.' Basically, the description of Nagalim, territories beyond Nagaland. That was off the table.

Part II: Article 1 announced: 'There shall be one-party-one-government system in Nagaland for such period of time as deemed necessary and expedient.' It claimed NSCN (I-M) as the 'only authentic National Council' and its Government of the People's Republic of Nagaland is its 'legitimate government'. Article 2. (b) mentioned that 'The Chairman, the Vice-Chairman and the General Secretary together form the Collective Leadership and the convening power of the National Hoho is vested in it.' They would have six-year terms. It assumed control for the 'Collective Leadership' and in effect nullified the powers of the Assembly and the Naga Hohos or tribal organisations.

Part III of the Yehzabo nominally delegated power to the chair a.k.a. the Yaruiwo, because all bills would be passed only with prime minister's assent. While the chairman would formally appoint every senior official, including 'the Chief Justice and Justices of the Supreme Court, the Chief Election Commissioner and the Longwibu of the Army ...' the applicator or executor remained the general secretary a.k.a. Ato Kilonser, or the prime minister. He would pull all strings and appointments and controlled all ministers and councils and controlled, through radiating authority, even the village 'ahng'—chief.

Women featured minimally in the twelve-page document, in three sentences.

A major mention was in Article 12 of Part III: 'There shall be a National Socialist Women Organization of Nagaland (NSWON) which is composed of the constituent regional women organizations.' And part IV, Article 3 (h) mentioned: 'Women in Nagaland shall enjoy equal right with men in all spheres of life—political, economic, cultural and social.'

While it was an excellent proposition, it would be somewhat uphill as in Nagaland homelands customary law provisions negated gender parity and affirmative political action. A male-dominated attitude reflected in the public diminution of women. Nagaland, for example, had not elected a single female MP, MLA, or village head and there was massive backlash, as we have read, whenever the subject came up. Female voice was largely absent in churches.

There were other incendiaries, so to speak.

The last item in Part IV announced: 'It is the bounden duty of every citizen of Nagaland to pay taxes to the state.'

This was big, considering one of the rallying cries of the earliest Naga rebels against both British and Indian domination was they wouldn't pay taxes to any government. Subsequent agreements with the government of India guaranteed Nagas of Nagaland from paying personal income tax. So what tax was I-M talking about, exactly? A progressive Nordic system that taxed citizens to provide welfare benefits and increase fiscal accountability and fiscal responsibility? Or simply a continuation of I-M's system of 'donations' and 'taxes' that often extorted for the 'national cause'—a system that had also weaponized the group, like all factions, and enriched several kilonsers and other leaders?

In 'Part V. Economic Systems,' the Yehzabo proposed nationalising nearly the entire economy, including minerals, as well as jurisdiction to nationalise commons.

That was also incendiary besides being totally controlling, considering that in Nagaland, traditional ownership of land and forests was already vested in tribes, and Article 371A of India's Constitution permitted Nagaland primacy of 'religious or social practices of the Nagas', 'Naga customary law and procedure', 'administration of civil and criminal justice involving decisions according to Naga customary law' and 'ownership and transfer of land and its resources'. (Other constitutional provisions safeguarded land ownership—as part of broader tribal ownership—in Manipur and Arunachal, for instance, as we have seen.)

A point on industries was somewhat confounding for a progressive, aspirational economy. 'All major means of production and industries shall be nationalised till such time as deemed necessary.' Like a command politics, it would be a command economy.

The root-Yehzabo was manifestly a manifesto for I-M-Land, not a constitution for a new Nagaland, and certainly not the Naga people—unless everybody wished to revert to a state of adulterated, whimsical socialism.

09/2019-10/2019:

Ironically, Ravi could be Muivah's ticket; the ticket for his family and coterie too, who, like that of other some other leaders, form the creamy layer of the rebellion. Indeed, the ticket for the top leadership of all Naga rebel groups in talks with the government for whom Ravi remains the common platform.

There are several steps to it all. A key one is that of disarming rebels. From my discussions, it appears that an arrangement has been reached with all Naga groups and factions currently in peace talks with the government.

My take, though, is that this will be a process of sleight of hand and photo-ops. There is every likelihood that plentiful rebel arms and ammunition will remain cached in both India and Myanmar—where several Naga groups have ethnic links, and where logistical links exist despite Myanmar's military crackdown in that region. ('Fragrant grease' has for long sustained Tatmadaw's economy.)

And, if there is a night of the long knives, it will be a matter between various factions within a rebel group as much as between one group and another.

So, the safest place for Muivah might not be Camp Hebron near Dimapur, which will be gradually dismantled after a final peace deal is signed, but his government-provided 'ceasefire' residence of several years in New Delhi's Lodi Estate—or any other designated fortress with a maximum-security cordon.

Because, while some leaders will certainly accept government sinecures, his is unlikely to be a simple case of a rebel leader being pensioned off to the Rajya Sabha. Will Muivah and I-M, an organisation that applied the heft of its army and weapons to effect a parallel administration and extortion network more effectively than its rivals, be safe from retaliation after the peace deal? That's a part of collective crunch. And, essentially, a deal-breaker element along with immunity and position. This factor has earlier been raised in a meeting between Muivah and Ravi in Chümu.

Meanwhile, arrangements and agreements of politics and political economy are being negotiated across the Naga spectrum.

Ravi is still pushing for an all-faction deal by 31/10/2019.

Push had come to shove. I-M—or at least an element of I-M—had cracked.

I received word from contacts in Nagaland in mid-October—and wrote of it in an article on 22 October—that some key members of I-M had become 'inaccessible'. It was a euphemism for decamping to relatively safe havens—in Myanmar, or through Myanmar to points further east in Thailand and southwest China—over the previous fortnight. Among them was Major General Absalom Tangkhul, Muivah's trusted arm, and the person government investigators speculate as being the person behind the assassination of Arunachal Pradesh MLA Tirong Aboh along with nine of his entourage, including his son, on 21 May. I was given to understand that Ravi had declined—and that was the soft description—to paper over Absalom's alleged involvement.

Phungthing Shimrang, a former chief of I-M's army, was similarly inaccessible. So was Apam Muivah, the Ato Kilonser's nephew and contentious heir apparent and keeper of the clan's golden keys since the death in 2016 of Grinder, another of Muivah's nephews. Muivah was for the time in New Delhi, in his government-provided bungalow in Lodi Estate, where entry of visitors to the compound was recorded by members of the Intelligence Bureau that formally guard and monitor the place with the help of Delhi Police.

There was little India's security establishment didn't know of, from several overseas holdings of rebel leaders, from bank accounts to property and businesses. For instance, that families of I-M's senior leadership own businesses in South Delhi and the National Capital Region, including a bungalow-and-Airbnb in a tony neighbourhood near the tomb of the Mughal emperor Humayun, and a boutique in an upscale shopping hub not far from Muivah's Lodi Estate bungalow.

It's routine for Indian intelligence agencies to pile on pressure to leverage a gain in position to lead into a peace deal or in the process of hammering out—and I use this phrase judiciously—a peace deal. There would always be pressure applied by one side or the other before the annual renewal of ceasefire with I-M; a practice discontinued after ceasefire was extended 'indefinitely' after several years. But the spectre of pressure always remained, and was applied at will—as it had begun to happen with the renewed squeeze on I-M.

But sometimes, I-M just stepped into a mess of its own—and all India's security apparatus did was gleefully watch, alongside showing off its long reach. It has happened several times over the years, and it happened spectacularly in 2000, when Muivah was arrested in Thailand.

On 18 January 2000, less than three years into a ceasefire with India, Thai authorities detained Muivah at Bangkok's Don Mueng airport. Well, they soon discovered it was Muivah. The passenger who had disembarked from a Thai Airways flight from Karachi identified himself as Hwan Soo Chung from South Korea. 'Chung's' swarthy features didn't look particularly Korean and, upon checking, the passport proved to be fake. At another time Muivah might have slipped through, but he hadn't counted on heightened security on account of a major United Nations trade conference in Thailand.

The Naga rebel establishment and its public relations machinery put out that Muivah was coming from Pakistan to Bangkok for the peace talks, and India's intelligence agencies had contrived to tip off Thai authorities to embarrass Muivah. The I-M boss' own defence was that he was on his way to the Netherlands to attend a conference. But the routing that snagged him was unusual. Why backtrack several thousand kilometres to travel from Karachi to Amsterdam via Bangkok?

Muivah's defence did have some credence. He, some members of his family and close associates, maintained residences in Bangkok, his chosen hub in the same manner as for his figurehead colleague, Swu, in later years a residence-and-hub was Manila. An NGO, Asian Indigenous Peoples' Pact, was one of I-M's fronts in Thailand, and such a presence helped to provide it affiliation with the Netherlands-based liberal platform Unrepresented Nations People's Organization, which had become a go-to NGO for several rebel groups worldwide. Several active rebels and many NGO representatives from across far-eastern India who have no active connections with rebel groups but seek to promote issues of ethnicity, identity and human rights were regulars at UNPO gatherings.

Even so, it wasn't illogical to think that the livid Indian establishment had indeed tripped Muivah because, as they saw it, even after signing a ceasefire agreement he made no pretence of his connections with Pakistan, and its powerful intelligence apparatus that maintained contact with several rebel groups fighting the Indian state and various provinces. The journalist and Southeast Asia analyst Bertil Lintner wrote at the time in an article with a Bangkok byline: 'Intelligence sources in Bangkok claim that Muivah was in the process of working out a major arms deal in Pakistan. Pakistan's Inter Services Intelligence has for decades been active in India's northeast, and its Bangkok station has been in touch with NSCN's local contacts.'

Lintner also detailed what happened next to Muivah. It was all Muivah's doing—India's intelligence agencies couldn't have scripted it any better had they tried.

Muivah spent close to a week in a holding cell for illegal immigrants before he made the bail of 200,000 Thai Baht (or about ₹230,000). Grinder arranged the bail bond. Muivah was released on bail and a court appearance fixed for 1 February.

Then it became a comedy of errors along with a compounding of errors. On 30 January, two days before the court appearance, Muivah took off.

'... (H)e jumped bail and tried to escape to Malaysia via the small Hat Yai airport in southern Thailand, using a false Singaporean passport,' Lintner wrote. The police caught him. On his charges of fake passport were added charges of jumping bail and a second charge for using a fake passport. He was placed in a prison in Songkhla, a coastal town in Hat Yai province.

Meanwhile, the government of India kept up the pressure. From some detailed media reports in early February which could have only come from sources in the intelligence services—the sometimes-compatible mix of R&AW and IB—it appeared that the government didn't just want to lift I-M's veil, it wished to rip it off.

An article in *The Telegraph* of Kolkata, with a New Delhi dateline of 1 February 2000 detailed how Muivah, Swu and 'about 50 leaders' had been living since the early 1990s in the west-Bangkok suburb of Sukhaphiban. It mentioned the road on which Muivah lived, and the mansion he lived in. 'His flat, guarded round-the-clock by no less than 10 cadre who live in smaller houses in the same locality, is close to the so-called Government of the People's Republic of Nagaland Coordination Centre office, which is a two-storeyed building located at 100/482 Ramintranivet, Ram Intra Road ... According to reports available with officials here, the windows of the office always remain shut.'

The article went on to detail the location of the post office, not too far from the I-M office south of Don Mueng airport (it was several years before Suvarnabhumi airport became Bangkok's primary air hub), that I-M used to send and receive mail. It detailed the post box, No. 81, and the code of the postal area, Bangkok 10230—'The mailing address available with the government ...'

'Indian security agencies have been able to track down at least one of the accounts which Muivah personally operates under the alias Muslimuddin'—the article listed a branch of Bangkok Bank, on Ramkhamhaeng. 'Muslimuddin is believed to be a Bangladeshi name and Muivah also holds a fake Bangladeshi passport ... Officials said of late they have received reports that the NSCN(I-M) has set up many front companies engaged in several kinds of businesses and activities, including real estate, toy manufacturing and tour guides within Thailand.

Officials believe the tour operating firms help the NSCN(I-M) cadre to move around the country and abroad covertly and conveniently. "The NSCN(I-M) leaders live pretty comfortably in Thailand as their cadre rough it out in Nagaland," an official said, describing the lifestyles of the outfit's members who have made Bangkok a haven.'

The piece carried a collateral message: 'Muivah's arrest twice has burst the bubble that Bangkok remains a haven for insurgent leaders on the run from the Indian government. Officials believe that the Thai police's action has sent a message to the Ulfa, National Democratic Front of Boroland and the People's Liberation Army of Manipur that Bangkok can no longer provide them with unhindered cover. "One positive fallout of the arrests is that the Northeast insurgent outfits will now find it difficult to strike arms deals in some of the South-East Asian countries," an official said.'

The deliberate burn ended with a 'possibility' that the Angami tribe and the Chakesang tribal collective were turning against I-M; and that the Congress government of chief minister S.C. Jamir—long considered a nemesis by I-M—was doing all it could to have Muivah extradited, or deported. (I-M would return the favour by 'banning' Jamir from entering the Naga Hills after he left office in 2003 after his fifth stint as chief minister.)

There followed another act in the play, and this was copybook spook—copybook Indian spook. Grinder arrived in Kolkata from Bangkok, and was promptly arrested. 'Grinder Muivah was arrested on an absurd charge that he was trying to hijack a plane from Mizoram to rescue Muivah in Bangkok,' related the lawyer Nandita Haksar, in an article. The apparent target was the Aizawl-Kolkata sector.

The signal was clear: don't mess around. If we can get to your uncle, we can get to you, official go-between for peace talks or not.

'I went to Kolkata and then to Aizawl to file for bail for Grinder,' continued Haksar in a somewhat unifocal manner. 'It was then I saw for myself how the intelligence agencies work to disrupt the peace process.

I got Grinder out on bail and he came to some arrangement with the intelligence agencies, so he withdrew his case against the attempt to frame him in a patently false case.'

Haksar, who also helped Muivah's case in Thailand, added: 'Three former prime ministers of India signed an appeal to the Thai authorities asking that Muivah be released so the peace talks could resume. I put the letter on record in the Thai courts. The peace talks did resume. The Indian intelligence agencies managed to get the NSCN to agree to hold all further talks within India.'

The process had become more sophisticated over the years, and the information increasingly more comprehensive.

The security and political establishment also knew about several holdings by some Naga politicians and elite—and that of politicians and the elite of other Northeast Indian states too—but that was clearly for quite another kind of negotiating table. (Disclosure: I once received a request from a 'Northeastern' politician who wished to take down, or at least embarrass, a chief minister; to favour a potential chief ministerial candidate. He asked me to put him in touch with 'someone' at the finance ministry who could track down the gentleman's bank accounts in Southeast Asia. I declined, insisting I knew nobody, and also indicated that his 'candidate' evidently lived in a glass house.)

In any case it had all come down to the rebels' manoeuvring room. The government was counting on a compromise that could come about upon the rebels being compromised.

The talk-talk-fight-fight mode continued, because that's how such things worked. It was clear Ravi's 31 October deadline for a deal wouldn't work because even with all the cracks I-M hadn't cracked wide enough to force the pace.

As October turned to November, word came of more laying down of boundaries, of threats and counter-threats that had become an integral part of the negotiation with I-M.

The government's aim was to demonstrate that rebels have no way out except settling for a process that included disarmament, integration of cadres and leaders into paramilitary structures and the political system that took care of both Naga honour, and other forms of rehabilitation we have discussed earlier, and concerns of the three states contiguous to Nagaland—Manipur, Arunachal Pradesh and Assam—that their borders wouldn't be affected on account of a peace deal effective across Naga homelands in these states.

Word also arrived about a sometimes-used negotiating ploy of I-M to use China as a counterbalance. Indeed, Muivah and his colleagues had brought it up in interviews, including with me. The word from the negotiating table was that Ravi and his colleagues had conveyed to I-M that its attempt to seek help from China—in a throwback to such assistance received from the 1960s to 1990s—wouldn't work, as India wouldn't stand idly by. Besides, I-M was reminded that Myanmar had turned from relatively safe to slippery haven not just for I-M—but on the lines of see-what-happened-to-NSCN (K)? Government negotiators also kept pushing to merge its parallel streams of negotiations with I-M and the so-called NNPGs. A deal would be signed by all on the same set of papers.

I-M for its part was holding on to its sense of primacy. Word arrived too that, although he had been told otherwise by Ravi, Muivah hadn't shaken off his intent to lead a pan-Naga organisation—an ethno-cultural organisation. But the Indian side was jittery about this, with all the ethno-political overhang across Nagaland and Naga homelands in other states; and a suspicion that Muivah would try to leverage for this organization an over-arching political role.

There was some history to this, and dated back more than a decade, to the years between 1999 and 2010 when K. Padmanabhaiah was the interlocutor. There was some drift during this time, according to Haksar.

'Neither the Nagas nor the Indians put forward any substantial document on which the negotiations could take place. The NSCN was being advised by Michael Van Walt, a Dutch lawyer who has been an advisor to the Dalai Lama,' she writes of this time. 'He did not have knowledge of the Indian Constitution and the NSCN refused to read the Indian Constitution on principle. They wanted a solution 'outside' the frame of the Indian Constitution.'

Things changed in 2010, when Raghav Sharan Pandey, a former chief secretary of Nagaland was appointed interlocutor. 'It was he who put forward a non-Plan which had some concrete proposals,' Haksar relates. 'The non-Plan suggested the possibility of a pan-Naga body which could unite all the Nagas in different states without changing the borders of the existing states.'

As the import wasn't clear, in 2011 I-M—Haksar used 'NSCN'— invited a group of overseas lawyers 'with the approval of the Indian government' who would help to shape the suggestion into a 'document on the basis of which the NSCN could negotiate.' They met in Delhi. They were quite a bunch. The Australian Anthony Regan 'had negotiated for a similar settlement in Papua New Guinea'. 'The senior-most lawyer amongst us was Prof. Yash Ghai, who a year before, had successfully drafted the new Constitution for Kenya. He was a personal friend of Prime Minister Manmohan Singh and the prime minister had hoped that he could help bring about a resolution to the Indo-Naga conflict.'

Haksar writes that her husband, Sebastian Hongray and she were 'deeply involved' in the two-day discussions, the outcome of which was a 'detailed document'. 'It got a positive response from the NSCN leaders. There was talk that the document would be made public so the Nagas could debate over the contents.'

'But the document never saw the light of day.'

She writes of a meeting on the subject that took place after the signing of the Framework Agreement as a 'fiasco', and claims it happened 'mainly because none of the lawyers who had been involved in the first one were present'.

It was a point, but the lack of her presence and that of her colleagues could have been partly compensated by the old document seeing the light of day.

There was also the matter of Muivah himself. As much as he once criticised Zapu Phizo for not standing up for the Naga cause during the political deals of the 1960s and 1970s, Muivah didn't possess the cross-tribe stature as Zapu Phizo did. Phizo's grave lies by Nagaland's assembly and secretariat complex. Even with his contradictions and weaknesses—I've been told by former NNC members, staunch ones, that a rebellion couldn't be run from a fireside in Kent—Zapu Phizo remains an icon. Muivah was in comparison a limited icon, a person who appeared to be consumed by his own legacy and security—even a divisive figure as seen by some Naga tribes, let alone non-Nagas.

Even as the cumulative aspects made a deal and reconciliation more difficult, an informal team of pro-government—and yet, pro-Naga— legislators and community leaders now began to reach out to non-Naga communities in Manipur, Arunachal and Assam to explain that a Naga peace deal didn't just require understanding between the government and Naga rebels, alongside the acceptance of Naga citizenry, but also the understanding and acceptance of non-Naga people in these three states.

They again elaborated several points of understanding as prerequisites to the deal. One was, as we have discussed a little earlier, of accommodating rebels into the political system by expanding the legislature in Nagaland into a bicameral one, but also a delimitation exercise to increase representation in the house. Delimitation exercises in the three other states, this outreach conveyed, oughtn't be seen through the lens of ethnicity but legitimate representation in an arguably under-represented assembly. So too, more autonomy in so-called autonomous district councils in the hill areas of Manipur—home to Naga, Kuki and Hmar-Zomi tribes—and similar accommodation, this outreach suggested, needed to be made in Arunachal and Assam as well. Intact territory required the quid pro quo of an open mind and open heart. Everyone had to walk part of the way, or there wouldn't be a way out.

36. A Matter of CorCommunication

09/11/2019. Big news. Rajkumar Meghen, former chairman of UNLF released from Guwahati Central Jail.

Meghen served out a 10-year sentence with some remission. Convicted in 2016 for waging war against the state, among other charges, but his incarceration since 2010 counted as time served.

Takes me back to a memory, of a conversation in 2009 wt Pradip Phanjoubam, at the time editor of Imphal Free Press. We'd been chatting about several things, from what he called the TINA factor with Ibobi, to state of protests to new gen pol/intellectual/biz leadership, to state of rebel play. On the last point, told Pradip I'd been given to understand by his colleagues in local media, NGO-wallahs & security establishment that among some Meitei groups it was already beginning to happen. I was told that KYKL which had earlier broken from UNLF, had in principle agreed to be united in purpose—even if a full integration with UNLF unlikely at this stage.

Et voila! CorCom arrives in 2011, begins coordinated/co-operative action in 2012.

Cut to conversation with senior Imphal NGO official in July 2014. Validates previous info + analyses. Transcript & notes:

'We asked the Meitei groups to consider coming together as far as ten years ago. We told them pressure would be building up against them. It was inevitable. The situation was changing in Bangladesh, Myanmar. There would be more focus on their activities in these areas. There would be greater pressure of politics. But they did not listen. They had their own ideas.'

'They realised it later ... they announced formation of CorCom. By then Raj Kumar Meghen was already arrested.'

(Good point. CorCom key players UNLF, PLA, KYKL, KCP ++ came together. But Meghen's arrest was a big blow as he has cachet even among other rebel groups & enormous goodwill among many Meiteis for his ideological moorings + romanticism on account of being related to Manipur royal family.)

'We told them that by coming together they could be in better position to defend, but more importantly, negotiate with the government. We told them negotiations were inevitable. Better to be in a position from which negotiations are possible to some advantage.'

Exactly my assessment. But would possibility of such negotiations hold if Naga settlement sparks resentment? Then it would seem like betrayal by government & CorCom or individual groups would gain emotional cachet to continue and/or pressure for greater eco/pol benefit for Valley/Manipur as leverage for continued negotiation. As things stood VBIGs—as security establishment calls them—under huge pressure. Got feedback in Imphal & Moreh about how even as Manipur establishment sometimes went slow even with Ibobi's heavy hand, central security forces cut no slack for VBIGs. 'They go after them like a cat after a mouse,' as a contact in Moreh tells me. No slack even during fests like Lai Haraoba, when some cadres of groups reach 'home' to be with family.

Contd. transcript/notes: 'I met R.K. Meghen in Guwahati Jail. He believes the time has come to look ahead—work towards negotiation.'

Cut to 2019.

Expectedly, GoI stepped in. Meghen had planned to head to Imphal for what was to be a hero's welcome at a public function. But after a day, Meghen, also known as Sana Yaima—precious son—was taken back into protective custody by NIA, and flown to New Delhi. There he remained closeted, in animated suspension, much like the peace process in Nagaland and Manipur.

If this seems complicated, that's because it is. Primarily, it's about who Meghen is, what he represents and the power he can wield to tip the balance in the Naga peace process—and peace in Manipur.

My take is that Meghen, who studied international relations at Kolkata's Jadavpur University, will again have received an outreach that he has received earlier: eschew the path of rebellion and be a reconciliatory force to bring UNLF and colleagues in other rebel groups which are part of CorCom, to the table of peace talks. The expediency which led CorCom to band together for survival and conducting war could be applied to survival and conducting peace. The thought regained currency as Meghen was taken to New Delhi by NIA. It isn't difficult to gauge the kind of people—and from which agencies—he met.

Meghen returned to Imphal to a hero's welcome on 28/11/2019, after nearly three weeks in New Delhi's evidently benign custody. Meghen spoke in a conciliatory manner upon his arrival in Imphal. He spoke of remaining 'with the people'. Asked about implications of the ongoing Naga peace process, which from time to time has flown the kite of an integrated Naga homeland—Manipur is home to several Naga tribes—Meghen was quoted as saying by local media: '... I don't think the Government of India will do anything to compromise the overall integrity of Manipur ...'

This instant elder-statesperson of Manipur could emerge as a leading political figure, like rebel leader Laldenga who turned chief minister in Mizoram as a consequence of a landmark peace deal in 1986. Meghen's presence in Manipur and the respect he is accorded, especially by the Meitei majority to which he belongs, could be a crucial factor in the near future—for politics and for peace.

37. Migration Matrix:
The Future Will Be Tense

This tremendously multi-ethnic, multi-linguistic, multi-religious region carries risks beyond the various identity and ethnic conflicts that have shaped it, in particular since the 1940s—and which continue to shape the region in war and peace.

Migration—and illegal migration—is one such, a defining characteristic that remains at the core of much stress and insecurity in far-eastern India. Almost without exception across this region there remains resentment about migration from 'Mainland India'. No amount of legislation or government assurance has entirely been able to alleviate concerns and fears. It's a historical loop of natural and man-made realities and fault lines.

One of the biggest migrations that contributes to the heartburn, rhetoric and occasional violence in this region is the decades-long movement of several million mostly Bengali-Hindu displaced persons arrived from 'East' Bengal—East Pakistan—on account of Partition in 1947 and subsequent religious persecution. There is the relatively lesser-known wave of 1950, when systematic pogroms took place in East Pakistan. Or that of 1964, when riots were triggered in East Pakistan in retaliation over rumours of the loss of a hair of Prophet Muhammad at the Hazratbal shrine, in faraway Kashmir. Besides the slaughter of numerous Bengali Hindus, and the flight of tens of thousands of Bengali Hindus, these riots also led to the forced eviction of several tens of thousands of tribal people like the Garos, Khasis and Hajongs from the northern part of what was then East Pakistan, who were also caught up in the rage of triggered Islamists.

What began during Partition peaked between March and December

1971. This was on account of the anti-Bengali massacres—irrespective of religion—conducted by Pakistan's government with the help of its army and paramilitaries during that time as a measure to quell political protests and a burgeoning guerrilla war against that government. And the brief, open battle in December that year between Pakistan and India as a direct consequence of Pakistan's brutality and India's ability to leverage the fallout to its advantage—which ultimately led to the creation of Bangladesh.

West Bengal has borne the brunt of that migration. The crush was so intense that tens of thousands of Hindu Bengali migrants, mostly of the lower castes, were resettled in eastern and central India. Several thousand were resettled in the Andaman Islands. Numerous settlers were killed in the Sunderbans, in what has come to be known as the Marichjhapi Massacre of January 1979 after the island where the incident took place, when security forces of West Bengal evicted them. They were acting under the direct orders of an elected Communist government, which had, ironically, invited them back to West Bengal from refugee settlements elsewhere in India.

There is another aspect. Through the Partition and post-Partition decades, the reality of Muslim Bengalis arriving in India largely from Bangladesh for better prospects—whether for settling or for seasonal work in farms, for instance—morphed into the bogeyman, identified through an acronym that a majority in the region knows: IBI. Illegal Bangladeshi Immigrant. A marginally gentler appellation is 'Miya'. This has persisted even with the sizeable number of Muslims who—much like in the rest of India—chose to not migrate to Pakistan in 1947. Long-time residents of India and relatively recent arrivals alike have often been painted with the same brush in far-eastern India.

In West Bengal, from the 2010s onwards, it became a point for vicious rhetorical head-butting between the Trinamool Congress and the BJP—whose local and national leaders openly played on the emotive threat of Muslims taking over that state and blamed Trinamool for pandering to them. This contentious claim has often tipped verbal duels to outright violence between the supporters of these two parties. The BJP and fellow-subsidiaries and adjuncts of the so-called Sangh Parivar ensured that in West Bengal, general elections to parliament in 2019 and general elections in 2021 to that state's Assembly were predicated on the majoritarian perception of this threat.

If such tinder can be primed in an ethno-linguistically similar geography with a generous dash of religious bigotry, imagine then its incendiary power in India's far east, where it is all mixed together and perceived as being more or less the same evil: non-local.

The migratory pressure has come mostly to Assam and Tripura, although it retains incendiary properties elsewhere too.

In Assam, the problem's genesis can truly be blamed on the British, although that doesn't absolve cynical post-Independence politics in Assam—more of which a little later.

The East India Company extended its conquest of Assam in 1826 with that of Cachar six years later and merged them with the Bengal Presidency. This also began a forced migration: the practice of bringing plantation workers into Assam primarily from some areas of present-day Jharkhand, Bihar and West Bengal; alongside the steady unforced stream, as it were, of mostly Bengali professionals—including bureaucrats, teachers, doctors and lawyers. The dual streams strengthened after the formal annexation of Assam by the British East India Company in 1838. In addition, the steady stream of migrant labourers, small traders and businesspersons that have continued into the present day have caused local heartburn. It continues to fuel rhetoric and occasional violence. (In Assam and Manipur in particular, rebels frequently targeted such folk from the 1980s through to the 2010s, with the graph tapering off in the later years.)

After administrative reorganisation in the wake of the 1857 mutiny, the largely Bengali speaking districts of Sylhet, Cachar and Goalpara—in what is known as Lower Assam—were with some hill districts merged into the new Chief Commissioner's Province of Assam.

The reason Sylhet and Cachar were merged with the new province, suggests Nabanipa Bhattacharjee, an academician specialising in ethnolinguistic conflicts in Assam, was to meet the 'inadequate revenue potential of Assam'. It cut off Bengali speakers from Bengal, besides isolating the Sylheti who tend to identify themselves as Sylheti first before associating with any other nationalistic, linguistic or religious group.

The merger also had an unintended effect: of clubbing Bengali-speaking areas to Assam even as hiving off Assam was also done to assuage Assamese needs of identity. 'The situation for the Assamese was nothing less than paradoxical,' Bhattacharjee writes. 'The move was a moment of liberation from Bengal, but hardly from the Bengalis; the much needed and desired freedom and right to articulate and nurture the Assamese identity seemed sabotaged from the start.

Matters became messier with Partition. In 1947, much of Muslim-majority Sylhet went over to newly-born Pakistan after a referendum that year, except for the eastern extremity of Sylhet where a majority were both Bengali-speaking and Hindu. This remained with Assam—and India. Trouble would soon brew in this cauldron of Bengalis, cut-off from West Bengal, now several hundred kilometres to the west; and cut off too from the very Bengali, adjacent East Pakistan.

Meanwhile, from the early 20th century there had been a steady trickle of Bengali agricultural migrants into Assam, encouraged by the colonial government to settle along the Brahmaputra, but Partition unlocked a flood of Bengali Hindu refugees into eastern Indian territories from East Pakistan, a movement spurred by anti-Hindu riots there in 1950. There was a massive influx into West Bengal and Tripura, with its own set of consequences—of which more shortly. And there was substantial influx into Assam, which had never hidden its general dislike of Bengali-speaking people, brought about in no small measure by the historical arrogance of some Bengalis towards the Assamese from the time of John Company.

While Assam's Congress government under Gopinath Bordoloi accepted the inevitable after some months, a circular it issued on 4 May 1948, essentially sent out a personae non grata message. It cited 'peace, tranquillity and social equilibrium in towns and villages', and that, 'in no circumstances' should any settlement of land be made to those not indigenous. The definition of non-indigenous people extended to 'non-Assamese settlers in Assam though they already have lands and houses of their own and have made Assam their home to all intents and purposes'.

Things would get worse. The Assam (Official) Language Act, 1960, promulgated in December of that year, made Assamese the official language of Assam. This touched a raw nerve in Bengali-dominated Barak Valley, especially as it followed what came to be called the Bongal Kheda campaign: get rid of Bengalis.

Beginning mid-1960 Bengalis were attacked in the Brahmaputra Valley. The district magistrate of Guwahati and a senior police officer were stabbed by mobs. Depending on Assamese or Bengali sources, it is estimated that between 50,000 and ten times that number fled the Brahmaputra Valley primarily to Bengali-majority Cachar and West Bengal.

There were large, successful islands of mini-Bengal in the heart of Assam. 'In the towns of Gauhati, Tezpur, Nowgong, Jorhat, Dibrugarh, Tinsukia etc., almost half the population consists of Bengalis,' wrote K. C. Chakravarti in a July 1960 issue of *Economic Weekly* (precursor of the *Economic and Political Weekly*). 'Many Bengalis are thriving as doctors, lawyers, teachers, clerks and occasionally as traders.'

Quite often students were at the forefront of such attacks. 'They were being incited by Assamese job-seekers and protected by college and university authorities. The local police often felt helpless...' wrote Chakravarti. 'Congress and non-Congress leaders, politicians of all shades of opinion, Rightists, Leftists, Hindus, Muslims, poets, priests, men of letters, sober educationists, unruly students—all have wonderfully cooperated.'

Some critics maintained that existing law permitted a monolingual approach only if an ethnic group counted for 70 per cent of the total population. In Assam's case, going by the 1951 census it was 55 per cent, and much of Assam's area at the time contained non-Assamese ethnicities—future Meghalaya, for instance. But several Assamese writers and thinkers justified the move. 'Bengali has been declared as the State Language for the Darjeeling District of West Bengal where it is spoken only by about 16 per cent of the population,' maintained

P. C. Goswami in the same issue of the *Economic Weekly*. 'So there should be no hesitation in declaring Assamese as the State Language of Assam for fear of offending the people of Cachar and Hill Districts, particularly when adequate safeguards are provided for the minorities.'

Language remained an issue of imposition in places that had never been Assamese. Language safeguards were perceived as inadequate, tied up in legal and bureaucratic knots.

By February 1961, a resistance began to coalesce, and spread from Silchar to the other significant towns of Barak Valley, Karimganj (which is today a district headquarters of an eponymous district) and Hailakandi (also the district headquarters of an eponymous district). An ultimatum of a shutdown strike was announced for 19 May, if the language law wasn't modified to include the full-fledged use of Bangla in Cachar. The government arrested leaders of the movement and requested troopers of the Assam Rifles and paramilitaries of the Central Reserve Police Force to conduct flag marches.

On 19 May, Cachar was shut down. Protesters were arrested. When a truck carrying some of them passed by Silchar's railway station, protesters gathered nearby freed the detainees and set the truck on fire. Security forces arrived and waded into the mob. Shots were fired. Nine protesters died then; two died later.

Curfew couldn't prevent subsequent protests. Negotiations followed. In October 1961, the Language Act was amended to include, only for Cachar, Bangla as an official language on par with Assamese. Areas of Lower Assam, as it is known, like Dhubri and Goalpara which today have large Muslim, Bengali-speaking populations, do not have similar linguistic benefits.

Meanwhile, a third of the people in Assam use Bengali as a first language. Ethnicity, language and religion continue to contribute to volatility. Alongside, vestiges of the political manoeuvring that led to Assam's inclusion in the Republic of India instead of what was then East Bengal (and which soon became East Pakistan and is today Bangladesh) have remained, and simply added another layer to existing tension.

By the time the 1980s came around, a militant students' movement strongly rooted in the need to reclaim Assamese—Axomiya—identity and dominion soon morphed into outright militancy. One such derivative, the United Liberation Front of Asom, or ULFA, remained indiscriminate in its targets of threats, kidnappings, assassinations, bombing of public places and facilities. It targeted any ethnically non-Assamese person large swathes of the state, especially in the central and north-eastern parts, even at the cost of those whose ancestry, at least for some hundreds of years, was located within the boundaries of Assam.

In Assam, where parliamentary and local elections have also been pitched in part over majoritarian political control—and, since the 2010s overt Hindu-majoritarianism married to the Axomiya identity—such migration has never sat comfortably. With such a narrative, the Miya, both legally arrived from other parts of India and illegally arrived, continue to bear the brunt of ire in Assam's ethnic politics. It is a matter of record that several politicians in far-eastern India, particularly Assam, have for several decades wooed immigrant populations to ramp up electoral support, over the years transforming illegal migration into legal by applying the Indian practice of 'regularising' an illegality by administrative and legislative fiat—for a range of things from illegal construction to zoning. Resentment accruing from such political manipulation has often exploded into chaos. The Nellie Massacre in Assam in 1983 that killed over 2,100 Bengali Muslim men, women and children near the eponymous village due east of Guwahati, was only the most infamous of such incidents, the first of several ethno-religious firestorms in the name of preserving nationhood and identity. Across Assam several thousands have died as a result of inter-ethnic and inter-religious butchery since the1980s.

More recently, especially in 2018, disagreements over updating the National Register of Citizens (NRC), and the Citizen (Amendment) Bill, 2016, again brought to surface tension over the Bengali—and, allegedly, Bangladeshi—population settled there.

Several Bengali organizations, especially in the Bengali-majority Barak Valley-Cachar area support both the NRC process and the bill—because the citizens bill would bring many migrants security. Many Axomiya feel the terms of the NRC update and provisions of the bill are pro-immigrant—the pro- and anti-peace talks factions of ULFA have also weighed in on this side.

Trouble between indigenous Bodos and immigrant Muslims and the Adivasi in the Bodo Territorial Council-administered districts of Kokrajhar, Chirang, Baksa and Udalguri in central Assam, in the northern bank of the Brahmaputra abutting Bhutan, also isn't rare. (The writer Sanjoy Hazarika noted in his landmark book, *Strangers of the Mist*, how in the early years of the rebellion Bodo militants walked in from camps in Bhutan and simply machine-gunned numerous Bengali-speaking Muslims.) In 2012, massive violence broke out with Muslim settlers in Bodo areas where indigenous Bodo communities have for long resented land and jobs being usurped by those seen as outsiders, perceived by Bodos as being helped by successive governments of Assam. The violence left scores dead—besides unsettling several hundred thousand—from both communities. On 25 December 2014, the body count from ethnic violence that began two days earlier between the Bodo and adivasi communities in Assam inched towards a hundred. Mainly Bengali-speaking Muslims and migrants were attacked and killed in large numbers during elections to the Bodo Territorial Council in 2015.

For its part migration, irrevocably propelled by politics, pogrom and geopolitics in the Bengal delta, transformed Tripura from an overwhelmingly tribal entity which answers to a 'Tripuri' or 'Tiprasa' umbrella comprising several ethnicities—principally Borok, Reang, Noatia, Halam, besides other tribes, and some Meitei—into an overwhelmingly Bengali Hindu one. Today, mainstream Tripura is Bengali—about 70 per cent Bengali.

It was not long ago the kingdom of Tripura, bound by Bengal to its north, west and south; to the east a slice of Cachar, the southernmost tip of Assam, and a slice of the Lushai Hills district (later to become the Indian state of Mizoram). The Manikya kings ruled in a nearly unbroken line since the 15th century CE—the 13th century, if you consider the semi-mythical Ratna Fa—until 1949.

In 1947, two days before India itself became independent, the queen regent Kanchan Prava Devi signed a treaty of accession to

India. The formal merger would take place in 1949, on the same day Manipur formally merged with India. For all practical purposes, it stopped being Twipra, the land by the water, jettisoned the British-colonial Hill Tipperah, and emerged fully as Tripura, the Sanskritised and mythical triple city-realm of earth, sky and heaven to which the original conjoining of *'tui'* and *'pra'* in the Kok Borok language was as different as earth and sky.

Partition also robbed Tripura of a direct link with 'Mainland India', with residents of Tripura now required to either fly to Kolkata, or to travel several days by bus and train to reach places beyond Guwahati: Kolkata, New Delhi and elsewhere. Trade and industry remained basic. Agriculture was for decades the primary activity. Only in this millennium would Tripura's resources, like natural gas, really come of age and new geopolitical realities would spark growth and hope and links leveraging its unique location and recent history—we shall read more of this a little later.

Meanwhile, Bengalis swamped Tripura, arriving as refugees in the Partition years. In 1952, close to a quarter of a million refugees poured in, dwarfing even the near 2,00,000 of a year earlier. Pakistan's piecemeal, drawn out conflict with India over 1964–1965 drew more than a hundred thousand. In 1971, Pakistan's butchery in its eastern aspect, soon-to-be-Bangladesh massively opened floodgates. Tripura's population of about a million and half at the time—already majority Bengali—swelled by a third, according to a US State Department memo. *Doinik Shongbad*, a daily newspaper in Agartala, in mid-1971 estimated refugees at nearly 1.3 million. Nearly all were Bengali.

Between 1941 and 1951, years of the decadal census, the percentage of tribal folk in Tripura dropped from a little over 53 percent to a little over 37 percent. By 1981 it had dropped below 30 percent. The Census of 2011 shows the tribal population hovering just above 30 percent. 'The final Partition of India was a disaster for Tripura,' journalist and Northeast India watcher Subir Bhaumik aptly put it. Tripura, he maintained, became an 'insignificant little pariah in India's backyard'.

(The government, administration, trade, discourse and language also began to turn Bengali from 1946 onwards. Indeed, an advertisement by the Tripura Public Service Commission in 2020 for jobs in the state's forest service advertised the knowledge of Bengali as 'Desirable' along with the prerequisites from a clutch of degrees in relevant subjects of science. Some jobs are more ethnically tempered, listing as 'Desirable' the 'Knowledge of Bengali or Kokborok'. The official languages of Tripura are Bangla and Kok Borok. The latter is a matter of form more than substance.)

Migration also led to issues over land. In the late 1970s, an article in *India Today* magazine estimated that a staggering 90 percent of land that did not belong to government was owned or controlled by non-tribals. Some land that was deeded to Tripuri communities by their former kings—a prescient intervention—was given over to settle refugees, and more was encroached upon.

For all practical purposes, the Tripuri had become aliens in their own land.

Protest was a given and it surprised few when such pressure eventually spawned a string of armed movements by Tripuris. As early as 1967 an indigenous youths' organisation, Tripura Upajati Juba Samiti was formed, with the intention of official recognition for Kok Borok and autonomous tribal councils as encouraged by India's Constitution. As importantly, perhaps, there was demand for the restoration of traditional tribal lands that successive non-monarchical government had either given to non-tribal settlers or kept silent as these were appropriated. In the early 1970s, an angry but half-hearted effort of Tripuri reclamation took root with Tripura Sena, or army. It took till 1978 with the formation of the armed group, Tripura National Volunteers, or TNV, for the largely Bengali government to pay attention.

Some observers, including Bhaumik, maintain trouble could have been averted had the incoming Left Front communist government, which took over from the electorally overwhelmed Congress, had nominated a tribal person as chief minister instead of a Bengali. At any rate, the communists did try to make amends. In early 1979, they moved to restore to tribals land grabbed by non-tribals and moved the Tripura Autonomous District Council Bill in the provincial assembly.

It had the opposite effect. Several hundred Bengalis, grouped under the radical Amra Bangali, or We are Bengalis, began a cycle of violent protest. Matters escalated. Eighteen hundred people, mostly Bengali, ultimately lost their lives in clashes between tribals and non-tribals. Several thousand homes were destroyed. The Indian Army had to intervene. Even as this fire abated, TNV was up and running, targeting government and Bengali civilians.

It would be nearly a decade before TNV entered peace negotiations for a better deal for tribal folk, which some analysts have dismissed as counter-productive—and Bhaumik, in his blunt manner, describes it as 'ridiculous', because it provided three more seats to tribals in Tripura's Assembly, 'and little else'. Even after peace deals, indigenous peoples' enclaves continue to be the most undeveloped.

A slew of militant groups sprang up subsequently and—in an irony that marks see-sawing relations between India and Bangladesh with nearly every change of government in that country—found shelter mainly in the Chittagong Hill Tracts of Bangladesh and sometimes in the vast plains—the very land that many Bengalis in Tripura had escaped from. The lessening of militancy and outright attacks against Bengali settlers in Tripura has taken a mixture of governance and a change of geopolitical equations, which led to a more India-friendly government of Sheikh Hasina for much of this millennium severely reducing sanctuary for all manner of rebels against India—Naga, Meitei, Assamese, Bodo and, of course, Tripuri. Such groups had found active sanctuary during the premiership of Hasina's most significant political foe for several decades, Khaleda Zia, the tenure of Khaleda's assassinated husband and dictator, Ziaur Rahman, and another general-turned-absolute president, Hussain Muhammad Ershad. They had all taken several hard-line Islamist-led positions, from security matters to trade, and were perceived by India as being against its interests.

And evidently, the reduction of militancy also came about on account of some surgical strikes, as it were, of Tripura's own making. Even here, the Bengali connection wouldn't be far.

B, who's plugged in every which way to Tripura govt & security tells me of a few incidents as we chat at the Cafe Coffee Day outlet at Ginger Agartala at end of a seminar to promote Tripura-BD trade & investment.

Basically: whatever works. Exasperated by increasing & vicious rebel incursions, Tripura govt/R&AW/IB got in touch with Abdul Sweden/Sweden Salam (B not sure of sequencing), a BD thug to 'eliminate' Ranjit Debbarma, chief of All Tripura Tiger Force. Sweden asked for location, was given mobile no. OK, can track, he said. ATTF chief attacked, injured, many colleagues/ cadres killed. Ranjit D stayed put in BD but was pushed out by BD in 2012 at Dawki (Meghalaya's a 'neutral' border in this case & anyway area is quite the transit point for black ops along with migrants & coal from Meghalaya). Deep background, so unattributable to B. B suggests citing source as v.v. close to CM!

B isn't exaggerating. In late-Nov/early-Dec 2014, Tripura's police worked with Indian & BD security for a cross-border raid in BD to attack National Liberation Front of Tripura camps (of the BM/ Biswamohan faction) in Chittagong Hill Tracts. 8 killed, several camps destroyed, weapons & ammo seized, one commander, Kwaplai Debbarma, arrested. Several dozen cadres escaped but tracked down. Bodies buried in BD. Made the media. (Telegraph ran a story. Institute of Conflict Management report had more details.)

Anyway, CM Manik Sarkar, for all his mild-mannered nature, outward simplicity & reputation for personal probity takes tough stand for insurgents/ rebels. A/c to B: 'Unafraid to take hard calls when security calls are to be made.' B boasts that Tripura 'only state' that sanctioned cross-border ops, no waiting for intelligence re-routing from Delhi, no waiting for sanctions for ops from Delhi. This CPI(M) CM listens to/reads briefs & then gives pithy orders in typical Baangaal dialect which is adequate & leaves no room for ambiguity even if CM creates plausible deniability with no paper or mail trail.

'Shaira fyalao,' he once cleared such an op. Do it. Finish it.

And to think that at one time, Bengalis were freely made welcome, celebrated. Tripura's royals didn't prevent Partition refugees from entering Tripura. Kings encouraged Bengali administrators and teachers, even cultivators. The *Rajmala*, a chronicle of the kings of Tripura, begun in the mid-15th century CE during the rule of Dharma Manikya I, was commissioned to be written in Bengali.

Rabindranath Tagore was a beloved guest of the Manikyas, beginning with Bir Chandra Manikya. A story goes like this: The king was desolate after the death of his queen, Bhanumati, in 1881 and found solace in the young Tagore's poem 'Bhogno Hridoy'—A Broken Heart. He sent word of appreciation to Tagore in Kolkata and offered to print his works on hearing that the poet was being dismissed by Bengali littérateurs. His successor, Radhakishore Manikya, invited Tagore to Tripura. Two successive kings, Birendra Kishore Manikya and Bir Bikram Kishore Manikya, continued the relationship. Tripura's treasury helped Visva-Bharati, Tagore's dream university in Shantiniketan, take shape. Tagore gushed, as later-day Tripura government public relations proclaimed: 'When the woodlands of Tripura have sent out invitations to their floral feast through their courier of the south wind, I have come as a friend.'

That's finished.

Nagaland, which has in its plains vast farms worked by what Nagas call 'IBI' and 'Miya' hired labour and contract farmers, added itself to an inglorious list in 2015. On 5 March that year, a Bengali Muslim youngster who was in Dimapur's main jail, a little to the south of the airport, was mysteriously released to the custody of a mob. This mob, comprising men and women, the relatively old and the young, cursed, beat and dragged him for several kilometres along Dimapur's streets, and then lynched him at a major crossroads in the centre of the city: he was finally strung up from a lamppost. To them it was revenge: that man was in jail on charges of molesting a Naga girl. The skinned, pulped man became the focus of anger against 'IBI'.

Widespread condemnation of the lynching followed in Nagaland's media, and by several local tribal organisations and students' groups, among others. The anger, which several people I spoke to maintain was triggered by a faction of extremists for political gain, seemed all the more troubling when it emerged within days that, the murdered person had family in Assam's Karimganj district and was domiciled in Nagaland with a Naga spouse. But the anger remains, erupting from time to time in letters to media, but more vociferously in neighbourhoods, and of course social networks, including The Naga Blog, an otherwise quite sedate and influential Facebook group that encourages debate over venom.

Ethnicity and religion have since driven the churn over India's controversial National Register of Citizens and the Citizenship Amendment Act, 2019. Here the issues have remained a part of electoral battles for parliament as well as state legislatures since 2014, and more acutely since 2019.

A BJP electoral plank was essentially to provide a category of non-Muslim immigrants the opportunity for naturalization by amending the Citizenship Act, 1955. Introduced through the Citizenship (Amendment) Bill in 2019 or CAB—which took on board suggestions of a parliamentary committee that reviewed a similar bill from 2016—the central government sought to reduce the residency requirements for '… persons belonging to minority communities, namely, Hindus, Sikhs, Buddhists, Jains, Parsis and Christians from Afghanistan, Bangladesh and Pakistan' from an aggregate of 'not less than eleven years' to 'not less than six years'.

It wasn't surprising that NDA's lead constituent BJP would attempt legislation to bolster its credentials by excluding Muslims from CAB's equation—a move which continued to pose a Constitutional issue of inequality on grounds of religion. But in north-east India, where migration has remained an explosive issue for several decades, concern over CAB over-rode frequent assurances by elements of the BJP, Sangh and NDA that local provisions protected tribal-indigenous rights over land.

That year, protests and tension flared across the region. In Assam the National Register and the Citizenship Bill proved a contradictory and volatile mix. As the Register sought to address long-time and occasionally violent, local feelings against 'outsiders' and 'illegal' immigrants—primarily aimed at Muslim immigrants but, as discussed a little earlier, also against 'outsiders' who were non-Muslim—to many in Assam the Citizenship Bill seemed to be an underhanded way to legitimise such migration. A massive outcry followed in Assam and elsewhere, including Tripura which since the 2010s emerged as a bridgehead for the BJP and aggressive Hindu nationalism.

The Citizenship (Amendment) Bill 2019 was passed by the Lok Sabha that January. The Bill wasn't introduced in the upper house, Rajya Sabha, for its necessary approval on account of great criticism and unfavourable numbers for the BJP-led coalition.

The Bill died a natural death with the end of the BJP-led parliament's term in May 2019. But a re-election victory for the BJP and its coalition later that month brought it right back on track, and prompted a re-run.

Tension had meanwhile ratcheted up over the Citizens' Register. The final NRC list for Assam that was due to be published on 31 August 2019 had already caused heartburn over who is a legal resident of Assam and who would be outed as illegal migrants. In the chaos of verification and enumeration across urban and vastly rural Assam, there were notable instances of even some former and serving personnel in India's armed forces and paramilitaries being judged by kangaroo court-like decisions as illegal migrants. The overall numbers of those with questionable antecedents thus far ran into several hundred thousand.

The fingers remained pointed to neighbouring Bangladesh as a major source for such, mostly Muslim, migrants.

Bangladesh has steadfastly denied the existence of such movement since the birth of that country in 1971.

Meanwhile, concerns were already being raised in some circles as to the security fallout. What would the newly dispossessed do? Would Bangladesh take any back? Would some go underground, as it were, and join cells of extremists worshipful of the radical Islamist groups that have wreaked such havoc in Bangladesh? Not all concerns were fanciful.

Even as the administration in Assam and the central government scrambled to both deliver on election promises as well as contain any violent fallout of the NRC exercise, it needed to consider the reaction of the country that India now geopolitically called a friend: Bangladesh. India shares a 4,000 km-plus border with Bangladesh, along West Bengal (which accounts for more than half), Assam (the least, after Mizoram), Meghalaya, Tripura and Mizoram. Some of the border is riverine and impossible to fence. Even with fenced aspects, the border remains porous.

I had done a deep dive on such migration and what is sometimes referred to as cross-border movement, for my book, *The Bengalis: A Portrait of a Community.* There was data and claims, both verified and pie-in-the-sky.

A World Bank publication from 2016 listed the Bangladesh-India 'migration corridor' as the busiest after Mexico-United States and Ukraine-Russia. India's deputy home minister told parliament in November 2016 that an estimated 20 million Bangladeshi immigrants were illegally in India. Even accounting for the nationalist bias of the BJP-led coalition that formed that government in mid-2014, the numbers were staggering. The estimates were enormous enough in 2004, when the Congress Party-led coalition's deputy home minister placed the number at 12 million, with 5 million in Assam and close to 6 million in West Bengal. A row erupted, mainly on account of objections by the Congress government of the time in Assam. The central government withdrew the statement citing the 'unreliability' of the report.

In a 2016 essay for the think-tank Carnegie India, Sanjeev Tripathi, a former chief of R&AW, admitted there were no reliable figures of exact numbers of illegal immigrants from Bangladesh in India, but maintained that 'analysis' of population growth figures and demographics for Bangladesh and India since 1981 'suggests with reasonable certainty that their number exceeds 15 million' of these mostly economic migrants.

Unsurprisingly, Bangladesh continues to dispute such estimates. Sometimes its officials make fun of it. Surely, the jibes go, the governments of India and its states aren't so incompetent or venal as to provide illegals several privileges like voter identity cards and the all-encompassing, biometrics-enhanced Aadhaar cards?

There is no acknowledgement of remittances from India in data from Bangladesh Bank, as I found while researching *The Bengalis*. In the 'Others' column—for sources other than major remitting geographies that Bangladesh freely acknowledges—an entry marked 'Wage Earners Remittance Inflows' mentioned a figure of $800 million for the years 2014–2015. On the other hand, 'Migrations and Remittances' data released by the World Bank placed remittances from India to Bangladesh at $4.45 billion for the same period.

Bangladeshi officials and some in local media have also claimed that half a million and more Indian workers are engaged in Bangladesh's booming garment export sector. And that, they were mostly illegal.

The NRC would hardly untangle such knots.

And just how fraught the entire exercise was became evident in early September 2019, when NRC data showed, much to the BJP governments' embarrassment in both Assam and New Delhi, that Assam was more in a state of flux than a state of illegal Muslim influx.

Less than a week after the final list was released on 31 August, uncertainty prevailed over the process that, almost overnight, made nearly two million people, mostly Hindu, stateless. It placed the BJP and the Sangh in a spot. To leave these Hindus in the lurch would be politically disastrous. Something needed to be done urgently, like the reintroduction of the Citizenship Amendment Bill in Parliament. But to co-opt these Hindus in a renewed embrace of the Citizenship Bill— and, in short order, the Citizenship Act—would upset many pro-BJP Axomiya who, as ever, would interpret this as legitimizing non-Assamese and 'foreigners.' The snare to catch 'IBI' had instead become a trap for IBI-hunters.

Those tagged by NRC could appeal within 120 days—they had until January 2020. But a majority weren't well-off and many lived in areas away from knee-jerk NRC tribunals. Nearly a dozen detention centres were being prepared for those who failed that bid. It looked like a looming humanitarian and political crisis with overtones of a security crisis.

That Assam may have bitten off more than it can chew was evident from the strident protests against the numbers—and the vast numbers of non-Muslim people out of the NRC net—by several parties, including the ruling BJP. Now as the party both in Delhi and Dispur remained tied in knots, perhaps no other place in Assam reflected the complexity as much as the Barak Valley-Cachar area to the southeast of the state, which was outside the Axomiya arc. Here, matters of religion (both Hinduism and Islam), language (Bengali) and ethnicity (non-Axomiya) remained incendiary, on account of the pre- and post-Partition history of divide-and-impose we have discussed earlier.

Cut to the present. The BJP won the Silchar Lok Sabha seat in Barak Valley from the Congress in 2019. In 2016, it had won the majority of assembly segments across Cachar district, of which Silchar is the headquarter. (Seats in Barak Valley districts of Hailakandi and Karimganj went to the Congress and the pro-Muslim All India United Democratic Front, or AIUDF.)

Here, the BJP was caught between assuaging deep misgivings over the NRC exercise in Assam as well as Cachar—for opposite reasons. Many non-Muslim Bengalis out of the final NRC register in Cachar area did not have the prophylactic the Citizenship Bill sought to provide. It was a confounding case of attempting to please a majority and ending up displeasing the majority. That Assam remained under the watchful eyes of greatly reinforced teams of paramilitary forces was only one indication that the NRC cauldron remained on the boil.

It also a remained a point of concern for the BJP's moral redoubt, the Rashtriya Swayamsevak Sangh. Media reported RSS's chief Mohan Bhagwat as saying at a meeting in Kolkata on 22 September 2019 that Hindus in Assam caught in the NRC net wouldn't be expelled from Assam. Bhagwat, like his Sangh colleagues and those in the BJP, were betting on the Citizenship Amendment Bill to bail them out.

As momentum was built up for the re-introduction of CAB, as the Bill had come to be known, in Parliament, there was an expected ratcheting up of nationalistic rhetoric. The CEO of a Sangh Parivar think-tank, the New Delhi-based Indraprastha Vishwa Samvad Kendra, used the phrase 'the figment of someone's imagination' in an opinion piece in a national daily in early December 2019. He downplayed the persistent concerns over CAB in north-east India, where in Manipur, Nagaland, Mizoram and Meghalaya protests against the proposed bill have been frequent and strikes total. The Kendra, like other institutions that sought to impress a nationalist agenda as a national one, missed the beat. Railroading the Bill had the potential to severely upset the balance in north-east India, and further the reputation of BJP as a superstructure that repeatedly chose exclusivist religion over inclusive respect.

But there was already an expanding humanitarian crisis. In the last week of November Assam's parliamentary affairs minister told the Assembly of several dozen deaths from illnesses in detention centres across the state—centres that had sprung up in anticipation of netting 'IBIs'. There were already six such centres. Assam's government even requested aid from India's government to set up more centres to contain NRC detainees.

It was clear that, whatever the BJP-led governments did in New Delhi and Dispur to contain the political fallout, the humanitarian and human rights crisis would only grow, as there was—unsurprisingly—no indication whatsoever that Bangladesh, from where most immigrants and illegal immigrants to India arrive, would take back those who failed NRC scrutiny, and who would pack detention centres.

Parliament passed the Bill on 11 December 2019. A day later, the president of India gave his formal—if rubber-stamp—assent. A day later, CAB became CAA: The Citizenship (Amendment) Act, 2019. On 20 December, seven who had arrived from Pakistan were ceremonially given Indian citizenship under the new law.

In the three days as CAB became CAA, much of Assam flamed on. Axomiya protesters and passersby were shot dead by the state's police, curfew imposed, and the internet curtailed. It was redolent of Kashmir.

The response was all quite different in Barak Valley, primarily the Bengali-majority districts of Cachar, Hailakandi and Karimganj.

Cachar remained pro-NRC and certainly pro-CAA, with its largely

Bengali-Hindu population secure in the belief that even if any were outed by NRC, then CAA offered a safety net. Nothing underscored this reality as well as incumbent Congress MP from Silchar, Sushmita Dev's support for the Citizenship (Amendment) Bill's first run in early 2019. (Dev lost to her BJP rival Rajdeep Roy in the 2019 Lok Sabha elections. Dev was essentially battling from a near-identical platform with the disadvantage of being perceived an underperformer.)

At any rate, the BJP stuck to its guns. BJP's leadership announced the party would stick with NRC and CAA, evidently an attempt to not appear weak during ongoing elections to Jharkhand's Assembly, and with elections due in Delhi in February 2020 and later in that year in Bihar. The Union Cabinet even decided, just days after the birth of CAA, to allocate ₹85 billion to carry out a census, the National Population Register.

Alongside, of course, it attempted to regain face and credibility in Assam, where an ally, the chauvinistic Asom Gana Parishad, or AGP saw its offices trashed by Assamese protesters. Senior AGP and BJP officials and ministers were also heckled by the protesters.

The BJP was caught in its own spin. In the wake of ongoing nationwide protests—the Shaheen Bagh neighbourhood in New Delhi had already become an iconic anti-CAB-CAA-NRC protest hub—statements by government leadership, that NRC was not related to CAA, or that the Population Register has nothing to do with NRC, didn't cut ice. Neither did knee-jerk statements by Central cabinet ministers that government has never discussed nationwide implementation of NRC.

There was good reason for such skepticism. A minister in the BJP-led National Democratic Alliance government in 2015 had actually termed the Population Register a necessary step to NRC. Various members of government have repeatedly discussed such matters in various forums. Indeed, the BJP's manifesto for the 2019 Lok Sabha elections specifically mentioned NRC. In the segment on security titled 'Nation First', the sub-head 'Combating Infiltration' made the following claim: 'There has been a huge change in the cultural and linguistic identity of some areas due to illegal immigration, resulting in an adverse impact on local people's livelihood and employment. We will expeditiously complete the National Register of Citizens process in these areas on priority. In future we will implement the NRC in a phased manner in other parts of the country.'

It also strained credulity that a BJP-led government hadn't discussed NRC. Especially as another item in the same manifesto, for amending citizenship requirements for a select group of people from Pakistan, Afghanistan and Bangladesh—'Hindus, Jains, Buddhists and Sikhs escaping persecution from India's neighbouring countries will be given citizenship in India'—found expression in triumphant follow-through as CAA.

The document added a softener for India's far-east: 'We will make all efforts to clarify the issues to the sections of population from the Northeastern states who have expressed apprehensions regarding the legislation. We reiterate our commitment to protect the linguistic, cultural and social identity of the people of Northeast.'

That's where it went wrong.

Now damage control rapidly kicked in. In BJP-ruled Assam, where protests were strongest, NRC and CAA's face, Himanta Biswa Sarma, announced the formation of new tribal autonomous councils and development funds for niche communities, on the lines of Karbi Anglong in Assam.

In BJP-ruled Manipur, chief minister Nongthombam Biren Singh leveraged the Inner Line Permit or ILP for that state, which sought to screen entry of visitors, often derided as 'foreigners'—'mayang' in Meiteilon—from 1 January 2020.

In Meghalaya, where the government was in alliance with BJP, chief minister Conrad Sangma also leveraged ILP to initiate a 'resolution' to implement ILP, currently applicable to Arunachal Pradesh, Nagaland and Mizoram, and on 18 December 2019 the state's Assembly unanimously adopted a resolution to that effect. (It was another matter that, in February 2021, the governor of Meghalaya, the long-time BJP loyalist Satya Pal Malik, would be quoted by the webzine *theprint.in* as saying: 'I have not understood how ILP will help people in Meghalaya. You will have no investment, no tourism, nobody will come to you, and ultimately it will be harmful ... This is not my opinion, but assessment.

Whether or not ILP should be implemented is the Centre's prerogative.' It added to the confusion, correctly interpreted by the state's citizens and the Opposition: if you can agree to measures in Assam, and ILP for Manipur, then why not ILP for Meghalaya?)

In any case these were salves, not solutions—and yet again exposed the entire citizenship exercise as a strident, knee-jerk process.

And, in any case, many in Assam remained angry over public perception that CAA nullified aspects of the Assam Accord of 1985 that marked 1971 as the cut-off date for determining a 'foreigner'. CAA provided a cut-off date of only five years.

Policy palliatives would do nothing to calm concerns among the Assamese—Hindu, Muslim, and those of other persuasions—that CAA provides backdoor entry to a million or more Hindu immigrants, primarily from Bangladesh, that NRC, currently applied only to Assam, had netted. Similarly, ILP wouldn't really calm nerves in other Northeastern states, nearly all with a bloody history of reaction to political ingress and immigration—illegal or legal, from Bangladesh or 'Mainland' India.

Besides, the Kashmir conundrum would remain: if the government could repeal protective laws and break that state ...

And it all brought international attention.

A week after structured rioting in Delhi began on 23 February, aimed at those who were protesting against CAA, and stunning the world with its brazenness and unapologetic aftermath, came scrutiny of a different kind. The Office of United Nations' High Commissioner for Human Rights filed what is called an intervention application, in India's Supreme Court over CAA.

The Geneva-based office of the high commissioner, Michelle Bachelet Jeria, tacked the application onto the writ petition challenging CAA that former diplomat Deb Mukharji filed in the Supreme Court in December, one of 60 that includes similar applications by human rights activists, politicians and political parties, including from Northeast India. Bachelet Jeria wanted her office to be amicus curiae, or impartial or 'friendly' advisor to the court, for the petition. The high commissioner wished to intervene with neutrality—suggesting there was need to ensure such neutrality—and, by extension, nudged the Supreme Court to do right.

The government of India officially acknowledged the UN high commissioner's plea on 3 March, when the foreign ministry put out a terse release stating that India's permanent mission in Geneva was notified of the move a day earlier. Usual rebuttals followed: '... internal matter ...', '... sovereign right of the Indian Parliament to make laws ...', and '... no foreign party has locus standi on issues pertaining to India's sovereignty ...'

The statement sourced to the foreign ministry's official spokesperson extended the rebuttal to a decidedly tricky plane that can be contested on several grounds, and, indeed, forms the bedrock of anti-CAA sentiment and protests against heavy-handed politics. 'We are clear that the CAA is constitutionally valid,' the spokesperson declared, 'and complies with all requirements of our constitutional values'. The ministry then extended its political neck. 'We are confident that our sound and legally sustainable position would be vindicated by the Hon'ble Supreme Court' which is part of 'our independent judiciary'.

That would fly in India, which was in any case the political marketplace for CAA, NRC and the recently-boosted National Population Register. But Bachelet Jeria's deliberate intervention, even as it displayed the former Chilean president's independent streak, also morally weakened India's current membership of UN's Human Rights Council.

Much like the petitioners who question CAA, the high commissioner decried the 'narrow scope of the CAA'. Her office also highlighted another aspect that, 'in light of the broad prohibition of refoulement'—the forcible return of asylum seekers or refugees and the possibility of continued persecution—'may not be sufficiently objective and reasonable ... under international human rights law'. In other words, as CAA excludes Muslims, even those Muslim sects persecuted in Pakistan, Afghanistan and Bangladesh, it distorts the parameters that ought to be in 'accordance with international human rights law, including the right to equality before the law, equal protection of the law, and the right to non-discrimination and the absolute and non-derogable principle of non-refoulement'.

Bachelet Jeria was within her rights to intervene—by a resolution adopted by UN's General Assembly in January 1994. Resolution 48/141 created the post of the high commissioner for human rights. Among other things it also empowered the high commissioner 'To play an active role in removing the current obstacles and in meeting the challenges to the full realization of all human rights and in preventing the continuation of human rights violations throughout the world, as reflected in the Vienna Declaration and Programme of Action' and 'To engage in a dialogue with all Governments in the implementation of his/her mandate with a view to securing respect for all human rights ...'

On the other hand, various governments of India had displayed a patchy, even disastrous, human rights record across the country against its own citizens, that mocked India's signing of the Universal Declaration of Human Rights in the 1940s—indeed, far-eastern India had borne the brunt of it since the 1950s. It was reasonable to believe that India's government of the day would continue the unlovely, heavy-handed tradition of sign-and-forget.

More than anything else though, it all demonstrated that a bludgeoning one-policy-fits-all approach was at best a recipe for blowback and loss of credibility. But there was little indication yet that lessons were being learnt, or even of acknowledgement that the only alternative to inclusive, stable India was an inconclusive, unstable India.

An unstable 'Northeast'. An unstable, insecure—and unguarded— Eastern Gate.

38. And What If the East Changed Completely?

As much as cynical politics poses a risk to the socio-economic and political well-being of northeast India, it is necessary to add another complex aspect to this already complex matrix—and one that has the potential of being uncontrollable.

Over the years, migration caused by religious discord has abated. It has given way to migration for livelihood. Whatever its ethnic and religious colouring, the issue will increasingly go beyond the realm of religion—Hinduism, Islam, Christianity, tribal animistic beliefs. The pressure on land, livelihoods and the need for protecting indigenous identities and futures means that the uneasiness is unlikely to stop. It all adds up to an issue of great magnitude and will continue to colour nearly everything, big and small.

I was part of a gathering in New Delhi in late-2014—the BJP and its allies had stormed to power in May—for what was described as the diaspora from the eight far-eastern states to share ideas for conflict resolution and development. Several of that region's young entrepreneurs, celebrities and politicians, well-connected women and men in their 30s and 40s some of whom came from considerable privilege, had organised the event, titled 'A Strong Northeast is India's Asset'. The plan was to engage those from the National Capital Region and from across India on various issues, including how media has misunderstood the region; economic growth being the driver of the future; questions around India's nationalistic slogan 'Unity in Diversity'; and re-branding the image of Northeast India for the world at large and, certainly, 'Mainland' India.

A Kuki student leader from Manipur had been brutally assaulted in Bengaluru earlier that week. Among choice racial epithets he was reminded by his attackers that India's software capital was in India, not China. It was one among a series of horrific incidents in the National Capital Region and elsewhere.

As the conference began I thought about the how such an interaction might go. To the people from Northeast India it would be relatively simple—though hardly easy—to explain such attacks as that by some very sick people with deep insecurities. And that would be true enough in a country that could collectively be tried at any human rights tribunal for ethnic and communal turmoil and gender and caste biases and atrocities—all without mentioning the word 'Northeast'.

But to the Mainlander, try explaining 'Northeast', let alone 'Kuki'. How would that conversation run with an aspirational, educated, global, wired, affluent urban Indian—The Indian Dream sort of Mainlander?

'Kuki? What is that? Who are they? Are they from India?'

Yes, they live mainly in Manipur.

'Ah, that Mary something's place; where that woman boxer that Priyanka Chopra played in *Mary Kom*, comes from. But what kind of name is Mary *Kom*?"

You see, the Kom are a small ethnic sub-group, and…

'Like all those people in the Chinese restaurants or that girl who does my mani-pedi. They are always smiling, so why are they so *angry* with India, always being anti-national? This is not *China* or something, no?'

Anyway, back to the conference. The mostly young audience ranged from students and activists to professionals and a handful of businesspersons. India's junior home minister at the time, Kiren Rijiju, who is from Arunachal Pradesh, India's national security adviser Ajit Doval, and R.N. Ravi, at the time freshly appointed chair of the Joint Intelligence Committee and one of Doval's deputies, attended a few sessions.

When talk turned to acting upon India's Act East Policy, to seek better relations with South-East Asia using the conduit of north-eastern India to integrate the Asian highway system for moving goods and people; and opening up of road, rail and waterway links between India and Bangladesh to enable the movement of goods, services and people between that region of India and the 'Mainland', tempers ran high in the audience. Even talk of ambitious projects like a localised version of the Delhi-Mumbai Industrial Corridor, sometimes dramatically billed as the 'Seven Sisters Corridor'—surprisingly leaving Sikkim out of the equation—and the Asian Highway project that mostly remains a paper-route, if you will, in this region, was distilled to one major concern. Would it all lead to the greater 'movement'—migration—of people primarily from Bangladesh and elsewhere in India, and, to a lesser extent from Myanmar, into North-East India? If so, forget it.

There was complete disengagement with the reasons behind migration, let alone the continual inevitability of it. Livelihood needs will push it. For instance, without rapid and sustained socioeconomic development of Bangladesh, both India and Bangladesh will be powerless to stem it. Importation of religious belief, by virtue of Bangladesh's largely Islamic construct, may be a corollary, but religion, whether out of fear or favour, has for long stopped being the motive for migration. Even the exercise to fence India's 4,000 km-plus border with Bangladesh, some of it riverine, will hardly be a barrier to what the future can hold.

I had the opportunity to speculate about this future in a position paper for the Kesroli Group, a think tank of top professionals, entrepreneurs and technocrats of Indian origin—some of whom subsequently joined the central government after the BJP-led coalition assumed power in 2014—for a presentation to senior policymakers and CEOs. The matrices of China and India, Bangladesh and India, and the violent ethno-political dynamics of North-East India make for an incendiary historical and geopolitical mix even without adding inputs by nature, I posited in the paper and to that audience during a weekend retreat at the sprawling campus of Infosys Limited in Mysuru.

This was in 2009. There was still relative amity and exchange in India among right-of-centre, centrist and left-of-centre views that together sought solutions instead of unilateral, often-unmitigable actions. My task was to present logical scenarios of the medium- and long-term future; offer a 'war-gaming' approach with the express purpose to offer solutions, mitigate 'worst-case' to 'manageable-case'.

In retrospect my take probably cut a bit too close to the bone. But

I would stand by its alarm bells—and so has a referee of that paper who in 2014 became a minister with the BJP-led central government—as long as there is no evidence to the contrary. The combination of China and India, Bangladesh and India, and the ethno-political dynamics of the far-eastern arc of India make for an incendiary historical and geopolitical mix even without adding 'natural' causes—caused by nature and man alike. Altogether it presented the most complex, interlinked, inter-dependent landscape.

What would happen if Bangladesh were to suffer a series of cataclysmic storms and inundation of its coastline on account of global warming? Unlike the relatively gentler inward migration forced by a similar inundation of the Indian coastline along the Bay of Bengal, the population pressure of Bangladesh, expected to be more acute than India's for several decades into the 21st century, would lead to its citizens literally forcing their way to every other point of the compass to escape the country's vulnerable south.

India would be powerless to stem this migration—another kind of flood. In this migration, livelihood needs—the brutal matter of survival—would trump any push of religion. There might even be the somewhat ironical instance of Bengali Muslim migrants to Bengali-majority and Muslim-majority districts of India bordering Bangladesh—Goalpara, Dhubri, Karimganj and Hailakandi in Assam, for instance, and nearly the entire strip along West Bengal's border—having to compete with ever newer arrivals. In any case, such a future would turn migration into territorial usurpation, driven by the influx from present-day Bangladesh.

India's east and North-East could change in a way that would make even the effects of the Citizenship Act and the National Register of Citizens look like tame fireworks.

Kolkata could implode. If this were to happen, the Government of India of the time would be compelled to deploy military along this area. This would be further west from the existing border fencing along India's border with Bangladesh in the territory of West Bengal. Such an eastern Line of Control—a cousin of the Line of Control along India's western border with Pakistan—could form the de facto eastern boundary of India, running north to south roughly from Barauni-Katihar in present-day Bihar and run continuously south along the eastern borders of present-day Bihar, Jharkhand and Odisha and the mining rich areas west of present-day Bardhaman in West Bengal. This would be additional impetus to secure India's key mining and industrial belts against the influx. Economics as much as security would surely drive this cauterising.

India's urban spaces would be particularly vulnerable to strife, as it would need to absorb extra millions driven by the force of the migratory explosion. This migratory traffic would also place severe stress on present-day agrarian and rural spaces. Further, driven by the needs of the burgeoning population, there could be a continuing push to extend habitation, farming and industry deeper into 'breathing rooms': forested areas.

To follow through with such an eventuality, India would be unable to prevent the breakdown of 'Northeast' India. The states of Meghalaya, the territory of Assam south of the Brahmaputra, and the present-day state of Tripura could entirely be overrun by migrants. It is entirely conceivable that, cut off, Nagaland, Manipur and Mizoram could revert to their micro tribal states, with Myanmar and China dominating this political geography. And what of Arunachal Pradesh and northern Myanmar? How much would the migration tip China's hand and move it to secure its southern borders, even if that meant effectively moving that border further south—into India?

And what if it all turns out all right, much of it at any rate? The future, while patchy, does have some economic and geopolitical bright spots that might help cement some of the fault lines wrought by population pressure, migration and ethnic tension for some years—even some decades if things go well.

Tripura is thus far the brightest spark in this easternmost arc. Its unique geography, history, hydrocarbon resources as well as a go-getting attitude have pushed it to being among the best performing provinces of this region of India—indeed, India—in terms of human development parameters: giving it a large literate pool of human resources and making it a bridgehead for sub-regional diplomacy and prosperity. Here, ironically, the earlier migrations from the time of Partition had placed Tripura at the forefront.

For all practical purposes this state has piggybacked on India's foreign policy gains, even contributed to it. Tripura's particular dynamic and restlessness ensured it: It wouldn't any longer remain isolated on account of the quirk of Partition which robbed it off direct access to Kolkata and the rest of India across East Pakistan—and later, Bangladesh.

Indeed, at a talk in Guwahati in May 2014 that discussed the future of India's eastern neighbourhood, I had proposed that, as part of India's Look East Policy (which the incoming BJP-led government in Delhi escalated later that year to 'Act East') and even for benefits that would accrue on account of location, these eight Indian states ought to boost economic contacts with Bangladesh and Southeast Asia. It would also do to establish representative offices in such countries—independently or in association with Indian diplomatic missions—in much the same way as, say, provinces in USA and Canada did, and some provinces of Germany. The suggestion was buoyed in great part by what Tripura had already achieved with Bangladesh. The stress was on Tripura-with-Bangladesh as much as India-with-Bangladesh, because Tripura had evidently decided it would chart its own course, not wait for India's foreign and trade policies to play catch-up.

Natural gas and the natural order of things led to Tripura's attitudinal and policy resurgence. After it was discovered in the 1970s, natural gas evolved to become one of two biggest tickets to prosperity for Tripura, the second being trade and transhipment. With the commissioning of a major power station in Palatana fuelled by that gas, the state was enabled to handle its own power needs and contribute to its neighbouring provinces, and also lessen the need for expensive hydroelectricity projects that bring the attendant misery of displacement. It's literally a productive grid. Alongside supplying electricity from ONGC-Tripura Power Company's Palatana project to Assam, Meghalaya, Manipur, Nagaland and Mizoram, Tripura has for several years exported electricity

to Bangladesh (similar to an arrangement Bangladesh has with West
Bengal), since 2015 a small though geopolitically significant amount
to Myanmar and since 2019 to Nepal.

India's evolving ties with Bangladesh is, in many ways, Tripura's
lifeline. India-Bangladesh relations really took off from 2009 when
Sheikh Hasina again assumed the premiership. Bangladesh permitted
trans-shipment of equipment for ONGC's gas-based power plant in
Palatana, Tripura, in March 2011, using waterways—in this case, up to
Ashuganj port on the Meghna—and then travelling by road southeast
to Akhaura close to the busy border. This route usually saw a steady
stream of trucks from Bangladesh carrying cement, fish, stone chips,
readymade garments, crockery and several other items; not much flowed
in the reverse direction except visitors. From the border checkpoint it's
a few short kilometres into the suburbs of Agartala.

This was followed in September 2011 by the first bilateral visit to
Bangladesh by an Indian premier, at the time Manmohan Singh, in
12 years.

Trans-shipment of rice by state-run Food Corporation of India to
Tripura through Bangladesh became an established precedent. Indian
companies hope to score big in Bangladesh's infrastructure sector.
Bilateral trade more than doubled to $6 billion-plus between the
2009–2010 and 2014–2015 financial years. In 2011, India allowed
duty-free access to Bangladeshi goods except for a handful of products.
Transshipment of rice by state-run Food Corporation of India to Tripura
through Bangladesh is today an established precedent.

The issue of swapping enclaves (the bizarre reality of a total of 160
enclaves of Indian territory within Bangladesh, and Bangladeshi territory
within India) gathered momentum during this time. It culminated in
an agreement in May 2015 between the governments of Sheikh Hasina
and her Indian counterpart, Narendra Modi. India even moved several
paces on another tricky issue, that of sharing river waters. The Ganga,
Brahmaputra, Teesta and Barak decant into Bangladesh.

Bangladesh, on its part, has massively curtailed sanctuary for rebels
from nearby Indian states, most spectacularly with the arrest of several
senior leaders of the United Liberation Front of Asom (ULFA)—and

their subsequent, mysterious appearance in custody of Indian authorities.

'These are all big gestures by both countries,' Abdul Matlub Ahmad, chairman of Dhaka-based Nitol Niloy Group that associates with Indian behemoth Tata Motors, told me in Agartala. We first met there in July 2014—at the time he was also chairman of the India-Bangladesh Chamber of Commerce and Industry. But the two countries needed more innovative moves, he complained. 'For example, we are asking our government's permission to invest 5–10 per cent of our export earnings in India, specifically north-east India. Indian companies in Bangladesh must also export from Bangladesh.'

For its part India hopes to increasingly use Bangladeshi territory for the movement of people as well as goods. An Agartala-Dhaka-Kolkata bus service that shaves over 1,000 kilometres off a roundabout route via Assam and northern Bengal, is one example. Such a service began in 2018. India is also eyeing greater connectivity to power grids in Bangladesh to trade and transport electricity; and hydrocarbon transshipment through pipelines, railways and roads. It is likely that Mizoram will join the local and regional hydrocarbon production and shipping grid as and when exploration of deposits in the states's north-western Kolasib district pays out. India has funded improvements to the road and rail link from Agartala to Akhaura, on the banks of the Titāsh—immortalised by the writer Adwaita Mallabarman and film-maker Ritwik Ghatak. Similarly, it is looking to improve the road and rail access south from Akhaura to Chittagong Port, the main attraction for Tripura and far-eastern India; and improving access to the river port of Ashuganj, only 40 kilometres from Agartala. A road and rail link south from Agartala to the border town of Sabroom is a priority, along with a bridge being built by India to reach Chittagong, a little over 70 kilometres south of Sabroom. And eastern India, and several other regions in far-eastern India besides Tripura, would benefit from greater access of people and goods across Bangladesh, a near-seamless web that ceased with Partition.

Tripura has been pushing hard for a while. (And, as surprising as it might appear, much of this push arrived during the latter half of the tenure of the state's elected communist government—the Communist

Party of India (Marxist) had a near-25-year run until it was succeeded by
a BJP-led government in April 2018.) I heard a former foreign minister
of Bangladesh, Dipu Moni, talk up that mutual future in Agartala as
far back as 2014, while leading a group of businesspersons like Ahmad,
and diplomats and officials to a seminar called the Tripura Conclave,
fronted by a Bengali emigrant to the United States from Tripura. The
purpose was really the geo-economic policy of Tripura.

Dipu Moni began her speech in polished, impeccable English,
sharing greetings of Sheikh Hasina, and spoke loftily yet realistically
of the 'enormous and incalculable potential' of Bangladesh, Tripura,
far-eastern India and India working together. After some minutes,
she switched to Bengali and stayed with it for the remainder of her
speech, invoking the commonality of Bengali between Bangladesh and
Tripura, acknowledging Tripura's role in welcoming Bengalis in their
times of trouble—this said without irony. She wasn't only playing with
history; she was playing the crowd, playing the future. The crowd loved
it. Those who didn't, like some Tiprasa tribal activists who pointedly
asked questions in English about the future of their people in the greater
scheme of things—for them, the Bengali scheme of things—first received
an embarrassed silence, then a belligerent rumbling from the largely
Bengali audience, and were then ironically lectured to by the hosts
about well-being for all. 'This is about us,' said one of the organisers, a
Bengali. 'We should not be left behind.'

Equitable economic prosperity is the one thing that could go a long
way to addressing a range of ills ranging from migration to extremism,
is economic growth. Bangladesh is today among the world's fastest
growing economies, keeping pace with its larger neighbour India. In
key human development indicators this country portrayed as that of
the archetypically poor is a leader in South Asia, ahead of India, and
ahead of West Bengal, which has spent much of this millennium trying
to position itself as a manufacturing and services hub after more than
four decades of economic disaster local governments visited upon it.

Bangladesh runs among the largest and the most successful rural credit networks in the world. BRAC is today a global legend in poverty reduction, empowerment, microfinance and social enterprise and so is its founder, Fazle Hasan Abed. The country's trajectory is in a way emblematic of the manner in which BRAC has changed its avatars: from Bangladesh Rehabilitation Assistance Committee when it was established in 1972, after the war, to Bangladesh Rural Advancement Committee, to its current avatar, Building Resources Across Communities. The winner of the country's only Nobel thus far, Muhammad Yunus, won the Peace Prize in 2006 along with the pathbreaking microfinance organisation he founded, Grameen Bank—today a commercial behemoth. Bangladesh is today a leading, respected exporter of expertise in microfinance and socio-economic empowerment in the developing world. In October 2020, after half a year of economic devastation on account of the Covid-19 virus, the International Monetary Fund projected that Bangladesh's per capita Gross Domestic Product would for the first time exceed that of India's—after steadily outperforming India with its rate of growth of its exports, savings and investment.

The largely agricultural country now has a fast-growing domestic manufacturing and services sector seen as among the most robust in the region. Bangladesh has evolved into a global textile export powerhouse, and, according to the World Trade Organization, accounted for nearly seven per cent of global textile exports in 2019, ahead of India.

Bangladesh has come of age, moved with aid in an attempt to move beyond aid, its abject leitmotif for several decades after a genocidal war in 1971. And it must remain robust: socio-economic growth continues to be Bangladesh's greatest bulwark against a radical implosion, a calling card for its raison d'être, its very being.

In its economy lies Bangladesh's absolution—and absolution for the region that abuts it on three sides.

39. Interlude: Natter with a Nabob

15/01/2020: Meeting in New Moti Nagar.

Those who rave about Lutyens' Delhi should see power quotient here. Like the 'old' Moti Nagar, packed with bureaucrats, only some high-range babus too, including a Nabob of the Naga peace process. It's strange to have my own public suggestions & analyses since 2012 thrown back at me as policy. Politely, over excellent pakoras and mint chutney and fine tea, but strange.

The more I see & hear, the more the 2015 Framework Agreement seems hollow. As I keep writing, telling anyone who'll listen: little more than photo-op for Modi govt and I-M, meaningless without involving other factions & civil soc/citizens, local govts. I-M is not sole rebel claimant to post-conflict world, lost that cachet especially since split with K way back in in 1988. So why play them up in the first place, increase I-M's ego/significance at the cost of entire process? Ergo: net-net of Framework Agreement is typical bluster mutating to miscalculation of govt & then climbing down/back-track by doing what should have been done in the first place, talking to everyone, bringing other groups on board & instead of saying, 'See, I-M's holding everything back!'

Not sure Nabob is responsible for miscalculation & recalibration. Grand Nabob is NSA. Grander nabobs in MHA and PMO. Who will take the fall for major mess in Nagaland/Manipur? Or climb down, as they are already beginning to in J&K?

And who will be held responsible for the bluster and miscalculations of I-M? Recovery strategy of I-M now is clearly to maintain status quo and reiterating flag-constitution trope is emotional hook.

And recovery strategy of govt now is S.O.P. of pure attrition. More hemming in of I-M. Discrediting I-M. Wearing down I-M. Nabob launched into how I-M leadership 'nothing but a bunch of thugs & car thieves'. Specific ref to Phungthing. He and government really seem to hate that guy & other cronies like Absalom Tangkhul. Brutal chaps, but made government repeatedly look foolish & literally run riot. So, they will continue to hunt him & others close to Uncle M like Apam & whittle away credibility, and wait out M's death & that of other leaders, benefit from I-M splitting into more factions which is inevitable if this plays out & peace deal is delayed, & reel in who they can by offering the moon like they've done for all other factions + saving skin of K breakaways who're now part of peace process.

Nabob smiles like Buddha when I ask about future of I-M yaruiwo Q Tuccu. Tuccu's daughter married to senior IAF officer. Both from major Sümi political families.

But it's all a stalemate in many ways. Current I-M structure won't give. Who will monitor disarmament? Even if I-M cracks many Nagaland political fat cats will resist giving up power whatever they may say, don't have vision/depth like in Mizoram. Manipur won't give any concession to Naga homelands/Tangkhuls/others without massive emotional + security + fiscal/development sops. Naga peace meaningless anyway without accommodation in Manipur + meaningful peace with Manipur rebels. More inter-linked dominoes. More drift.

Why don't you make Muivah the governor of Nagaland? I suggest before I leave.

It's a jest, but it's enough to make Nabob place his cup of tea back on the table. He smiles. I plough on. Seriously: Muivah wants face-saving, pomp, splendour, immunity, security. Manipur doesn't want him even if Ukhrul does. Nagaland won't accept him in politics. So make him governor. He'll have people saluting him morning, noon and night. He can be a figurehead under the control of government of India. He'll be protected. Win-win.

Nabob smiled. Probably overstayed my welcome.

40. 2020: Same-Same But Different

It was all about timing and context.

After the rapid process that led to a peace deal with Bodo rebels on 27 January 2020, there was naturally some speculation that three extant conflicts in far-eastern India would soon be settled. One was of course the ongoing Naga peace process, which has been on a last-mile trot since mid-2018. The second involved Paresh Baruah, who led the at-war 'Independent' faction of ULFA. The third was with half a dozen Manipuri rebel groups that made up CorCom, or Coordination Committee.

Four factions of the National Democratic Front of Bodoland (NDFB) along with an influential Bodo students' organisation and a Bodo civilian pressure group signed the peace agreement with central and Assam governments. Among other concessions, the Bodoland Territorial Area Districts, the name given to Kokrajhar, Baksa, Chirang and Udalguri, the four contiguous districts of Assam bordering Bhutan and Arunachal Pradesh would now be known as Bodoland Territorial Region.

The changed nuance from 'districts' to 'region' was significant as it acknowledged a Bodo homeland within the state of Assam, without separating from Assam. This was dialled down from earlier rebel demands for a breakaway state and, later, suggestions for union territory status, which would have brought it under the administrative ambit of the central government. So, on the face of it, the arrangement satisfied the identity and aspirations of the Bodo people as well as solved for the BJP-led government of Assam the politically tricky matter of ceding territory. Ceding territory would set off the Assamese chauvinist and territorialist, as it were, and could trigger similar demands in other parts of Assam such as Karbi Anglong, Dima Hasao and Cachar, which also have homelands of non-Ahom ethnicities. And, as far as the Indian government was concerned, played into Naga demands for integrated homelands.

But the deal was inherently vulnerable and merited attention for other peace process in the region. Would the ₹1,500 crore (₹15 billion) promised to the Bodo territory as part of the peace deal, the amount to be shared equally by the central and Assam governments and disbursed over three years, lead to real development? Or would it continue to provide candy for the Council and Assam's paymasters, who oversaw the 'Bodo' region that includes some of the most under-developed districts in Assam? How much independence would Bodoland Territorial Council, now nominally responsible for administration and development, actually be accorded? (As it is the deal was remarkably, and uncomfortably, close to what a watered-down Alternative Arrangement in Manipur might resemble!)

The vulnerability of the Bodo peace deal was rooted in the birth of the Bodo rebellion in the first place—which began in the 1980s not on account of slights from India, but administrative and development apathy of the state of Assam, and a feeling that Bodo—the people, the language, the identity—were subsumed by the Assamese. The initial demand for Bodoland, which grew out of a students' movement (in much the same way, ironically, as a movement led by students in Assam which later birthed armed rebellion by ULFA), came even earlier, in the early 1970s.

This vulnerability extended to other parts of Assam and far-eastern India and indeed any geography in India that either had active conflict, or neutralized conflict with military or policing dominance and now hoped to seed positivity with governance and development.

It was not intemperate to remain sceptical of the Bodo—or Boro—peace deal, even though it brought the very welcome prospect of peace returning to a long-neglected, diminished and roiled part of northern Assam. It was on account of the quick-fix nature of the deal itself.

And this concern extended to these other conflicts, of quick-fix deals purportedly for the greater good undermined by expediency—

the Naga process and the Framework Agreement being cases in point. Essentially, such deals involved the integration of leaders more than cadres—who were usually calmed with modest government rehabilitation packages—into the political-economy food chain of a civilian administration. Typically, much benefit accrued to former rebel leaders, and little to the people on whose behalf they claimed to be fighting. This government-sponsored buyout of rebels was tied to a system of government-provided jobs for the local population. Examples abound, from Mizoram to Assam. (Besides massive central government funds and grants nearly all states in India's far-east record a staggering proportion of government jobs in employment statistics. An article in *Employment News*, a Government of India publication, even carried this plea from the author, a Mizo academic: 'In the absence of industries worth mentioning, state government has to be the main provider of job/ employment.')

But there was also the matter of the timing and context of the deal—the core reason.

The Bodo deal came together quickly when four factions of the National Democratic Front of Bodoland (NDFB) signed up. Some factions were already in 'peace camps.' The leader of a key faction, Ranjan Daimary, was released from jail just days before the deal, and flown to Delhi for the signing. It was a canny presaging of a possible Naga deal—indeed, it mirrored the release of key Naga leaders, the changing situation in Myanmar, and so on. The trigger for it all was the arrival from Myanmar of a faction of NDFB led by B. Saoraigwra. This faction was bereft of refuge in Myanmar on account of that country's army hammering away at the north-western Myanmar headquarters and base area of what remained of NSCN-K which, among other things, provided safe haven—for considerations in cash and kind—to Saoraigwra's NDFB faction, Baruah's faction of ULFA, CorCom groups and other minor rebel splinters of Indian origin such as the remnants of Kamtapur Liberation Organisation that has for some decades sought a homeland in northern Bengal—which began with the feeling of their not-Bengali identities being subsumed and their livelihoods threatened.

Saoraigwra's group provided the most recent example of the policy quid pro quo between the governments of India and Myanmar to deny rebels bases and flush them out. This denial of refuge by Myanmar was now expected to bring several rebel groups above ground and impel them to talk peace with the government of India.

Only, it wasn't that simple. While several ULFA factions continued their tortuous peace talks with central government agencies to seek political accommodation from Assam's government, Baruah, from all available indications, had invoked his China option, as an Indian security analyst told me during a conversation to exchange notes. Baruah's faction, and those still operating from Myanmar, would find among the Tatmadaw some financially sympathetic ear, as it were, to continue to provide refuge. To bring him—and them—on board would require more than pressure. Baruah brought to bear an extreme position for Assamese identity and sovereignty, much like what was practiced by his former colleagues now in talks with the Indian and Assam governments—sentiments that had not dissipated even with Assam's helter-skelter run for economic prosperity and, since 2014, greater dalliance with a Hindu majoritarian ethic.

This position, as we have seen, twinned well with the ongoing and highly contentious exercise of the National Register of Citizens, which sought to expose illegal immigrants in Assam. But it certainly clashed with provisions of the Citizenship (Amendment) Act, 2019, that sought to provide Indian citizenship—and, by extension, continued Assamese residency—to non-Muslim immigrants from Bangladesh and elsewhere. This opposition remains explosive in Assam, and has a cachet among those who hold Axomiya identity and nationalism close to their hearts—ULFA's heart.

The mechanics of pressure and a food-chain peace was also uncertain with Manipuri rebel groups. Ideologically strong CorCom were certainly hamstrung by developments in Myanmar, but members of CorCom had for long had arrangements with that country's establishment. The likelihood of their jettisoning conflict was also directly dependent on massive accommodation by the current BJP dispensation in Manipur—as well as the outcome of the Naga peace process. Any mis-step there would make CorCom's purpose and appeal stronger. Indeed, it could draw recruits for future rebellion.

19/06/2020

GoI's pressure tactic with I-M is yielding more fracture—but these are dangerous fractures. Just received copy of open letter dated today written by 'Major General A. Raman, Deputy Longvibu, General Headquarters, Naga Army' on I-M's letterhead, but it's obviously from a 'camp office'—where? Naga refuge in NW Myanmar? Shan State? Sichuan province?—and relayed/ released via loyalists/ friends to Nagaland/ Naga/ NE media.

Raman is a.k.a. Absalom Tangkhul, ops chief of I-M, former I-M army chief Gen. Phungthing's right-hand man and, like Phungthing, a target for Ravi/Govt. Letter reads like an open, direct threat to both GoI and I-M leadership: Muivah & Co., V.S. Atem, Anthony Shimray, the lot, even though they aren't specifically named. Letter accuses I-M leadership in Hebron of selling out to GoI and its agencies. Significant clarification: Absalom absolves Phungthing & himself of everything. Invokes all-for-the-cause clause. Seems like a progression to likelihood of Phungthing & Absalom becoming a core of opposition/ rebellion/ pushback with China & others backing—well, at least a leveraging point—as I wrote in Oct 2019 after I got information of Phungthing, Absalom & Muivah's nephew, Apam, disappearing off the radar into Myanmar and beyond. (But just China, or will Pak lend a hand as they had earlier? Is a hardline faction rearing its head among BD army/intel? They'll probably hedge their bets to see how effective Phungthing & Co are before offering support, maybe just keep them for propaganda leverage from time to time.)

Absalom's letter:

'On 14 Jun 2020, National Investigation Agency (NIA) of India has filed charge sheet against an innocent Naga lady Mrs Alemla Jamir, who is also the wife of our revered National Leader Lt Gen (retd) Phungthing Shimrang ... There have been a lot of arrests & operations by NIA against my soldiers in the last six months therefore, I am compelled to write & make things clear now ... Indian government and its god forsaken Intelligence Agencies are just going around and picking anyone and everyone from their home, workplace *or even while they are travelling. My house was also raided some days ago by NIA in Dimapur & my family members who have no hand in anything are being constantly harassed by Indian Government.'*

Absalom then hammered his own (former?) colleagues.

'I am highly surprised & appalled by the behavior & reaction of my own organization during this complete scene. The national workers sitting in Hebron have either become puppets of Indian government or have lost their complete fire and fervor ... I along with my soldiers ... felt betrayed & lost out due to the level of inaction of our senior officers sitting in Hebron & also in Delhi.

'I announce today that since my own organisation is not able to take any action therefore, if there is one more incident of harassment carried out by the Indian government or their agencies towards my soldiers or our family members, it would draw serious consequences. I along with Lt Gen (retd) Phungthing Shimrang, Maj Gen Hangshi & my soldiers will retaliate & retaliate like never before. I therefore, warn Indian government and their agencies to refrain from harassing people in my land if they don't want to put the life of their soldiers in danger. I also pray to my seniors in Hebron to take note of my words and not be pet dogs of the Indians.'

In response, the government of India ignored Abasalom and his patron, Phungthing, and cranked up the pressure on I-M's core—in an operation that roped in both Assam Rifles and, significantly, Nagaland Police. A first information report, or FIR, registered by Nagaland Police detailed how the raid snagged nearly ₹1.59 crore (₹15.9 million) from the residence of Rayilung Nsarangbe, a top I-M bagman, along with two kilos of the explosive RDX, several weapons including an AK-56 assault rifle, a handgun, and a CZ 99 .22 calibre rifle—a precision Czech weapon usually used for hunting. Investigators also detailed a cash trail of several million rupees that began with an Agra-based construction firm engaged in road construction projects in Nagaland and Manipur and, via Naga and non-Naga middlemen—all named—ended with Nsarangbe, who was arrested on 5 July from his Dimapur residence along with two associates.

An article detailing the FIR and bust, published on 8 July 2020 in *Deccan Chronicle*, took care to mention that Nsarangbe 'happens to be a close associate of NSCN (IM) general secretary Thuingaleng Muivah,' referred to Muivah's office as 'self-style Prime Minister's Office'—'self-styled' being a long-used phrase of briefings by India's police forces, paramilitaries, Army and intelligence backgrounders in the same manner rebels in India's far east were often referred to as 'bandits' by many army officers posted there from the 1950s to 1990s. The article offered calibrated praise for a letter Ravi wrote to Rio on 16 June 2020 that had meanwhile set off a mini-storm of indignation in Naga political and rebel circles: 'In what has also corroborated the hard-hitting letter of Nagaland Governor R.N. Ravi …'

Five days later, the same correspondent wrote that Nsarangbe's wife, whom security agencies accused of having withdrawn ₹4 crore (₹40 million) from Nsarangbe's bank account the day after his arrest, had also been taken into custody, and the hunt was on to trace the recipient of this money. Meanwhile, a pastor with links to the network had been arrested with over a million rupees in cash and he in turn had fingered 'an IAS officer of Manipur' as being part of the gravy train that diverted money from central government-funded rural roadworks and employment schemes to I-M's coffers.

More tantalising details followed. Nsarangbe 'had acquired 800-acre land and was in possession of Rs. 5.59 crore'—nearly ₹60 million. NIA had taken over the case. And a plainly sensationalist tid-bit even allowing for the fact that there were indeed people in Nagaland's politics and administration keen to play down the case, and trip up NIA's involvement: 'Admitting that some forces deliberately delayed the NIA's entry into the investigation security sources said that NIA team had arrived Dimapur on July 6 to be the part of investigation but in the name of COVID formalities they could not join investigation.'

NIA would file a chargesheet against Nsarangbe and three others—Lamci Iralu, Zingshongam Muinao a.k.a. Ruth Chawang, Ramningle Pame—in the last week of December 2020, but in the super-charged game of pressure-the-rebel, that amounted to a distant future.

Meanwhile, the squeeze on I-M, recent breakaways like the trigger-happy warlord Absalom and his other colleagues on the run, and other rebel factions, and even some elements of the government of Nagaland, would just keep increasing. The entire peace process, the government face of which was Ravi—backed by the strategic vice of the national security advisor and the tactical hammer of the intelligence and investigative agencies—had now descended to the level of a dangerous farce. And except for the relatively benign public approach towards the Naga rebel groups and factions clustered into the grab-all 'NNPG', the gloves were all off.

The often-bizarre developments came thick and fast and would be the hallmarks of the year of talk-talk-fight-fight.

On 7 July, the political branch of Nagaland's home department issued a memo to all government employees. I received a ready-to-print file:

GOVERNMENT OF NAGALAND
HOME DEPARTMENT::POLITICAL BRANCH

NO. CON-6/LOR-5/2007 (Pt File)   *Dated Kohima, the 7th July, 2020*

OFFICE MEMORANDUM

As per instructions, all the Administrative Heads of Departments and all the Heads of Departments and all the Heads of Department are directed to obtain information in the self declaration form attached herewith, from all Government servants under his/her department/office, regarding family members and relatives in underground organizations, and submit to the Home Department, Political Branch latest by 7th August, 2020 positively.

Enclosed: As stated

Sd/-
TEMJEN TOY, IAS
Chief Secretary, Nagaland

To
All AHODs/ HODs for compliance

Sd/-
(ABIJIT SINHA) IAS
Principal Secretary, Home

It had a separate page for a 'self-declaration', which only added to the unprecedented nature of the move.

Self—declaration

Name of Government Servant:

Department & Designation:

A) Is there any family member or close relative a member of a Naga Underground Organization—Yes/No

B) If Yes: Name of the person who is member of an UG Organization—

Nature of Relationship with the Govt. Employee—

Name of Underground Organization of which he/she is a member—

Position/Rank presently held in the UG Organization—

It is certified that the information provided is true to the best of my knowledge.

Signature of the Govt. Servant

NOTE:

- *Family member shall consist of spouse, sons/daughters, sibling and parents of the Govt. Employee.*
- *Relative shall consist of anyone who is directly related to any of the family member of the Govt. employee.*

Then on 11 July arrived word of a major clash in Longding district of Arunachal Pradesh of six I-M cadres being killed in a joint operation of Arunachal police and Assam Rifles. Besides the body count, the early morning raid fetched assault rifles with Chinese markings. Media quoted R.P. Upadhyaya, Arunachal's director general of police, as saying that one of the killed, Sonyam Tangkhul, was involved in the killing of the MLA Tirong Aboh. The news groups Assam Alert and @ *datelinedelhi* offered these details within minutes of the announcement. *@datelinedelhi* would add: '... the team of six was sent by Absalom, a self-styled major general of the NSCN(IM) also the main accused in Aboh case ... Absalom remains absconding ... Police say militants fired as many as 400 rounds in the encounter ...'

Meanwhile, Hebron continued its journey around the sun like an asteroid that had broken away from earth's gravity but retained the option to visit from time to time. It also appeared that the conglomerate of CorCom and its alliance with an ULFA faction had found second wind—but it wasn't clear yet whether it was in anticipation of continued warlordism, renewed support from China, fresh logistical inputs and alliances with the on-the-run elements of I-M, a push to create greater visibility and leverage for a settlement with the governments of Myanmar and India; or, to use an examination-colloquialism, all of the above.

The developments and assertions arrived fast-and-furious.

04/07/2020: News in nagalandpage.com
NSCN (IM) REDUCES TAX FROM 5% TO 3%
'This is for general information that in the context of the prevailing Covid-19 pandemic crisis and the economic situation that followed because of the continued lockdown, the 5% tax payable to the Government of the People's Republic of Nagalim (GPRN) shall henceforth be reduced to 3% with immediate effect,' said an emailed release issued by the MIP, NSCN/GPRN.

21/07/2020 (Whatsapp chat)

Me: So, Uncle M left Dimapur for Delhi on a chartered plane? Papers say with wife and seven others ...

Kohima: Yes!!

Me: What's this 'treatment' for which he needs to rush? Is he being careful because of Covid?

Kohima: Lol

Me: Checked. VT-HGL. Dassault-Falcon 2000. Sweet ride. Shows as registered to Hinduja Group/Ashok Leyland, then pvt air operator. But companies charter or lend their aircraft, I mean Modi flew Adani jet to his 2014 inaug, so ... but it's expensive even for a relatively short ride, DMU-DEL.

Kohima: Nothing fr them. One new AK56 costs same.

30/07/2020 (WhatsApp chat)

Kohima: https://easternmirrornagaland.com/yung-aung-led-nscn-k-splits-further/

+ Indo-Naga talks NH pushes for change in interlock

Me: Yeah, it broke yesterday afternoon.

Kohima: Yes

Me: Did you see this item in Nagaland Page?

Me: 'Indo-Naga Talks: NH pushes for change in interlocutor, Dimapur, July 29: The Naga Hoho has pushed for replacement of the current interlocutor to the Indo-Naga peace talk by stating that a peaceful settlement cannot be achieved "with an interlocutor without empathy and without understanding of our history and our aspiration ..." said NH president HK Zhimomi and general secretary K Elu Ndang in a representation to the Prime Minister of India ...'

Me: Fat chance. It's a stranglehold now. Who's pushing Hoho?

Kohima: Naga Hoho has no membership from any Naga tribes in Nagaland and yet some section of the media gives it the primary space.

Me: So they're now I-M proxies?

Kohima: Yes. The mistake that Muivah and his family made with the help of T R Zeliang still persists—it has led to the break up of the Naga Hoho which was a creation of so many years of hard work by all sections of the society! But now they want to manipulate it like they manipulate the NSCN IM...

Kohima: They captured it and it became their downfall ... Otherwise these were platforms for all tribes to come together and ventilate or share ideas.

Me: Hmm.

Kohima: Muivah wanted control of all Naga tribes much more than a solution to the Naga Issue in which he supposedly stood for more than 60 years ... And while seeking to control everything he lost the plot.

Me: Hmm.

This stand appeared to be validated by an item dated 12 August I came by on the Instagram page of Eastern Mirror with the headline: Naga Hoho doesn't have mandate of Nagas of Nagaland, says 14 tribes: 'The 14 tribal hohos of Nagaland on Wednesday said the representation of the Naga Hoho to the government of India doesn't represent the Nagas of Nagaland as not a single Naga tribe from Nagaland is affiliated to it. The press and media cell of the 14 tribes stated that "Naga Hoho doesn't have the mandate of Nagas of Nagaland."'

But the battle of pushing, and pushing back, the negotiatory attitude of talk-talk-fight-fight, escalated all around.

30/07/2020 (Joint statement by MNPF, RPF & ULFA-I)

Internationally 'the era of expansionism is over' but not the Indian expansionism. As the entire world has made up its mind against expansionism, the people of WeSEA are also countering against the expansionism of India. Therefore, the people of WeSEA are still fighting against colonial ruler India for our independence. As a course of independence struggle against Indian colonisation and expansionism, a combined force of Manipur Naga People's Front (MNPF), Revolutionary People's Front (RPF) and United Liberation Front of Asom—Independent (ULFA-I) had conducted a joint military offensive against IOF (Indian Occupation Forces) on July 29, 2020 at Sajik Tampak area of Manipur. During this joint military offensive around 4 IOF personnel were killed in action and many more wounded.

We deeply regret that in our liberation struggle our brothers of WeSEA are killed or wounded in action. We know that joining the Indian Occupation Force is not right because rougish [Sic] India makes enmity among our brothers. Therefore we would like to ask our brothers and sisters of WeSEA to please withdraw from the Indian forces and instead fight against the rougish India for our independence.

We are also calling upon the people of WeSEA to stay away from the Indian Forces as they are the super spreader of infectious Coronavirus Disease 2019 (COVID-19).

Ruichumhao	*MM Ngouba*	*Paresh Asom*
Defence Secretary, MNPF	*Chief of Army Staff, PLA*	*Vice Chairman &*
		Chief of Army Staff
		ULFA[I]

The paragraph about 'regret' was particularly significant as the incident didn't go down well in terms of optics. Indeed, for 'WeSEA' it was a PR disaster. 'Around 4 IOF killed' were actually three, and all from the region—'Northeast India' as popularized by the Indian government, and 'West South East Asia' of this particular rebel grouping which once counted on S.S. Khaplang as its chief patron. In the photo of the three coffins circulated by Assam Rifles, they were placed left to right. Havildar Pranay Kalita was from Assam, Rifleman Metha Konyak of Nagaland, and Rifleman Ratan Salam of Manipur. All from the 4th Battalion, they were on their way back to their operational base in Khongtai on 29 July around 6:30 pm—a time of dusk-to-darkness in this IST-mandated region—when the patrol was attacked with a combination of an IED or improvised explosive device and then fired upon. Six others troopers were injured.

The news had reached me at 11 pm that night by way of a typically staccato, and clinical yet chilling Whatsapp message. It was a forward from a contact who was on a government group. From the type of message one could infer it had come from someone in the police, army or intelligence:

'Likely Stand Off/ IED cum Ambush on a party ex 4 AR in Gen A Sajik Tampak near BP 41. Speculations of fatal cas (being ascertained). Time 1845 approx. PLA/CORCOM.'

41. Framework Disagreement

12/08/2020—Via Morung Express & Others

FRAMEWORK AGREEMENT BETWEEN THE GOVERNMENT OF INDIA (GoI) AND NATIONAL SOCIALIST COUNCIL OF NAGALAND (NSCN)

The political conflict is about six decades old. Attempts have been made for its comprehensive Resolution through discussions between the Govt. of India and the representatives of the Naga people from time to time. A fresh attempt in this regard was initiated through a political dialogue between the Govt. of India and the NSCN in 1997.

The GoI and the NSCN dialogue led to a better mutual understanding. While the GoI in the expression of the understanding recognized the unique history and position of the Nagas; the NSCN understood and appreciated the intricacies of the Indian system. With such an understanding and with due appreciation of the imperative of the contemporary realities and regard for the future vision both sides have agreed to reach and agreement that will end the violent confrontation once and for all and will usher in comprehensive progress in consonance with the genius of the Naga people.

Both sides have understood each other's respective positions and are cognizant of the universal principle that in a Democracy sovereignty lies with the people. Accordingly, the Govt. of India and the NSCN, respecting wishes of the people for sharing the sovereign power as defined in the competencies reached an agreement on the 3rd August, 2015 as an honorable solution. It is a matter of great satisfaction that dialogue between the Govt. of India and the NSCN has successfully concluded and we are confident it will provide for an enduring inclusive relationship of peaceful co-existence of two entities.

The two sides agree that within this Framework Agreement details and execution plan will be worked out and implemented shortly.

Sd/-	*Sd/-*	*Sd/-*
(Isak Chishi Swu)	*(Th. Muivah)*	*(RN Ravi)*
Chairman	*General Secretary*	*Representative of Government*
National Socialist	*National Socialist*	
Council of Nagaland	*Council of Nagaland*	

On a personal note it was yet again a validation of my years-long stand that the Framework Agreement had been little more than an agreement to talk settlement and bereft of any specific commitment by either party except to dial down and move on. The leak of the agreement evidently capped an I-M-led public relations onslaught with the leak of the purported Framework Agreement—a long-delayed response to Ravi and the government's pincer movement of the previous three years. It did seek to offer a substantial bite. Along with its proxies among the Naga tribes and civil society organisations, I-M sought to turn the government's narrative on its head.

An official response from I-M was that Ravi had become a 'liability' and it was all on account of his 'misdoings'. Indeed, I-M went as far as to release a copy of what it called a 'manipulated' version of the Framework Agreement of 3 August 2015. This purported document was released to media, with the offending sentence underlined. In it, I-M maintained, Ravi had contrived to delete the word 'new' from the phrase '… an enduring exclusive new relationship …' thereby changing the meaning of the Agreement.

I-M also took exception to a couple of clauses in a government report as indicating Ravi's duplicity. It was Report No. 213 of the Department-Related Parliamentary Standing Committee On Home Affairs, and titled 'Security Situation In The North Eastern States Of India.' It had been presented to Parliament on 19 July 2018.

I-M specifically pointed out two parts, both in Chapter III of the Report. These two sub-sections were:

3.1.4 During the course of the last several years, the Government started opening out and reaching out to civil society organisations, Naga Tribal bodies and other stakeholders to get the views of the stakeholders other than NSCN (IM). In 2015, the Government reached an understanding with the NSCN (IM), which agreed for a settlement within Indian federation, with a special status. The Interlocutor informed the Committee that this was a departure from their earlier position of 'with India, not within India' and the Government called it 'Framework Agreement' and signed it.

And the other:

3.1.8 The Committee was informed that the contours of the agreement had not been spelt out in the framework agreement. The framework agreement was just about the recognition of the uniqueness of Naga history by the Government of India, and an understanding that inclusive settlement will be within the Indian federation with due regards to the uniqueness of the Naga history. However, the Interlocutor stated that it was implied in the agreement that some special arrangement will have to be made for the Nagas.

This, I-M maintained, amounted to misleading Parliament, along with the subsequent public omission of the word 'new'—the very word that had implied 'with India, not within India'. According to I-M, the second part merely buttressed Ravi's lie.

In the battle of pressure and counter-pressure, it was easy to forget that, in the tightly calibrated nature of the process, Ravi, firmly a part of the establishment, answered to a master's voice. More precisely, a collective, with its own dynamic of command and control: the national security advisor, home minister—with whom the office of NSA was often engaged in turf wars—and the prime minister. As an intelligence officer who now owed his resurgence beyond Doval to this trinity, with an additional layer of approval of the Sangh—invitations he received to events organised by Sangh fronts and affiliated organisations were only one of the indications—Ravi would, or could, do little without his controllers' imprimatur.

There were also other matters to consider. Ridding Ravi would simply mean getting another interlocutor who would follow the same institutional guidelines and establishment approach—and overlayed by the ever-changing landscape of turf battles. And, for the moment, Ravi would remain governor of Nagaland, which allowed him every opportunity to continue to play hardball.

I-M also neglected to present its own convincing argument of the Framework Agreement, in their PR spin cleverly conflating their interpretation as Ravi's misinterpretation. In any case, even allowing for reinstating the word 'new', in the government of India's scheme it altered absolutely nothing in letter and spirit. The acknowledgement of 'with a special status' and 'that some special arrangement will have to be made for the Nagas' was really all that would happen.

And, this was in a parliamentary committee report presented in 2018. Ravi and the government of India's position towards I-M had begun to harden in 2017 and has steadily ramped up since. After the fair accompli of the splitting of J&K in mid-2019, the writing on the wall was that it would all be 'within' India and 'with' India, or not at all. Ravi was following a collective script. He wasn't an outlier. He was an insider who now had more than the peace negotiations to protect. The massive squeeze on I-M, and the isolating of I-M—with, it must be said, substantial help from I-M's own predilections—was now only part of the plan.

The real play would be in Manipur, Arunachal Pradesh and Assam. It would go back to that old loop: how to assuage both Naga and non-Naga interests in an honourable manner with a feeling that everyone would win. For the government it was clear: So what if a few ageing, cornered leaders of I-M lost?

Or even: a few ageing leaders of Nagaland who protected them?

On 16 June 2020, Ravi had written a four-page letter of which I have a copy, to Nagaland's chief minister, Neiphiu Rio.

After a cordial 'My dear Chief Minister' it was a broadside

unprecedented in its venom in recent political history, and directed as much at the government as all rebel groups. Ravi wrote of 'Day to day unrestrained depredations by over half a dozen organized armed gangs, brazenly running their respective so called "Governments" challenging the legitimacy of the State Government without any resistance from the State law and order machinery has created a crisis of confidence in the system.'

When parts of the letter leaked shortly, it created an uproar and, unsurprisingly, started the wheels churning about how to rid Nagaland—and the peace process—of Ravi, who clearly had the go-ahead to push everyone to the wall, in the same manner they pushed citizens to the wall. For several weeks there was little else that dominated Naga communication channels:

'... The State Government development departments are under duress to give regular ransom to the armed gangs. "Town Commands" of these armed gangs keep the people in towns and its neighbourhood terrorised. Brazen display of fire power by the rival gangs for turf control drive the people to panic.

'Situation has deteriorated to such an extent that the armed miscreants appoint their own "dealers" for every commodity from salt to construction materials coming into the State. They decide and levy illegal "Taxes" on every item. They run "syndicates", for contrabands including alcoholic drinks. They are operating check gates for this purpose at almost every entry points [sic] to the State with the full knowledge of the State law and order machinery.'

This leads to as much as a trebling of costs to the consumer, Ravi continued, also driving home the point that the same system effected goods travelling south to Manipur—that being the key artery for supply. All this was on the first page. The governor-interlocutor was just getting warmed up.

He wrote of a 'steady down-slide in all parameters of development in Nagaland—e.g. road connectivity, health and education infrastructures and livelihood' on account of siphoning of government funds, which— he hinted at this—besides being skimmed by intermediaries was 'attributed to institutionalised systemic ransom to the armed gangs'. He referred to CAG reports to make his point.

'During periodic monitoring of the progress of construction of National Highways in the State, the NHIDCL authorities and project contractors have frequently complained of the armed gangs stopping the work unless 5-7% of the project cost is given to them as ransom. There have been instances of kidnapping and assault on project engineers and managers for defiance or delay in ransom payment.' Investigations moved slowly or not at all.

Entire Forests were being handed to these 'armed miscreants', and forest department employees evicted from their homes with full connivance of 'direction from above'. Land was being encroached.

Ravi then tore into the police and local judiciary.

'Reports of the DGP on police action against the armed gangs during the last over three years reveal disconcerting facts on the abysmal status of law and order in the State. Whatever actions against the armed miscreants that have been occasionally taken are only against the foot soldiers. I did not come across a case in which senior members of gangs have been implicated. In over 98% of the cases, the accused are at large or on bail within a couple of days of arrest. Even in grave offences such as those under the Indian Arms Acts and Explosive Substance Act where minimum punishment under law is prescribed for five years or more, the convicted accused are awarded 5-10 days sentence often with the concurrence of the Public Prosecutor. Whenever the cases are charge-sheeted under Section 7 of the Nagaland Security Regulations (NSR) 1962 which carries punishment of imprisonment upto 5 years, the charges are not pressed at the trial ...'

Nothing had happened even after repeatedly raising 'serious concerns with you from time to time ...' '... The scenario in the State is grim. The law and order has collapsed ...'

From now on, Ravi wrote, he would keep an eye on things, from postings to the state of law and order.

The 'regards' at the end was hardly a salve.

This play of being a bull inside a China shop had its effect of laying on the pressure some more. The government of Nagaland had been put on notice as an impediment to the peace process alongside lack of development. The satrapies within Nagaland and the Northeast and their backers in New Delhi had been put on notice—cementing a power shift that had begun the previous years within the Sangh superstructure in relation to Northeast India. I-M and every other rebel faction had been put on notice; only I-M would attempt to push back, every other group had acquiesced in principle to what a conclusive peace deal would bring them. The arguments that corruption was a pandemic in the Mainland, central government policies had led directly to the ills of Nagaland, that the central government had signed ceasefire agreements that permitted Naga rebels to retain arms, train and recruit and that for decades every governor of Nagaland and every government of India had papered over precisely the financial misdemeanours being dredged up, cut little ice. Ravi and his cohorts had managed to change the narrative. (In a year, the narrative would extend to citizens, including groups like ACAUT, demanding clarifications from I-M and others about leaching funds meant for treatment and prevention of Covid-19, an infection Muivah himself would test positive for.)

On 15 August 2020, Ravi's expression at a photo-op during an 'At Home' he hosted to mark India's 74th Independence Day seemed to say it all. There he was, smiling with a smug expression as he sat at the head of the Governor's table, flanked by his wife, Laxmi, Rio and his wife Kaisa, and the speaker of Nagaland Assembly, Sharingain Longkumer. It was as if he knew he would remain both governor and interlocutor for a while longer.

A month later, the government of India's stand would visibly harden. Word was conveyed through media that the government wasn't going to 'concede' I-M's renewed demand about a separate flag and constitution. It was also conveyed that this government stand was already communicated the previous year, on 31 October 2019, the last day of Ravi's previous ultimatum to I-M to conclude talks. As we read, this led to a crisis management meeting in New Delhi and of a renewed chain reaction of punches and counter-punches with raids on I-M, accusations by on-ground or on-the-run I-M officials about government overreach, a propaganda and public relations war by both sides—or, more precisely, every side. The government's message-by-media also held out the deadline of 30 September 2020 to conclude the peace process. Word came that the media leaks this time around were reportedly primed by Doval and not, as I had rudely impugned to a peace-talks insider, that it had come 'From the desk of Ravi via his court stenographer' in that particular newspaper.

The structured media leaks conveyed a further reiteration that I-M had indeed again brought up the matter of a separate flag and constitution in 'informal talks' with Intelligence Bureau officials—an outcome of the ongoing chill between I-M and Ravi—but the demand was again turned down. This, government 'sources' clarified to media, was only the continuation of an agreement reach on 31 October 2019, that the matter of a separate flag and constitution would remain a matter of discussion even after a peace accord was signed—but this did not imply that it meant a 'yes'.

Indeed, it appeared to be a gentler way of saying: do the deal with everything that has already been agreed. There can be no other deal in the current situation. It also seemed that while I-M had trumped itself, so had the government. Both would need to regain face even as the dangerous game of attrition continued and the world outside the bubble that India and I-M had created went about its business.

42. 'Do You Think the Movement Will End with Mr Muivah?'

05/10/2020

 Call from Dimapur with this central msg: 'Muivah has decided he cannot die leaving a legacy of surrender.'

 Muivah is 85. He appears to have chosen status quo and to be remembered as a leader who didn't bow to India. I-M did sign the Framework Agreement, first group to get on board. But pro-I-M and pro-Muivah folks will spin it the way that marks their 'interpretation' as a victory (that insistence on flag and constitution) and not a climbdown.

 And this way he saves face and status quo clout and privileges. But what of his people? What do they save besides a prolonging of this peace without peace? Scraps at a post Muivah, post I-M banquet?

 It's not easy. The talks are now ever more talk-talk-fight-fight. This story is far from ended.

I shall always remember the meeting with Muivah in his government-provided bungalow in Lodi Estate—provided as a gesture of conciliation and accepted as such. In those days good faith counted for something, even on the face of it.

It was in end-April 2010, about two months after his return to India. Manmohan Singh was prime minister, P. Chidambaram the home minister. I had attempted to meet Muivah in Hebron that March. I had based myself in Nagaland for some weeks for just that opportunity, but he was too busy. Besides, the right words hadn't yet been conveyed to his ears by the right people, as it were—by way of friends, acquaintances, and contacts in Ukhrul—for the interview to come through.

We met in Delhi on a day Muivah had a surgery to his cheek at the All India Institute of Medical Sciences. It's why he declined a photo that day, with a smile and an apologetic 'another time'.

(It is remarkable that his public stand about autonomy and insistent applicability of the Naga constitution—the Yehzabo, based on a patriarchal model modified by NSCN—tied to any peace hadn't changed at all in a decade although that reality has steadily receded since our conversation—and, certainly, even more since Modi became prime minister in May 2014. The signing of the Framework Agreement a little over a year later changed nothing.)

Muivah's rasping but forceful voice came through as I replay the interview. He remained calm through the hour-long interaction but lost his temper when, after building rapport through the interview, towards the end I pressed him on a couple of points, fully aware it might be cutting too close to the bone.

The Indian government appears to just want to play a waiting game.

'Yes!' Muivah immediately sat straighter.

I came to the point tangentially, referring to the conflict of several decades and traversing many generations of Nagas, the urgent need for closure, the need to fulfil the aspirations of youngsters. It was done so as to not offend him as that could jeopardise the interview and display bad form with bad manners—at least in the tribal tradition, while speaking to an elder and a person of some importance—but he figured the tack as soon as I began. Because his eyes changed, his face became firmer. I had touched one of his raw nerves. Muivah became more upset as I continued.

'Wouldn't it be incumbent, wouldn't it be right, after so much sacrifice and torment all around, to offer your people a greater root to that hope?' For me to say it any plainer in front of Muivah—for heaven's sake, stop fighting and start living, as I'd written elsewhere—would be too direct, impolite.

'In your presence,' I added, signalling his legacy—his age—while mentioning the transparent, typical Indian modus operandi of attrition, which was for Muivah's generation of rebel leadership to pass on.

'We never think that Indians would do the best for us, that they would have the greatest love for us. We don't think that.' Here Muivah spoke slowly. I recall his face had begun to flush, darken in anger.

'They want to wear us out, for days, for years. They do not learn from the bitterness of their failure, the failures from which they suffered. They are going to repeat the same mistake. Do you think the movement will end with Mr Muivah?'

'Who am I?' He raised his voice nearly to a shout. '*Who* am I?

'That is a serious mistake. You may not like to hear it, but this is a fact: more than a thousand people will come and do much better than what we have done. We have that kind of belief, faith; that Nagas will become stronger all the time. Let us see how strong the Indians will be.'

Muivah went into flashback mode, reminiscing about what he told K. Padmanabhaiah, the interlocutor during whose stint the ceasefire-extension fracas happened; and how Nehru was a show off.

'Mr Nehru claimed big, big things. He went to the extent of saying, "No, the Chinese will be thrown out of Indian soil, in 1962." In two weeks' time Chinese forces reached up to the banks of the Brahmaputra. Do you want to repeat the mistake of Mr Nehru today also? Do you think China has become weaker and you have become stronger?'

'Nations rise,' Muivah marked what he implied as India's arrogance. 'Nations fall. This time also if they cannot take positive steps forward soon, Nagas will take steps. We know the techniques. We have tried it before. They won't be able to wear us out.'

Ten years later, the words ring as hollow as the Framework Agreement. Isak Chishi Swu, the I in I-M, is dead. Shangwang Shangyung Khaplang is dead. Muivah is in his late 80s. I-M is weakened, its leadership structure stressed, and K is fractured, nearly finished. I-M is ranged against the rest of the rebel groups and its own identity among most Naga tribes.

But it is ironical too that with all the showboating of Modi and his government, the best his government and the security apparatus could hope for as a solution was Muivah's death & I-M's subsequent implosion—perhaps controlled implosion—and create some more manageable disorder from the chaos. The standard government play but very dangerous play, because there was no telling who would next light the fire, and how, and where. In the Naga rebel construct, the angry, the rejected and the hunted have usually done so, and reinvented themselves with the logistical assistance of India's geopolitical adversaries and well-crafted emotional appeal to the intellectual and unemployed in equal measure.

Muivah gifted me a Tangkhul jacket as I left. I still have the jacket, as I do all my notes and recordings—and wishful thought for a headline that I would dearly love to see for Nagaland, Manipur, and all of far-eastern India:

Peace Breaks Out.

Epilogue

India's far-east will remain in churn in the foreseeable future.

Assam leaned heavily to the Hindu-right through 2021, with politics resembling the communal horrors and chauvinism of the 1980s. CAA remained the Sword of Damocles—or, perhaps, the dual sword of Amit Shah and Himanta Biswa Sarma, as the two BJP strongmen waved it about, in turn fuelling chauvinism and paranoia. The BJP's sledgehammer sway continued in Manipur, with an eye to imminent elections—but hardly towards peace and reconciliation. Manipuri rebels weren't helping either: word came from Myanmar that several rebel groups had thrown in their lot with the Tatmadaw for pure survival, and taken to putting down citizens of Myanmar in whose land they sheltered.

Tripura found an indigenous bulwark to the Hindu-right and Bengali impulses with the formation of a party by a Tripuri—not-Bengali—royal, who swore fealty to Tripura over religion. Arunachal Pradesh remained at the forefront of China's mission-creep more than a year after a massive flare-up of cross-border tensions; as that giant economy took hits and prepared for diverting attention from public unrest, sabre-rattling at the borders would continue, at once hampering Arunachal and cocooning it with an overload of Indian defence preparedness. Meghalaya remained a blip battled over by local political dynasts. Mizoram was buffeted by the goings-on in Myanmar, dealing with a refugee influx alongside flux of a pandemic.

Ravi was fired as the governor of Nagaland in the first week of September, which media in the region—Naga and pro-Naga—immediately touted as a victory for I-M. He would resign as interlocutor in days.

On 14 September Ravi received a formal farewell at the State

Banquet Hall in in the chief minister's residential complex in Kohima. In attendance was a smug Rio and his colleagues—the Opposition had now united under a common political umbrella of convenience, ostensibly in preparation for a peace deal. They gave speeches. Ravi spoke of futures. Before dinner, they listened as a young Naga lady crooned an immensely popular soppy song of eternal friendship, *Yeh Dosti*, from the 1975 Bollywood hit *Sholay*: '…*Tera saath na chhorenge* …' Shall never leave you …

The next day Ravi was gone, to New Delhi and then to Tamil Nadu to take up position as governor of that state. New interlocutors moved in within days, also signalling a not-so-subtle power shift from the national security advisor to the home ministry—culmination of another turf battle that formally began on 30 May 2019, the day Amit Shah took office as minister for home. On 5 October 2021, a large team of NSCN (I-M) leadership travelled to Delhi, with Muivah, Tuccu and Wangnao—I-M's paper-trinity—at its head. Representatives of the so-called NNPGs and the ever-flashy Niki, the one-man showboat, were already in Delhi for talks. Word came of a peace deal by Christmas—as it had for the three previous years.

If a deal arrived, it would be—in an irony in this game of blinding ironies—the one hammered out by Ravi and the prime minister's office, with a face-saving cushion of the Naga flag in exchange for India's primacy and the defanging of I-M and other groups. In any case, it would need to be in tandem with the emotional and political needs in Manipur, Arunachal and Assam, or there would be no deal at all, just decorative status quo a step away from hellish ethno-political chaos.

Meanwhile, connectivity and livelihoods would redeem the east, not cantankerousness. In that the future remained hazy.

After several years of effort, a patchy on-again-off-again bus service to link Manipur's capital Imphal to Mandalay, northern Myanmar's commercial and administrative hub, through the Moreh-Tamu gateway was scheduled for a formal launch in April 2020, but closure of the border on account of the fast-spreading Covid-19 outbreak stalled that. The same as it stalled efforts to make regular the occasional effort to fly from Imphal to Mandalay.

Dislocation caused by a military-led coup in Myanmar in early 2021 added to the years-long conflict in Rakhine state and exacerbated this stasis. The so-called Kaladan Multi-Modal Project to link the hub of Aizawl to the Rakhine port of Sittwe and have a sea-link with Kolkata (one of several possibilities of trade links), slowed. Work on two integrated immigration and customs check points to Myanmar in Mizoram, at Zorinpui in Lawngtlai district and Kawrpuichhuah in Lunglei district, slowed; as has also happened in Suterkandi in Assam.

This disparate nature, this very uniqueness of each aspect in India's far-east, unique needs, and the need for unique responses, took me back to a conversation I had in Imphal several years ago—just weeks before Modi's first government took office in May 2014—with the respected economist and regional policy don, Amar Yumnam. 'It is imperative that we develop perspectives which are alive to the diversity of this country,' Professor Yumnam had told me over his favourite cups of Sichuan and Korean teas at his books-and-documents-laden office in Manipur University, within sight of an Assam Rifles camp on a hill—within the campus. 'Forget other countries. It is in our own interest—in the interest of India—that we develop perspectives; not the imposing, or imposed generalised perspectives from Delhi. Delhi's interest will not serve the interest of Jammu & Kashmir. Jammu & Kashmir's interest will not solve the issues of Northeast or Manipur. So, it is best that we develop perspectives of dealing with this region and our neighbouring countries based on the reality of this country.'

The sentiment held true then. It holds truer now.

But while the India and the region waited out the ebb and flow of the diseases of politics and pandemic, there was some positive news for connectivity.

On 2 July 2021, a train on a trial run rolled into Jiribam station in Manipur from Silchar. Jiribam is Manipur's major western town and entry point from lower Assam—literally the western arm of a compass which converges on the hub of Imphal. There's the highway to the north that descends from Kohima, the highway east from Myanmar that winds its way via Moreh, and the old Teddim Road that travels up from Mizoram to the south and which, one day, hopes to reach into Myanmar with minimal border controls for the movement of goods and people along the coast and beyond.

The trial train later carried on to the village of Vangaichungpao in the hills in Tamenglong. Although several years and several central government administrations behind schedule, this railway link, even this little journey into Manipur, was a hugely symbolic boost.

I can't wait to take a train to Imphal. It would save hours and a visit to the chiropractor because like millions of others I wouldn't have to take the wretched highway from Silchar that's even worse than the wretched highway from Dimapur.

2023. 2025. 2030 … It will be worth waiting for.

A journey to the future.

To the Eastern Gate.

Acknowledgements

While I look to the ongoing future in India's far-east and its hinterland, and more books that wait to be written by my colleagues in academia, media and the literary world, it is time to thank so very many who provided empathy, time, knowledge, opportunity, generosity, connections and, occasionally, protection. Their individual and collective contributions carry *The Eastern Gate*.

In terms of attempting to understand the root causes for conflict in 'Northeast' India, and aspects of resolution of that conflict, my work goes back several years. But the idea for this book began to take shape over 2013 and 2014, over two speaking engagements. One was at St Joseph's College, Jakhama, to which I was invited by Father Abraham Lotha and his colleague, Dihe Mao. It was for a seminar in 2013 on India's 'Look East Policy'—soon to be amped up to 'Act East Policy'—in the context of Northeast India. The talk I gave there, and one on regional security and development for the inaugural Sarat Mahanata Memorial Lecture in Guwahati, in 2014, at the invitation of Partha Mahanta, coalesced my thoughts that formed the framework for *The Eastern Gate*. Further research and reportage soon followed—and hasn't really ended!—the region remains ever-dynamic.

Nobokishor Urikhimbam and his colleagues at United NGOs Mission-Manipur, especially R. Boipu Koireng and a person I can only identify as M, opened several doors and enabled travel to some areas of Manipur without which this book could not have been completed. Seth Shatsang, president of All Naga Students' Association, Manipur from 2013 to 2018, continued to enable the opening of doors among Naga hearts, minds and histories.

Alongside those interviewed specifically for this work, there are others who have informed and encouraged me over the years with their time, insights and conversations that transcend acknowledgement for any one book. In no particular order they are: Ram Wankheirakpham, Thockchom Nandini, Babloo Loitongbam, Laifungbam Debabrata 'Bobby' Roy, Basanta Wareppa, Sanjoy Hazarika, Pradip Phanjoubam, Professor Amar Yumnam, Neichute Doulo, Tsibu Haralu, Pranab Bora, Naheed Hazarika, Mmhonlümo Kikon, Kaushik Deka, Ningreichon Tungshang, Robert Lyngdoh, Temsula Ao, Barun Mitra, Ngachonmi Chamroy …

There are so many others from Nagaland, Manipur, Assam, Tripura, Meghalaya, Arunachal Pradesh and Mizoram—and so many associated with the central and provincial governments and various government agencies—I cannot name. They are sources, colleagues and friends. Naming them could—and certainly would in several instances—endanger their lives and jobs; for some, naming would also compromise their positions in public life.

I must thank some of my publishers. In this work I have discussed certain aspects about migration and ethno-political tension in Northeast India, which first found voice, though in far less detail, in *The Bengalis: A Portrait of a Community*, published by Aleph Book Company in 2017. Thank you, David Davidar and Aienla Ozukum. A few historical and anecdotal aspects are mirrored from *Highway 39: Journeys through a Fractured Land*, published by 4th Estate, an imprint of HarperCollins India, in 2012—such history doesn't change, hence. Karthika V.K., editor of HarperCollins at the time, understood the need for the book, and Shantanu Ray Choudhury and she ensured its empathetic editing. Some core thoughts on the peace processes that encompass Nagaland, Manipur, Arunachal Pradesh, Assam, and a future that also encompasses Tripura, Mizoram and Meghalaya have found expression in some of my Root Cause columns in *Mint* during the column's run from 2009 to 2020; a few such are acknowledged in the select bibliography. My thanks to Sukumar Ranganathan for creating space for the column.

Himanjali Sankar, editor of Simon and Schuster India and her colleague Sayantan Ghosh pushed for and, then, shepherded *The Eastern Gate*. Their colleague Megha Mukherjee took the manuscript to publication. They sensed the need and urgency for the work, unlike another publisher who was content to stall the book after actually commissioning it, because 'We know you love Northeast India but who will read about Northeast India?'

The short answer to that is: Enough and more will. Because here, history and futures affect the lives of not only the 50 million or so in that ethnically diverse and complex region, but the lives of hundreds of millions of people in the Subcontinent. The 'Northeast' won't wait for elegant denial over aromatic coffee and rich cake in New Delhi delicatessens.

If not then, now. If not this book, others. If not books, then media, both corporate and independent. If not such media, then free communication by groups of people and individuals through every possible channel and on every possible forum. The 'Northeast' is a force of history, a force of nature, a force of people. She *will* travel. I hope she travels well, accompanied by peace and prosperity.

Select Bibliography

Books

Allen, B.C., *Gazetteer of Naga Hills and Manipur*, Mittal Publications, New Delhi, (Reproduced) 2009.

Assam Administration Report 1882-1940 (accessed at *lib.cam.ac.uk* in 2010, 2017).

Balagopal, C., *On a Clear Day You Can See India: The Little World of the District Official*, HarperCollins Publishers India, Noida, 2013.

Barpujari, H.K., *The American Missionaries and North-east India (1836-1900 A.D.): A Documentary Study*, Spectrum Publications, Guwahati/ New Delhi, 1986.

Barua, Lalit Kumar, *India's North-East Frontier (Incorporating the Continuation of John Michell's Report)*,Spectrum Publications, Guwahati, 2010.

Baruah, Sanjib
_____*Beyond Counter-insurgency: Breaking the Impasse in Northeast India* (Ed.), Oxford University Press, New Delhi, 2009.
_____*Durable Disorder: Understanding the Politics of Northeast India*, Oxford University Press, New Delhi, 2005.

Bhattacharyya, Rajeev, *Rendezvous with Rebels: A Journey to Meet India's Most Wanted Men*, HarperCollins Publishers India, Noida, 2014.

Bhattacharyya, N.N., *North East India: A Systematic Geography*, Rajesh Publications, New Delhi, 2005.

Chakravarti, Sudeep
_____*Highway 39: Journeys through a Fractured Land*, 4th Estate (an imprint of HarperCollins India), Noida, 2012.
_____*The Bengalis: A Portrait of a Community*, Aleph Book Company, New Delhi, 2017.

Elwin, Verrier
_____*A Philosophy for NEFA (With a Foreword by the Prime Minister of India)*, North-East Frontier Agency, Shillong, second edition, 1959.
_____*India's North-East Frontier in the Nineteenth Century* (Ed.), Oxford University Press, London, 1959.
_____*Nagaland*, Published by P. Datta for the Research Department, Adviser's Secretariat, Shillong, 1961.

Gill, Preeti (Ed.), *The Peripheral Centre: Voices from India's Northeast*, Zubaan, New Delhi, 2010.

Government of Nagaland, Department of Parliamentary Affairs, *Naga Referencer: Orientation Programme for Legislators of Nagaland*, Kohima, 2006.

Haksar, Nandita; Hongray, Sebastian M., *The Judgement that Never Came: Army Rule in North East India*, Chicken Neck (an imprint of Bibliophile South Asia), New Delhi, 2011.

Haokip, P.S., *Zale'n-Gam: The Kuki Nation*, Kuki National Organisation, Privately published, 2008 (Revised edition with additional text).

Hazarika, Sanjoy, *Strangers of the Mist: Tales of War & Peace from India's Northeast*, Viking, Penguin Books India, New Delhi, 1994, 1995.

Heath, Ian; Perry, Michael, *The North-East Frontier (1837-1901)*, Men-At-Arms Series, Osprey Military, Osprey Publishing, Oxford, 1999.

Hodson, Brian Houghton, *Miscellaneous Essays Relating to Indian Subjects, Vol. II*, Trübner & Co, London, 1880.

Hodson, T.C.,

_____*The Meitheis*, Published under the orders of the Government of Eastern Bengal and Assam, David Nutt, London, 1908.

_____*The Naga Tribes of Manipur*, Published under the authority of the Government of Eastern Bengal and Assam, Macmillan and Co., Limited, London, 1911.

Iralu, Kaka D., *Nagaland and India: The Blood and the Tears*, Privately Published, Kohima, 2003 (second edition).

Jeyaseelan, Lazar (Ed.), *Conflict Mapping and Peace Processes in Northeast India*, North Eastern Social Research Centre, Guwahati, 2008.

Johnstone, James, *My Experiences in Manipur and the Naga Hills (With an Introductory Memoir)*, Sampson Low, Marston and Company Limited, London, 1896.

Kaplan, Robert D., *Monsoon: The Indian Ocean and the Future of American Power*, Random House Trade Paperbacks, New York, 2011.

Keyho, Biseto Medom, *My Journey in the Nagaland Freedom Movement*, Privately Published, Kohima, 2008.

Lintner, Bertil, *Great Game East: India, China and the Struggle for Asia's Most Volatile Frontier*, HarperCollins Publishers India, Noida, 2012.

Mackenzie, Alexander, *History of the Relations of the Government with the Hill tribes of the North-East Frontier of Bengal*, The Home Department Press, Calcutta, 1884.

Majumdar, Nivedita, (Ed.), *The Other Side of Terror: An Anthology of Writings on Terrorism in South Asia*, Oxford University Press, New Delhi, 2009.

Mehrotra, Deepti Priya, *Burning Bright: Irom Sharmila and the Struggle for Peace in Manipur*, Penguin Books India, New Delhi, 2009.

Nag, Sajal, *India and North-East India: Mind, Politics and the Process of Integration (1946-1950)*, Regency Publications, New Delhi, 1998.

Nath, D. (Ed.), *Reopening of the Stilwell Road: Prospects and Problems*, Maulana Abul Kalam Azad Institute of Asian Studies, Kolkata and Anamika Publishers & Distributors (P) Ltd, Delhi, 2004.

Nshoha, A. *Traditional Naga Village System and Its Transformation*, Maulana Abul Kalam Azad Institute of Asian Studies, Kolkata and Anshah Publishing House, Delhi, 2009.

Parrat, Saroj Nalini, *The Religion of Manipur*, Firma KLM (Private) Limited, Calcutta, 1980.

Phanjoubam, Pradip, *The Northeast Question: Conflicts and frontiers*, Routledge, New Delhi, 2016.

Rammohan E.N., *Insurgent Frontiers: Essays from the Troubled Northeast*, India Research Press, New Delhi, 2005.

Saikia, Jaideep, *Terror Sans Frontiers: Islamist Militancy in Northeast India*, Vision Books, New Delhi, 2008 (revised edition).

Sengupta, Dipankar and Singh, Sudhir Kumar, (Eds), *Insurgency in North-East India: The Role of Bangladesh*, Authorspress, in association with Spandan, New Delhi, 2004.

Shimray, Atai A.S., *Let Freedom Ring: Story of Naga Nationalism*, Promilla & Co., Publishers, in association with Bibliophile South Asia, New Delhi, 2005.

Singh, Karam Manimohan, *Nupi Lan [Women's War of Manipur]*, K. Premlata Devi, Imphal, 2000.

Singh, N. Joykumar (Ed.), *Ethnic Relations Among the People of North-East India*, Centre for Manipur Studies, Manipur University and Akansha Publishing House, New Delhi, 2006.

Singh, Thingnam Kishan (Ed.), *Look East Policy and India's North East: Polemics and Perspectives,* Centre for Alternative Discourse, Manipur and Concept Publishing Company, New Delhi, 2009.

Vungzamawi, K. (Ed. et al), *Prism of the Zo People,* Zomi Human Rights Foundation, Lamka, 2013 (Revised & enlarged edition).

Yadav, Anil (Trans. Basnet, Anurag), *Is That Even a Country, Sir!*, Speaking Tiger, 2017.

Articles, Essays, Reports, Journals

Anand, Manoj,
_____'India refuses separate flag and constitution to Naga negotiators,' *Deccan Chronicle*, 21 September 2020.
_____'NSCN (IM) extortion racket busted, 5 held,' *Deccan Chronicle*, 8 July 2020.
_____'Nagaland extortion racket: NIA arrests NSCN (IM) treasurer's wife,' *deccanchronicle.com*, 13 July 2020 (accessed 13 July 2020).
'Asian Highway Network,' UN-ESCAP (United Nations Economic and Social

Commission for Asia and the Pacific), downloaded from *unescap.org* on 4 June 2014.

'ATTF chief Ranjit Debbarma held on sedition charges,' *Press Trust of India*, Agartala, 13 November 2017.

Bagchi, Indrani, 'For first time, northeastern states to play a big role during India-ASEAN summit,' *Times of India*, 27 November 2017.

Bhaumik, Subir

_____'Book arson "a Taleban-style" act', 14 April 2005 (Downloaded from http://news.bbc.co.uk/2/hi/south_asia/4443565.stm)

_____'Disaster in Tripura', *Seminar*, No. 510, 2002.

Bhattacharjee, Nabanipa,

_____'Language of Love and Death: Fifty Years of Assam's Language Movement', *Mainstream*, Vol L, No 9, 18 February 2012.

_____'Negotiating Marginality: The Bangla-speakers of Assam', *Mainstream*, Vol LI, No 34, 10 August 2013.

_____'Speaking the Devil's Tongue: The Bengalis of Assam', Abstract of lecture at Department of History and Culture, Faculty of Humanities and Languages, New Delhi: Jamia Millia Islamia, 24 January 2013.

'Budget Speech of Shri Neiphiu Rio Chief Minister, Minister-In-Charge, Finance For 2021-22,' Government of Nagaland, 18 February 2021(via Centre for Budget and Governance Accountability).

Chakravarti, K. C., 'Bongal Kheda Again', *Economic Weekly*, 30 July 1960.

Chakravarti, Sudeep

_____'Armymen's plea has brought AFSPA into spotlight,' *Mint*, 6 September 2018.

_____'Balancing the Naga accord,' *Mint*, 7 August 2015.

_____'Between rebels' compromises lies fate of Naga peace,' *Mint*, 24 October 2019.

_____'Cleaning up Nagaland,' *Mint*, 2 October 2015.

_____'East By North-east: The Way Ahead for India's Security and Prosperity,' Parts I, II, III, *The Sentinel* (14, 15, 16 May 2014), (Reprint of a talk delivered at The 1st Sarat Mahanta Memorial Lecture, Guwahati, 1 May 2014).

_____'Extra-judicial killings in Manipur: Justice delayed,' *Mint*, 2 August 2018.

_____'Indian business and Myanmar,' *Mint*, 23 August 2013.

_____'India's Demographic Tsunami,' position paper for The Kesroli Group, 2009; republished by Gateway House: Indian Council on Global Relations, July 2010 at *www.gatewayhouse.in*; partially republished in *OPEN*, 10 July 2010.

_____'In Naga peace talks lie the fate of rebels' own deal,' *Mint*, 12 September 2019.

_____'Manipur and the visitation of vultures,' *Mint*, 22 December 2016.

_____'Manipur's staged encounters: How far can CBI, Supreme Court, push? *Mint*, 1 February 2018.

_____'Nagaland's ACAUT displays immense courage against a corrupt state machinery,' *firstpost.com*, 20 June 2017.

_____'Naga framework agreement remains an inside job between the signatories,' *Hindustan Times*, 4 July 2016.

_____'Naga peace process: New equations,' *Mint*, 3 April 2015.

_____'Revocation of 35A may ring alarm bells in other states,' *Mint*, 8 August 2019.

_____'Sudeep Speak,' *thethumbprintmag.com*, 1 January 2013 (accessed 31 January 2013).

_____'The balancing act in Manipur,' *Mint*, 10 April 2015.

_____'Time to bell the fat cats,' *Mint*, 26 June 2015.

_____'Tripura: BJP, IPFT and Tiprasa angst, *Mint*, 8 March 2018.

_____'Twipraland demand: Legitimate agitation for separate tribal state in Tripura or BJP grab to topple CPM govt?', *firstpost.com*, 17 July 2017.

Chandra, Madhu, 'The Effects of the Burning of Meitei Puyas (The Sacred Writings of Manipur,' *e-pao.net*, 1 September 2018 (downloaded 1 September 2018).

China Report: A Journal of East Asian Studies, Vol. 50, No. 3, Institute of Chinese Studies, New Delhi, August 2014.

Choudhury, Ratnadip, 'After 15 Years, Nagas Of Ukhrul Welcome Manipur Chief Minister With Red Carpet,' *ndtv.com*, 13 April 2017 (downloaded 13 April 2017).

'Chronology for Nagas in India,' Minorities at Risk Project, Refworld/UNHCR, 2004 (At *refworld.org/docid/469f38981e.html* downloaded 2009).

Das, Ram Upendra, *Enhancing India-Myanmar Border Trade: Policy and Implementation Measures*, Department of Commerce, Ministry of Commerce and Industry, Government of India, New Delhi, 2016.

Datta Sekhar, '8 NLFT rebels killed: Report,' *The Telegraph*, 10 December 2014.

'Dimapur lynching: "One act of barbarism has shamed Nagas"', *Eastern Mirror*, 13 March 2015.

'Doval, Ravi in Myanmar to attend NCA signing event,' *Nagaland Post*, 15 October 2015.

'8 ethnic armed groups to sign NCA on Oct 15,' Nagaland Post News, *Nagaland Post*, 12 October 2015.

Fifth Report, Second Administrative Reforms Commission: Public Order (Justice for each…Peace for all), Second Administrative Reforms Commission, Government of India, 2007.

Forino, Giuseppe, von Meding, Jason & Johnson, Thomas, 'The oil economics and land-grab politics behind the Rohingya genocide,' *Quartz* in *ecologies.in*, 22 September 2017 (accessed 22 September 2017).

Goswami, P. C., 'Tragedy of Political Tactlessness', *Economic Weekly*, 30 July 1960.

Government of the People's Republic of Nagalim, *Nagas at a Glance*, Privately Published, 2006.

Hasnat, Karishma, 'Meghalaya Governor warns Inner Line Permit will harm state's economy & tourism,' *theprint.in*, 6 February 2021 (accessed 7 February 2021).

Haksar, Nandita, 'Road to peace gets longer,' *Force*, issue dated September 2020.

Haokip, Helam (Ed.), *Souvenir: The 19th General Assembly cum Election (2012-2015)*, Kuki Inpi, Manipur, 2012.

Hassan, Mohammad Sajjad, *The State and Societies in Northeastern India: Explaining Manipur's Breakdown and Mizoram's Order*, PhD in Development Studies, London School of Economics & Political Science, 2007 (*etheses.lse.ac.uk/2569/1/U615518.pdf* downloaded 2014).

'India, Myanmar resolve to fight militancy,' *Press Trust of India*, 16 July 2015.

India-Myanmar Border Trade, Working Paper 378, Indian Council for Research on International Economic Relations, June 2019.

India-Myanmar Trade and Investment: Prospects and Way Forward, Working Paper No. 90, Export-Import Bank of India, June 2019.

Jiribam Correspondent, *Imphal Free Press*, 'Trial passenger train arrives at Jiribam railway station,' *Imphal Free Press*, 3 July 2021 (accessed at *ifp.co.in* on 3 July 2021).

'Joint patrolling with Myanmar to turn heat on cross-border insurgents,' TNN, *Times of India*, 1 November 2016.

Katju, Markandeya, 'The right to criticise: the sedition judgment on Kishorechandra Wangkhem,' *The Hindu*, 10 April 2019.

Konthoujam, Indrakumar, *Alternative Perspectives: Economy, Polity, History & Culture, (Vol. III Issue IV), Colonialism and Resistance: Framework, Administration and Democratic Movements*, Centre for Alternative Discourse, Manipur, 2008.

Kramer, Tom, *Neither War nor Peace: The Future of Ceasefire Agreements in Burma*, Transnational Institute, July 2009.

'KSDC releases map of proposed 'Kuki state,' Times News Network, *Times of India*, Kolkata, 14 November 2012.

Kuki Movement for Human Rights, *The Plight of the Indigenous Kuki People: Unraveling the Story of Deception, Suppression and Marginalization in the Tri Border Areas of India, Myanmar and Bangladesh*, 2009.

'Kuki Tribal Union Message to KSO,' *The Morung Express*, 8 February 2011.

Lepcha, Irani Sonowal, 'How "NSCN(IM)" threatened Arunachal NPP before Aboh killing,' *eastmojo.com*, 22 June 2019 (accessed article and audio clip of conversation on 23 June 2019).

Lianzela, 'Employment Scenario in Mizoram,' *Employment News*, Vol. XXXVII, No. 25, Ministry of Information and Broadcasting, Government of India, 22-28 September, 2012.

Linter, Bertil, 'NSCN leader T. Muivah's imprisonment in Thailand may split the militant outfit,' *The Week* (issue dated 5 March 2000).

Mahadevan, Prem, *Crossing the Line: Geopolitics and Criminality at the India-Myanmar Border*, Global Initiative Against Transnational Organized Crime, Geneva, November 2020.

'Manipur BJP spokesperson's son found guilty in 2011 case, charged with homicide not amounting to murder,' Express News Service, *indianexpress.com*, 7 January 2017 (accessed 7 January 2017).

Mitra, Sumit, 'Tripura: The Promised Land?', *India Today*, 1-15 August 1979.

'Myanmar army attacks ULFA-I camp,' Agencies, *Nagaland Post*, 3 February 2019 (accessed at *nagalandpost.com* on 4 February 2019).

'Myanmar army continue offensive against NSCN (K), NE insurgents,' *Nagaland Post*, 16 May 2019.

'Myanmar army vows to throw out Indian rebels,' *mizzima.com* via *nagalandpost.com*, 7 November 2017 (accessed 7 November 2017).

Nag, Sajal, 'Nehru and the Nagas: Minority Nationalism and the Post-Colonial State,' *Economic and Political Weekly*, Vol. 44, Issue No. 49, 05 December 2009.

'Naga peace talks: PMO overrules MHA on key appointment,' Express News Service, *The Indian Express*, 30 August 2014.

'Nagaland Home Minister Arrested; Arms, Cash Seized,' *outlookindia.com*, 18 February 2013 (accessed 18 February 2013).

Nandy, Chandan, 'Muivah arrest bursts Bangkok bubble,' *The Telegraph*, 1 February 2000.

North Eastern Region: Vision 2020, Government of India and North Eastern Council, Ministry of Development of North Eastern Region, 2008.

'NSA Ajit Doval meets Myanmar President, top defence officials,' *Press Trust of India*, 17 June 2015.

'ONGC strikes gas in Mizoram,' *The Telegraph*, 10 June 2014.

Patranobis, Sutirtho, 'India, China to resume stalled dialogue on corridor with Myanmar, Bangladesh,' *Hindustan Times*, 19 April, 2017.

'Passports To Rohingya Muslims,' Government Of India Ministry Of Home Affairs, Lok Sabha Unstarred Question No.782 To Be Answered On The 01st March, 2016.

People and Guns: Naga People's Struggle for Peace, Naga Peoples Movement for Human Rights, DVD: 90 minutes, 2009.

Rajagopal, Krishnadas, 'SC ends impunity for armed forces,' *The Hindu*, 9 July 2016.

Rana, Kishan S., Uberoi, Patricia, *India's North East States, the BCIM Forum and Regional Integration* (Monograph), Institute of Chinese Studies, Delhi, No. 1, December 2012.

Report of the Committee to Review the Armed Forces (Special Powers) Act, 1958,

Ministry of Home Affairs, Government of India, Ministry of Home Affairs, 2005.

Report of the Comptroller and Auditor General of India on Social, Economic, Revenue and General Sectors For the year ended 31 March 2014, GOVERNMENT OF NAGALAND Report No. 1 of 2015, Comptroller and Auditor General of India, 2015.

Report of the Comptroller and Auditor General of India on State Finances For the Year ended 31 March 2013 (laid on the table of the State Legislature Assembly on 16-07-2014), GOVERNMENT OF MANIPUR, Comptroller and Auditor General of India, 2014.

Roy, Subhajit, 'At the UN, India for restraint in Rakhine, praises Bangladesh,' *Indian Express*, 20 September 2017.

'Rs.1 cr seized from Nagaland candidate,' Hindustan Times Correspondent, Guwahati, *Hindustan Times*, 17 February 2013.

'Rs 3.06 Crore Worth Drugs Seized in Mizoram,' *northeasttoday.in*, 19 October 2015 (accessed 20 October 2015).

Rutsa, Xavier, 'Naga peace talks: R.N. Ravi holds talks with rebel groups,' Times New Network, 24 October 2017 (accessed at *timesofindia.com* on 24 October 2017).

Sharma, Sushil Kumar (Brig.), 'Taxation and Extortion: A Major Source of Militant Economy in Northeast India,' Occasional Paper, Vivekananda International Foundation, July 2016.

Singh, Manmohan, 'PM's speech at handing over of the Kangla Fort to the Government of Manipur,' 20 November 2004 (accessed at *archivepmo.nic.in* on 17 June 2016).

Singh, Vijaita, 'Naga leader Isak Chishi Swu passes away in Delhi hospital,' *thehindu.com*, 28 June 2016 (accessed 28 June 2016).

'Study Tour of Standing Committee on Finance to Guwahati, At Shillong On 19th June 2012,' PowerPoint presentation by Northeast Frontier Railway (Construction Organisation), received on 7 June 2014.

Subramanian, Nirupama, 'On Rohingya Refugees' return, Home says one thing but MEA said another, *Indian Express*, 20 September 2017.

The Manipur Land Revenue and Land Reforms Act, 1960. Legislative Department, Ministry of Law and Justice, Government of India. (Downloaded from *legislative.gov.in*, 2017).

THE NAGALAND OWNERSHIP AND TRANSFER OF LAND AND ITS RESOURCES IN RESPECT OF MINERALS INCLUDING PETROLUEM AND NATURAL GAS RESOLUTION, 2010 By Legislative Assembly of Nagaland Under Article 371 of the Constitution of India, Nagaland Legislative Assembly, 26 July 2010.

'Time has not come for any rethink on AFSPA: Army Chief Gen. Rawat,' *Press Trust of India*, 28 January 2018.

Turner, Mandy, 'Armed violence and poverty in Northeast India: a mini case
        study for the Armed Violence and Poverty Initiative,' Centre of
        International Cooperation and Security, Department of Peace Studies,
        University of Bradford. AVPI Case Studies, 2004.
'Two Hundred Thirteenth Report Security Situation In The North Eastern States
        Of India, Department-Related Parliamentary Standing Committee On
        Home Affairs,' Parliament Of India Rajya Sabha, (Presented To Rajya
        Sabha On 19th July, 2018) (Laid On The Table Of Lok Sabha On
        19th July, 2018), Rajya Sabha Secretariat, New Delhi July, 2018/
        Ashadha, 1940 (Saka).
'2 ZUF cadres killed, one "K" man injured in clash with NSCN-IM,' Hueiyen
        News Service / Daniel Kamei and Newmai News Network, published in
        e-pao.net, 30 May 2012 (Downloaded from *http://e-pao.net/
        GP.asp?src=17..310512.may12* on 31 May 2012).
'UNHCR: The refugee status case of Mr Muivah,' Urgent Appeals Case, Asia,
        Asian Human Rights Commission, 29 November 2000.
'Won't allow anti-India insurgency: Myanmar,' *Nagaland Post*, 19 October 2015.
Yehzabo, Government of the Peoples' Republic of Nagalim, 1980, 1996 (sourced
        by the author).

Resources

arunachaltimes.in
burmalibrary.org
censusindia.gov.in
Central Archaeological Library, New Delhi
eastmojo.com
Economic and Political Weekly (and *epw.in*)
e-pao.net
Google Earth (*google.com/earth*)
Imphal Free Press (and *ifp.co.in*)
indianarmy.nic.in
ipsnews.net
irrawaddy.com
kanglaonline.com
manipurpolice.gov.in
mdoner.gov.in (Ministry of Development of North Eastern Region,
Government of India)
mizzima.com
Nagaland Post (and *nagalandpost.com*)
nagalim.nl
Nehru Memorial Museum & Library, New Delhi
nscn.livejournal.com

nytimes.com
Press Trust of India (and *ptinews.com*)
South Asia Terrorism Portal *(satp.org)*
The Assam Tribune (and *assamtribune.com*)
The Hindu (and *thehindu.com*)
The Morung Express (and *morungexpress.com*)
The Naga Blog (Facebook group)
thenagarepublic.com
The Sangai Express (and *thesangaiexpress.com*)
The Sentinel (and *sentinelassam.com*)
The Telegraph (and *telegraphindia.com*)
thethumbprintmag.com
The Week (and *theweek.in*)
trackingterrorism.org
tuensang.nic.in
un.org
unescap.org
United News of India (and *uniindia.com*)

Note on Interviews: While the period and location for numerous interviews have been provided in the narrative, the precise location for some have been masked, especially interviews with some rebels, narcotic and weapons smugglers and sellers, security and intelligence personnel of the Indian government and various Indian states, and various levels of conflict resolution negotiators, both from government and not, in Nagaland, Manipur, Assam, Tripura, Meghalaya and New Delhi. Some identities have also been masked for reasons of confidentiality as requested by those being interviewed. All interviews for this book were conducted between mid-2008 and early-2021. Most interviews were conducted face-to-face, with the remainder conducted over email, telephone and social network applications.

Index